Contents

Preface   v

Chapter 1   The European Conquest of America   1

Interpretive Essay
The Americas . . .   *L. S. Stavrianos*   2

Sources
The Indians as Seen by European Artists   11
   Illustrations: John White's engraving of Indians making a canoe near
   Roanoke, 1588; a settlement of Virginia Indians; Florida battle scene, 1564

Broken Spears: The Aztec Account of the Conquest of Mexico   13
   The Broken Spears: The Aztec Account of the Conquest of Mexico, edited by
   Miguel Leon-Portilla

Race War: The New England Experience   20
   The Old Indian Chronicle, edited by Samuel G. Drake

Chapter 2   Jamestown   23

Interpretive Essay
The Labor Problem at Jamestown, 1607–1618   *Edmund S. Morgan*   24

Sources
Jamestown: The Physical Setting   36
   Illustrations of Jamestown

Life and Death in Virginia: Richard Frethorne's Account, 1623   37

Chapter 3   Puritan Order   42

Interpretive Essay
Deputy Husbands   *Laurel Thatcher Ulrich*   43

Sources
New England Primer, 1690   55

Harvard, 1636–1642   *56*
    From "New England's First Fruits," 1643

Three Early New England Portraits   *60*
    Illustrations: Henry Gibbs; Thomas Smith's Self-Portrait; Ann Pollard

The Trial of Anne Hutchinson, 1637   *62*
    From *The History of the Colony and Province of Massachusetts Bay* by
    Thomas Hutchinson

Chapter 4   The Have-Nots in Colonial Society   *67*

Interpretive Essay
White Servitude   *Richard Hofstadter*   *68*

Sources
Portraits of Poverty   *86*
    Illustrations: Hogarth engraving; an Elizabethan Beggar

The Experience of Bondage: Gottlieb Mittelberger's Account, 1754   *87*

Wanted: Runaway Servants   *90*
    Newspaper advertisements for runaway servants, eighteenth century

Chapter 5   Black Slavery   *94*

Interpretive Essay
The Middle Passage   *Daniel P. Mannix and Malcolm Cowley*   *95*

Sources
Portraits of Slavery   *108*
    Illustrations: Slaves on the bark *Wildfire;* bartering for slaves on the Gold
    Coast; engraving by Alexander Anderson; shock of enslavement; diagram
    of the slave ship *La Vigilante de Nantes;* standard equipment for the
    middle passage; advertisement in a Charleston, S.C., newspaper, 1766

Wanted: Runaway Slaves   *113*
    Newspaper advertisements, eighteenth and early nineteenth centuries

Chapter 6   Toward Revolution   *117*

Interpretive Essay
The Spirit of '76   *Carl Becker*   *119*

Sources
George III   *138*
    Illustrations: George III, woodcut frontispiece to Watts *Speller,* 1770;
    pulling down the statue of George III

Common Sense, 1776   *Thomas Paine*   *140*

The
American
Record

Images of the Nation's Past

Volume One: To 1877

The
American
Record

Images of the Nation's Past

Second Edition

Volume One: To 1877

Edited by

William Graebner
State University of New York, College at Fredonia

Leonard Richards
University of Massachusetts, Amherst

Alfred A. Knopf   New York

Second Edition
987654321
Copyright ©1982, 1988 by Alfred A. Knopf, Inc.

Library of Congress Cataloging-in-Publication Data

The American record.

  Contents: v. 1. To 1877—v. 2. Since 1865.
  1. United States—History. 2. United States—
History—Sources. I. Graebner, William.
II. Richards, Leonard L.
E178.6.A4145 1987   973   87–3523
ISBN 0–394–35620–9 (v. 1)
ISBN 0–394–35621–7 (v. 2)

Text design: Leon Bolognese
Cover design: Nadja Furlan-Lorbek

Cover illustration: "The Residence of David Twining," by Edward Hicks. Courtesy of the Abby Aldrich Rockefeller Folk Art Collection, Williamsburg, Virginia.

Preface

During the past two or three decades, the study of history in the United States has become in many ways more sophisticated and, we think, more interesting. Until the 1950s the dominant tradition among American historians was to regard the historian's domain as one that centered on politics, diplomacy, and war. Now, in the late 1980s, historians are eager to address new kinds of subjects, and to include whole sections of the population that were neglected in the traditional preoccupation with presidential administrations, legislation, and treaties. Women and children, the poor and economically marginal, have moved nearer the center of the historians' stage. And we have become almost as eager to know how our ancestors dressed, ate, reared their children, made love, and buried their dead as we are to know how they voted in a particular presidential election. The result is a collective version of our national past that is more inclusive, more complicated, and less settled.

The second edition of *The American Record* continues the effort begun in the first. We have attempted to bridge the gap between the old history and the new, to graft the excitement and variety of modern approaches to history on an existing chronological and topical framework with which most of us feel comfortable. Most of the familiar topics are here. We have included essays on the early colonial settlements, the Revolutionary War, the Founding Fathers, immigration, Progressivism, and the civil rights movement. But by joining these essays to primary sources, we have tried to make it possible for teachers and students to see links between the early settlements and European poverty; between the Revolutionary War and the colonial class structure; between the Founding Fathers and the physical layout of the nation's capital; between immigration and the prairie houses of Frank Lloyd Wright; between Progressivism and the proclamation of Mother's Day; between the civil rights movement and rock 'n' roll. This is a book that teaches the skill of making sense out of one's whole world.

Throughout, we have attempted to incorporate materials with *texture:* documents that are not only striking but that can be given more than one interpretation; photographs that invite real examination and discussion; tables and maps that have something new and interesting to contribute; and essays, such as Laurel Thatcher Ulrich's examination of Puritan women and Allen Matusow's treatment of the New Left, that are at once superb examples of recent historical scholarship and accessible to undergraduates.

From the beginning, we realized that our approach to American history would require adjustment for many students and teachers. It was one thing to expect a student to place an address by Teddy Roosevelt in the context of turn-of-the-century imperialism, yet quite another to expect students to do the same with Edgar Rice Burroughs's *Tarzan of the Apes*. For this reason, we have offered a good deal of guidance. Introductions to primary and secondary materials are designed not just to provide basic background information, but to suggest productive avenues of interpretation. Interpretive essays and questions are intended to create a kind of mental chemistry in which students will have enough information to experience the excitement of putting things together, and yet not so much guidance that conclusions become obvious.

We remain indebted to R. Jackson Wilson, who inspired the first edition of this book. We also wish to thank our editors at Alfred A. Knopf—first David Follmer and then Chris Rogers—for their patient supervision of a difficult project. And we are especially grateful to the teachers and students who used the first edition of *The American Record* and showed us how to make the book better.

William Graebner
State University of New York, College at Fredonia

Leonard Richards
University of Massachusetts, Amherst

Chapter 7   The American Revolution   *145*

Interpretive Essay
Mobilizing Armed Force in the American Revolution   *John Shy   147*

Sources
A Spy's View of Washington's Army, 1775   *156*
  Observations by Benjamin Thompson

Three Views of the American Soldier   *159*
  British, American, and French illustrations

Silencing the Tories   *162*
  A London cartoon; letter from Ann Hulton to Mrs. Lightbody, 1774;
  records of the Committee of Safety, New York, 1775

Chapter 8   Creating the Constitution   *166*

Interpretive Essay
The Creation of a More Perfect Union   *John C. Miller   167*

Sources
Ratification   *179*
  Table and map

The Virginia Debates   *181*
  *The Debates in the Several State Conventions on the Adoption of the Federal
  Constitution,* edited by Jonathan Elliott

The Meaning of the Slave Trade Provision   *186*
  Charles Cotesworth Pinckney and James Wilson

Designing the Nation's Capitol   *188*
  Illustrations: Designs of the Capitol by Samuel Dobie, Charles
  Wintersmith, Etienne Hallet, James Diamond, and William Thornton;
  portrait of William Thornton

Chapter 9   Federalists and Republicans   *191*

Interpretive Essay
Jefferson and the Strategy of Parties   *James MacGregor Burns   192*

Sources
Roughhouse Politics   *206*
  Cartoon lampooning Lyon–Griswold brawl

Truth versus Treason   *207*
  Federalist cartoon; Republican handbills, 1804 and 1807

The Nature of American Aristocracy, 1813   *209*
  Thomas Jefferson and John Adams

Chapter 10   The Transformation of Northern Society   215

Interpretive Essay
Civilizing the Machine   *John F. Kasson*   216

Sources
Lowell: As It Was and As It Is, 1845   *Henry A. Miles*   238

Portraits of Industrialism   242
  Illustrations: View of Lowell, Massachusetts; the title page of the *Lowell Offering;* textile workers of Lawrence, Massachusetts; the women strikers of Lynn

Chapter 11   Jacksonian Democracy   245

Interpretive Essay
Jacksonian Democracy   *Leonard L. Richards*   246

Sources
The Election of 1828   257
  Anti-Jackson cartoons

"King Andrew"   259
  Anti-Jackson cartoons

The Art of Democratic Politics   *Davy Crockett*   260

The Election of 1840   262
  Painting depicting Harrison campaign; "Rally for William Henry Harrison in St. Louis, Missouri," as reported by the St. Louis *New Era*

The Artist's View of Politics   *George Caleb Bingham*   266
  "Canvassing for a Vote"; "County Election"; "Verdict of the People"; "Stump Speaking"

Chapter 12   Antislavery   270

Interpretive Essay
The Commitment to Immediate Emancipation   *James Brewer Stewart*   271

Sources
Commission to Theodore Dwight Weld, 1834   281
  From *Letters to Theodore Dwight Weld, Angelina Grimke Weld, and Sarah Grimke,* 1822–1844, edited by Gilbert H. Barnes and Dwight L. Dumond

The Anti-Slavery Record, 1835–1836   285
  Six illustrations from the front page of *The Anti-Slavery Record*

"Fathers and Rulers" Petition   288
  From *Letters of Theodore Dwight Weld, Angelina Grimke Weld and Sarah Grimke, 1822–1844,* edited by Gilbert H. Barnes and Dwight L. Dumond

Slavery as It Is, 1839   *Theodore Dwight Weld*   289

Chapter 13   Western Expansion   *291*

Map showing expansion of the United States across the continent   *292*

Interpretive Essay
The Quest for Room   *William L. Barney*   *292*

Sources
The Kansas–Nebraska Act, 1854   *304*
  Map showing the United States in 1854

Two Portraits of the West   *304*
  Illustrations: John Gast's "Manifest Destiny"; "Forcing Slavery Down the
  Throat of a Freesoiler"

The Lincoln–Douglas Debates, 1858   *307*
  From *Political Debates between Abraham Lincoln and Stephen A. Douglas in
  the Celebrated Campaign of 1858 in Illinois;* photographs of Stephen A.
  Douglas and Abraham Lincoln

Chapter 14   The Civil War   *315*

Map: The Union Disintegrates; table: Deaths in the Civil War and Other
Wars   *316*

Interpretive Essay
Hayfoot, Strawfoot   *Bruce Catton*   *317*

Sources
The Photographers' War   *326*
  Illustrations: Abraham Lincoln, 1860 and 1865; Civil War dead; Private
  Edwin Francis Jennison; the 107th U.S. Colored Infantry; powder
  monkey, USS *New Hampshire;* ruins of Charleston, S.C.; Union dead;
  Union wounded; the Richmond and Petersburg Railroad Depot;
  Richmond at war's end; freedmen in Richmond; John Wilkes Booth's
  accomplices

Sherman's March Through Georgia, 1865   *David P. Conyngham*   *333*

Chapter 15   Reconstruction   *341*

Interpretive Essay
Promised Land   *Elizabeth Rauh Bethel*   *342*

Sources
The Meaning of Freedom   *355*
  Letter from Jourdon Anderson to His Former Master from *The
  Freedmen's Book,* edited by Lydia Maria Child, 1865

The Cartoonist's View of Reconstruction   *357*
  Ten Political cartoons by Thomas Nast, 1865–1876

The South Redeemed   *366*
  Maps of the Barrow plantation, 1860 and 1880

The
American
Record

Images of the Nation's Past

Volume One: To 1877

1

The European
Conquest of America

The idea that Europeans discovered America in 1492 is of course
absurd. And so are the maps of the Mediterranean area that describe it as the "known" world. The Western Hemisphere, and other
areas that Europeans thought of as "terra incognita," were discovered and known to those who lived in them many centuries before
white Europeans set sail on their momentous voyages. The importance of 1492 is not that Columbus stumbled on the New World—
new, that is, to Europeans—in that year. What made his voyage, and
those of other European explorers, important is what they set in
motion: the conquest of vast areas of the world by a newly energized
Europe. What the Europeans discovered was not new continents
only, but new continents they could subject to their power. The expansion of Europe was an event in *world* history.

Innovations in navigational technology, combined with the economic and political development of Europe, created a vast new arena
for domination. "Native" societies in Africa and Asia proved to be
more resistant than Europeans hoped. But in the Americas, Indian
cultures fell with relative ease before the European onslaught. Some
of the native American societies were weak and disunited, and were
technologically little advanced beyond the levels achieved in the
Stone Age. But there were mighty and sophisticated empires in the
Americas, too, particularly those of the Aztecs in Mexico and the Incas in Peru. One of the major mysteries of world history is the explanation for the speed and the completeness of their defeat, the
rapid and total European conquest that has made North and South
America modern extensions of European culture.

How have historians accounted for this astonishing fact? On the
surface, differences in technology seem to provide an easy answer.
The horse, gunpowder, and other devices certainly made a differ-

ence—even the most advanced American cultures do not seem to have grasped the principle of the wheel. But technology cannot fully explain how a tiny handful of European adventurers managed to defeat Indian populations with hundreds of thousands of skillful and resourceful warriors. Disunity among the Indians, all over both North and South America, has also been invoked as a part of the explanation. But the native civilizations were hardly more disunited and contentious than their European conquerors.

More recently, historians have begun to pay attention to a silent factor that few of the participants in the European conquest were fully aware of—and that few used intentionally. For countless generations, Europe had been ravaged by diseases like tuberculosis and smallpox. In the process, Europeans had developed natural immunities to the worst effects of their illnesses. The isolated Americans, on the other hand, had not been exposed to these diseases and had no immunities. They could be slain by the hundreds of thousands by sicknesses as harmless to whites as the measles. Such diseases literally wiped out entire tribes and their cultures and made it possible for Europeans to simply walk in and take over.

The conquest of the Americas was a complex process, and there are no clear-cut answers to our questions about it. What we know for certain is this: very few events in the history of the human race have had more far-reaching consequences, for the conquerors and their victims alike.

Interpretive Essay

L. S. Stavrianos

The Americas . . .

The following essay, by the noted world historian L. S. Stavrianos, explores the reasons behind the European success. As you read it, you may want to think carefully about the types of factors Stavrianos introduces, and the order of importance in which you think they should be ranked. You should also classify those that suggest European "strengths" and Indian "weaknesses." Finally, you will want to be aware that a "strength" is only a strength for specific purposes, and in comparison to some other factor that makes an opponent vulnerable. Can you detect any cultural or ethnic biases in Stavrianos's

essay, or does he appear to maintain a balanced and humane view toward all parties?

The Vikings had stumbled upon North America in the eleventh century, and for about one hundred years they tried to maintain settlements there, but without success. In the fifteenth century Columbus likewise stumbled upon the New World, but this time the sequel was altogether different. Instead of failure and withdrawal, discovery now was followed by massive and overwhelming penetration of both North and South America. The contrast reflected the extent of the increase in European power and dynamism during the intervening half millennium.

Equally striking was the contrast between the rapid European penetration and exploitation of the Americas, and the centuries that elapsed before the same could be done in Africa. One reason was geography; the New World was physically more accessible and inviting. The other reason, as noted by Adam Smith, was "the miserable and helpless" plight of the Indians. Although they were far from all being at the same level of development, yet the overall nature of the Indian cultures was such that effective resistance was impossible. . . .

I. Land and People

The Americas, in contrast to Africa, were exceptionally open to newcomers from Europe. No sandbars obstructed the approaches to the coasts. Harbors were much more frequently available along the indented coastline of the Americas than along the unbroken coastline of Africa. Also the Americas had a well-developed pattern of interior waterways that were relatively free of impediments and offered easy access to the interior. There was no counterpart in Africa to the majestic and smooth-flowing Amazon, Plata, Mississippi, or St. Lawrence. The climate of the Americas, too, is generally more attractive than that of Africa. The Amazon basin, it is true, is hot and humid, and the polar extremities of both continents are bitterly cold, but the British and the French settlers flourished in the lands they colonized north of the Rio Grande, and the Spaniards likewise felt at home in Mexico and Peru, which became their two principal centers.

Until recently it was believed that the Indians first began crossing over from Siberia to the Americas about 10,000 years ago. New archaeological findings, together with the use of carbon-14 dating, have forced drastic revision of this estimate. It is now generally agreed that man certainly was in the New World 20,000 years ago, and probably 20,000 years or more before that. The last major migration of Indians took place about 3,000 years ago.

From L. S. Stavrianos, *Man's Past and Present,* 2nd ed., © 1975, pp. 212–218. Reprinted by permission of Prentice-Hall, Inc., Englewood Cliffs, N.J.

The actual crossing to the New World presented little difficulty to these early newcomers. The last of the Ice Ages had locked up vast quantities of sea water, lowering the ocean level by 460 feet and thus exposing a 1,300-mile-wide land bridge connecting Siberia and Alaska. A "bridge" of such proportions was, in effect, a vast new subcontinent, that allowed ample scope for the vast diffusion of plants and animals that now took place. Even after rising temperatures lifted the sea level and submerged the connecting lands, the resulting narrow straits easily could have been crossed in crude boats without even losing sight of shore.

Most of those who crossed to Alaska moved on into the heart of North America through a gap in the ice sheet in the central Yukon plateau. They were impelled to press forward by the same forces that led them to migrate to America—the search for new hunting grounds and the continual pressure of tribes from the rear. In this manner both the continents were soon peopled by scattered tribes of hunters. Definite evidence has been found that indicates that the migrants from Asia reached the southern tip of South America by 11,000 years ago.

As regards racial traits, all Indians may be classified as Mongoloids. They have the characteristic straight black hair, sparse on the face and body; high cheekbones; and the Mongolian spot that appears at the base of the spine in young children. Considerable variation exists, however, among the different tribes: the earliest varieties of American Indian are much less Mongoloid than the later ones, because they left Asia before the Mongoloids, as we know them today, had fully evolved. That the immigrants at once spread out and settled in small, inbred groups in a variety of climates also explains the presence of individual physical types.

II. Cultures

The migrants to the New World brought little cultural baggage with them since they came from northeast Siberia, one of the least advanced regions of Eurasia. They were, of course, all hunters, organized in small bands, possessing only crude stone tools, no pottery, and no domesticated animals, except perhaps the dog. Since they were entering an uninhabited continent they were completely free to evolve their own institutions. . . .

During the ensuing millennia the American Indians did develop an extraordinarily rich variety of cultures, adapted to one another as well as to the wide range of physical environments they encountered. Some remained at the hunting band stage while others developed kingdoms and empires. Their religions encompassed all known categories, including monotheism. They spoke some 2,000 distinct languages, some as different from one another as Chinese and English. This represents as much variation in speech as in the entire Old World, where about 3,000 languages are known to have existed in A.D. 1500. Nor were these languages primitive, either in vocabulary or in any other respect. Whereas Shakespeare used about 24,000 words, and the

King James Bible about 7,000, the Nahuatl of Mexico used 27,000 words, while the Yahgans of Tierra del Fuego, considered to be one of the world's most retarded peoples, possess a vocabulary of at least 30,000 words.

Taking all types of institutions and practices into account, anthropologists have defined some twenty-two culture areas in the New World—the Great Plains area, the Eastern Woodlands, the Northwest Coast area, and so forth. A simpler classification, on the basis of how food was obtained, involves three categories: hunting, gathering, and fishing cultures; intermediate farming cultures; and advanced farming cultures. This scheme is not only simpler but it is also meaningful from the viewpoint of world history, for it helps to explain the varied responses of the Indians to the European intrusion.

The advanced farming cultures were located in Mesoamerica (central and southern Mexico, Guatemala, and Honduras) and the Andean highland area (Ecuador, Peru, Bolivia, and northern Chile). The intermediate farming cultures were generally in the adjacent regions, while the food-gathering cultures were in the more remote regions—the southern part of South America, and the western and northern part of North America.

This geographic distribution of culture points up the fact that, in contrast to Africa, the most advanced regions in the Americas were not located closest to Eurasia. One reason is that northeast Siberia was not a greater center of civilization, as was the Middle East and the Mediterranean basin that contributed so much to the Africans. Also, climatic conditions in Alaska and the Canadian Arctic obviously were not conducive to rapid cultural development as was the case in the Sudan savannah zone. Thus the tempo of advance in the Americas depended not on proximity to Eurasia but rather on suitability for the development of agriculture. It is significant, then, that agriculture was first developed in the Americas in regions that were strikingly similar to the Middle East where agriculture originated in Eurasia—that is, highland regions not requiring extensive clearing of forests to prepare the fields for crops, with enough rainfall to allow the crops to mature, and with a supply of potentially high-yielding native plants available for domestication.

. . . The Indians domesticated over one hundred plants, or as many as were domesticated in all Eurasia, a truly extraordinary achievement. Agriculture in turn made possible the development of large empires and sophisticated civilizations comparable in certain respects to those of West Africa. Unfortunately, these indigenous American civilizations were suddenly overwhelmed by the Spaniards and thus left little behind them other than their precious domesticated plants.

III. Civilizations

The three major Amerindian civilizations were the Mayan, in present-day Yucatan, Guatemala, and British Honduras; the Aztec, in present-day Mexico; and the Inca, stretching for 3,000 miles from mid-Ecuador to mid-Chile. The Mayans were outstanding for their remarkable development of the arts and sciences. They alone evolved an ideographic form of writing in which characters or signs were used as conventional symbols for ideas. They also studied the movements of the heavenly bodies in order to measure time, predict the future, and set propitious dates for sacrifices and major undertakings. So extensive was the astronomical knowledge compiled by highly trained priests that it is believed to have been at least equal to that of Europe at that time.

Maya cities, if they may be so called, were ceremonial centers rather than fortresses or dwelling places or administrative capitals. This was so because the Mayans practiced slash and burn agriculture, which exhausted the soil within two or three years, requiring constant moving of the village settlements. To balance this transitory mode of life, the Maya cultivators expressed their social unity by erecting large stone buildings in centers that were devoted primarily to religious ceremonies. These buildings were large temple pyramids and also community houses in which the priests and novices probably lived. This architecture, produced entirely with stone tools, was decorated with sculpture that was unsurpassed in the Americas and that ranks as one of the great world arts.

The Maya civilization flourished between the fourth and tenth centuries, but then declined for reasons that remain obscure. It may have been soil exhaustion, or epidemic disease, or, more plausibly, peasant revolutions against the burden of supporting the religious centers with their priestly hierarchies. In any case the great stone structures were abandoned to decay and were swallowed by the surrounding forest, to be unearthed only in recent decades with archaeological excavations.

The Aztecs were brusque and warlike compared to the artistic and intellectual Mayas—a contrast reminiscent of that between the Romans and the Greeks in the Old World. The Aztecs actually were latecomers to Mexico, where a series of highly developed societies had through the centuries succeeded one another. These had been vulnerable to attacks by barbarians from the arid north who naturally gravitated down in response to the lure of fertile lands. The last of these invaders were the Aztecs, who had settled on some islands on Lake Texcoco, then filling much of the floor of the valley of Anáhuac. As their numbers grew and the islands became overcrowded, the Aztecs increased their arable land by making *chinampas,* floating islands of matted weeds, covered with mud dredged from the lake floor, and anchored to the bottom by growing weeds. To the present day, this mode of cultivation is carried on in certain regions. Before each planting the farmers scoop up fresh mud and spread it over the *chinampa,* whose level steadily rises with the succession of crops. The farmers then excavate the top layers of mud, which they use to build a new *chinampa,* thus beginning a new cycle.

The *chinampas* enabled the Aztecs to boom in numbers and wealth. Early in the fifteenth century they made alliances with towns on the lake shore, and from that foothold they quickly extended their influence in all directions. Raiding expeditions went out regularly, forcing other peoples to pay tribute in kind and in services. By the time the Spaniards appeared on the scene, Aztec domination extended to the Pacific on the west, to the Gulf of Mexico on the east, almost to Yucatan on the south, and to the Rio Grande on the north. The capital, Tenochtitlán, was by then a magnificent city of 200,000 to 300,000 people, linked to the shore by causeways. The conqueror Cortes compared the capital to Venice and judged it to be "the most beautiful city in the world."

Aztec power was based on constant war preparedness. All men were expected to bear arms, and state arsenals were always stocked and ready for immediate use. With their efficient military machine the Aztecs were able to extract a staggering amount of tribute from their subjects. According to their own extant records, they collected in one year fourteen million pounds of maize, eight million pounds each of beans and amaranth, and two million cotton cloaks in addition to assorted other items such as war costumes, shields, and precious stones.

The Spaniards were not only dazzled by the wealth and magnificence of the Aztec state, but also horrified by the wholesale ritual massacre of a continual procession of human victims. These were slaughtered at the top of the ceremonial pyramids that abounded everywhere and that the Spaniards soon realized functioned as altars for human sacrifice. Indeed the Aztecs waged war to take captives for sacrifice as well as to exact tribute for their capital. The first objective they considered even more important than the second, for their priests taught that the world was in constant danger of cataclysm, especially the extinguishing of the sun. Hence the need for offering human victims to propitiate the heavenly deities. But this practice trapped the Aztecs in a truly vicious circle: sacrificial victims were needed to forestall universal disaster; these could be obtained only through war; successful war could be waged only by sacrificing victims, but these in turn could be secured only through war.

Finally, the Incas of Peru were one of the numerous tribes of Quechua stock and language that raised llamas and grew potatoes. In the twelfth century they established themselves in the Cuzco valley which they soon dominated. At this early stage they evolved a dynasty from their war chiefs, while their tribesmen constituted an aristocracy amongst the other tribal peoples. The combination of a hereditary dynasty and aristocracy, which was unique in the New World, constituted an effective empire-building instrument. From their imperial city of Cuzco in the Peruvian highlands, the Incas sent forth armies and ambassadors, west to the coastal lands, and north and south along the great mountain valleys. By the time of the Spanish intrusion they had extended their frontiers some 2,500 miles from Ecuador to central Chile, a much larger empire than that of the Aztecs.

This empire was held together physically by a road system which still can be traced for hundreds of miles and which included cable bridges of plaited aloe fibre and floating bridges on pontoons of buoyant reeds. Equally important was an extensive irrigation system, parts of which are still in use, and which made the Inca empire a flourishing agricultural unit. Communications were maintained by a comprehensive system of post-stations and relays of runners who conveyed messages swiftly to all parts of the empire.

Imperial unity was furthered also by elaborate court ritual and by a state religion based on worship of the sun, of which the king, or Inca, was held to be a descendant, and in whose ceremonial worship he played an essential role. Other techniques of imperial rule included state ownership of land, mineral wealth, and herds, careful census compilations for tax and military purposes, deposition of local hereditary chieftains, forced population resettlement for the assimilation of conquered peoples, and mass marriages under state auspices. Not surprisingly, the Inca empire is considered to be one of the most successful totalitarian states the world has ever seen.

IV. Conclusion

Impressive as were these attainments of the American Indians, the fact remains that a handful of Spanish adventurers was able to easily overthrow and completely uproot all three of the great New World civilizations. And this despite the fact that the Aztec empire had a population of over ten million, and the Inca empire, over six million. The explanation for the one-sided Spanish triumph is to be found ultimately in the isolation of the Americas. This isolation, it should be noted, was, as in the case of Africa, internal as well as external. That is to say, not only were the American Indian civilizations cut off from stimulating interaction with civilizations on other continents, but also they were largely isolated from each other.

"With respect to interrelations between Peru and Mesoamerica," reports an archaeologist, "it is sufficient to state that not a single object or record of influence or contact between these areas has been accepted as authentic from the long time span between the Formative period [about 1000 B.C.] and the coming of the Spaniards. . . ." In other words, there is no reliable evidence of interaction between the Mesoamerican and Peruvian civilizations over a span of 2,500 years. And during those millennia, as we have seen, the various regions of Eurasia, and to a lesser extent sub-Saharan Africa, were in continual fructifying contact. The end result was that the American Indians—even those of the Andes and Mesoamerica—lagged far behind the Eurasians and especially behind the technologically precocious Europeans. By A.D. 1500 the New World had reached the stage of civilization that Egypt and Mesopotamia had attained about 2500 B.C.

Precisely what did this mean when the confrontation occurred with the arrival of the Spaniards? It meant, in the first place, that the Indians found themselves economically and technologically far behind the civilization represented by the invaders. The highly developed art, science, and religion of the Indians should not be allowed to obscure the fact that they lagged seriously in more material fields. The disparity was most extreme in Mesoamerica, but it also prevailed in the Andean area. In agriculture, the Indians were brilliantly successful in domesticating plants but much less effective in actual production. Their cultivation techniques never advanced beyond the bare minimum necessary for feeding populations that rarely reached the density of those of the Old World. Their tools were made only of stone, wood, or bone. They were incapable of smelting ores, and though they did work with metal, it was almost exclusively for ornamental purposes. The only ships they constructed were canoes and seagoing rafts. For land transportation they made no use of the wheel, which they knew but used only as a toy. Only the human back was available for transportation, with the exception of the llama and the alpaca, which were used in the Andes but which could not carry heavy loads.

The immediate significance of this technological lag should not be exaggerated. The Indians obviously were at a grave disadvantage with their spears and arrows against the Spaniards' horses and guns. But after the initial shock, the Indians became accustomed to firearms and cavalry. Furthermore, the Spaniards soon discovered that the Indian weapons were sharp and durable, and they came to prefer the Indian armor of quilted cotton to their own.

This suggests that factors in addition to technological disparity lay behind the Spanish victories. One was the lack of unity amongst the Indian peoples. In both Mexico and Peru the Spaniards were able to use disaffected subject tribes that had been alienated by the oppressive style of Cuzco and Tenochtitlán. The Indians were also weakened by over-regimentation. They had been so indoctrinated and accustomed to carrying out orders without question that when their leaders were overthrown they were incapable of organizing resistance on their own.

This passivity was compounded by religious inhibitions. Both Cortes in Mexico and Pizarro in Peru were at first believed by the natives to be gods returning in fulfillment of ancient prophecies. This explains the suicidal vacillations of Atahualpa in Cuzco and of Montezuma in Tenochtitlán. To Atahualpa the Spaniards were the creator-god Viracocha and his followers, and, for this reason, the ruler waited meekly for Pizarro, who with his 180 men quickly seized control of the great empire. Likewise, to Montezuma, Cortes was the god Quetzalcoatl who was returning to claim his rightful throne, so that again the ruler waited listlessly for the Spaniards to ensconce themselves in his capital.

Equally disastrous for the Aztecs was their concept of war as a short-term ritual endeavor. Their main interest in war was to capture prisoners, whose hearts they offered to their gods. Accordingly their campaigns frequently were ceremonial contests during which prisoners were taken with minimal dislocation and destruction. This type of military tradition obviously was a serious handicap. The Spaniards killed to win; the Aztecs tried to take prisoners.

If the great civilizations of the New World lacked the power and the cohesion to resist the Europeans, this was even more true of the less developed food gathering and intermediate farming culture areas. Precisely because they were less developed, they also had smaller populations, so that when the

Europeans appeared they simply lacked the numbers to hold their ground. Their weakness in this respect was accentuated by the diseases that the first explorers brought with them. The Indians, lacking immunity, were decimated by the epidemics, so that the early colonists often found abandoned fields and deserted village sites that they could take over.

Later, when the full flood of immigration from Europe got under way, the Indians were hopelessly overwhelmed. First came the traders who penetrated throughout the Americas with little competition or resistance, for the Americas, unlike Africa, had no rival native merchant class. Then appeared the settlers who, attracted by the combination of salubrious climate and fertile land, came in ever-increasing numbers and inundated the hapless Indians. When the latter occasionally took up arms in desperation, they were foredoomed to failure because they lacked both unity and the basic human and material resources. Thus, the unequal contest ended relatively quickly with the victorious white man in possession of the choice lands and the Indians relegated to reservations or to the less desirable regions that did not interest the new masters.

It is apparent that the balance of forces was quite different in America from what it was in Africa. Geography, relatively small population, and a comparatively low level of economic, political, and social organization all worked against the Indian to make it possible for the Europeans to take over the Americas at a time when they were still confined to a few toeholds on the coasts of Africa. Adam Smith was indeed justified in referring to the Indians as "miserable and helpless Americans" in contrast to the Africans.

Sources

The Indians as Seen by European Artists

Europeans formed a fantastic variety of mental pictures of the lives and behavior of the natives of the Americas. On one hand, they might portray the Indians as vicious cannibals, with almost no social organization. On the other hand, Europeans often pictured Indian society as being rather orderly, advanced, and "civilized." Here are three very famous sixteenth-century representations. Pictures, we like to believe, tell us more than words. Suppose you were to try to translate these pictures into a few words, however. What would they be? Can you imagine other ways of depicting the Indians that Europeans might have used?

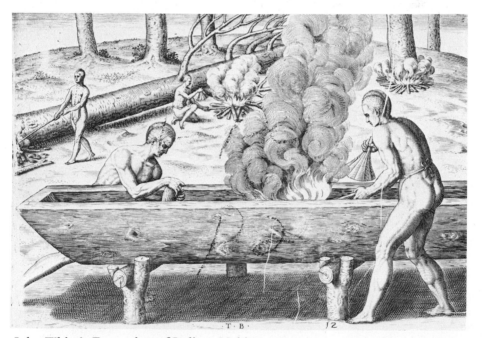

John White's Engraving of Indians Making a Canoe near Roanoke, 1588. *Rare Book Division, New York Public Library.*

A Settlement of Virginia Indians. *From Part I, Plate XX, in Theodore DeBry's*
America. *Arents Collection/New York Public Library.*

Florida Battle Scene, 1564. *American Antiquarian Society.*

Broken Spears: The Aztec Account of the Conquest of Mexico

What about the Indians' side of the story? How did they react to their conquerors? Such information is hard to come by, of course, since the various Indian groups kept many fewer written records than the Europeans. But the Mexican anthropologist Miguel León Portilla has pieced together a moving Aztec account of the fall of Mexico to the Cortés expedition. Some of these accounts were written as early as 1528, just seven years after the Spaniards took Mexico City. As you read this story of the way Montezuma and his people experienced the shock of invasion and the bitterness of their defeat, keep these questions in mind: What do the Aztecs give as the *cause* of the European victory? Technology? Divine intervention? Does the Aztec interpretation of what happened accord with Stavrianos's picture of the European conquest? If there are disagreements, whose story do you think is more believable, and why?

From *The Broken Spears*, edited and with an introduction by Miguel Leon-Portilla (Boston: Beacon Press, 1962), pp. 29–149. Copyright © 1962 by Beacon Press. Originally published in Spanish under the title *Vision de los Vencidos*, copyright © 1959 by Universidad Nacional Autonoma de Mexico. Reprinted by permission of Beacon Press.

Motecuhzoma Goes Out to Meet Cortes

The Spaniards arrived in Xoloco, near the entrance to Tenochtitlan. That was the end of the march, for they had reached their goal.

Motecuhzoma now arrayed himself in his finery, preparing to go out to meet them. The other great princes also adorned their persons, as did the nobles and their chieftains and knights. They all went out together to meet the strangers.

They brought trays heaped with the finest flowers—the flower that resembles a shield; the flower shaped like a heart; in the center, the flower with the sweetest aroma; and the fragrant yellow flower, the most precious of all. They also brought garlands of flowers, and ornaments for the breast, and necklaces of gold, necklaces hung with rich stones, necklaces fashioned in the petatillo style.

Thus Motecuhzoma went out to meet them, there in Huitzillan. He presented many gifts to the Captain and his commanders, those who had come to make war. He showered gifts upon them and hung flowers around their necks; he gave them necklaces of flowers and bands of flowers to adorn their breasts; he set garlands of flowers upon their heads. Then he hung the gold necklaces around their necks and gave them presents of every sort as gifts of welcome. . . .

Motecuhzoma Awaits Word from the Messengers

While the messengers were away, Motecuhzoma could neither sleep nor eat, and no one could speak with him. He thought that everything he did was in vain, and he sighed almost every moment. He was lost in despair, in the deepest gloom and sorrow. Nothing could comfort him, nothing could calm him, nothing could give him any pleasure.

He said: "What will happen to us? Who will outlive it? Ah, in other times I was contented, but now I have death in my heart! My heart burns and suffers, as if it were drowned in spices . . . ! But will our lord come here?"

Then he gave orders to the watchmen, to the men who guarded the palace: "Tell me, even if I am sleeping: 'The messengers have come back from the sea.' " But when they went to tell him, he immediately said: "They are not to report to me here. I will receive them in the House of the Serpent. Tell them to go there." And he gave this order: "Two captives are to be painted with chalk."

The messengers went to the House of the Serpent, and Motecuhzoma arrived. The two captives were then sacrificed before his eyes: their breasts were torn open, and the messengers were sprinkled with their blood. This was done because the messengers had completed a difficult mission: they had seen the gods, their eyes had looked on their faces. They had even conversed with the gods!

The Messengers' Report

When the sacrifice was finished, the messengers reported to the king. They told him how they had made the journey, and what they had seen, and what food the strangers ate. Motecuhzoma was astonished and terrified by their report, and the description of the strangers' food astonished him above all else.

He was also terrified to learn how the cannon roared, how its noise resounded, how it caused one to faint and grow deaf. The messengers told him: "A thing like a ball of fire comes out of its entrails: it comes out shooting sparks and raining fire. The smoke that comes out with it has a pestilent odor, like that of rotten mud. This odor penetrates even to the brain and causes the greatest discomfort. If the cannon is aimed against a mountain, the mountain splits and cracks open. If it is aimed against a tree, it shatters the tree into splinters. This is a most unnatural sight as if the tree had exploded from within."

The messengers also said: "Their trappings and arms are all made of iron. They dress in iron and wear iron casques on their heads. Their swords are iron; their bows are iron; their shields are iron; their spears are iron. Their deer carry them on their backs wherever they wish to go. These deer, our lord, are as tall as the roof of a house.

"The strangers' bodies are completely covered, so that only their faces can be seen. Their skin is white, as if it were made of lime. They have yellow hair, though some of them have black. Their beards are long and yellow, and their moustaches are also yellow. Their hair is curly, with very fine strands.

"As for their food, it is like human food. It is large and white, and not heavy. It is something like straw, but with the taste of a cornstalk, of the pith of a cornstalk. It is a little sweet, as if it were flavored with honey; it tastes of honey, it is sweet-tasting food.

"Their dogs are enormous, with flat ears and long, dangling tongues. The color of their eyes is a burning yellow; their eyes flash fire and shoot off sparks. Their bellies are hollow, their flanks long and narrow. They are tireless and very powerful. They bound here and there, panting, with their tongues hanging out. And they are spotted like an ocelot."

When Motecuhzoma heard this report, he was filled with terror. It was as if his heart had fainted, as if it had shriveled. It was as if he were conquered by despair. . . .

The Spaniards Take Possession of the City

When the Spaniards entered the Royal House, they placed Motecuhzoma under guard and kept him under their vigilance. They also placed a guard over Itzcuauhtzin, but the other lords were permitted to depart.

Then the Spaniards fired one of their cannons, and this caused great confusion in the city. The people scattered in every direction; they fled without rhyme or reason; they ran off as if they were being pursued. It was as if they had eaten the mushrooms that confuse the mind, or had seen some dreadful apparition. They were all overcome by terror, as if their hearts had fainted. And when night fell, the panic spread through the city and their fears would not let them sleep.

In the morning the Spaniards told Motecuhzoma what they needed in the way of supplies: tortillas, fried chickens, hens' eggs, pure water, firewood and charcoal. Also: large, clean cooking pots, water jars, pitchers, dishes and other pottery. Motecuhzoma ordered that it be sent to them. The chiefs who received this order were angry with the king and no longer revered or respected him. But they furnished the Spaniards with all the provisions they needed—food, beverages and water, and fodder for the horses.

The Spaniards Reveal Their Greed

When the Spaniards were installed in the palace, they asked Motecuhzoma about the city's resources and reserves and about the warriors' ensigns and shields. They questioned him closely and then demanded gold.

Motecuhzoma guided them to it. They surrounded him and crowded close with their weapons. He walked in the center, while they formed a circle around him.

When they arrived at the treasure house called Teucalco, the riches of gold and feathers were brought out to them: ornaments made of quetzal feathers, richly worked shields, disks of gold, the necklaces of the idols, gold nose plugs, gold greaves and bracelets and crowns.

The Spaniards immediately stripped the feathers from the gold shields and ensigns. They gathered all the gold into a great mound and set fire to everything else, regardless of its value. Then they melted down the gold into ingots. As for the precious green stones, they took only the best of them; the rest were snatched up by the Tlaxcaltecas. The Spaniards searched through the whole treasure house, questioning and quarreling, and seized every object they thought was beautiful.

The Seizure of Motecuhzoma's Treasures

Next they went to Motecuhzoma's storehouse, in the place called Totocalec [Place of the Palace of the Birds], where his personal treasures were kept. The Spaniards grinned like little beasts and patted each other with delight.

When they entered the hall of treasures, it was as if they had arrived in Paradise. They searched everywhere and coveted everything; they were slaves to their own greed. All of Motecuhzoma's possessions were brought out: fine bracelets, necklaces with large stones, ankle rings with little gold bells, the royal crowns and all the royal finery—everything that belonged to the king and was reserved to him only. They seized these treasures as if they were their own, as if this plunder were merely a stroke of good luck. And when they had taken all the gold, they heaped up everything else in the middle of the patio.

La Malinche called the nobles together. She climbed up to the palace roof and cried, "Mexicanos, come forward! The Spaniards need your help! Bring them food and pure water. They are tired and hungry; they are almost fainting from exhaustion! Why do you not come forward? Are you angry with them?"

The Mexicans were too frightened to approach. They were crushed by terror and would not risk coming forward. They shied away as if the Spaniards were wild beasts, as if the hour were midnight on the blackest night of the year. Yet they did not abandon the Spaniards to hunger and thirst. They brought them whatever they needed, but shook with fear as they did so. They delivered the supplies to the Spaniards with trembling hands, then turned and hurried away. . . .

The Massacre in the Main Temple During the Fiesta of Toxcatl

At this moment in the fiesta, when the dance was loveliest and when song was linked to song, the Spaniards were seized with an urge to kill the celebrants. They all ran forward, armed as if for battle. They closed the entrances and passageways, all the gates of the patio: the Eagle Gate in the lesser palace, the Gate of the Canestalk and the Gate of the Serpent of Mirrors. They posted guards so that no one could escape, and then rushed into the Sacred Patio to slaughter the celebrants. They came on foot, carrying their swords and their wooden or metal shields.

They ran in among the dancers, forcing their way to the place where the drums were played. They attacked the man who was drumming and cut off his arms. Then they cut off his head, and it rolled across the floor.

They attacked all the celebrants, stabbing them, spearing them, striking them with their swords. They attacked some of them from behind, and these fell instantly to the ground with their entrails hanging out. Others they be-headed: they cut off their heads, or split their heads to pieces.

They struck others in the shoulders, and their arms were torn from their bodies. They wounded some in the thigh and some in the calf. They slashed others in the abdomen, and their entrails all spilled to the ground. Some attempted to run away, but their intestines dragged as they ran; they seemed to tangle their feet in their own entrails. No matter how they tried to save themselves, they could find no escape.

Some attempted to force their way out, but the Spaniards murdered them at the gates. Others climbed the walls, but they could not save themselves. Those who ran into the communal houses were safe there for a while;

so were those who lay down among the victims and pretended to be dead.
But if they stood up again, the Spaniards saw them and killed them.

The blood of the warriors flowed like water and gathered into pools.
The pools widened, and the stench of blood and entrails filled the air. The
Spaniards ran into the communal houses to kill those who were hiding. They
ran everywhere and searched everywhere; they invaded every room, hunting
and killing.

The Siege of Tenochtitlan

Now the Spaniards began to wage war against us. They attacked us by land
for ten days, and then their ships appeared. Twenty days later, they gathered
all their ships together near Nonohualco, off the place called Mazatzintamalco.
The allies from Tlaxcala and Huexotzinco set up camp on either side of the
road.

Our warriors from Tlatelolco immediately leaped into their canoes and
set out for Mazatzintamalco and the Nonohualco road. But no one set out
from Tenochtitlan to assist us: only the Tlatelolcas were ready when the
Spaniards arrived in their ships. On the following day, the ships sailed to
Xoloco.

The fighting at Xoloco and Huitzillan lasted for two days. While the
battle was under way, the warriors from Tenochtitlan began to mutiny. They
said: "Where are our chiefs? They have fired scarcely a single arrow! Do
they think they have fought like men?" Then they seized four of their own
leaders and put them to death. The victims were two captains, Cuauhnochtli
and Cuapan, and the priests of Amantlan and Tlalocan. This was the second
time that the people of Tenochtitlan killed their own leaders. . . .

The Fighting Is Renewed

The Spaniards made ready to attack us, and the war broke out again. They
assembled their forces in Cuepopan and Cozcacuahco. A vast number of
our warriors were killed by their metal darts. Their ships sailed to Texopan,
and the battle there lasted three days. When they had forced us to retreat,
they entered the Sacred Patio, where there was a four-day battle. Then they
reached Yacacolco.

The Tlatelolcas set up three racks of heads in three different places. The
first rack was in the Sacred Patio of Tlilancalco [Black House], where we
strung up the heads of our lords the Spaniards. The second was in Acacolco,
where we strung up Spanish heads and the heads of two of their horses.
The third was in Zacatla, in front of the temple of the earth-goddess Cihua-
coatl, where we strung up the heads of Tlaxcaltecas.

The women of Tlatelolco joined in the fighting. They struck at the enemy and shot arrows at them; they tucked up their skirts and dressed in the regalia of war.

The Spaniards forced us to retreat. Then they occupied the market place. The Tlatelolcas—the Jaguar Knights, the Eagle Knights, the great warriors— were defeated, and this was the end of the battle. It had lasted five days, and two thousand Tlatelolcas were killed in action. During the battle, the Spaniards set up a canopy for the Captain in the market place. They also mounted a catapult on the temple platform.

Epic Description of the Besieged City

And all these misfortunes befell us. We saw them and wondered at them; we suffered this unhappy fate.

> Broken spears lie in the roads;
> we have torn our hair in our grief.
> The houses are roofless now, and their walls
> are red with blood.
>
> Worms are swarming in the streets and plazas,
> and the walls are splattered with gore.
> The water has turned red, as if it were dyed,
> and when we drink it,
> it has the taste of brine.
>
> We have pounded our hands in despair
> against the adobe walls,
> for our inheritance, our city, is lost and dead.
> The shields of our warriors were its defense,
> but they could not save it.
>
> We have chewed dry twigs and salt grasses;
> we have filled our mouths with dust and bits of adobe;
> we have eaten lizards, rats and worms. . . .

When we had meat, we ate it almost raw. It was scarcely on the fire before we snatched it and gobbled it down.

They set a price on all of us: on the young men, the priests, the boys and girls. The price of a poor man was only two handfuls of corn, or ten cakes made from mosses or twenty cakes of salty couch-grass. Gold, jade, rich cloths, quetzal feathers—everything that once was precious was now considered worthless.

The captains delivered several prisoners of war to Cuauhtemoc to be sacrificed. He performed the sacrifices in person, cutting them open with a stone knife. . . .

Race War:
The New England Experience

As the Aztecs' memory of their defeat indicates, the European conquest of America involved a good deal of brutality and terrorism.
And brutality was not confined to Central or South America, either.
Wherever Indians were able to mount a significant resistance, the European retaliation was likely to be swift and very harsh. The following selections attempt to justify the beheading and quartering—the
cutting into four pieces—of an Indian leader, King Philip. He was
the leader of Indian resistance in New England that culminated in
what the English settlers called King Philip's War (1675–1676). The
second selection was written by the most highly educated man in
New England, Increase Mather, and thus represents the most "enlightened" view of the Indian in New England. Do you believe the
two descriptions of the Indians' behavior? How does Mather explain
the causes of the Indians' attacks on whites? How does he explain the
white victory?

King Philip's War:
A Contemporary Account

A True but Brief Account of our Losses sustained since this Cruel and
Mischievous War began, take as follows:

In *Narraganset* not one House left standing.
At *Warwick,* but one.
At *Providence,* not above three.
At *Potuxit,* none left.
Very few at *Seaconicke.*
At *Swansey,* two, at most.
Marlborough, wholy laid in Ashes, except two or three Houses.
Grantham and Nashaway, all ruined but one House or two.
Many Houses burnt at *Springfield, Scituate, Lancaster, Brookfield* and
Northampton.
The greatest Part of *Rehoboth* and *Taunton* destroyed.
Great Spoil made at *Hadley, Hatfield* and *Chelmsford.*
Deerfield wholy, and *Westfield* much ruined.
At *Sudbury,* many Houses burnt, and some at *Hingham, Weymouth,* and
Braintree.

From "A New and Farther Narrative of the State of New-England, July 22, 1676" by N. S.,
from *The Old Indian Chronicle,* Samuel G. Drake, ed. (Boston, 1867), pp. 244–246.

Besides particular Farms and Plantations, a great Number not be reckoned up, wholly laid waste, or very much damnified.

And as to Persons, it is generally thought, that of the English there hath been lost, in all, Men Women and Children, above Eight Hundred, since the War began. Of whom many have been destroyed with exquisite Torments, and most inhumane Barbarities; the Heathen rarely giving Quarter to those that they take, but if they were Women, they first forced them to satisfie their filthy Lusts and then murdered them; either cutting off the Head, ripping open the Belly, or skulping the Head of Skin and Hair, and hanging them up as Trophies; wearing Men's Fingers as Bracelets about their Necks, and Stripes of their Skins which they dress for Belts, They knockt one Youth of the Head, and laying him for dead, they flead (or skulp'd) his Head of Skin and Hair. After which the Boy wonderfully revived, and is now recovered, only he hath Nothing but the dry Skull, neither Skin nor Hair on his Head. Nor have our Cattle escaped the Cruelty of these worse than Brute and Savage Beasts: For what Cattle they took they seldom killed outright: or if they did, would eat but little of the Flesh, but rather cut their Bellies, and letting them go several Days, trailing their Guts after them, putting out their Eyes, or cutting off one Leg, &c.

Defeat of King Philip: Increase Mather's Account

August 6. An *Indian* that deserted his Fellows, informed the inhabitants of *Taunton* that a party of *Indians* who might be easily surprised, were not very far off, and promised to conduct any that had a mind to apprehend those *Indians* in the right way towards them, whereupon about twenty Souldiers marched out of *Taunton,* and they took all those *Indians,* being in number thirty and six, only the *Squaw-Sachem of Pocasset,* who was next unto *Philip* in respect to the mischief that hath been done, and the blood that hath been shed in this Warr, escaped alone; but not long after some of *Taunton* finding an *Indian Squaw* in *Metapoiset* newly dead, cut off her head, and it happened to be *Weetamoo,* i.e. *Squaw-Sachem* her *head.* When it was set upon a pole in *Taunton,* the *Indians* who were prisoners there knew it presently, and made a most horrid and diabolical Lamentation, crying out that it was their Queens head. Now here it is to be observed, that God himself by his own hand brought this enemy to destruction. For in that place, where the last year, she furnished *Philip* with Canooes for his men, she her self could not meet with a Canoo, but venturing over the River upon a Raft, that brake under her, so that she was drowned, just before the *English* found her. Surely *Philips* turn will be next.

From Increase Mather, *A History of King Philip's War* (Albany, 1862), pp. 191–195.

August 10. Whereas *Potock* a chief Counsellor to the old Squaw-Sachem of *Narraganset,* was by some of Road Island brought into *Boston,* and found guilty of promoting the War against the *English,* he was this day shot to death in the Common at *Boston.* As he was going to his execution, some told him that now he must dy, he had as good speak the truth, and say how many *Indians* were killed at the Fort-Fight last winter. He replyed, that the *English* did that day kill above seven hundred fighting men, and that three hundred who were wounded, dyed quickly after, and that as to old men, women and Children, they had lost no body could tell how many; and that there were above three thousand *Indians* in the Fort, when our Forces assaulted them, and made that notable slaughter amongst them.

August 12. This is the memorable day wherein *Philip,* the perfidious and bloudy Author of the War and wofull miseryes that have thence ensued, was taken and slain. And God brought it to pass, chiefly by *Indians* themselves. For one of *Philips* men (being disgusted at him, for killing an *Indian* who had propounded an expedient for peace with the *English*) ran away from him, and coming to Road-Island, informed that *Philip* was now returned again to *Mount-Hope,* and undertook to bring them to the swamp where he hid himself. Divine Providence so disposed, as that Capt. *Church* of *Plymouth* was then in Road-Island, in order to recruiting his Souldiers, who had been wearied with a tedious march that week. But immediately upon this Intelligence, he set forth again, with a small company of *English* and *Indians.* It seemeth that night *Philip* (like the man, in the Host of *Midian*) dreamed that he was fallen into the hands of the *English,* and just as he was saying to those that were with him, that they must fly for their lives that day, lest the *Indian* that was gone from him should recover where he was. Our Souldiers came upon him and surrounded the *Swamp* (where he with seven of his men absconded). Thereupon he betook himself to flight; but as he was coming out of the Swamp, an *English-man* and an *Indian* endeavoured to fire at him, the *English-man* missed of his aime, but the *Indian* shot him through the heart, so as that he fell down dead. The *Indian* who thus killed *Philip* did formerly belong to Squaw-Sachim of *Pocasset,* being known by the name of *Alderman.* In the beginning of the war, he came to the Governour of *Plymouth,* manifesting his desire to be at peace with the *English,* and immediately withdrew to an Island not having engaged against the *English* nor for them, before this time. Thus when *Philip* had made an end to deal treacherously, his own Subjects dealt treacherously with him. This Wo was brought upon him that spoyled when he was not spoyled. And in that very place where he first contrived and began his mischief, was he taken and destroyed, and there was he (like as Agag was hewed in pieces before the Lord) cut into four quarters, and is now hanged up as a monument of revenging Justice, his head being cut off and carried away to *Plymouth,* his Hands were brought to *Boston. So let all thine Enemies perish, O Lord!*

2

Jamestown

We all know the story of Jamestown—or think we do. There was Captain John Smith, who put lazy gentlemen to work. There was Pocahontas, who made peace possible between whites and Indians. And there was John Rolfe, who figured out how to grow the "noxious weed," tobacco, successfully, and so insured the struggling colony's eventual triumph.

But this familiar story had no meaning whatever to the original settlers of the colony of Virginia. For them, Virginia was not a setting for personal dramas. Life there was ugly, brutal, and very likely to be short. In fact, death was the most prominent feature of life. It came often and quickly—through illness, accident, and Indian resistance—but mainly through starvation.

The toll was awesome. The Virginia Company of London sent 144 colonists to Virginia late in 1606. Of these, thirty-nine died at sea. Forty-six more died within a few months of landing. Only thirty-eight were still alive when the next ship arrived in 1608. New settlers from England brought the population up to about five hundred. All but sixty of these died during the "starving time" of the winter of 1609–1610.

The figures for the longer run are almost as appalling. Between 1607 and 1624, four out of every five colonists who came over to Jamestown died.

Those who had been sent out to lose their lives in this deathtrap were the advance guard of a commercial concern, the Virginia Company. It had been chartered in 1606 by the English Crown for the purpose of colonizing an area that was about half the size of the present United States. The investors in the company expected it to pay quick profits, perhaps from the discovery of gold or silver, or of an easy water passage through the continent (whose size no one yet knew) to the fabled markets of Asia.

The enterprise was, in short, a capital venture by a group of stockholders to whom the New World was an opportunity for investment. The investment failed. The stockholders eventually sank about 100,000 pounds (worth about 12 million of today's dollars) in their speculation. In return, they got nothing. The company paid no dividends and its stock became worthless paper within a dozen years.

Why did the settlers and the investors alike fare so poorly? In the early years, the company did send over large numbers of "gentlemen," who wouldn't work. The original settlers also spent a lot of their time quarreling with each other and searching for gold. But surely such explanations do not account for the fact that Englishmen with the advantages of Iron Age technology had such difficulties, why they starved to death in an area where Indians had lived successfully for years.

Interpretive Essay

Edmund S. Morgan

The Labor Problem at Jamestown, 1607–1618

The following selection is by the most distinguished historian of the colonial period at work in the United States today. In it, he confronts the vexed problem of Jamestown. More precisely, he addresses a simple but puzzling question: why seventeenth-century Englishmen had so much difficulty coping with the wilderness, why they starved to death rather than put in a hard day's work getting food. Morgan traces the problem back to English attitudes toward work and comes to the unhappy conclusion that the only way Virginians could solve their labor problem was to introduce black slavery. As you read, you should pay particular attention to the *logic* of the essay, which governs the introduction of its factual detail. Does that logic seem plausible? Or could other kinds of connections explain the facts that Morgan introduces?

The story of Jamestown, the first permanent English settlement in America, has a familiar place in the history of the United States. We all know of

From Edmund S. Morgan, "The Labor Problem at Jamestown, 1607–18," *American Historical Review* 76 (1971): 595–610. Copyright by Edmund S. Morgan.

the tribulations that kept the colony on the point of expiring: the shortage of supplies, the hostility of the Indians, the quarrels among the leaders, the reckless search for gold, the pathetic search for a passage to the Pacific, and the neglect of the crucial business of growing food to stay alive. Through the scene moves the figure of Captain John Smith, a little larger than life, trading for corn among the Indians and driving the feckless crew to work. His departure in October 1609 results in near disaster. The settlers fritter away their time and energy, squander their provisions, and starve. Sir Thomas Gates, arriving after the settlement's third winter, finds only sixty men out of six hundred still alive and those sixty scarcely able to walk.

In the summer of 1610 Gates and Lord La Warr get things moving again with a new supply of men and provisions, a new absolute form of government, and a new set of laws designed to keep everybody at work. But when Gates and La Warr leave for a time, the settlers fall to their old ways. Sir Thomas Dale, upon his arrival in May 1611, finds them at "their daily and usuall workes, bowling in the streetes." But Dale brings order out of chaos. By enlarging and enforcing the colony's new law code (the famous *Lawes Divine, Morall and Martiall*) he starts the settlers working again and rescues them from starvation by making them plant corn. By 1618 the colony is getting on its feet and ready to carry on without the stern regimen of a Smith or a Dale. There are still evil days ahead, as the Virginia Company sends over men more rapidly than the infant colony can absorb them. But the settlers, having found in tobacco a valuable crop for export, have at last gone to work with a will, and Virginia's future is assured.

The story probably fits the facts insofar as they can be known. But it does not quite explain them. The colony's long period of starvation and failure may well be attributed to the idleness of the first settlers, but idleness is more an accusation than an explanation. Why did men spend their time bowling in the streets when their lives depended on work? Were they lunatics, preferring to play games rather than clear and plow and plant the crops that could have kept them alive?

The mystery only deepens if we look more closely at the efforts of Smith, Gates, La Warr, and Dale to set things right. In 1612 John Smith described his work program of 1608: "the company [being] divided into tennes, fifteenes, or as the businesse required, 4 hours each day was spent in worke, the rest in pastimes and merry exercise." Twelve years later Smith rewrote this passage and changed the figure of four hours to six hours. But even so, what are we to make of a six-hour day in a colony teetering on the verge of extinction?

The program of Gates and La Warr in the summer of 1610 was no more strenuous. William Strachey described it:

> it is to be understood that such as labor are not yet so taxed but that easily they perform the same and ever by ten of the clock have done their morning's work: at what time they have their allowances [of food] set out ready for them, and until it be three of the clock again they take their own pleasure, and afterward, with the sunset, their day's labor is finished.

The Virginia Company offered much the same account of this period. According to a tract issued late in 1610, "the setled times of working (to effect all themselves, or the Adventurers neede desire) [requires] no more pains than from six of clocke in the morning untill ten, and from two of the clocke in the afternoone till foure." The long lunch period described for 1610 was also a feature of the *Lawes Divine, Morall and Martiall* as enforced by Dale. The total working hours prescribed in the *Lawes* amounted to roughly five to eight hours a day in summer and three to six hours in winter.

It is difficult, then, to escape the conclusion that there was a great deal of unemployment or underemployment at Jamestown, whether it was the idleness of the undisciplined in the absence of strong government or the idleness of the disciplined in the presence of strong government. How are we to account for this fact? By our standards the situation at Jamestown demanded hard and continuous work. Why was the response so feeble?

One answer, given by the leaders of the colony, is that the settlers included too many ne'er-do-wells and too many gentlemen who "never did know what a dayes work was." Hard work had to wait until harder men were sent. Another answer may be that the Jamestown settlers were debilitated by hunger and disease. The victims of scurvy, malaria, typhoid, and diphtheria may have been left without the will or the energy to work. Still another answer, which has echoed through the pages of our history books, attributed the difficulty to the fact that the settlement was conducted on a communal basis: everybody worked for the Virginia Company and everybody was fed (while supplies lasted) by the company, regardless of how much he worked or failed to work. Once land was distributed to individuals and men were allowed to work for themselves, they gained the familiar incentives of private enterprise and bent their shoulders to the wheel. These explanations are surely all valid—they are all supported by the testimony of contemporaries—and they go far toward explaining the lazy pioneers of Jamestown. But they do not reach to a dimension of the problem that contemporaries would have overlooked because they would have taken it for granted. They do not tell us what ideas and attitudes about work, carried from England, would have led the first English settlers to expect so little of themselves in a situation that demanded so much. The Jamestown settlers did not leave us the kind of private papers that would enable us to examine directly their ideas and attitudes, as we can those of the Puritans who settled New England a few years later. But in the absence of direct evidence we may discover among the ideas current in late sixteenth- and early seventeenth-century England some clues to the probable state of mind of the first Virginians, clues to the way they felt about work, whether in the Old World or the New, clues to habits of thinking that may have conditioned their perceptions of what confronted them at Jamestown, clues even to the tangled web of motives that made later Virginians masters of slaves.

Englishmen's ideas about the New World at the opening of the seventeenth century were based on a century of European exploration and settlement. The Spanish, whose exploits surpassed all others, had not attempted to keep their success a secret, and by the middle of the sixteenth century Englishmen interested in America had begun translating Spanish histories and memoirs in an effort to rouse their countrymen to emulation. The land that emerged from these writings was, except in the Arctic regions, an Eden, teeming with gentle and generous people who, before the Spanish conquest, had lived without labor, or with very little, from the fruits of a bountiful nature. There were admittedly some unfriendly exceptions who made a habit of eating their more attractive neighbors; but they were a minority, confined to a few localities, and in spite of their ferocity were scarcely a match for Europeans armed with guns. Englishmen who visited the New World confirmed the reports of natural abundance. Arthur Barlowe, for example, reconnoitering the North Carolina coast for Walter Raleigh, observed that "the earth bringeth foorth all things in aboundance, as in the first creation, without toile or labour," while the people were "most gentle, loving and faithfull, void of all guile, and treason, and such as lived after the manner of the golden age. . . ."

English and European readers may have discounted the more extravagant reports of American abundance, for the same authors who praised the land often gave contradictory accounts of the hardships they had suffered in it. But anyone who doubted that riches were waiting to be plucked from Virginia's trees had reason to expect that a good deal might be plucked from the people of the land. Spanish experience had shown that Europeans could thrive in the New World without undue effort by exploiting the natives. With a mere handful of men the Spanish had conquered an enormous population of Indians in the Caribbean, Mexico, and Peru and had put them to work. In the chronicles of Peter Martyr Englishmen learned how it was done. Apart from the fact that the Indians were naturally gentle, their division into a multitude of kingdoms, frequently at odds with one another, made it easy to play off one against another. By aiding one group against its enemies the Spaniards had made themselves masters of both.

The story of English plans to imitate and improve on the Spanish strategy is a long one. It begins at least as early as Francis Drake's foray in Panama in 1572–73, when he allied with a band of runaway slaves to rob a Spanish mule train carrying treasure from Peru across the isthmus to Nombre de Dios on the Caribbean. The idea of joining with dissident natives or slaves either against their Spanish masters or against their wicked cannibalistic neighbors became an important ingredient in English plans for colonizing the New World. Martin Frobisher's experiences with the Eskimos in Baffin Land and Ralph Lane's with the Indians at Roanoke should perhaps have disabused the English of their expectations; but they found it difficult to believe that any group of natives, and especially the noble savages of North America, would fail to welcome what they called with honest pride (and some myopia) the "gentle government" of the English. If the savages first encountered by a colonizing expedition proved unfriendly, the thing to do was to make contact with their milder neighbors and rescue them from the tyranny of the unfriendly tribe, who must be their enemies and were probably cannibals to boot.

The settlers at Jamestown tried to follow the strategy, locating their settlement as the plan called for, near the mouth of a navigable river, so that they would have access to the interior tribes if the coastal ones were hostile. But as luck would have it, they picked an area with a more powerful, more extensive, and more effective Indian government than existed anywhere else on the Atlantic Coast. King Powhatan had his enemies, the Monacans of the interior, but he felt no great need of English assistance against them, and he rightly suspected that the English constituted a larger threat to his hegemony than the Monacans did. He submitted with ill grace and no evident comprehension to the coronation ceremony that the Virginia Company arranged for him, and he kept his distance from Jamestown. Those of his warriors who visited the settlement showed no disposition to work for the English. The Monacans, on the other hand, lived too far inland (beyond the falls) to serve as substitute allies, and the English were thus deprived of their anticipated native labor.

They did not, however, give up their expectations of getting it eventually. In 1615 Ralph Hamor still thought the Indians would come around "as they are easily taught and may be lenitie and faire usage . . . be brought, being naturally though ingenious, yet idlely given, to be no lesse industrious, nay to exceed our English." Even after the massacre of 1622 Virginians continued to dream of an Indian labor supply, though there was no longer to be any gentleness in obtaining it. Captain John Martin thought it better to exploit than exterminate the Indians, if only because they could be made to work in the heat of the day, when Englishmen would not. And William Claiborne in 1626 invented a device (whether mechanical or political is not clear) that he claimed would make it possible to keep Indians safely in the settlements and put them to work. The governor and council gave him what looks like the first American patent or copyright, namely a three-year monopoly, to "have holde and enjoy all the benefitt use and profitt of this his project or inventione," and they also assigned him a recently captured Indian, "for his better experience and tryall of his inventione."

English expectations of the New World and its inhabitants died hard. America was supposed to be a land of abundance, peopled by natives who would not only share that abundance with the English but increase it under English direction. Englishmen simply did not envisage a need to work for the mere purpose of staying alive. The problem of survival as they saw it was at best political and at worst military.

Although Englishmen long remained under the illusion that the Indians would eventually become useful English subjects, it became apparent fairly early that Indian labor was not going to sustain the founders of Jamestown. The company in England was convinced by 1609 that the settlers would have to grow at least part of their own food. Yet the settlers themselves had to be driven to that life-saving task. To understand their ineffectiveness in coping with a situation that their pioneering descendants would take in stride, it may be helpful next to inquire into some of the attitudes toward work that these first English pioneers took for granted. How much work and what kind of work did Englishmen at the opening of the seventeenth century consider normal?

The laboring population of England, by law at least, was required to work much harder than the regimen at Jamestown might lead us to expect. The famous Statute of Artificers of 1563 (re-enacting similar provisions from the Statute of Laborers of 1495) required all laborers to work from five in the morning to seven or eight at night from mid–March to mid–September, and during the remaining months of the year from day break to night. Time out for eating, drinking, and rest was not to exceed two and a half hours a day. But these were injunctions not descriptions. The Statute of Laborers of 1495 is preceded by the complaint that laborers "waste much part of the day . . . in late coming unto their work, early departing therefrom, long sitting at their breakfast, at their dinner and noon-meat, and long time of sleeping after noon." Whether this statute or that of 1563 (still in effect when Jamestown was founded) corrected the situation is doubtful. The records of local courts show varying efforts to enforce other provisions of the statute of 1563, but they are almost wholly silent about this provision, in spite of the often-expressed despair of masters over their lazy and negligent laborers.

It may be said that complaints of the laziness and irresponsibility of workmen can be met with in any century. Were such complaints in fact justified in sixteenth- and early seventeenth-century England? There is some reason to believe that they were, that life during those years was characterized by a large amount of idleness or underemployment. The outstanding economic fact of the sixteenth and early seventeenth century in England was a rapid and more or less steady rise in prices, followed at some distance by a much smaller rise in wages, both in industry and in agriculture. The price of provisions used by a laborer's family rose faster than wages during the whole period from 1500 to 1640. The government made an effort to narrow the gap by requiring the justices in each county to readjust maximum wages at regular intervals. But the wages established by the justices reflected their own nostalgic notions of what a day's work ought to be worth in money, rather than a realistic estimate of what a man could buy with his wages. In those counties, at least, where records survive, the level of wages set by the justices crept upward very slowly before 1630.

Wages became so inadequate that productivity was probably impaired by malnutrition. From a quarter to a half of the population lived below the level recognized at the time to constitute poverty. Few of the poor could count on regular meals at home, and in years when the wheat crop failed, they were close to starvation. It is not surprising that men living under these conditions showed no great energy for work and that much of the population was, by modern standards, idle much of the time. The health manuals of the day recognized that people normally slept after eating, and the laws even prescribed a siesta for laborers in the summer time. If they slept longer and more often than the laws allowed or the physicians recommended, if they loafed on the job and took unauthorized holidays, if they worked slowly and ineffectively when they did work, it may have been due at least in part to undernourishment and to the variety of chronic diseases that undernourishment brings in its train.

Thus low wages may have begot low productivity that in turn justified low wages. The reaction of employers was to blame the trouble on deficiencies, not of diet or wages, but of character. A prosperous yeoman like Robert Loder, who kept close track of his expenses and profits, was always bemoaning the indolence of his servants. Men who had large amounts of land that they could either rent or work with hired labor generally preferred to rent because labor was so inefficient and irresponsible.

Even the division of labor, which economists have customarily regarded as a means of increased productivity, could be a source of idleness. Plowing, for example, seems to have been a special skill—a plowman was paid at a higher rate than ordinary farm workers. But the ordinary laborer's work might have to be synchronized with the plowman's, and a whole crew of men might be kept idle by a plowman's failure to get his job done at the appropriate time. It is difficult to say whether this type of idleness, resulting from failure to synchronize the performance of related tasks, was rising or declining; but cheap, inefficient, irresponsible labor would be unlikely to generate pressures for the careful planning of time.

The government, while seeking to discourage idleness through laws requiring long hours of work, also passed laws that inadvertently discouraged industry. A policy that might be characterized as the conservation of employment frustrated those who wanted to do more work than others. English economic policy seems to have rested on the assumption that the total amount of work for which society could pay was strictly limited and must be rationed so that everyone could have a little, and those with family responsibilities could have a little more. It was against the law for a man to practice more than one trade or one craft. And although large numbers of farmers took up some handicraft on the side, this was to be discouraged, because "for one man to be both an husbandman and an Artificer is a gatheringe of divers mens livinges into one mans hand." So as not to take work away from his elders, a man could not independently practice most trades until he had become a master through seven years of apprenticeship. Even then, until he was thirty years old or married, he was supposed to serve some other master of the trade. A typical example is the case of John Pikeman of Barking, Essex, a tailor who was presented by the grand jury because he "being a singleman and not above 25 years of age, does take in work of tailoring and works by himself to the hindrance of other poor occupiers, contrary to the law."

These measures doubtless helped to maintain social stability in the face of a rapid population increase, from under three million in 1500 to a probable four and a half million in 1640 (an increase reflected in the gap between wages and prices). But in its efforts to spread employment so that every able-bodied person would have a means of support, the government in effect discouraged energetic labor and nurtured the workingman's low expectations of himself. By requiring masters to engage apprentices for seven-year terms and servants (in agriculture and in most trades) for the whole year rather than the day, it prevented employers from hiring labor only when there was work to be done and prevented the diligent and effective worker from replacing the ineffective. The intention to spread work is apparent in the observation of the Essex justices that labor by the day caused "the great depauperization of other labourers." But labor by the year meant that work could be strung out to occupy an unnecessary amount of time, because whether or not a master had enough work to occupy his servants they had to stay and he had to keep them. The records show many instances of masters attempting to turn away a servant or apprentice before the stipulated term was up, only to have him sent back by the courts with orders that the master "entertain" him for the full period. We even have the extraordinary spectacle of the runaway master, the man who illegally fled from his servants and thus evaded his responsibility to employ and support them.

In pursuit of its policy of full employment in the face of an expanding population, the government often had to create jobs in cases where society offered none. Sometimes men were obliged to take on a poor boy as a servant whether they needed him or not. The parish might lighten the burden by paying a fee, but it might also fine a man who refused to take a boy assigned to him. To provide for men and women who could not be foisted off on unwilling employers, the government established houses of correction in every county, where the inmates toiled at turning wool, flax, and hemp into thread or yarn, receiving nothing but their food and lodging for their efforts. By all these means the government probably did succeed in spreading employment. But in the long run its policy, insofar as it was effective, tended to depress wages and to diminish the amount of work expected from any one man.

Above and beyond the idleness and underemployment that we may blame on the lethargy and irresponsibility of underpaid labor, on the failure to synchronize the performance of related tasks, and on the policy of spreading work as thinly as possible, the very nature of the jobs to be done prevented the systematic use of time that characterizes modern industrialized economies. Men could seldom work steadily, because they could work only at the tasks that could be done at the moment; and in sixteenth- and seventeenth-century England the tasks to be done often depended on forces beyond human control: on the weather and the seasons, on the winds, on the tides, on the maturing of crops. In the countryside work from dawn to dusk with scarcely an intermission might be normal at harvest time, but there were bound to be times when there was very little to do. When it rained or snowed, most farming operations had to be stopped altogether (and so did some of the stages of cloth manufacture). As late as 1705 John Law, imagining a typical economy established on a newly discovered island, assumed that the persons engaged in agriculture would necessarily be idle, for one reason or another, half the time.

To be sure, side by side with idleness and inefficiency, England exhibited the first signs of a rationalized economy. Professor J. U. Nef has described the many large-scale industrial enterprises that were inaugurated in England in the late sixteenth and early seventeenth centuries. And if the development of systematic agricultural production was advancing less rapidly than historians once supposed, the very existence of men like Robert Loder, the very complaints of the idleness and irresponsibility of laborers, the very laws prescribing hours of work all testify to the beginnings of a rationalized economy. But these were beginnings only and not widely felt. The laborer who seemed idle or irresponsible to a Robert Loder probably did not seem so to himself or to his peers. His England was not a machine for producing wool or corn. His England included activities and pleasures and relationships that systematic-minded employers would resent and that modern economists would classify as uneconomic. At the opening of the seventeenth century, England was giving him fewer economic benefits than she had given his grandfathers so that he was often ready to pull up stakes and look for a better life in another county or another country. But a life devoted to more and harder work than he had known at home might not have been his idea of a better life.

Perhaps we may now view Jamestown with somewhat less surprise at the idle and hungry people occupying the place: idleness and hunger were the rule in much of England much of the time; they were facts of life to be taken for granted. And if we next ask what the settlers thought they had come to America to do, what they thought they were up to in Virginia, we can find several English enterprises comparable to their own that may have served as models and that would not have led them to think of hard, continuous disciplined work as a necessary ingredient in their undertaking.

If they thought of themselves as settling a wilderness, they could look for guidance to what was going on in the northern and western parts of England and in the high parts of the south and east. Here were the regions, mostly wooded, where wastelands still abounded, the goal of many in the large migrant population of England. Those who had settled down were scattered widely over the countryside in isolated hovels and hamlets and lived by pasture farming, that is, they cultivated only small plots of ground and ran a few sheep or cattle on the common land. Since the gardens required little attention and the cattle hardly any, they had most of their time to themselves. Some spent their spare hours on handicrafts. In fact, they supplied the labor for most of England's minor industries, which tended to locate in pasture-farming regions, where agriculture made fewer demands on the inhabitants, than in regions devoted to market crops. But the pasture farmers seem to have offered their labor sporadically and reluctantly. They had the reputation of being both idle and independent. They might travel to the richer arable farming regions to pick up a few shillings in field work at harvest time, but their own harvests were small. They did not even grow the wheat or rye for their own bread and made shift to live in hard times from the nuts and berries and herbs that they gathered in the woods.

Jamestown was mostly wooded, like the pasture-farming areas of England and Wales; and since Englishmen used the greater part of their own country for pasture farming, that was the obvious way to use the wasteland of the New World. If this was the Virginians' idea of what they were about, we should expect them to be idle much of the time and to get grain for bread by trading rather than planting (in this case not wheat or rye but maize from the Indians); we should even expect them to get a good deal of their food, as they did, by scouring the woods for nuts and berries.

As the colony developed, a pasture-farming population would have been quite in keeping with the company's expectation of profit from a variety of products. The Spaniards' phenomenal success with raising cattle in the West Indies was well known. And the proposed employment of the settlers of Virginia in a variety of industrial pursuits (iron works, silk works, glass works, shipbuilding) was entirely fitting for a pasture-farming community. The small gardens assigned for cultivation by Governor Dale in 1614 will also make sense: three acres would have been far too small a plot of land to occupy a farmer in the arable regions of England, where a single man could handle thirty acres without assistance. But it would be not at all inappropriate as the garden of a pasture farmer. In Virginia three acres would produce more than enough corn to sustain a man for a year and still leave him with time to make a profit for the company or himself at some other job—if he could be persuaded to work.

Apart from the movement of migrant workers into wastelands, the most obvious English analogy to the Jamestown settlement was that of a military expedition. The settlers may have had in mind not only the expeditions that subdued the Irish but also those dispatched to the European continent in England's wars. The Virginia Company itself seems at first to have envisaged the enterprise as partly military, and the *Lawes, Divine, Morall and Martiall* were mostly martial. But the conception carried unfortunate implications for the company's expectations of profit. Military expeditions were staffed from top to bottom with men unlikely to work. The nucleus of sixteenth-century English armies was the nobility and the gangs of genteel ruffians they kept in their service, in wartime to accompany them into the field (or to go in their stead), in peacetime to follow them about as living insignia of their rank. Work was not for the nobility nor for those who wore their livery. According to the keenest student of the aristocracy in this period, "the rich and well-born were idle almost by definition." Moreover they kept "a huge labor force . . . absorbed in slothful and parasitic personal service." Aside from the gentlemen retainers of the nobility and their slothful servants the military expeditions that England sent abroad were filled out by misfits and thieves whom the local constables wished to be rid of. It was, in fact, government policy to keep the able-bodied and upright at home and to send the lame, the halt, the blind, and the criminal abroad.

The combination of gentlemen and ne'er-do-wells of which the leaders at Jamestown complained may well have been the result of the company's using a military model for guidance. The Virginia Company was loaded with noblemen (32 present or future earls, 4 countesses, 3 viscounts, and 19 barons). Is it possible that the large number of Jamestown settlers listed as gentlemen and captains came from among the retainers of these lordly stock-holders and that the rest of the settlers included some of the gentlemen's personal servants as well as a group of hapless vagabonds or migratory farm laborers who had been either impressed or lured into the enterprise by tales of the New World's abundance? We are told, at least, that persons designated in the colony's roster as "laborers" were "for most part footmen, and such as they that were Adventurers brought to attend them, or such as they could perswade to goe with them, that never did know what a dayes work was."

If these men thought they were engaged in a military expedition, military precedent pointed to idleness, hunger, and death, not to the effective organiza-tion of labor. Soldiers on campaign were not expected to grow their own food. On the other hand they *were* expected to go hungry often and to die like flies even if they never saw an enemy. The casualty rates on European expeditions resembled those at Jamestown and probably from the same causes: disease and undernourishment.

But the highest conception of the enterprise, often expressed by the lead-ers, was that of a new commonwealth on the model of England itself. Yet this, too, while it touched the heart, was not likely to turn men toward hard, effective, and continuous work. The England that Englishmen were saddled with as a model for new commonwealths abroad was a highly complex society in which the governing consideration in accomplishing a particular piece of work was not how to do it efficiently but who had the right or the duty to do it, by custom, law, or privilege. We know that the labor shortage in the New World quickly diminished considerations of custom, privilege, and specialization in the organization of labor. But the English model the settlers carried with them made them think initially of a society like the one at home, in which each of them would perform his own special task and not encroach on the rights of other men to do other tasks. We may grasp some of the assumptions about labor that went into the most intelligent plan-ning of a new commonwealth by considering Richard Hakluyt's recommenda-tion that settlers include both carpenters and joiners, tallow chandlers and wax chandlers, bowyers and fletchers, men to rough-hew pike staffs and other men to finish them.

If Jamestown was not actually troubled by this great an excess of special-ization, it was not the Virginia Company's fault. The company wanted to establish at once an economy more complex than England's, an economy that would include not only all the trades that catered to ordinary domestic needs of Englishmen but also industries that were unknown or uncommon in England: a list of artisans the company wanted for the colony in 1611 included such specialists as hemp planters and hemp dressers, gun makers and gunstock makers, spinners of pack thread and upholsterers of feathers. Whatever idleness arose from the specialization of labor in English society was multiplied in the New World by the presence of unneeded skills and the absence or shortage of essential skills. Jamestown had an oversupply of glassmakers and not enough carpenters or blacksmiths, an oversupply of gentlemen and not enough plowmen. These were Englishmen temporarily baffled by missing links in the economic structure of their primitive community. The later jack-of-all-trades American frontiersman was as yet unthought of. As late as 1618 Governor Argall complained that they lacked the men "to set their Ploughs on worke." Although they had the oxen to pull them, "they wanted men to bring them to labour, and Irons for the Ploughs, and harnesse for the Cattell." And the next year John Rolfe noted that they still needed "Carpenters to build and make Carts and Ploughs, and skilfull men that know how to use them, and traine up our cattell to draw them; which though we indeavour to effect, yet our want of experience brings but little to perfection but planting Tobacco."

Tobacco, as we know, was what they kept on planting. The first shipload of it, sent to England in 1617, brought such high prices that the Virginians stopped bowling in the streets and planted tobacco in them. They did it without benefit of plows, and somehow at the same time they managed to grow corn, probably also without plows. Seventeenth-century Englishmen, it turned out, could adapt themselves to hard and varied work if there was sufficient incentive.

But we may well ask whether the habits and attitudes we have been examining had suddenly expired altogether. Did tobacco really solve the labor problem in Virginia? Did the economy that developed after 1618 represent a totally new set of social and economic attitudes? Did greater opportunities for profit completely erase the old attitudes and furnish the incentives to labor that were needed to make Virginia a success? The study of labor in modern underdeveloped countries should make us pause before we say yes. The mere opportunity to earn high wages has not always proved adequate to recruit labor in underdeveloped countries. Something more in the way of expanded needs or political authority or national consciousness or ethical imperatives has been required. Surely Virginia, in some sense, became a success. But how did it succeed? What kind of success did it have? Without attempting to answer, I should like very diffidently to offer a suggestion, a way of looking ahead at what happened in the years after the settlement of Jamestown.

The founders of Virginia, having discovered in tobacco a substitute for the sugar of the West Indies and the silver of Peru, still felt the lack of a native labor force with which to exploit the new crop. At first they turned to their own overpopulated country for labor, but English indentured servants brought with them the same haphazard habits of work as their masters. Also like their masters, they were apt to be unruly if pressed. And when their terms of servitude expired—if they themselves had not expired in the "seasoning" that carried away most immigrants to Virginia—they could be persuaded to continue working for their betters only at exorbitant rates. Instead they struck out for themselves and joined the ranks of those demanding rather than supplying labor. But there was a way out. The Spanish and Portuguese had already demonstrated what could be done in the New World when a local labor force became inadequate: they brought in the natives of Africa.

Sources

Jamestown: The Physical Setting

These pictures are modern—and probably very accurate—representations of Jamestown as it looked in its early years. If these were the only sources of information you had about Jamestown, how would you describe the relationship between the town center and the outlying land? Why would you think the settlers chose this particular site for their point of beginning? Look back at the picture of the Indian village in Chapter 1 (p. 12). What similarities can you see between it and these representations of Jamestown? What details would signal you that Jamestown was more technologically advanced?

Painting by Sidney King/Photo by Thomas L. Williams.

Jamestown-Yorktown Foundation.

Life and Death in Virginia: Richard Frethorne's Account, 1623

Today it is virtually impossible for us to fully understand those who lived and died in Virginia. Our world is much different, and most of us have never experienced the anxiety, suffering, and isolation that was so much a part of everyday life in early Virginia. Fortunately, a few personal documents have survived those miserable years, and they help us to understand the predicament of the first settlers. Most of these documents were written by leaders. But the one that follows was written by an indentured servant, Richard Frethorne, in 1623, to his parents in England. All we know of Frethorne is contained in this letter.

Loving and kind father and mother:

My most humble duty remembered to you, hoping in God of your good health, as I myself am at the making hereof. This is to let you understand that I your child am in a most heavy case by reason of the nature of the

Richard Frethorne, Letter to his father and mother, March 20, April 2 and 3, 1623, in Susan M. Kingsbury, ed., *The Records of the Virginia Company of London,* IV (Washington, D.C.: Government Printing Office, 1935), pp. 58–62. Reprinted from Report of the Royal Commission on Historical Manuscripts, *Report on the Mss. of His Grace the Duke of Manchester* (London, 1881), VIII Report, Appendix II, pp. 40–41.

country, [which] is such that it causeth much sickness, [such] as the scurvy and the bloody flux and diverse other diseases, which maketh the body very poor and weak. And when we are sick there is nothing to comfort us; for since I came out of the ship I never ate anything but peas, and loblollie (that is, water gruel). As for deer or venison I never saw any since I came into this land. There is indeed some fowl, but we are not allowed to go and get it, but must work hard both early and late for a mess of water gruel and a mouthful of bread and beef. A mouthful of bread for a penny loaf must serve for four men which is most pitiful. [You would be grieved] if you did know as much as I [do], when people cry out day and night—Oh! that they were in England without their limbs—and would not care to lose any limb to be in England again, yea, though they beg from door to door. For we live in fear of the enemy every hour, yet we have had a combat with them on the Sunday before Shrovetide, and we took two alive and made slaves of them. But it was by policy, for we are in great danger; for our plantation is very weak by reason of the death and sickness of our company. For we came but twenty for the merchants, and they are half dead just; and we look every hour when two more should go. Yet there came some four other men yet to live with us, of which there is but one alive; and our Lieutenant is dead, and [also] his father and his brother. And there was some five or six of the last year's twenty, of which there is but three left, so that we are fain to get other men to plant with us; and yet we are but 32 to fight against 3000 if they should come. And the nighest help that we have is ten miles of us, and when the rogues overcame this place [the] last [time] they slew 80 persons. How then shall we do, for we lie even in their teeth? They may easily take us, but [for the fact] that God is merciful and can save with few as well as with many, as he showed to Gilead. And like Gilead's soldiers, if they lapped water, we drink water which is but weak.

And I have nothing to comfort me, nor is there nothing to be gotten here but sickness and death, except [in the event] that one had money to lay out in some things for profit. But I have nothing at all—no, not a shirt to my back but two rags (2), nor no clothes but one poor suit, nor but one pair of shoes, but one pair of stockings, but one cap, [and] but two bands. My cloak is stolen by one of my own fellows, and to his dying hour [he] would not tell me what he did with it; but some of my fellows saw him have butter and beef out of a ship, which my cloak, I doubt [not], paid for. So that I have not a penny, nor a penny worth, to help me to either spice or sugar or strong waters, without the which one cannot live here. For as strong beer in England doth fatten and strengthen them, so water here doth wash and weaken these here [and] only keeps [their] life and soul together. But I am not half [of] a quarter so strong as I was in England, and all is for want of victuals; for I do protest unto you that I have eaten more in [one] day at home than I have allowed me here for a week. You have given more than my day's allowance to a beggar at the door; and if Mr. Jackson had not relieved me, I should be in a poor case. But he like a father and she like a loving mother doth still help me.

For when we go to Jamestown (that is 10 miles of us) there lie all the ships that come to land, and there they must deliver their goods. And when we went up to town [we would go], as it may be, on Monday at noon, and come there by night, [and] then load the next day by noon, and go home in the afternoon, and unload, and then away again in the night, and [we would] be up about midnight. Then if it rained or blowed never so hard, we must lie in the boat on the water and have nothing but a little bread. For when we go into the boat we [would] have a loaf allowed to two men, and it is all [we would get] if we stayed there two days, which is hard; and [we] must lie all that while in the boat. But that Goodman Jackson pitied me and made me a cabin to lie in always when I [would] come up, and he would give me some poor jacks [to take] home with me, which comforted me more than peas or water gruel. Oh, they be very godly folks, and love me very well, and will do anything for me. And he much marvelled that you would send me a servant to the Company; he saith I had been better knocked on the head. And indeed so I find it now, to my great grief and misery; and [I] saith that if you love me you will redeem me suddenly, for which I do entreat and beg. And if you cannot get the merchants to redeem me for some little money, then for God's sake get a gathering or entreat some good folks to lay out some little sum of money in meal and cheese and butter and beef. Any eating meat will yield great profit. Oil and vinegar is very good; but, father, there is great loss in leaking. But for God's sake send beef and cheese and butter, or the more of one sort and none of another. But if you send cheese, it must be very old cheese; and at the cheesemonger's you may buy very good cheese for twopence farthing or halfpenny, that will be liked very well. But if you send cheese, you must have a care how you pack it in barrels; and you must put cooper's chips between every cheese, or else the heat of the hold will rot them. And look whatsoever you send me—be it never so much—look, what[ever] I make of it, I will deal truly with you. I will send it over and beg the profit to redeem me; and if I die before it come, I have entreated Goodman Jackson to send you the worth of it, who hath promised he will. If you send, you must direct your letters to Goodman Jackson, at Jamestown, a gunsmith. (You must set down his freight, because there be more of his name there.) Good father, do not forget me, but have mercy and pity my miserable case. I know if you did but see me, you would weep to see me; for I have but one suit. (But [though] it is a strange one, it is very well guarded.) Wherefore, for God's sake, pity me. I pray you to remember my love to all my friends and kindred. I hope all my brothers and sisters are in good health, and as for my part I have set down my resolution that certainly will be; that is, that the answer of this letter will be life or death to me. Therefore, good father, send as soon as you can; and if you send me any thing let this be the mark.
    ROT

Richard Frethorne,
Martin's Hundred

The names of them that be dead of the company [that] came over with us to serve under our Lieutenants:

John Flower	George Goulding
John Thomas	Jos. Johnson
Thos. Howes	our lieutenant, his father and
John Butcher	brother
John Sanderford	Thos. Giblin
Rich. Smith	George Banum
John Olive	a little Dutchman
Thos. Peirsman	one woman
William Cerrell	one maid
	one child

All these died out of my master's house, since I came; and we came in but at Christmas, and this is the 20th day of March. And the sailors say that there is two-thirds of the 150 dead already. And thus I end, praying to God to send me good success that I may be redeemed out of Egypt. So *vale in Christo*.

Loving father, I pray you to use this man very exceeding kindly, for he hath done much for me, both on my journey and since. I entreat you not to forget me, but by any means redeem me; for this day we hear that there is 26 of [the] Englishmen slain by the Indians. And they have taken a pinnace of Mr. Pountis, and have gotten pieces, armor, [and] swords, all things fit for war; so that they may now steal upon us and we cannot know them from [the] English till it is too late—[till the time] that they be upon us—and then there is no mercy. Therefore if you love or respect me as your child, release me from this bondage and save my life. Now you may save me, or let me be slain with infidels. Ask this man—he knoweth that all is true and just that I say here. If you do redeem me, the Company must send for me to my Mr. Harrod; for so is this Master's name. April, the second day.

Your loving son,
Richard Frethorne

Moreover, on the third day of April we heard that after these rogues had gotten the pinnace and had taken all furnitures [such] as pieces, swords, armor, coats of mail, powder, shot and all the things that they had to trade withal, they killed the Captain and cut off his head. And rowing with the tail of the boat foremost, they set up a pole and put the Captain's head upon it, and so rowed home. Then the Devil set them on again, so that they furnished about 200 canoes with above 1000 Indians, and came, and thought to have taken the ship; but she was too quick for them—which thing was very much talked of, for they always feared a ship. But now the rogues grow very bold and can use pieces, some of them, as well or better than an Englishman; for an Indian did shoot with Mr. Charles, my master's kinsman, at a mark of white paper, and he hit it at the first, but Mr. Charles could not hit it. But see the envy of these slaves, for when they could not take the ship, then our men saw them threaten Accomack, that is the next plantation. And now there is no way but starving; for the Governor told us and Sir George that except the *Seaflower* [should] come in or that we can fall foul of these rogues and get some corn from them, above half the land will surely be starved. For they had no crop last year by reason of these rogues, so that we have no corn but as ships do relieve us, nor we shall hardly have any crop this year; and we are as like to perish first as any plantation. For we have but two hogshead of meal left to serve us this two months, if the *Seaflower* do stay so long before she come in; and that meal is but three weeks bread for us, at a loaf for four [men] about the bigness of a penny loaf in England—that is but a halfpennyloaf a day for a man. Is it not strange to me, think you? But what will it be when we shall go a month or two and never see a bit of bread, as my master doth say we must do? And he said he is not able to keep us all. Then we shall be turned up to the land and eat barks of trees or molds of the ground; therefore with weeping tears I beg of you to help me. Oh, that you did see my daily and hourly sighs, groans, and tears, and [the] thumps that I afford mine own breast, and [the way I] rue and curse the time of my birth, with holy Job. I thought no head had been able to hold so much water as hath and doth daily flow from mine eyes.

But this is certain: I never felt the want of father and mother till now; but now, dear friends, full well I know and rue it, although it were too late before I knew it.

I pray you talk with this honest man. He will tell you more than now in my haste I can set down.

Your loving son,
Richard Frethorne

Virginia, 3rd April, 1623

3

Puritan Order

The settling of Jamestown was proclaimed to be God's work, in which spreading the Gospel took precedence over everything else. But few Englishmen set off for Virginia to establish a holy community. The first to embark on such a venture were the Pilgrims, a small group of Puritan extremists who had separated from the Church of England on the grounds that the king's church was hopelessly corrupt. After a brief spell in Holland, they came to Plymouth in 1620 hoping to establish a Zion in the wilderness. Ten years later, a much larger and more affluent group of Puritans settled just north of the Pilgrims, in and around Boston. They too hoped to establish a holy commonwealth. In both the Pilgrim colony at Plymouth and the Puritan settlement in Massachusetts Bay order was a primary goal and value. The Puritans and Pilgrims both felt that they had escaped an England that was in decline. There, they believed, the poor, servants, children—the powerless in general—no longer felt bound to submit to authority. And those with power—the court and the nobility—had become hopelessly corrupt. New England was more than a new beginning, then. It was an attempt to recover something that had been lost in the Old World. And recovery meant discipline, the sacrifice of individual interests to the community's paramount interest in order. To the leaders, discipline also meant the rounding off of individual beliefs to fit an agreed-upon consensus. At both Plymouth and Massachusetts Bay, there was a heavy preoccupation with compacts and covenants—agreements signed by the adult males who were heads of households, efforts to ward off dissent and disruption.

Despite their compacts and covenants, both groups had trouble with internal dissension. One of the ironies of Puritanism—with Protestantism generally—was its tendency to split into warring factions. Puritans never abandoned the ideal of establishing a single universal church. But the Bible—their sole source of authority—was subject to various interpretations. Truths that seemed self-evident to one Puritan did not seem so to others who were equally eager to find the true path to salvation. Ministers denounced one another for teaching false doctrine. Congregations split into bickering cliques. And community leaders constantly had to worry about firebrands such as Roger Williams and Anne Hutchinson who challenged established norms.

To overcome disunity, and to establish a godly community in an ungodly world, Puritans relied not only on deep religious faith but also on such basic social institutions as the family. Early Virginia was settled mainly by bachelors. New England Puritans would not even permit single persons to live as bachelors. Puritan New England was settled by families, and all single persons had to live within a family. Outside the family, so Puritans believed, ungodliness and anarchism were sure to gain the upper hand. In turn, all families had to live within a specified distance of the church, which was seen as the larger family to which all individual families were subordinate.

Interpretive Essay

Laurel Thatcher Ulrich

Deputy Husbands

In the following selection, Professor Laurel Thatcher Ulrich, a historian at the University of New Hampshire, examines the role of women in Puritan New England. Puritan society was male-dominated and father-oriented. But Ulrich finds that in everyday life women were regarded as fully capable of handling male duties, and were expected to do so if it furthered the good of their families and was acceptable to their husbands. As you read, think about the way Puritans dealt with questions of sex differentiation. Were they basically rigid or flexible? Do you see any contradictions? Think also about how the Puritan family may have been a model of the problem of the larger society: how to keep order and still allow a measure of "Christian liberty" to all participants.

Many historians have assumed, with Page Smith, that "it was not until the end of the colonial era that the idea of a 'suitable' or 'proper' sphere of feminine activities began to emerge." For fifty years historians have relied upon the work of Elizabeth A. Dexter, who claimed that there were more "women of affairs" proportionally in eighteenth-century America than in 1900. Colonial newspapers yield evidence of female blacksmiths, silversmiths, tinworkers, shoemakers, shipwrights, tanners, gunsmiths, barbers, printers, and butchers, as well as a great many teachers and shopkeepers. Partly on the basis of such evidence, Richard Morris concluded in his pioneering study of female legal rights that American women in the colonial period attained "a measure of individuality and independence in excess of that of their English sisters."

Recently, however, a few historians have begun to question these assumptions. Mary Beth Norton has carefully studied the claims of 468 loyalist women who were refugees in Great Britain after the American Revolution. Only forty-three of these women mentioned earning money on their own or even assisting directly in their husbands' business. As a group, the loyalist women were unable to describe their family assets, other than household possessions, and they repeatedly described themselves as "helpless" to manage the business thrust upon them. She has concluded that these women were "almost wholly domestic, in the sense that that word would be used in the nineteenth-century United States." In a study of widowhood in eighteenth-century Massachusetts, Alexander Keyssar came to similar conclusions. Economic dependency, first upon husbands, then upon grown sons, characterized the lives of women in the agricultural village of Woburn.

Both groups of historians are right. The premodern world did allow for greater fluidity of role behavior than in nineteenth-century America, but colonial women were by definition basically domestic. We can account for these apparently contradictory conclusions by focusing more closely upon the economic relationship of husband and wife. There is a revealing little anecdote in a deposition recorded in Essex County in 1672. Jacob Barney of Salem had gone to Phillip Cromwell's house to negotiate a marriage. Although both Cromwell and his wife were present, Barney had turned to the husband, expecting, as he said, "to have their minds from him." But because Cromwell had a severe cold which had impaired his hearing, he simply pointed to his wife and said that whatever she agreed upon, "he would make it good." This incident dramatizes three assumptions basic to family government in the traditional world:

1. The husband was supreme in the external affairs of the family. As its titular head, he had both the right and the responsibility to represent it in its dealings with the outside world.

2. A husband's decisions would, however, incorporate his wife's opinions and interest. (Barney expected to hear *their* minds from *him*.)

3. Should fate or circumstance prevent the husband from fulfilling his role, the wife could appropriately stand in his place. As one seventeenth-century Englishman explained it, a woman "in her husband's absence, is

wife and deputy-husband, which makes her double the files of her diligence. At his return he finds all things so well he wonders to see himself at home when he was abroad.''

To put it simply, Dexter's evidence points to what was permissible in colonial society, Norton's to what was probable. As deputy husbands a few women, like Mistress Cromwell, might emerge from anonymity; most women did not. Yet both sets of evidence must be analyzed apart from modern assumptions about the importance of access to jobs in expanding female opportunity. The significance of the role of deputy husband cannot be determined by counting the number of women who used it to achieve independence. To talk about the independence of colonial wives is not only an anachronism but a contradiction in logic. A woman became a wife by virtue of her dependence, her solemnly vowed commitment to her husband. No matter how colorful the exceptions, land and livelihood in this society were normally transmitted from father to son, as studies like Keyssar's have shown.

One can be dependent, however, without being either servile or helpless. To use an imperfect but nonetheless suggestive analogy, colonial wives were dependent upon patriarchal families in somewhat the same way seventeenth-century ministers were dependent upon their congregations or twentieth-century engineers are dependent upon their companies. That is, they owned neither their place of employment nor even the tools of their trade. No matter how diligently they worked, they did not expect to inherit the land upon which they lived any more than a minister expected to inherit his meetinghouse or an engineer his factory. Skilled service was their major contribution, secure support their primary compensation. Unlike professionals in either century, they could not resign their position, but then neither could they be fired. Upon the death of a husband they were entitled to maintenance for life—or until they transferred their allegiance (symbolized by their name) from one domestic establishment to another.

The skilled service of a wife included the specialized housekeeping skills described in the last chapter, but it also embraced the responsibilities of a deputy husband. Since most productive work was based within the family, there were many opportunities for a wife to "double the files of her diligence." A weaver's wife, like Beatrice Plummer, might wind quills. A merchant's wife, like Hannah Grafton, might keep shop. A farmer's wife, like Magdalen Wear, might plant corn.

Looking backward to the colonial period from the nineteenth century, when "true womanhood" precluded either business enterprise or hard physical labor, historians may miss the significance of such work, which tells us less about economic opportunity (which for most women was limited) than about female responsibility (which was often very broad). Most occupations were indeed gender-linked, yet colonial Englishmen were far less concerned with abstract notions like "femininity" than with concrete roles like "wife" or "neighbor." Almost any task was suitable for a woman as long as it furthered the good of her family and was acceptable to her husband. This approach was both fluid and fixed. It allowed for varied behavior without really challenging the patriarchal order of society. There was no proscription against female farming, for example, but there were strong prescriptions toward dutiful wifehood and motherhood. Context was everything.

In discussing the ability of colonial women to take on male duties, most historians have assumed a restrictive ideology in Anglo-American society, an essentially negative valuation of female capacity. Some historians have argued that this negative ideology was offset by the realities of colonial life; others have concluded it was not. This chapter reverses the base of the argument, suggesting that even in America ideology was more permissive than reality. Under the right conditions any wife not only *could* double as a husband, she had the responsibility to do so. In the probate courts, for example, widows who did not have grown sons were routinely granted administration of their husbands' estates. Gender restrictions were structural rather than psychological. Although there was no female line of inheritance, wives were presumed capable of husbanding property which male heirs would eventually inherit.

To explain fully the contradictions in such a system, we must return to the day-to-day behavior of individual husbands and wives, first examining the factors which enhanced the role of deputy husband and then exploring conditions which muted its significance for colonial women.

Historians can read wills, account books, and tax records, documents in which males clearly predominate, but they cannot so easily explore the complex decision-making behind these records. Scattered glimpses of daily interaction suggest that there was as much variation in seventeenth- and eighteenth-century families as there is today. Some wives were servile, some were shrews, others were respected companions who shared the authority of their spouses in the management of family affairs. Important conditions, however, separated the colonial world from our own. The most basic of these was spatial. Earlier we described an imaginary boundary stretching from house to yard, separating the domain of the housewife from the world of her husband. It is important to recognize that in reality no such barrier existed. Male and female space intersected and overlapped. Nor was there the sharp division between home and work that later generations experienced. Because servants and apprentices lived within the household, a family occasion—mealtime or nightly prayer—could become a business occasion as well.

In June of 1661 a young maid named Naomi Hull described a discussion which took place in the parlor of the Samuel Symonds' home in Ipswich, Massachusetts, early in that year. The case concerned the length of indenture of two Irish servants. According to the maid, all of the family had gathered for prayer when one of the Irishmen asked if a neighbor's son was coming the next day to plow. *Mistress* Symonds said she thought so. One of the men asked who would plow with him. *Mistress* Symonds said, "One of you." When the two men announced that their indenture was up and that they would work no longer, both the master and the mistress questioned the servants. At one point Mistress Symonds interrupted her husband. "Let them alone," she said. "Now they are speaking let them speak their own minds."

Because the involvement of Mistress Symonds was not at issue, this casual description of her participation is all the more impressive. Such an anecdote shows the way in which boundaries between male and female domains might blur in a common household setting.

Ambitious men in early America were often involved in many things at once—farming and running a gristmill, for example, or cutting timber and fishing. Because wives remained close to the house, they were often at the communications center of these diverse operations, given responsibility for conveying directions, pacifying creditors, and perhaps even making some decisions about the disposition of labor. On a day-to-day basis this might be a rather simple matter: remembering to send a servant to repair a breach in the dam after he finished in the field, for example, or knowing when to relinquish an ox to a neighbor. But during a prolonged absence of her husband a woman might become involved in more weighty matters.

Sometime in the 1670s Moses Gilman of Exeter, New Hampshire, wrote to his wife from Boston:

> Loving wife Elisabeth Gillman these are to desire you to speake to John Gillman & James Perkins and so order the matter thatt Mr. Tho. Woodbridge may have Twelve thousand fott of merchantable boards Rafted by thirsday night or sooner if poseble they Can for I have Absolutly sould them to him & if John Clough sen or any other doe deliver bords to make up the sum Give Receits of whatt you Receive of him or any other man and lett no bote bee prest or other ways disposed of untill I Returne being from Him who is yos till death
>
> Moses Gilman

If Gilman had doubted his wife's ability to "order the matter," he could have written a number of separate letters—to John Gilman, James Perkins, John Clough, and perhaps others. But securing a shipment of twelve thousand feet of merchantable boards entirely by letter would have been complicated and time-consuming. Instead, Gilman relied on the good sense of his wife, who would be respected as his surrogate, and who probably had acquired some expertise in making out receipts for forest products and in conveying instructions to lumbering and shipping crews. A "loving wife" who considered herself his "till Death" was more trustworthy than a hired servant or business associate. As a true consort, she would know that by furthering her husband's interest she furthered her own.

Thus, a wife with talent for business might become a kind of double for her husband, greatly extending his ability to handle affairs. This is beautifully illustrated in a document filed with the New Hampshire court papers. In February of 1674 Peter Lidget of Boston signed a paper giving Henry Dering of Piscataqua full power of attorney "to collect all debts due to him in that place and thereabout." On the reverse side of the document Dering wrote: "I Henry Dering have, and do hereby Constitute, ordaine, and appoint my loveing wife, Anne Dering my Lawful Attourney" to collect and sue for Peter Lidget's debts "by virtue of the Letter of Attourney on the other side." (Anne Dering was the widow of Ralph Benning of Boston. She left her married name—and perhaps some of her business acumen—to her great-grandson, Governor Benning Wentworth of New Hampshire.)

Court cases involving fishermen give some glimpses of the kinds of responsibility assumed by their wives, who often appear in the foreground as well as the background of the documents. Depositions in an action of 1660 reveal Anne Devorix working alongside her husband, "taking account" as a servant culled fish from a spring voyage. She herself delivered a receipt from the master of the ship to the shop where the final "reckoning" was made. When her husband was at sea, she supervised spring planting on the family corn land as well as protecting the hogsheads, barrels, and flakes at the shore from the incursions of a quarrelsome neighbor. Even more visible in the records is Edith Creford of Salem, who frequently acted as an attorney for her husband, at one point signing a promissory note for £33 in "merchantable cod fish at price current." Like the fishwives of Nantucket whom Crèvecoeur described a hundred years later, these women were "necessarily obliged to transact business, to settle accounts, and in short, to rule and provide for their families."

At a different social level the wives of merchant sea captains played a similar role. Sometime in the year 1710 Elizabeth Holmes of Boston sat down with Patience Marston of Salem and settled accounts accumulated during a voyage to Newfoundland. Neither woman had been on the ship. They were simply acting as attorneys for their husbands, Captain Robert Holmes, who had commanded the brigantine, and Mr. Benjamin Marston, who owned it. Family letters give a more detailed picture of Mistress Marston's involvement in her husband's business.

In the summer of 1719 Benjamin Marston took command of one of his own ships, taking his twenty-two-year-old son Benjamin with him. Young Benjamin wrote his mother complete details of the first stage of the journey, which ended at Casco Bay in Maine. He included the length of the journey, the state of the family enterprises in Maine, and the price of lumber and staves, adding that he was "Sorry you should sett so long in ye house for no Adv[ance] but perhaps to ye prejudice of your health." Patience was obviously "keeping shop." A week later Benjamin wrote again, assuring his mother that he was looking after the business in Maine. "My father w[oul]d have been imposed upon by m——c had I not interposed and stood stiffly to him," he explained. Was the son acting out some Oedipal fantasy here, or was he perhaps performing as his *mother's* surrogate, strengthening the resolve of the presumably more easygoing father? The next day he wrote still another letter, asking for chocolate, complaining boyishly that "ye Musketo's bitt me so prodigiously as I was writing that I can hardly tell what it was I wrote," and conveying what must by then have been a common request from the absent husband. Mrs. Marston was to get a witnessed statement regarding a piece of family business and send it by "the first Oppertunity."

Because the business activities of wives were under the "wing, protection, and cover" of a husband (to repeat Blackstone's phrase), they are difficult to measure by standard methods. Patience Marston was a custodian of messages, guardian of errands, preserver of property, and keeper of accounts. Yet without the accidental survival of a few family papers there would be no way of knowing about her involvement in her husband's business. In Benjamin's will she received the standard "thirds." She may have become impatient with her chores or anxious about her husband's business acumen, but there is no indication of this in the only writings preserved in her hand. She served as "deputy husband" as circumstances demanded, and when her husband perished from smallpox soon after arriving in Ireland, she declared herself grateful for the dear son who returned "as one from the dead" to take over his father's business.

The role of deputy husband deserves more careful and systematic study. But two cautions are in order. First, the biases of the twentieth century may tempt historians to give undue significance to what were really rather peripheral enterprises. Acting as attorney to one's husband is not equivalent to practicing law. To colonial women, it may even have been less desirable than keeping house. This leads to the second point. The value of any activity is determined by its meaning to the participant, not to the observer. In early America position was always more important than task. Colonial women might appear to be independent, even aggressive, by modern standards, yet still have derived their status primarily from their relationship to their husbands.

This is well illustrated in a New Hampshire court record of 1671. A carpenter named John Barsham testified about an argument he had heard between Henry Sherburne and his second wife, Sarah, who was the widow of Walter Abbott. Barsham had come to the house to get some nails he needed for repairing a dwelling he had rented from them. According to Barsham, Sarah became so angry at her husband's opposition that she "rose off from the seat where she was setting & came up to him with her arms akimbo saying we should have nayles & he had nothing to [do] in it." As if to add the final authority to her demand, she asked him "why he trode upon Walter Abbotts floor & bid him get out of doors, & said that he had nothing to do there." Sarah Sherburne was an experienced and assertive woman. She had kept tavern "with two husbands and none." The house in which she and Sherburne lived had been part of her inheritance from her first husband. But in the heat of the argument she did not say, "Get out of *my* house" or "Get out of the house *I* provided." She said, "Get out of Walter Abbott's house." Her identity was not as property owner, but as wife. To assert her authority over her husband, she invoked the memory of his predecessor.

For some women, the realities of daily life in coastal New England enhanced the role of deputy husband. For others, discrepancies in education as well as the on-again-off-again nature of the role made involvement in the family business just another chore. A woman who worked effectively as an assistant, especially with the authority of a living husband behind her, could still be insecure in handling complex business arrangements. Finally (and

perhaps the most important point of all), most woman had other things to
do. A closer examination of female economic life suggests not only separate
education and separate duties but separate lines of trade.

Selectman's indentures from mid–eighteenth–century Newbury show the
contrasting training offered boys and girls at the lowest end of the social
spectrum in a commercial town. Between 1743 and 1760 the selectman indentured sixty children of the town poor. Forty-nine of these were boys, who
were apprenticed to blacksmiths, shipwrights, cordwainers, coopers, weavers,
tanners, tailors, joiners, blockmakers, riggers, mastmakers, and even a perri-
wig-maker in the town. The eleven girls, on the other hand, were promised
instruction in the generalized skills of "housewifery" or "women's work,"
though occasionally spinning, carding, sewing, and knitting were also specified. Often the phrase "Art, Trade, or Mystery" on these printed forms
was crossed out in the girls' indentures. All of the children were assured
instruction in reading, but only the boys were to learn "to write a Ledgable
hand & cypher as far as the Gouldin Rule" or "to write & Cypher as far as
ye Rule of three or so far as to keep a Tradesmans Book."

That more than four times as many boys as girls were apprenticed suggests that the support of poor girls was usually handled in some other way.
Either they remained with their families or were placed as day workers or
maids on a less formal basis among the housewives of the town. The crossed-
out passages in the indentures highlight the anomalous position of these female
apprentices. Clearly, the training of artisans and the training of their wives
were two separate processes belonging to two separate systems. A female
might learn the mysteries of blacksmithing or tanning—but only informally,
by working as a helper to the men in her family. Predictably, in the region
as a whole, women lagged far behind men in their ability to write, a dis-
crepancy which actually increased over the eighteenth century.

What this meant in the daily lives of ordinary women is suggested by
extant account books from the period. Although many such books survive,
in the entire century between 1650 and 1750 there is not a single one known
to have been kept by a woman. Purchasing an account book was a significant
step for a farmer or village craftsman. A Topsfield weaver recognized this
when he wrote in the inside of his new book, "John Gould his Book of
accounts I say my Book my owne book and I gave one shillin and four
pence for it so much and no more." Books like Gould's fall somewhere
between the systematic, literate, merchant-oriented economy which came to
dominate the external trade of New England and the local, personal, largely
oral trade networks which were central to village life. As deputy husbands a
few women might participate in the former, but for most wives economic
life was centered in the latter.

Something of the range of bookkeeping methods employed in colonial
America is preserved in an anonymous account book from Portsmouth, New
Hampshire. One segment of this record was kept in the unformed scrawl
typical of ordinary craftsmen and farmers; another was neatly posted in the
hand of a professional clerk. But evidence of a third and quite different method

is preserved in entries for a laborer named Richard Trip, who traded work in the "gundalow" (a Piscataqua sailing vessel) for "75 meals of victualls" and "75 nights of lodging brot from the acco[un]t kept in chaulk on the wall." The wife of the unknown shopkeeper may have been responsible for the chalk account as well as for providing the "diet," "washing," and "mittins" recorded in Trip's debits. For this sort of bookkeeping she had no need for "cyphering."

Judging only from the account books, one might conclude that most married women were seldom involved in trade even on the village level. Yet account books represent but one strand of the village economy. Other sources point to an extensive, less systematic, and largely oral trade network in which women predominated. A court case of 1682 provides an interesting example. When a woman named Grace Stout appeared to answer several charges of theft, the witnesses against her included thirty-four persons, among them twenty-one housewives who were able to give precise accounts of the value of work performed or goods received. These were petty transactions— kneading bread for one woman, purchasing stockings knitted by another— not the sort of thing to turn up in a colonial trade balance but nevertheless an essential part of the fabric of economic life.

The account books themselves give negative evidence of a separate female network. Although most ledgers include a few female names, the great majority of written accounts are with men, with credits reflecting the dominant commodities in each community. Ipswich farmers traded grain, farm labor, and animal products for shoes, weaving, rum, tobacco, skillets, and cotton wool. Householders from Marblehead paid for the same items in cash and fish, while those from Exeter usually offered pine, oak, and hemlock boards as well as labor. Entries for the products of female craft are infrequent; most sustained accounts for butter, cheese, sewing, or spinning are listed under the names of widows. This pattern is especially striking in the few accounts which shift from the name of a husband to the name of his widow. Thomas Bartlett, a Newbury shoemaker, listed twenty-one entries under the name of Ephraim Blesdel from March 13, 1725, until October 16, 1730. Until the middle of July 1728 the credits included hides, cider, onions, codfish, veal, and cash. But on that date Bartlett reckoned with "the widow Debrath Blesdel." Nine of the twelve credits which follow are for spinning. There is pathos in a second series recorded in Bartlett's book. From November 1729 until September 1733 he listed twenty-seven debits under John Wood's name, all for making and mending shoes. The credits already included some spinning as well as cash and skins when, on June 8, 1732, he noted in a taciturn entry: "husbands shoes sent back." From that point on, the account was with "Widow Anne Wood," who now attempted to pay for her shoes in dried sage from her garden and in additional spinning.

Anne Wood was probably trading small amounts of sage long before her husband's death. The accumulation of minor transactions which composed female trade could become substantial without ever appearing in written accounts. Suggestive evidence of this appears in the account book of Thomas

Chute, a tailor from Marblehead, Massachusetts, who became one of the first settlers of New Marblehead in frontier Maine. In May of 1737 Chute reckoned with Joseph Griffin of Marblehead, matching his own charges for tailoring against £8 debited in Griffin's book, finally balancing the whole with £4 pending, "By you[r] wives accoumpt with mine." A similar entry appears forty years later, in 1766, when he added to a £25 total accumulated by John Farrow of New Marblehead the sum of £3 "by yr wifes & mine acoumpts." For the most part, the trade of Thomas Chute and the trade of his wife were harmoniously separate.

Informal, oral, local, petty—female enterprise appears as the merest flicker on the surface of male documents. That it existed seems clear enough. The problem is in determining its value to the participants.

Potentially at least, managing a female specialty might be even more attractive than simply helping in a husband's work. An Ipswich woman known in the records only as Mistress Hewlett became so successful in the poultry business that she was able to loan money to her husband. When a friend expressed surprise at this arrangement, arguing that the wife's income really belonged to him if he needed it, Ensign Hewlett replied, "I meddle not with the geese nor the turkeys for they are hers for she has been and is a good wife to me." To the neighbor, loaning money to one's spouse was contradictory, an assertion of individual rather than communal values. But to Hewlett, no such threat was implied. His wife had "been a good wife." As long as independent female trade remained a minor theme within a larger communal ethic, it did not threaten either male supremacy or the economic unity of the family.

Yet consider the case of Mary Hunt of Portsmouth. Her encounter with Samuel Clark suggests both the opportunities and the limitations of female trade. When she found a cheese missing from her house after the fast day in October of 1675, she suspected Clark, who was a near neighbor. Storming into his house, she opened a drawer. There between two pieces of biscuit was the evidence she needed, an uneaten morsel notched, as she later testified, "with the very same marke which I put upon my best cheeses." Mary Hunt's accusation was brash, for Clark had once served on a jury which convicted her of stealing from the prominent Cutt family when she lived with them as a maidservant. Her new status as a housewife and as a cheese dealer had obviously given her a sense of power as well as an opportunity for revenge.

The story does not end there, however. A marked cheese does not have the durability of a marked tankard or clock. Unfortunately, Mary Hunt's cheese did not make it to court in November, much less into the stream of physical artifacts from which we derive our understanding of a culture. Clark's servant apparently swallowed the evidence. Though Hunt won her case in the fall, Clark successfully appealed in June, standing on his dignity as a man never before suspected of "any crime much less so base a crime as theft and for so sorry a matter as cheese." Part of his long—and professionally inscribed—defense was a counter-accusation: it was well known in the neighborhood, he said, that Goody Hunt sold her products to "one and another" and was apt to do so without her husband's knowledge, crying theft if called to reckon.

Clearly, the informal nature of female trade might work to the advantage of a woman who wanted a little extra income independent of her husband, yet ultimately the economic power of any woman was inseparable from her larger responsibility as wife. The role of housewife and the role of deputy husband were two sides of the same coin. Whether trading cheese or shipping barrel staves, a good wife sustained and supported the family economy and demonstrated her loyalty to her husband.

In the absence of a husband, the same skills might prove inadequate to independence. An anonymous document in the Essex Institute at Salem, Massachusetts, reveals the chasm which might develop between "female trade" and "male business." The unknown author of this little treatise had been accused of fraudulently securing a deed from an aged widow. In his defense he methodically itemized the charges against him, then answered each in turn. Two are of particular interest here—first, that the woman knew but little of the "common commerce of life," and, second, that she was unable to form a "just idea" of what belonged to her or its value. The man answered the first charge with a flat denial:

> I nor no other Person In this Neaborrhood I donte believe Ever heard of her not knowing how for to Trade.

But he at least partly acknowledged the second:

> How could she or any other Person forme any just Idia of what they are worth when it is Eveadent that Part of it was In Another Persons hands . . . and She Not Knowing how for to Right so as for to keep my Acc[ount] nor she could not Read Righting nor she could not Chipher so as for to Cast up my Acc[ount].

These two statements summarize much of what we have said here. A talent for trade was one thing; the ability to handle complex business affairs was another. Although northern New England produced many Elizabeth Gilmans and Edith Crefords, women who successfully handled business in the absence of their husbands, it probably produced even more women like this anonymous widow of Salem. In her years as a housewife she had acquired considerable skill in the "common commerce of life" but little that would prepare her to deal with a sophisticated and aggressive assault on her property, especially when legal documents were involved. No longer able to rely upon a spouse or a son, she had truly become a "relict."

In February of 1757 Mary Russell of Concord, Massachusetts, wrote a letter to her brother-in-law Samuel Curwen of Salem in which she joked, "I should have answered Your letter long before this had I known when we were to come to Boston but you know I am a Femme Covert and cannot act for my self." Her wit betrays a deeper feeling—if not yet a *feminist* sense of injustice, certainly a quite consciously *feminine* annoyance at the officious pedantry of the law, at least as it was discussed in her own parlor. Mary Russell knew that the restrictions of the common law had little relationship to the ordinary decisions of her daily life. Within her own domain she acted confidently and independently.

Yet the predicament which she described in jest became a reality for at least some women in the course of the eighteenth century as both business and law became increasingly sophisticated. The loyalist widows whom Mary Beth Norton described were in this position. Without their husbands or the familiar surroundings of home, they were forced to deal with the complexities of an English court. Little wonder that they declared themselves "helpless."

Norton's more recent work has shown, however, that the American Revolution affected many patriot women in a strikingly different way. At first reluctantly and then with increasing confidence and skill, these wives took up the management of farms and businesses while their husbands were away at war. Norton believes that the war had dissolved traditional bound-aries, altering a "line between male and female behavior, once apparently so impenetrable." Our evidence from early New England suggests a quite differ-ent conclusion. If there was an "impenetrable" gender barrier in mid-eigh-teenth-century America, it was a new one. The avowed helplessness of the loyalist women may be a measure of increasing specialization in economic life just before the revolution. The competence of the patriot women is even clearer evidence of the persistence of the old role of deputy husband. That patriot women failed to establish permanent changes in female roles is hardly surprising, since they acted within rather than against traditional gender defini-tions.

The economic roles of married women were based upon two potentially conflicting values—gender specialization and identity of interest. A wife was expected to become expert in the management of a household and the care of children, but she was also asked to assist in the economic affairs of her husband, becoming his representative and even his surrogate if circumstances demanded it. These two roles were compatible in the premodern world be-cause the home was the communication center of family enterprise if not always the actual place of work. As long as business transactions remained personal and a woman had the support of a familiar environment, she could move rather easily from the role of housewife to the role of deputy husband, though few women were prepared either by education or by experience to become "independent women of affairs."

The role of deputy husband reinforced a certain elasticity in premodern notions of gender. No mystique of feminine behavior prevented a woman from driving a hard bargain or chasing a pig from the field, and under ideal conditions day-to-day experience in assisting with a husband's work might prepare her to function competently in a male world—should she lose her husband, should she find herself without a grown son, should she choose not to remarry or find it impossible to do so. But in the immediate world such activities could have a far different meaning. The chores assigned might be menial, even onerous, and, whatever their nature, they competed for attention with the specialized housekeeping responsibilities which every woman shared.

Sources

New England Primer, 1690

Puritan New England may have been the most literate community in the world. The ability to read was essential to these Protestant reformers. Even more than other Protestants, they were committed to the idea of the "priesthood of all believers"—the notion that the individual church member had to understand God's truth as well as any priest. The ability to read the Bible was the most important key to this possibility. Therefore, the Puritans tried to make sure that their children learned to read by requiring each town to maintain a public school, long before any European country had such an educational system. One of the first books published in the English-speaking colonies was a reading book for children, the *New England Primer* (1690). In format it was an alphabet book. But it was also a way of teaching morality and religion. How do the ideas presented in this alphabet book resemble those discussed in Ulrich's essay? Can you detect any differences between these ideas and the attitudes of the Virginia settlers discussed by Morgan in the preceding chapter?

(12)

A.
In ADAM's Fall
We sinned all.

B.
Heaven to find,
The BIBLE mind.

C.
CHRIST crucify'd,
For Sinners dy'd.

D.
The DELUGE drown'd
The Earth around.

E.
ELIJAH hid
By Ravens fed.

F.
The Judgment made
FELIX afraid.

(13)

G.
As runs the GLASS,
Our Life doth pass.

H.
My Book and HEART
Must never part.

J.
JOB feels the Rod,
Yet blesses GOD.

K.
Proud KORAH's Troop
Was swallow'd up.

L.
LOT fled to *Zoar*,
Saw fiery Shower
On *Sodom* pour.

M.
MOSES was he
Who *Israel's* Host
Led through the Sea.

American Antiquarian Society.

Harvard, 1636–1642

The New England colonists not only wanted to make certain that all the members of their society could read. They also wanted a supply of learned ministers. And they knew they could not count on the English universities to give them the preachers they needed. In 1636, very shortly after the first large migration to Massachusetts Bay, the colony founded a college, Harvard, to train its ministers. The following documents will give you considerable insight into the reasons why the college was created, its rules, and its program of study. How do the ideas that guided the college match up with the kinds of attitudes discussed in Ulrich's essay? Or do they coincide at all? How would you compare this educational system with the one you have experienced? Many differences are obvious, but are there any continuities and similarities? What does the administration of the college tell you about the relationship of church and state in Massachusetts?

After God had carried us safe to New England, and we had builded our houses, provided necessaries for our livelihood, reared convenient places for God's worship, and settled the civil government, one of the next things we longed for, and looked after, was to advance learning and perpetuate it

From "New England's First Fruits" (London, 1643) in *Sabin's Reprints* (New York, 1865), Quarto Series, no. vii.

to posterity, dreading to leave an illiterate ministry to the churches when our present ministers shall lie in the dust. And as we were thinking and consulting how to effect this great work, it pleased God to stir up the heart of one Mr. Harvard (a godly gentleman and a lover of learning, there living amongst us) to give the one half of his estate (it being in all about 1700 £) towards the erecting of a College, and all his library. After him another gave 300 £, others after them cast in more, and the public hand of the state added the rest. The College was, by common consent, appointed to be at Cambridge (a place very pleasant and accommodate), and is called (according to the name of the first founder) Harvard College.

The edifice is very fair and comely within and without, having in it a spacious hall (where they daily meet at commons, lectures, [and] exercises), and a large library with some books to it, the gifts of divers of our friends, their chambers and studies also fitted for and possessed by the students, and all other rooms of office necessary and convenient, with all needful offices thereto belonging. And by the side of the College a fair grammar school, for the training up of young scholars, and fitting of them for academical learning, that still, as they are judged ripe, they may be received into the College of this school; Master Corlet is the master, who hath very well approved himself for his abilities, dexterity, and painfulness in teaching and education of the youth under him.

Over the College is Master Dunster placed, as President, a learned, conscionable, and industrious man, who hath so trained up his pupils in the tongues and arts, and so seasoned them with the principles of Divinity and Christianity, that we have to our great comfort, (and in truth) beyond our hopes, beheld their progress in learning and godliness also.* The former of these hath appeared in their public declamations in Latin and Greek, and disputations logical and philosophical which they have been wonted (besides their ordinary exercises in the college hall) in the audience of the magistrates, ministers, and other scholars, for the probation of their growth in learning, upon set days, constantly once every month to make and uphold. The latter hath been manifested in sundry of them by the savory breathings of their spirits in their godly conversation. Insomuch that we are confident, if these early blossoms may be cherished and warmed with the influence of the friends of learning and lovers of this pious work, they will by the help of God come to happy maturity in a short time.

Over the College are twelve Overseers chosen by the General Court. Six of them are of the magistrates, the other six of the ministers, who are to promote the best good of it and (having a power of influence into all persons in it) are to see that every one be diligent and proficient in his proper place.

---

*Henry Dunster (1609–1658/59), the first president of Harvard, was forced to resign in 1654 because of his heretical beliefs regarding the efficacy of infant baptism although he was a satisfactory president in all other respects.

Rules and Precepts that are observed in the College

1. When any scholar is able to understand Tully, or such like classical Latin author *extempore,* and make and speak true Latin in verse and prose . . . and decline perfectly the paradigms of nouns and verbs in the Greek tongue, let him then and not before be capable of admission into the College.

2. Let every student be plainly instructed and earnestly pressed to consider well [that] the main end of his life and studies is *to know God and Jesus Christ which is eternal life,* John 17:3, and therefore to lay Christ in the bottom, as the only foundation of all sound knowledge and learning. And seeing the Lord only giveth wisdom, let everyone seriously set himself by prayer in secret to seek it of him . . .

3. Everyone shall so exercise himself in reading the Scriptures twice a day that he shall be ready to give such an account of his proficiency therein, both in theoretical observations of the language and logic, and in practical and spiritual truths, as his tutor shall require, according to his ability . . .

4. That they, eschewing all profanation of God's name, attributes, word, ordinances, and times of worship, do study with good conscience carefully to retain God and the love of His truth in their minds, else let them know that (notwithstanding their learning) God may give them up to strong delusions, and in the end to a reprobate mind . . .

5. That they studiously redeem the time: observe the general hours appointed for all the students, and the special hours for their own classes, and then diligently attend the lectures without any disturbance by word or gesture. And if in anything they doubt, they shall inquire, as of their fellows, so (in case of *non satisfaction*), modestly of their tutors.

6. None shall, under any pretence whatsoever, frequent the company and society of such men as lead an unfit and dissolute life. Nor shall any without his tutors leave, or (in his absence) the call of parents or guardians, go abroad to other towns.

7. Every scholar shall be present in his tutor's chamber at the seventh hour in the morning, immediately after the sound of the bell, at his opening the Scripture and prayer; so also at the fifth hour at night, and then give account of his own private reading, as aforesaid in particular the third, and constantly attend lectures in the hall at the hours appointed. But if any (without necessary impediment) shall absent himself from prayer or lectures, he shall be liable to admonition, if he offend above once a week.

8. If any scholar shall be found to transgress any of the laws of God, or the school, after twice admonition, he shall be liable, if not *adultus,* to correction; if *adultus,* his name shall be given up to the Overseers of the College, that he be admonished at the public monthly act.

The times and order of their studies, unless experience shall show cause to alter:

[1.] The second and third day of the week, read lectures as followeth:

To the first year at eight of the clock in the morning Logic the first three quarters, Physics the last quarter.

To the second year, at the ninth hour, Ethics and Politics at convenient distances of time.

To the third year at the tenth [hour] Arithmetic and Geometry the three first quarters, Astronomy the last.

Afternoon The first year disputes at the second hour.

The second year at the third hour.

The third year at the fourth, everyone in his Art.

[2.] The fourth day read Greek.

To the first year the Etymology and Syntax at the eighth hour.

To the second at the ninth hour, Prosodia and Dialects.

Afternoon The first year at second hour practice the precepts of Grammar in such authors as have a variety of words.

The second year at third hour practice in Poesy, Nonnus, Duport, or the like.

The third year perfect their Theory before noon, and exercise Style, Composition, Imitation, Epitome, both in Prose and Verse, afternoon.

[3.] The fifth day read Hebrew and the Eastern Tongues.

Grammar to the first year hour the eighth.

To the second, Chaldee at the ninth hour.

To the third, Syriac at the tenth hour.

Afternoon The first year practice in the *Bible* at the second hour.

The second in Ezra and Daniel at the third hour.

The third at the fourth hour in Trostius' New Testament.

[4.] The sixth day read Rhetoric to all at the eighth hour.

Declamations at the ninth. So ordered that every scholar may declaim once a month. The rest of the day [free from studies].

[5.] The seventh day read Divinity Catechetical at the eighth hour.

Commonplaces at the ninth hour.

Afternoon The first hour reads history in the winter, the nature of plants in the summer.

The sum of every lecture shall be examined before the new lecture be read.

Every scholar, that on proof is found able to read the originals of the Old and New Testament into the Latin tongue, and to resolve them logically, withal being of godly life and conversation, and at any public act hath the approbation of the Overseers and Master of the College, is fit to be dignified with his first degree.

Every scholar that giveth up in writing a system, or synopsis, or sum of Logic, Natural and Moral Philosophy, Arithmetic, Geometry and Astronomy, and is ready to defend his theses or positions, withal skilled in the originals as abovesaid, and of godly life and conversation, and so approved by the Overseers and Master of the College, at any public act, is fit to be dignified with his second degree.

Three Early New England Portraits

Our knowledge of the literate Puritans comes mostly from their own writings. But they left to posterity other kinds of evidence, including a number of individual portraits. The first is of a young boy, Henry Gibbs. Do you think he was really like that? Or do you think the portrait was a Puritan dream of what little boys should be like? What do you make of his clothing? What does the background—the tessellated floor—tell you about his society? The second portrait is a self-portrait of Thomas Smith. Do you think it is more revealing than young Henry's portrait? Why? What does the background say about his life, his concerns? The third portrait is of an ancient Puritan named Ann Pollard. Painted in 1721, she was one of the original settlers of Boston, coming over on one of the first ships as a "romping girl" of ten. She had outlived all her generation, and the portrait was done in honor of her one-hundredth birthday. Does she share any traits with young Henry Gibbs or with Thomas Smith?

"Henry Gibbs" (1670), Anonymous. *Collection of Mrs. David M. Giltinan/ Photo by Richard Lee.*

**Thomas Smith's
Self-Portrait (ca. 1675).**
Worcester Art Museum.

**"Ann Pollard" (1721),
Anonymous.** *Massachusetts
Historical Society/Photo by
George M. Cushing.*

The Trial of Anne Hutchinson, 1637

The Puritans might indoctrinate small children with their *Primer*. They might create tight rules at Harvard for the education of their ministers. But their world was full of dissent, despite their efforts. They never achieved their ideal of a community of Christian believers firm and secure in their shared faith. One of the sharpest controversies in Massachusetts erupted in the early 1630s and centered on a woman named Anne Hutchinson. Mrs. Hutchinson, a devout wife and mother of a large, well-to-do family, was in some ways a model Puritan. She studied scripture and listened intently to sermons. She held discussions with her neighbors in her home. But she began to argue, publicly, that the ministers were preaching too much about "works," or the behavioral obligations of Christians, and not enough about *grace:* God's free gift of salvation to the saved, a gift they could not earn through their own efforts. The leaders of the colony gradually recognized a threat to their authority and to the stability of their little society. They decided to try Anne Hutchinson and brought her into court in 1637. The colony's governor, John Winthrop, took the role of prosecutor. How would you describe Mrs. Hutchinson's attitude toward authority? toward law?

November 1637

The Examination of Mrs. Anne Hutchinson at the Court of Newtown

Mr. Winthrop, Governor: Mrs. Hutchinson, you are called here as one of those that have troubled the peace of the commonwealth and the churches here; you are known to be a woman that hath had a great share in the promoting and divulging of those opinions that are causes of this trouble, and to be nearly joined not only in affinity and affection with some of those the court had taken notice of and passed censure upon, but you have spoken divers things as we have been informed very prejudicial to the honour of the churches and ministers thereof, and you have maintained a meeting and an assembly in your house that hath been condemned by the general assembly as a thing not tolerable nor comely in the sight of God nor fitting for your sex, and notwithstanding that was cried down you have continued the same, therefore we have thought good to send for you to understand how things are, that if you be in an erroneous way we may reduce you that so you may become a profitable member here among us, otherwise if you be obstinate in your course that then the court may take such course that you may trouble

From Thomas Hutchinson, *The History of the Colony and Province of Massachusetts Bay* (Boston: Thomas and John Fleet, 1767), Vol. II, Appendix II, pp. 366–391.

us no further, therefore I would intreat you to express whether you do not assent and hold in practice to those opinions and factions that have been handled in court already, that is to say, whether you do not justify Mr. Wheelwright's sermon and the petition.

Mrs. Hutchinson: I am called here to answer before you but I hear no things laid to my charge.

Gov.: I have told you some already and more I can tell you.

Mrs. H.: Name one Sir.

Gov.: Have I not named some already?

Mrs. H.: What have I said or done?

Gov.: Why for your doings, this you did harbour and countenance those that are parties in this faction that you have heard of.

Mrs. H.: That's matter of conscience, Sir.

Gov.: Your conscience you must keep or it must be kept for you.

Mrs. H.: Must not I then entertain the saints because I must keep my conscience.

Gov.: Say that one brother should commit felony or treason and come to his brother's house, if he knows him guilty and conceals him he is guilty of the same. It is his conscience to entertain him, but if his conscience comes into act in giving countenance and entertainment to him that hath broken the law he is guilty too. So if you do countenance those that are transgressors of the law you are in the same fact.

Mrs. H.: What law do they transgress?

Gov.: The law of God and of the state.

Mrs. H.: In which particular?

Gov.: Why in this among the rest, whereas the Lord doth say honour thy father and thy mother.

Mrs. H.: Ey Sir in the Lord. . . .

Gov.: Why do you keep such a meeting at your house as you do every week upon a set day?

Mrs. H.: It is lawful for me to do so, as it is all your practices and can you find a warrant for yourself and condemn me for the same thing? The ground of my taking it up was, when I first came to this land because I did not go to such meetings as those were, it was presently reported that I did not allow of such meetings but held them unlawful and therefore in that regard they said I was proud and did despise all ordinances, upon that a friend came unto me and told me of it and I to prevent such aspersions took it up, but it was in practice before I came therefore I was not the first. . . .

Gov.: Well, we see how it is we must therefore put it away from you or restrain you from maintaining this course.

Mrs. H.: If you have a rule for it from God's word you may.

Gov.: We are your judges, and not you ours and we must compel you to it.

Mrs. H.: If it please you by authority to put it down I will freely let you for I am subject to your authority. . . .

Dep. Gov.: I would go a little higher with Mrs. Hutchinson. About three years ago we were all in peace. Mrs. Hutchinson from that time she came hath made a disturbance, and some that came over with her in the ship did inform me what she was as soon as she was landed. I being then in place dealt with the pastor and teacher of Boston and desired them to enquire of her, and then I was satisfied that she held nothing different from us, but within half a year after, she had vented divers of her strange opinions and had made parties in the country, and at length it comes that Mr. Cotton and Mr. Vane were of her judgment, but Mr. Cotton hath cleared himself that he was not of that mind, but now it appears by this woman's meeting that Mrs. Hutchinson hath so forestalled the minds of many by their resort to her meeting that now she hath a potent party in the country. Now if all these things have endangered us as from that foundation and if she in particular hath disparaged all our ministers in the land that they have preached a covenant of works, and only Mr. Cotton a covenant of grace, why this is not to be suffered, and therefore being driven to the foundation and it being found that Mrs. Hutchinson is she that hath depraved all the ministers and hath been the cause of what is fallen out, why we must take away the foundation and the building will fall.

Mrs. H.: I pray Sir prove it that I said they preached nothing but a covenant of works. . . .

Dep. Gov.: I do but ask you this, when the ministers do preach a covenant of works do they preach a way of salvation?

Mrs. H.: I did not come hither to answer to questions of that sort.

Dep. Gov.: Because you will deny the thing.

Mrs. H.: Ey, but that is to be proved first.

Dep. Gov.: I will make it plain that you did say that the ministers did preach a covenant of works.

Mrs. H.: I deny that.

Dep. Gov.: And that you said they were not able ministers of the new testament, but Mr. Cotton only.

Mrs. H.: If ever I spake that I proved it by God's word.

Court: Very well, very well. . . .

Gov.: Here are six undeniable ministers who say it is true and yet you deny that you did say that they did preach a covenant of works and that they were not able ministers of the gospel, and it appears plainly that you have spoken it. . . .

Mrs. H.: That I absolutely deny. . . .

Gov.: Mrs. Hutchinson, the court you see hath laboured to bring you to acknowledge the error of your way that so you might be reduced, the time now grows late, we shall therefore give you a little more time to consider of it and therefore desire that you attend the court again in the morning.

The Next Morning   Mrs. H.: If you please to give me leave I shall give you the ground of what I know to be true. Being much troubled to see the falseness of the constitution of the church of England, I had like to have turned separatist; whereupon I kept a day of solemn humiliation and pondering of the thing; this scripture was brought unto me—he that denies Jesus Christ to be come in the flesh is antichrist—This I considered of and in considering found that the papists did not deny him to be come in the flesh, nor we did not deny him—who then was antichrist? Was the Turk antichrist only? The Lord knows that I could not open scripture; he must by his prophetical office open it unto me. So after that being unsatisfied in the thing, the Lord was pleased to bring this scripture out of the Hebrews. He that denies the testament denies the testator, and in this did open unto me and give me to see that those which did not teach the new covenant had the spirit of antichrist, and upon this he did discover the ministry unto me and ever since, I bless the Lord, he hath let me see which was the clear ministry and which the wrong. Since that time I confess I have been more choice and he hath left me to distinguish between the voice of my beloved and the voice of Moses, the voice of John Baptist and the voice of antichrist, for all those voices are spoken of in scripture. Now if you do condemn me for speaking what in my conscience I know to be truth I must commit myself unto the Lord.

Mr. Nowel: How do you know that that was the spirit?

Mrs. H.: How did Abraham know that it was God that bid him offer his son, being a breach of the sixth commandment?

Dep. Gov.: By an immediate voice.

Mrs. H.: So to me by an immediate revelation.

Dep. Gov.: How! an immediate revelation.

Mrs. H.: By the voice of his own spirit to my soul. . . .

Gov.: The case is altered. . . . The ground work of her revelations is the immediate revelation of the spirit and not by the ministry of the word, . . . and this hath been the ground of all these tumults and troubles, and I would that those were all cut off from us that trouble us, for this is the thing that hath been the root of all the mischief.

Court: We all consent with you. . . .

Dep. Gov.: These disturbances that have come among the Germans have been all grounded upon revelations, and so they that have vented them have stirred up their hearers to take up arms against their prince and to cut the throats of one another, and these have been the fruits of them, and whether the devil may inspire the same into their hearts here I know not, for I am fully persuaded that Mrs. Hutchinson is deluded by the devil, because the spirit of God speaks truth in all his servants.

Gov.: I am persuaded that the revelation she brings forth is delusion.

All the court but some two or three ministers cry out we all believe it—we all believe it.

. . . Gov.: The court hath already declared themselves satisfied concerning the things you hear, and concerning the troublesomeness of her spirit and the danger of her course amongst us, which is not to be suffered. Therefore if it be the mind of the court that Mrs. Hutchinson for these things that appear before us is unfit for our society, and if it be the mind of the court that she shall be banished out of our liberties and imprisoned till she be sent away, let them hold up their hands.

All but three. . . .

Gov.: Mrs. Hutchinson, the sentence of the court you hear is that you are banished from out of our jurisdiction as being a woman not fit for our society, and are to be imprisoned till the court sends you away.

Mrs. H.: I desire to know wherefore I am banished?

Gov.: Say no more, the court knows wherefore and is satisfied.

4

The Have-Nots in Colonial Society

Once the colonies were established, colonial leaders faced a long-term problem. If they were to become rich, they had to recruit a labor force. Acquiring land was easy for a man of means, since land in America was so plentiful. But acquiring *labor* was a constant problem. The small farmer could rely on his family, but a man with broad acres needed extra hands. Where were they to be found?

One possible source was obviously the Indian. And colonists repeatedly tried to enslave the Indian. As late as 1708 South Carolina held 1,400 red men in bondage as compared to 4,100 Africans. But colonists found to their chagrin that enslaving the Indian was more trouble than it was worth. In any case, the supply of Indian labor was minute compared to the need. Since enslaving the Indians proved unworkable, the earliest planters had to look to Europe—particularly to England—for their solutions. (They would later, of course, look even farther, to Africa. But at first, black slavery was not an important factor in colonial life.) The most immediate solution to the labor problem seemed to lie in the English practice of "indentured" or contractual servitude. The arrangement was basically simple: in return for a promise of some kind—a promise to be fed and housed and trained in some work, for example—men or women could bind themselves to work for a master for a period of years. The most common term in England, and then in the colonies, was seven years. An agreement, called an indenture, would then be written and signed, and for the agreed-upon period of years, the servant would become the virtual property of the master.

As it happened, England in the seventeenth century contained thousands of young men and women who were desperate enough to bind themselves into servitude and risk the hazards of the Atlantic crossing—all in return for little more than the vague hope that they would somehow be better off at the end of their term. It is impossible to know just how many came, but probably as many as half of the immigrants of the seventeenth and eighteenth centuries came in bondage of one kind or another. Most were indentured servants; others were "redemptioners," who had only to work off the costs of their passage. But, no matter what the form, their servitude had much in common with slavery. Their contracts could be bought and sold. They could not live where they pleased, or marry without their masters' permission, or work for themselves. They had no guarantee of fair treatment or of decent food, clothing, and shelter.

The English government occasionally tried an even more drastic way of populating the colonies—and in the process ridding itself of social problems. A small but significant number of criminals and juvenile delinquents were simply "transported" to the New World.

Among them, the Indian slaves, the indentured servants, the redemptioners, and the convicts constituted a severely oppressed underclass. Traditionally, American historians have pictured white servitude in rosy colors, emphasizing the hard-working indentured servant who became a successful farmer after serving his time. But the rags-to-riches experience was truly exceptional, and indentured servants who ended up owning vast estates have always been more conspicuous in history textbooks than in history itself.

Interpretive Essay

Richard Hofstadter

White Servitude

In the following essay, the distinguished historian Richard Hofstadter paints a realistic picture of the lives of indentured servants. Hofstadter is anxious for his readers to understand that the early American experience was in many ways an "anguish," a terrible trial of human suffering and exploitation. If, as he points out, there was little sense of risk for the bondservants who peopled the English colonies, it was only because there was "so little at stake" for people whose lives in the Old World were worth little in any case. Why do you think that a historian like Hofstadter, writing at the end of the 1960s, might

have been more aware of the "anguish" of the colonial experience than his more traditional predecessors had been?

1

The transportation to the English colonies of human labor, a very profitable but also a very perishable form of merchandise, was one of the big businesses of the eighteenth century. Most of this labor was unfree. There was, of course, a sizable corps of free hired laborers in the colonies, often enjoying wages two or three times those prevalent in the mother country. But never at any time in the colonial period was there a sufficient supply of voluntary labor, paying its own transportation and arriving masterless and free of debt, to meet the insatiable demands of the colonial economy. The solution, found long before the massive influx of black slaves, was a combined force of merchants, ship captains, immigrant brokers, and a variety of hard-boiled recruiting agents who joined in bringing substantial cargoes of whites who voluntarily or involuntarily paid for their passage by undergoing a terminable period of bondage. This quest for labor, touched off early in the seventeenth century by the circulars of the London Company of Virginia, continued by William Penn in the 1680's and after, and climaxed by the blandishments of various English and continental recruiting agents of the eighteenth century, marked one of the first concerted and sustained advertising campaigns in the history of the modern world.

If we leave out of account the substantial Puritan migration of 1630–40, not less than half, and perhaps considerably more, of all the white immigrants to the colonies were indentured servants, redemptioners, or convicts. Certainly a good many more than half of all persons who went to the colonies south of New England were servants in bondage to planters, farmers, speculators, and proprietors. The tobacco economy of Virginia and Maryland was founded upon the labor of gangs of indentured servants, who were substantially replaced by slaves only during the course of the eighteenth century. "The planters' fortunes here," wrote the governor of Maryland in 1755, "consist in the number of their servants (who are purchased at high rates) much as the estates of an English farmer do in the multitude of cattle." Everywhere indentured servants were used, and almost everywhere outside New England they were vital to the economy. The labor of the colonies, said Benjamin Franklin in 1759, "is performed chiefly by indentured servants brought from Great Britain, Ireland, and Germany, because the high price it bears cannot be performed in any other way."

Indentured servitude had its roots in the widespread poverty and human

dislocation of seventeenth-century England. Still a largely backward economy
with a great part of its population permanently unemployed, England was
moving toward more modern methods in industry and agriculture; yet in
the short run some of the improvements greatly added to the unemployed.
Drifting men and women gathered in the cities, notably London, where they
constituted a large mass of casual workers, lumpenproletarians, and criminals.
The mass of the poverty-stricken was so large that Gregory King, the pioneer
statistician, estimated in 1696 that more than half the population—cottagers
and paupers, laborers and outservants—were earning less than they spent.
They diminished the wealth of the realm, he argued, since their annual expenses exceeded income and had to be made up by the poor rates, which
ate up one-half of the revenue of the Crown. In the early eighteenth century,
this situation made people believe the country was overpopulated and emigration to the colonies was welcomed; but in the latter part of the century, and
in the next, the overpopulation theory gave way to the desire to hoard a
satisfactory labor surplus. Yet the strong outflow of population did not by
any means cease. From the large body of poor drifters, many of them diseased,
feckless, or given to crime, came a great part of the labor supply of the rich
sugar islands and the American mainland. From the London of Pepys and
then of Hogarth, as well as from many lesser ports and inland towns, the
English poor, lured, seduced, or forced into the emigrant stream, kept coming
to America for the better part of two centuries. It is safe to guess that few
of them, and indeed few persons from the other sources of emigration, knew
very much about what they were doing when they committed themselves
to life in America.

    Yet the poor were well aware that they lived in a heartless world. One
of the horrendous figures in the folklore of lower-class London in the seventeenth and eighteenth centuries was the "spirit"—the recruiting agent who
waylaid, kidnapped, or induced adults to get aboard ship for America. The
spirits, who worked for respectable merchants, were known to lure children
with sweets, to seize upon the weak or the gin-sodden and take them aboard
ship, and to bedazzle the credulous or weak-minded by fabulous promises
of an easy life in the New World. Often their victims were taken roughly
in hand and, pending departure, held in imprisonment either on shipboard
or in low-grade hostels or brothels. To escaped criminals and other fugitives
who wanted help in getting out of the country, the spirits could appear as
ministering angels. Although efforts were made to regulate or check their
activities, and they diminished in importance in the eighteenth century, it
remains true that a certain small part of the white colonial population of
America was brought by force, and a much larger portion came in response
to deceit and misrepresentation on the part of the spirits.

    With the beginnings of substantial emigration from the Continent in
the eighteenth century the same sort of concerted business of recruitment
arose in Holland, the Rhenish provinces of Germany, and Switzerland. In
Rotterdam and Amsterdam the lucrative business of gathering and transship-
ping emigrants was soon concentrated in the hands of a dozen prominent

English and Dutch firms. As competition mounted, the shippers began to employ agents to meet the prospective emigrants at the harbor and vie in talking up the comforts of their ships. Hence the recruiting agents known as *Neülander*—newlanders—emerged. These newlanders, who were paid by the head for the passengers they recruited, soon branched out of the Dutch ports and the surrounding countryside and moved up the Rhine and the Neckar, traveling from one province to another, from town to town and tavern to tavern, all the way up to the Swiss cantons, often passing themselves off as rich men returned from the easy and prosperous life of America in order to persuade others to try to repeat their good fortune. These confidence men—"soul sellers" as they were sometimes called—became the continental counterparts of the English spirits, profiteers in the fate of the peasantry and townspeople of the Rhineland. Many of the potential emigrants stirred up by the promises of the newlanders were people of small property who expected, by selling some part of their land or stock or furnishings, to be able to pay in full for their passage to America and to arrive as freemen. What the passage would take out of them in blood and tears, not to speak of cash, was carefully hidden from them. They gathered in patient numbers at Amsterdam and Rotterdam often quite innocent of the reality of what had already become for thousands of Englishmen one of the terrors of the age— the Atlantic crossing.

2

In 1750 Gottlieb Mittelberger, a simple organist and music master in the Duchy of Württemberg, was commissioned to bring an organ to a German congregation in New Providence, Pennsylvania, and his journey inspired him to write a memorable account of an Atlantic crossing. From Heilbronn, where he picked up his organ, Mittelberger went the well-traveled route along the Neckar and the Rhine to Rotterdam, whence he sailed to a stopover at Cowes in England, and then to Philadelphia. About four hundred passengers were crowded onto the ship, mainly German and Swiss redemptioners, men pledged to work off their passage charges. The trip from his home district to Rotterdam took seven weeks, the voyage from Rotterdam to Philadelphia fifteen weeks, the entire journey from May to October.

What moved Mittelberger, no literary man, to write of his experiences was first his indignation against the lies and misrepresentations used by the newlanders to lure his fellow Germans to America, and then the hideous shock of the crossing. The voyage proved excruciating and there is no reason to think it particularly unusual. The long trip down the Rhine, with constant stops at the three dozen customs houses between Heilbronn and Holland, began to consume the limited funds of the travelers, and it was followed by an expensive stop of several weeks in Holland. Then there was the voyage at sea, with the passengers packed like herring and cramped in the standard bedsteads measuring two feet by six. "During the journey," wrote Mittelberger, "the ship is full of pitiful signs of distress—smells, fumes, horrors, vomiting, various kinds of sea sickness, fever, dysentery, headaches, heat, constipation, boils, scurvy, cancer, mouth-rot, and similar afflictions, all of them caused by the age and the highly-salted state of the food, especially of the meat, as well as by the very bad and filthy water, which brings about the miserable destruction and death of many. Add to all that shortage of food, hunger, thirst, frost, heat, dampness, fear, misery, vexation, and lamentation as well as other troubles. Thus, for example, there are so many lice, especially on the sick people, that they have to be scraped off the bodies. All this misery reached its climax when in addition to everything else one must suffer through two or three days and nights of storm, with everyone convinced that the ship with all aboard is bound to sink. In such misery all the people on board pray and cry pitifully together."

Even those who endured the voyage in good health, Mittelberger reported, fell out of temper and turned on each other with reproaches. They cheated and stole. "But most of all they cry out against the thieves of human beings! Many groan and exclaim: 'Oh! If only I were back at home, even lying in my pig-sty!' Or they call out: 'Ah, dear God, if I only once again had a piece of good bread or a good fresh drop of water.' " It went hardest with women in childbirth and their offspring: "Very few escape with their lives; and mother and child, as soon as they have died, are thrown into the water. On board our ship, on a day on which we had a great storm, a woman about to give birth and unable to deliver under the circumstances, was pushed through one of the portholes into the sea because her corpse was far back in the stern and could not be brought forward to the deck." Children under seven, he thought (though the port records show him wrong here), seldom survived, especially those who had not already had measles and smallpox, and their parents were condemned to watch them die and be tossed overboard. The sick members of families infected the healthy, and in the end all might be lying moribund. He believed disease was so prevalent because warm food was served only three times a week, and of that very little, very bad, very dirty, and supplemented by water that was often "very black, thick with dirt, and full of worms . . . towards the end of the voyage we had to eat the ship's biscuit, which had already been spoiled for a long time, even though no single piece was there more than the size of a thaler that was not full of red worms and spiders' nests."

The first sight of land gave heart to the passengers, who came crawling out of the hatches to get a glimpse of it. But then for many a final disappointment lay in wait: only those who could complete the payment of their fare could disembark. The others were kept on board until they were bought, some of them sickening within sight of land and, as they sickened, losing the chance of being bought on good terms. On landing some of these families were broken, when despairing parents indentured their children to masters other than their own.

Not even passengers of means who paid their way, moved more or less freely about ship, occupied cabins or small dormitories, and had superior rations could take an Atlantic crossing lightly. In addition to the hazards of winds too feeble or too violent, of pirates, shipwrecks, or hostile navies, there were under the best of circumstances the dangers of sickness. Travelers in either direction frequently died of smallpox or other diseases on board or soon after arrival. Anglican colonials often complained of the high mortality rate among their young would-be clergymen crossing to England to be ordained. The Dutch Reformed preacher Theodorus Frelinghuysen lost three of his five sons on their way to be ordained in Amsterdam. The evangelist George Whitefield on his first crossing to the colonies in 1738 saw a majority of the soldiers on board afflicted with fever and spent much of his time "for many days and nights, visiting between twenty and thirty sick persons, crawling between decks upon his knees, administering medicines and cordials" and giving comfort. On this voyage the captain's Negro servant died, was wrapped in a hammock and tossed into the sea. In the end all but a handful of the passengers took the fever, including Whitefield, who survived treatment by bleeding and emetics. The ship on which he returned a few months later was afflicted by a "contrary wind," drifted for over a week to the point at which crew and passengers were uncertain where they were, and took so long to arrive at Ireland that water rations, which had been cut to a pint a day, were just about to run out.

When paying passengers were exposed to such afflictions, how much worse must have been the sufferings of the servants and redemptioners packed into the holds, frequently at a density that violated the laws, and without adequate ventilation. Food provisions were calculated to last fourteen weeks, which was normally sufficient, but the rations deteriorated rapidly, especially in summer. Water turned stale, butter turned rancid, and beef rotted. If Mittelberger's voyage ranked among the worst, Atlantic crossings were frequently at or near the worst, and many more disastrous ventures were recorded. With bad luck, provisions could give out. The *Love and Unity* left Rotterdam for Philadelphia in May 1731 with more than 150 Palatines and a year later landed with 34, after having put in toward the end at Martha's Vineyard for water and food. On the way rations became so low that water, rats, and mice were being *sold,* and the storage chests of the dead and dying were broken open and plundered by the captain and crew. A ship called the *Good Intent*—the names of eighteenth century vessels often reek with irony—arrived off the American coast in the winter of 1751 but found herself unable to make port because of the weather; she was able to put in to harbor in the West Indies only after twenty-four weeks at sea. Nearly all of the passengers had died long before. The *Sea Flower,* which left Belfast with 106 passengers in 1741, was at sea sixteen weeks, and lost 46 passengers from starvation. When help arrived, six of the corpses had been cannibalized.

It is true that given adequate ventilation, a stock of lemon juice and vegetables, and good luck with the winds, decent sanitary arrangements were possible. The philanthropic Georgia Trustees, who were concerned about the health of their colonists, "put on board turnips, carrots, potatoes, and onions, which were given out with the salt meat, and contributed greatly to prevent the scurvy." Out of some fifteen hundred people who had gone to Georgia at the public expense, it was claimed in 1741, not more than six had died in transit. A traveler to Jamaica in 1739 reported that the servants on his ship "had lived so easily and well during the voyage, that they looked healthful, clean and fresh, and for this reason were soon sold," yet he saw another vessel arrive not long afterward with "a multitude of poor starved creatures, that seemed so many skeletons: misery appeared in their looks, and one might read the effects of sea-tyranny by their wild and dejected countenances."

3

The situation in which the indentured servant or the redemptioner found himself upon his arrival depended in large measure upon his physical condition. There would be a last-minute effort to clean up and appear presentable, and in some ports the healthy were separated from the sick, once colonial officials adopted quarantine measures. Boston, the most vigilant of the ports, had long kept a pesthouse on an island in the harbor and fined captains who disregarded the regulations. "As Christians and men," the governor of Pennsylvania urged in 1738, "we are obliged to make a charitable provision for the sick stranger, and not by confining him to a ship, inhumanly expose him to fresh miseries when he hopes that his sufferings are soon to be mitigated." Pennsylvania then designated Province Island for quarantine and built a pesthouse to harbor sick immigrants. In 1750 and again in 1765 it passed laws to bar overcrowding on ships. Laws passed by Virginia and Maryland in the 1760's providing for the quarantine of convict ships were frowned upon in London, and Virginia's law was disallowed.

Buyers came on shipboard to take their pick of the salably healthy immigrants, beginning a long process of examination and inspection with the muscles and the teeth, and ending with a conversational search for the required qualities of intelligence, civility, and docility. At Philadelphia buyers might be trying to find Germans and eschew the Scotch-Irish, who were reputed to be contumacious and work resistant and disposed to run away. Some buyers were "soul drivers" who bought packs of immigrants and brutally herded them on foot into the interior where they were offered along the way to ready purchasers. On the ships and at the docks there were final scenes of despair and frenzy as servants searched for lost articles of indenture, or lamented the disappearance of baggage, unexpected overcharges, the necessity of accepting indentures longer than their debts fairly required, the separation of families.

The final crisis of arrival was the process we would call acclimatization, in the eighteenth century known as "seasoning." Particularly difficult in the tropical islands, seasoning also took a heavy toll in the Southern colonies of the mainland. People from the cities and from the mild English climate found the summer hard going in any colony from Maryland southward, especially on plantations where indentured servants were put to arduous field labor by owners whose goal it was to get a maximum yield of labor in the four or five years contracted for. Fevers, malaria, and dysentery carried many off, especially in their first years of service. Seasoning was thought to be more or less at an end after one year in the new climate, and servants who had been wholly or partly seasoned were at a premium.

During the voyage, thoughtful servants might have recalled, quite a number of persons had battened on their needs—the spirit or the newlander, the toll collectors and the parasites of the seaports, the ship captain or merchant; now there was the master. Any traffic that gave sustenance to so many profiteers might well rest on a rather intense system of exploitation. A merchant who would spend from six to ten pounds to transport and provision an indentured servant might sell him on arrival—the price varied with age, skill, and physical condition—for fifteen to twenty pounds, although the profits also had to cover losses from sickness and death en route. The typical servant had, in effect, sold his total working powers for four or five years or more in return for his passage plus a promise of minimal maintenance. After the initially small capital outlay, the master simply had to support him from day to day as his services were rendered, support which was reckoned to cost about thirteen or fourteen pounds a year. In Maryland, where exploitation was as intense as anywhere, the annual net yield, even from unskilled labor, was reckoned at around fifty pounds sterling. The chief temptation to the master was to drive the servant beyond his powers in the effort to get as much as possible out of him during his limited years of service. The chief risk was that the servant might die early in service before his purchase price had been redeemed by his work. That he might run away was a secondary risk, though one against which the master had considerable protection. Still, hard as white servitude bore on servants, it was nevertheless not always a happy arrangement for owners, especially for those with little capital and little margin for error; shiftless and disagreeable servants, as well as successful runaways, were common enough to introduce a significant element of risk into this form of labor.

Indentured servants lived under a wide variety of conditions, which appear to have softened somewhat during the eighteenth century. Good or bad luck, the disposition of the master, the length of the term of work, the size of the plantation or farm, the robustness or frailty of the worker—all these had a part in determining the fate of each individual. Servants in households or on small farms might be in the not uncomfortable situation of familiar domestic laborers. Tradesmen who were trying to teach special skills to their workers, or householders who wanted satisfactory domestic service, might be tolerable masters. The most unenviable situation was that of servants on Southern plantations, living alongside—but never with—Negro slaves, both groups doing much the same work, often under the supervision of a relentless overseer. One has to imagine the situation of a member of the English urban pauper class, unaccustomed to rural or to any sustained labor, thrust into a hot climate in which heavy field labor—including, worst of all, the backbreaking task of clearing new land of rocks, trees, and shrubs—was his daily lot. Even as late as 1770 William Eddis, the English surveyor of customs at Annapolis, thought that the Maryland Negroes were better off than "the Europeans, over whom the rigid planter exercises an inflexible severity." The Negroes, Eddis thought, were a lifelong property, so were treated with a certain care, but the whites were "strained to the utmost to perform their allotted labour; and, from a prepossession in many cases too justly founded, they were supposed to be receiving only the just reward which is due to repeated offenses. There are doubtless many exceptions to this observation, yet, generally speaking, they groan beneath a worse than Egyptian bondage." Yet in Virginia, as the blacks arrived in greater numbers, white laborers seemed to have become a privileged stratum, assigned to lighter work and more skilled tasks.

The status and reputation of Southern indentured laborers were no doubt kept lower than elsewhere because there were a considerable number of transported convicts among them. Colonies to the north were not completely free of convict transportees, but the plantation system regularly put honest unfortunates alongside hardened criminals and lumped all together as rogues who deserved no better than what was meted out to them. Among the byproducts of English social change of the seventeenth and eighteenth centuries was a very substantial pool of criminal talents. The laws devised to suppress the criminal population were so harsh—scores of crimes were defined as felonies and hanging was a standard punishment for many trivial offenses—that England would have been launched upon mass hangings far beyond the point of acceptability had it not been for two devices that let many accused off the penalties prescribed for felons. One was the benefit of clergy—a practice inherited from the Middle Ages and continued until the early nineteenth century—which permitted a convicted felon to "call for the book" and prove his literacy. On the ancient assumption that those who could read were clerics and thus exempt from severe punishments by the secular state, the relatively privileged class of literate felons could be permitted to escape with the conventional branding on the thumb.

A second practice, however, the predecessor of convict transportation, was to secure royal pardons for ordinary offenders deemed by the judges to be worthy of some indulgence. Until the end of the French wars in 1713 it was customary to send them into the army, but in peacetime England did not know what to do with felons and drifters. In 1717 Parliament passed an act which in effect made royal clemency contingent upon transportation to the colonies for a term of labor; in consequence the large-scale shipping of convicts began which continued to the time of the American Revolution. To America at large, including the island colonies, around thirty thousand felons were transported in the eighteenth century, of whom probably more than two-thirds reached Virginia and Maryland, where they were readily snapped up by the poorer planters.

The whole procedure, though clearly intended to be a humane and useful alternative to wholesale hangings, was dreadfully feared by convicts, who may have guessed, quite rightly, that whoever bought their services would try to get the most out of them during their seven-year terms (fourteen years in the case of transmuted death penalties) of hard labor. In transit felons probably were fed somewhat better than they were used to, but usually they were kept below deck and in chains during the entire voyage, and on the average perhaps one in six or seven would die on the way. "All the states of horror I ever had an idea of," wrote a visitor to a convict ship, "are much short of what I saw this poor man in; chained to a board in a hole not above sixteen feet long, more than fifty with him; a collar and padlock about his neck, and chained to five of the most dreadful creatures I ever looked on." Mortality could run very high: on one ship, the *Honour,* which arrived in Annapolis in 1720, twenty of the sixty-one convicts had died. Merchants transporting felons on government contracts pleaded for subsidies to cover losses that hit them so hard.

While some planters rushed to the seaports to find convicts for their field labor supply, others were disturbed by the effect they expected criminals would have on the character of the population. These hazardous importations caused most anxiety in the colonies that received masses of transported felons. Pennsylvania subjected the importation of convicts to constant statutory harassment after 1722. Virginia at mid-century seems to have thought herself in the midst of a crime wave. The Virginia *Gazette* complained in 1751: "When we see our papers fill'd continually with accounts of the most audacious robberies, the most cruel murders, and infinite other villainies perpetrated by convicts transported from Europe, what melancholy, what terrible reflections it must occasion! What will become of our posterity? These are some of thy favours Britain. Thou art called our Mother Country; but what good mother ever sent thieves and villains to accompany her children; to corrupt some with their infectious vices and murder the rest? What father ever endeavour'd to spread a plague in his family? . . . In what can Britain show a more sovereign contempt for us than by emptying their jails into our settlements; unless they would likewise empty their jakes [privies] on our tables!" The concluding metaphor seems to have come quite naturally to the colonials: Franklin also used it, although he is better remembered for his suggestion that the Americans trade their rattlesnakes for the convicts. But all laws rejecting transported convicts were disallowed in England by the Board of Trade and the Privy Council, while subterfuge measures designed to impede or harass the trade were looked at with suspicion.

4

The system of indenture was an adaptation, with some distinctively harsh features, of the old institution of apprenticeship. In fact, a few native-born colonials, usually to discharge a debt or answer for a crime but sometimes to learn a trade, entered into indentures not altogether unlike those undertaken by immigrants. In law an indenture was a contract in which the servant promised faithful service for a specified period of time in return for his housing and keep and, at the end of his term of work, that small sum of things, known as "freedom dues," which his master promised him upon their parting. The typical term was four or five years, although it might run anywhere from one or two years to seven. Longer terms were commonly specified for children, and were calculated to bring them to freedom at or just past the time they reached majority. Most indentures followed a standard pattern: as early as 1636 printed forms were available, needing only a few details to be filled out by the contracting parties. Often an emigrant's original indenture was made out to a merchant or a ship's captain and was sold with its holder to an employer on arrival. Indentures became negotiable instruments in the colonies, servants bound under their terms being used to settle debts, even gambling debts. In theory the contract protected the servant from indefinite exploitation, but in practice it had quite limited powers. It was a document vulnerable to loss, theft, or destruction, and when one considers both the fecklessness and inexperience of most indentured servants and the lack of privacy under which they lived, it is little wonder that their contracts often disappeared.

During the eighteenth century, however, circumstances began to alter the prevailing system of indentures and to lessen its severities, particularly when a special class of bonded servants, the redemptioners, became numerous. The redemptioner appeared at the beginning of the century, coming largely from the Continent, often emigrating with a family and with a supply of tools and furnishings. The passengers who traveled with Mittelberger were mostly redemptioners. Indentured servants were simply a part of a ship's cargo, but redemptioners were low-grade, partially paid-up passengers. The redemptioner embarked without an indenture, sometimes having paid part of the money for his own and his family's passage, and arranged with the shipping merchant to complete payment within a short time after landing. Once here, he might try to find relatives or friends to make up his deficit; failure to pay in full meant that he would be sold to the highest bidder to redeem whatever part of his fare was unpaid. The length of his servitude would depend upon the amount to be redeemed. It could be as short as one or two years, although four years seems to have been much more common. Redemptioners would try to go into service as a whole family group. Although redemptioners were often swindled because of their lack of English and were overcharged for interest, insurance, and the transportation of their baggage, it was less profitable to carry them than indentured servants. Still, merchants were eager to fill their ships as full as possible with a ballast of redemptioners.

All bonded servants, indentured and redemptionist, were chattels of their masters, but the terminability of their contracts and the presence of certain legal rights stood between them and slavery. A servant could be freely bought and sold, except in Pennsylvania and New York where laws required the consent of a court before assigning a servant for a year or more. His labor could be rented out; he could be inherited on the terms laid down in his master's will. Yet he could own property, although he was forbidden to engage in trade. He could also sue and be sued, but he could not vote. It was expected that he would be subject to corporal punishment by his master for various offenses, and whipping was common; but a master risked losing his servant on the order of a court for a merciless or disfiguring beating. The right of a servant to petition the courts against abuse was more than a negligible protection. Penniless servants were, of course, at a disadvantage in courts manned by representatives of the master class: in effect they were appealing to the community pride, compassion, or decency of the magistrates, and the sense that there were certain things that ought not be done to a white Christian. Yet the frequency of complaints by servants makes it clear that the prerogative of appeal was widely used, and the frequency of judgments rendered for servants shows that it was not used in vain. No colony recognized the validity of agreements between master and servant made *during* servitude unless both parties appeared before a magistrate and registered their consent. Statutes regulated the terms of servitude in cases in which no papers of indenture existed.

For many thousands of servants their term of indentured servitude was a period of enforced celibacy. Marriage without the consent of the master was illegal, and the crimes of fornication and bastardy figure importantly in the records of bound servitude—not surprisingly, when we realize how many of the servant population were between the ages of eighteen and thirty. The sexuality of redemptioners, since they commonly came in families, was a much less serious problem for them and their masters. Among indentured servants as a whole, however, there were many more men than women. The situation of maidservants was full of both opportunities and hazards. Their services were considerably prized, and a clever or comely woman, as mistress or wife, might escape from the dreariest exactions of servitude. Still, women were also vulnerable to sexual abuse, and the penalties for simply following their own inclinations were high. Masters were unwilling to undergo the loss of time, the expense of rearing a child, or the impairment of health or risk of death in childbirth, and thus were unlikely to give consent to marriage. But the laws contrived to give masters the chance to turn such events to their own account. For fornication and bastardy there were ceremonial whippings, usually of twenty-one lashes; more to the point, sentences of from one to two or three years of extra service were exacted, an overgenerous compensation for the loss of perhaps no more than a few weeks of work. From Pennsylvania southward, Richard B. Morris has concluded, the master was often enriched far beyond his actual losses. Where a manservant fathered a child, he could be required to do whatever extra service was necessary to provide for its maintenance. Merely for contracting unsanctioned marriages, servants could be put to a year's extra service. If a maidservant identified her master as the father of her child, he could be punished for adultery, and she removed from him and resold. A keen disrelish for miscegenation provided an additional term of punishment: for bearing a mulatto bastard a woman might get heavy whipping and seven years of extra service. Despite such restraints, there were a substantial number of illegitimate births, mulatto and otherwise.

However, the commonest crime committed by servants, not surprisingly, was running away—not an easy thing to get away with, since in the colonies everyone had to carry a pass, in effect an identity card, and stiff penalties ranging from fines and personal damages to corporal punishment were imposed upon persons harboring fugitives. Runaways were regularly advertised in the newspapers, rewards were offered, and both sheriffs and the general public were enlisted to secure their return. Returned they often were, and subjected to what were regarded as suitable penalties; captured servants who were unclaimed were resold at public auction. On the whole, and especially in Pennsylvania and colonies to the south, the laws turned the punishment of the recovered runaway into an advantage for the master. The standard penalty in the North, not always rigorously enforced, was extra service of twice the time the master had lost, though whipping was also common. In Pennsylvania, a five-to-one penalty was fixed and commonly enforced, while in Maryland, the harshest of all the colonies, a ten-to-one penalty was authorized by a law of 1661 and very often enforced to the letter. A habitual runaway, or one who succeeded in getting away for weeks, could win himself a dreary extension of servitude. There was one horrendous case of a maidservant in Anne Arundel County, Maryland, who ran off habitually for short terms, and whose master quietly kept a record, true or false, of her absences. Finally taking her to court, the master rendered an account of 133 accumulated days of absence. Since it was impossible for her to deny her frequent absences, she had no shadow of an answer, and was booked for 1,330 days of extra service. Hers was an unusual but not a singular case: there are recorded penalties of 1,530 days, 2,000 days, and even one of 12,130 days, which the master handsomely commuted to an even five years. Virginia assessed double time, or more if "proportionable to the damages" which could be high in tobacco-harvesting time, plus an additional punishment, more commonly inflicted in the seventeenth than the eighteenth century, of corporal punishment. On the eve of the Revolution, Negro slavery had largely replaced indentures in the tidewater plantations but indentures were still important on the accessible and inviting edges of settlement, and there runaways became a critical problem. In South Carolina, where fear of insurrection had been a dominant motive, a law of 1691 had authorized a week's extra service for a day of absence, and for absences that ran as long as a week, a year for a week—a fifty-two-to-one ratio that made Maryland seem relaxed. In 1744 the week-for-a-day ratio was still kept, but the maximum penalty was set at a year's service. Whipping was also routine.

The problem of preventing and punishing runaways was complicated by what was held to be the "pirating" of labor by competing employers—and it became necessary to establish a whole series of penalties for enticing or distracting indentured labor. Plainly, if neighbors could entice bound laborers from their owners for occasional or even permanent service by offering money or promising better treatment, a rudimentary subterranean labor market would begin to replace servitude, and property in servants would become increasingly hazardous. Pirating was not taken lightly in the law, and enticers of labor were subject to personal damage suits as well as to criminal prosecution, with sentences ranging from whipping or sitting in the stocks to fines. The penalties were so heavy in the tobacco colonies that law-abiding planters might even hesitate to feed or shelter a servant who had apparently been deserted by his master. Indeed, innkeepers in these colonies were often fined simply for entertaining or selling liquor to servants. Suits for damages for brief enticements were hardly worth the trouble in the case of servants whose work was valued at a few pence a day. But in New York a skilled cabinetmaker and chair carver indentured in 1761 was lured away by a competitor at frequent intervals, and a few years later his master won a smashing judgment of £128.

Plots hatched by several servants to run away together occurred mostly in the plantation colonies, and the few recorded servant uprisings were entirely limited to those colonies. Virginia had been forced from its very earliest years to take stringent steps against mutinous plots, and severe punishments for such behavior were recorded. Most servant plots occurred in the seventeenth century: a contemplated uprising was nipped in the bud in York County in 1661; apparently led by some left-wing offshoots of the Great Rebellion, servants plotted an insurrection in Gloucester County in 1663, and four leaders were condemned and executed; some discontented servants apparently joined Bacon's Rebellion in the 1670's. In the 1680's the planters became newly apprehensive of discontent among the servants "owing to their great necessities and want of clothes," and it was feared they would rise up and plunder the storehouses and ships; in 1682 there were plant-cutting riots in which servants and laborers, as well as some planters, took part.

By the eighteenth century, either because of the relaxed security of the indenture system or the increasing effectiveness of the authorities, disturbances were infrequent, although in 1707 a gang of runaways planned to seize military stores, burn Annapolis, steal a ship, and set up as pirates, but were stopped. Again in 1721 a band of convict servants conspired unsuccessfully to seize military stores at Annapolis. An insurrection of some consequence did actually break out among white servants under the British regime in East Florida during the summer of 1768, when three hundred Italians and Greeks in that very heterogeneous colony revolted against hard work and stern treatment, seized the arms and ammunition in the storehouse, and prepared to set sail from a ship at anchor in the river at New Smyrna. They were intercepted by a government vessel and promptly surrendered. Three leaders were convicted of piracy, one of whom was pardoned on condition that he execute his two comrades. Discontent and dissension, reaching into the local elite, were still rife in Florida at the time of the Revolution.

A serious threat to the interests of masters, one which gives testimony to the onerousness of servitude, was the possibility of military enlistment. In New England, where there were not many servants, military service was obligatory and seems to have posed no major temptation to escape servitude, but in Pennsylvania and the tobacco colonies, where servants were numerous and essential, the competing demand by the army for manpower in the intercolonial war of the 1740's, and, even more, in the French and Indian War of the 1750's, aroused great anxiety among the masters. In the 1740's, more than a third of the Pennsylvania enlistments were from men in the servant class whose masters were compensated at the colony's expense; in Maryland, during the French and Indian War, Governor Horatio Sharpe reported not only that "servants immediately flocked in to enlist, convicts not excepted," but also that recruits among freemen were extremely scarce, and in Virginia George Washington urged that servants be allowed to enlist in the Virginia volunteers lest they seize the alternative and join the regular army. The resistance of the Pennsylvania Assembly to enlistments during the 1750's became provocatively stubborn and in Maryland there was armed resistance and rioting against recruitment. Parliament, whose interest it was to increase the army, passed a measure in 1756 authorizing officers to enlist indentured servants regardless of restraining colonial laws or practices. The best that masters could hope for was compensation from their colony's legislature, a practice that was repeated in Pennsylvania in 1763, or suing the recruiting officer for civil damages. During the Revolution, the Continental Congress and some of the states encouraged the enlistment of servants, but Pennsylvania and Maryland exempted them from military service. When despite this recruiting officers in Pennsylvania continued to enlist servants, a group of Cumberland County masters complained with magnificent gall that apprentices and servants "are the property of their masters and mistresses, and every mode of depriving such masters and mistresses of their property is a violation of the rights of mankind. . . ." A good number of servants ran off to the British forces, especially in Virginia, but neither the wars nor the Revolution ended the practice of servitude, which declined but did not die until the nineteenth century.

5

Numerous as are the court records of penalties which lengthened service, most servants did not run afoul of the law; their periods of servitude did at last come to an end, entitling them to collect "freedom dues" if they could, and to start in life for themselves. Freedom dues were usually specified by law, but little seems to be known about their payment. Virginia and North Carolina laws of the 1740's required £3 in money, and North Carolina added an adequate suit of clothes. The Crown provided 50 acres of land, free of quitrent for ten years, in South Carolina. A Pennsylvania law of 1700 specified two complete suits of clothes, one of which was to be new, one new ax, one grubbing hoe, and one weeding hoe. Massachusetts long before in the seventeenth century had provided in biblical fashion that servants after seven years' labor should "not be sent away empty," but what this maxim was actually worth to servants is difficult to say. Like the dues of ordinary apprentices, freedom dues may have functioned most importantly as a kind of inducement to servants to carry out in good faith the concluding months and weeks of servitude. Where the labor of a servant was particularly valuable, his master might strengthen that inducement by a cash payment considerably beyond what had been promised.

What was the economic situation of the servant after completing his servitude? It varied, no doubt, from colony to colony, and with the availability of lands. In the mainland colonies, it appears to have been assumed that an ex-servant was to be equipped for work as a free hired man with enough clothes and tools or money to give him a small start. It was assumed that wages for a freeman were high enough to enable him to earn an adequate competence or to provide himself with a plot of land within a fairly short time. Some ex-servants no doubt went westward and took up new lands. "The inhabitants of our frontiers," wrote Governor Alexander Spotswood of Virginia in 1717, "are composed generally of such as have been transported hither as servants, and being out of their time, settle themselves where land is to be taken up that will produce the necessaries of life with little labour." But it is quite likely that Spotswood erred considerably on the side of optimism. For example, in Maryland, where a freed servant in the seventeenth century was entitled to 50 acres of land upon showing his certificate of freedom at the office of the land office secretary, the records show that relatively few became farmers, though many assumed their land rights and sold them for cash. Abbott E. Smith, in one of the most authoritative studies of colonial servitude, estimates that only one out of ten indentured servants (not including redemptioners) became a substantial farmer and another became an artisan or an overseer in reasonably comfortable circumstances. The other eight, he suggests, either died during servitude, returned to England when it was over, or drifted off to become the "poor whites" of the villages and rural areas. There is reason to think that in most places servants who had completed a term of bondage and had a history of local residence met the prevailing parochial, almost tribal qualifications for poor relief, and were accepted as public charges. Redemptioners, Smith remarks, did a good deal better, but the scrappy evidence that has thus far been found does not yet allow much precision. Sir Henry Moore, governor of New York, thought them so anxious to own land that they made great sacrifices to do so: "As soon as the time stipulated in their indentures is expired, they immediately quit their masters, and get a small tract of land, in settling which for the first three or four years they lead miserable lives, and in the most abject poverty; but all this is patiently borne and submitted to with the greatest cheerfulness, the satisfaction of being land holders smooths every difficulty, and makes them prefer this manner of living to that comfortable subsistence which they could procure for themselves and their families by working at the trades in which they were brought up." An Englishman who traveled in America in the opening years of the nineteenth century noticed "many families, particularly in Pennsylvania, of great respectability both in our society and amongst others, who had themselves come over to this country as redemptioners; or were children of such."

As for the indentured servants, the dismal estimate that only two out of ten may have reached positions of moderate comfort is an attempt to generalize the whole two centuries of the experience of English servitude, taking the seventeenth century when the system was brutal and opportunities were few with the eighteenth, when it became less severe. In the early years more servants returned to England, and mortality was also higher. But it will not do simply to assume that freed servants, especially those from the tobacco fields, were in any mental or physical condition to start vigorous new lives, or that long and ripe years of productivity lay ahead for them. If we consider the whole span of time over which English indentured servitude prevailed, its heavy toll in work and death is the reality that stands out.

The Horatio Alger mythology has long since been torn to bits by students of American social mobility, and it will surprise no one to learn that the chance of emergence from indentured servitude to a position of wealth or renown was statistically negligible. A few cases to the contrary are treasured by historians, handed down from one to another like heirlooms—but most of them deal with Northern servants who came with education or skills. The two most illustrious colonial names with servitude in their family histories are Benjamin Franklin and the eminent Maryland lawyer Daniel Dulany. Franklin's maternal grandfather, Peter Folger of Nantucket, a man of many trades from teacher and surveyor to town and court clerk and interpreter between whites and Indians, had bought a maidservant for £20 and later married her. Dulany, who came from a substantial Irish family, arrived in 1703 with two older brothers; the brothers melted into the anonymity that usually awaited indentured arrivals, but Daniel was picked up by a lawyer who was pleased to buy a literate servant with some university training to act as his clerk and help with his plantation accounts. The closest thing to a modest, American-scale family dynasty to come out of servitude was that of the New England Sullivans. John Sullivan and Margery Browne both came to Maine as indentured servants in the 1720's. After Sullivan earned his freedom he became a teacher, bought Margery out of servitude, and married her. Their son John became a lawyer, a Revolutionary patriot, one of Washington's leading generals, and governor of New Hampshire. His younger brother, James, also a lawyer, became a congressman from Massachusetts and in time governor of the state. In the third generation, John's son, George, became a Federalist congressman and the attorney general of New Hampshire; James's son, William, pursued a successful legal career in Boston, played a prominent role in state politics, and was chosen to be one of the three delegates to take the manifesto of the Hartford Convention to Washington. John Lamb, a leader of the Sons of Liberty and later an officer in the Revolution, was the son of Anthony Lamb who had followed an improbable career: an apprentice instrument maker in London, Anthony became involved with a notorious burglar who ended on the gallows at Tyburn; as a first offender, Lamb was sentenced to be transported, served out an indenture in Virginia, moved to New York, and became a reputable instrument maker and a teacher of mathematics, surveying, and navigation. Charles Thomson, one of six children orphaned by the death of their father on shipboard in 1739, began his American life as an indentured servant and became a teacher in Philadelphia, a merchant, a Revolutionary patriot, and Secretary of the Continental Congress. Matthew Thornton, whose parents came to Maine in the Scotch-Irish emigration of 1718, began life under indenture, became a physician, a patriot leader in New Hampshire, and a signer of the Declaration of Independence. Matthew Lyon, who won notoriety as a peppery Republican congressman from Vermont and as a victim of the Sedition Act, emigrated from Ireland in 1765 and paid off his passage by three years of indentured service on farms in Connecticut before he bought his own farm in Vermont. And there were others, brands snatched from the burning, triumphs of good fortune or strong character over the probabilities.

6

Thoreau, brooding over the human condition in the relatively idyllic precincts of Concord and Walden Pond, was convinced that the mass of men lead lives of quiet desperation. His conviction quickens to life again when we contemplate the human costs of what historians sometimes lightly refer to as the American experiment. It is true that thousands came to the colonies in search of freedom or plenty and with a reasonably good chance of finding them, and that the colonies harbored a force of free white workers whose wages and conditions might well have been the envy of their European counterparts. Yet these fortunate men were considerably outnumbered by persons, white or black, who came to America in one kind of servitude or another. It is also true that for some servants, especially for those who already had a skill, a little cash, or some intelligence or education or gentility, servitude in America might prove not a great deal worse than an ordinary apprenticeship, despite the special tribulations and hazards it inflicted. But when one thinks of the great majority of those who came during the long span of time between the first settlements and the disappearance of white servitude in the early nineteenth century—bearing in mind the poverty and the ravaged lives which they left in Europe, the cruel filter of the Atlantic crossing, the high mortality of the crossing and the seasoning, and the many years of arduous toil that lay between the beginning of servitude and the final realization of tolerable comfort—one is deeply impressed by the measure to which the sadness that is natural to life was overwhelmed in the condition of servitude by the stark miseries that seem all too natural to the history of the poor. For a great many the journey across the Atlantic proved in the end to have been only an epitome of their journey through life. And yet there must have seemed to be little at risk because there was so little at stake. They had so often left a scene of turbulence, crime, exploitation, and misery that there could not have been much hope in most of them; and as they lay in their narrow bedsteads listening to the wash of the rank bilge water below them, sometimes racked with fever or lying in their own vomit, few could have expected very much from American life, and those who did were too often disappointed. But with white servants we have only begun to taste the anguish of the early American experience.

Sources

Portraits of Poverty

The following pictures are eloquent testimony about one of the social conditions in England that had fateful consequences for the
American colonies: poverty. The first is an engraving by the great
satirist William Hogarth. How would you describe the attitude toward the poor the illustration suggests was dominant in the upper
classes? The beggar in the second illustration is an Elizabethan figure.
Does he look pitiful? Or threatening? Would he fit Hofstadter's description of the candidate for indentured servitude?

The Granger Collection.

The Experience of Bondage: Gottlieb Mittelberger's Account, 1754

One of our richest sources of information about the life of the white bondsmen and women is the following autobiographical account. It was written by Gottlieb Mittelberger, a German who came to Pennsylvania in 1750 and spent four years in bondage. Mittelberger was a schoolmaster, and we can see his education and intelligence at work in this story. But the conditions he encountered were probably typical of those met by other indentured servants. What kind of impression do you think Mittelberger is trying to make on his German audience? Why do you think Mittelberger uses the term "serf"?

Both in Rotterdam and in Amsterdam the people are packed densely, like herrings so to say, in the large sea vessels. One person receives a place of scarcely 2 feet width and 6 feet length in the bedstead, while many a ship carries four to six hundred souls; not to mention the innumerable implements, tools, provisions, water-barrels and other things which likewise occupy much space.

On account of contrary winds it takes the ships sometimes 2, 3 and 4 weeks to make the trip from Holland to Kaupp [Cowes] in England. But when the wind is good, they get there in 8 days or even sooner. Everything is examined there and the custom-duties paid, whence it comes that the ships ride there 8, 10 to 14 days and even longer at anchor, till they have taken in their full cargoes. During that time every one is compelled to spend his last

From Gottlieb Mittelberger, *Journey to Pennsylvania in the Year 1750 and Return to Germany in the Year 1754* (Philadelphia: J. J. McVey, 1898), pp. 19–20, 22, 24.

remaining money and to consume his little stock of provisions which had been reserved for the sea; so that most passengers, finding themselves on the ocean where they would be in greater need of them, must greatly suffer from hunger and want. Many suffer want already on the water between Holland and Old England.

When the ships have for the last time weighed their anchors near the city of Kaupp [Cowes] in Old England, the real misery begins with the long voyage. For from there the ships, unless they have good wind, must often sail 8, 9, 10 to 12 weeks before they reach Philadelphia. But even with the best wind the voyage lasts 7 weeks.

But during the voyage there is on board these ships terrible misery, stench, fumes, horror, vomiting, many kinds of seasickness, fever, dysentery, headache, heat, constipation, boils, scurvy, cancer, mouth-rot, and the like, all of which come from old and sharply salted food and meat, also from very bad and foul water, so that many die miserably.

Add to this want of provisions, hunger, thirst, frost, heat, dampness, anxiety, want, afflictions and lamentations, together with other trouble, as *c. v.* the lice abound so frightfully, especially on sick people, that they can be scraped off the body. The misery reaches the climax when a gale rages for 2 or 3 nights and days, so that every one believes that the ship will go to the bottom with all human beings on board. In such a visitation the people cry and pray most piteously. . . .

Many sigh and cry, "Oh, that I were at home again, and if I had to lie in my pigsty!" Or they say: "O God, if I only had a piece of good bread, or a good fresh drop of water." Many people whimper, sigh and cry piteously for their homes; most of them get home-sick. Many hundred people necessarily die and perish in such misery and must be cast into the sea, which drives their relatives or those who persuaded them to undertake the journey, to such despair that it is almost impossible to pacify and console them. In a word, the sighing and crying and lamenting on board the ship continues night and day so as to cause the hearts even of the most hardened to bleed when they hear it. . . .

At length, when, after a long and tedious voyage, the ships come in sight of land, so that the promontories can be seen, which the people were so eager and anxious to see, all creep from below on deck to see the land from afar, and they weep for joy, and pray and sing, thanking and praising God. The sight of the land makes the people on board the ship, especially the sick and the half-dead, alive again, so that their hearts leap within them; they shout and rejoice, and are content to bear their misery in patience, in the hope that they may soon reach the land in safety. But alas!

When the ships have landed at Philadelphia after their long voyage, no one is permitted to leave them except those who pay for their passage or can give good security; the others, who cannot pay, must remain on board the ships till they are purchased, and are released from the ships by their purchasers. The sick always fare the worst, for the healthy are naturally preferred and purchased first; and so the sick and wretched must often remain on board in front of the city for 2 or 3 weeks, and frequently die, whereas many a one, if he could pay his debt and were permitted to leave the ship immediately, might recover and remain alive. . . .

The sale of human beings in the market on board the ship is carried on thus: Every day Englishmen, Dutchmen and High-German people come from the city of Philadelphia and other places, in part from a great distance, say 20, 30, or 40 hours away, and go on board the newly arrived ship that has brought and offers for sale passengers from Europe, and select among the healthy persons such as they deem suitable for their business, and bargain with them how long they will serve for their passage money, which most of them are still in debt for. When they have come to an agreement, it happens that adult persons bind themselves in writing to serve 3, 4, 5 or 6 years for the amount due by them, according to their age and strength. But very young people, from 10 to 15 years, must serve till they are 21 years old.

Many parents must sell and trade away their children like so many head of cattle; for if their children take the debt upon themselves, the parents can leave the ship free and unrestrained; but as the parents often do not know where and to what people their children are going, it often happens that such parents and children, after leaving the ship, do not see each other again for many years, perhaps no more in all their lives. . . .

It often happens that whole families, husband, wife, and children, are separated by being sold to different purchasers, especially when they have not paid any part of their passage money.

When a husband or wife has died at sea, when the ship has made more than half of her trip, the survivor must pay or serve not only for himself or herself, but also for the deceased.

When both parents have died over halfway at sea, their children, especially when they are young and have nothing to pawn or to pay, must stand for their own and their parents' passage, and serve till they are 21 years old. When one has served his or her term, he or she is entitled to a new suit of clothes at parting; and if it has been so stipulated, a man gets in addition a horse, a woman, a cow.

When a serf has an opportunity to marry in this country, he or she must pay for each year which he or she would have yet to serve, 5 to 6 pounds. But many a one who has thus purchased and paid for his bride, has subsequently repented his bargain, so that he would gladly have returned his exorbitantly dear ware, and lost the money besides.

If some one in this country runs away from his master, who has treated him harshly, he cannot get far. Good provision has been made for such cases, so that a runaway is soon recovered. He who detains or returns a deserter receives a good reward.

If such a runaway has been away from his master one day, he must serve for it as a punishment a week, for a week a month, and for a month half a year. But if the master will not keep the runaway after he has got him back, he may sell him for so many years as he would have to serve him yet.

Wanted: Runaway Servants

We have learned a considerable amount about colonial servitude from documents like the following. They are advertisements for runaway servants, placed by their masters in eighteenth-century newspapers in Virginia, Georgia, and South Carolina. Do they suggest any conclusions to you that were not reached by Hofstadter? Why did the masters describe the clothes their servants were wearing when they ran away? Why would the servants not simply discard those clothes for others? In terms of purchasing power, the rewards offered were very large. What kinds of trades and skills did the runaways represent? These advertisements were published in an area where black slavery was already well established. Does that fact make any sense? If there were slaves, why were there indentured servants?

Virginia *Gazette,* April 16, 1767. Advertisement.

Run away from King William court-house, on the 14th of March last, three apprentice boys, viz. James Axley, a carpenter, about 5 feet 8 inches high, and wears his own black hair cued behind; had on when he went away a gray cloth coat, without pockets or flaps, and a pair of leather breeches much daubed with turpentine. William Arter, a carpenter, rather taller and better set than the former, of a dark complexion, has black hair, but his clothes no way remarkable. William Kindrick, a bricklayer, which business he understands well, and is supposed to be gone with a view of carrying it on with the other boys; he is a fresh complexioned youth, wears a cap, and had on a bearskin coat with metal buttons, a dark brown waistcoat, and a pair of lead coloured serge breeches. It is supposed they are gone to Bedford, or into Carolina. Whoever brings the said apprentices to King William or Hanover court-houses shall have forty shillings reward for each, besides their expenses defrayed.

Francis Smith, Sen.-James Geddy

Virginia *Gazette,* Nov. 1767.

Prince George, November 10, 1767.
Supposed to be run away from the subscriber (having liberty about three weeks ago to go up to Osborne's and Warwick, on James river, to look for

From U. B. Phillips, ed., "Plantation and Frontier," Part I in John R. Commons et al., eds., *A Documentary History of American Industrial Society.* Copyright 1909, 1937 by John R. Commons; copyright 1958 by Russell & Russell (New York: Russell & Russell, 1958), pp. 352–354, 346–348.

work, and not since heard of) an indented servant man named Alexander Cuthbert, by trade a bricklayer, born in Perth in Scotland, but came last from London in one Captain Grigg to Potowmack river. He is about 5 feet 6 or 7 inches high, about 22 years of age, wears his own hair of a dark brown colour, is a little pitted with the smallpox, and, as he was some time in England, has not much of the Scotch accent. Had with him when he went away a blue coarse cloth coat, blue and red striped silk and cotton jacket, blue breeches, several white and check linen shirts, and many other articles of apparel. He carried with him his bricklayer's and plaistering tools, a sliding rule, some books of architecture and mensuration, etc. From the little time I have had him, he appeared a harmless inoffensive lad, entirely sober and obliging, and if he has gone off must have been advised to such a measure by some more designing than himself. It is probable he may make to the northward and so to Philadelphia, having been heard to speak of some acquaintances gone that way. Whoever takes up the said servant (if run away) and delivers him to the subscriber, shall have five pounds if taken within the colony, and ten pounds if taken at any considerable distance out of it, paid by

William Black

N.B. All masters of vessels are desired to be cautious of not carrying such a person out of the country.

Virginia *Gazette,* March 26, 1767

Run away from the subscriber, in Northumberland county, two Irish convict servants named William and Hannah Daylies, tinkers by trade, of which the woman is extremely good; they had a note of leave to go out and work in Richmond county and Hobb's Hole, the money to be paid to Job Thomas, in said county; soon after I heard they were run away. The man wore a light coloured coarse cloth frock coat, a blue striped satin jacket, and plaid one, a pair of leather breeches, a pair of Russia drill white stockings, a little brown bog wig, and his hat cocked up very sharp. He is about 5 feet 8 inches high, of a sandy complexion, and freckled; is a well made fellow, somewhat bow legged. The woman had on an old stuff gown and a light coloured petticoat, and under petticoat of cotton with a blue selvedge at the bottom, a blue striped satin gown, the same with his jacket, two check aprons, and a pair of pale blue calimanco shoes. They both wore white shirts, with very short ruffles, and white thread stockings. They had a complete set of tinkers tools. They were seen to have two English guineas and a good deal of silver, and said in Essex county they lived in Agusta, and inquired the road that way. Whoever will apprehend both or either of said servants, and brings them to me, shall have five pounds reward for each, and reasonable travelling charges allowed by

William Taite.

Virginia *Gazette,* Feb. 26, 1767. Advertisement.

Run away from the subscriber in Augusta, on the 17th of January last, a convict servant man named John Jones, an Englishman, about 35 years of age, about 5 feet 7 inches high, of a fair complexion, and fair short hair; had on when he went away a blue homemade drugget jacket lined with striped linen, a blue broad cloth do. under it, leather breeches, coarse spun shirt made out of hemp linen, sheep gray stockings, and country made shoes; he has been a sailor, and I suppose will endeavour to get on board some vessel. I have heard that he has altered his name at Fredericksburg, and stole from thence a ruffed shirt, a pair of everlasting breeches, an old whitish coloured jacket, and two razors. Whoever takes up the said servant, and brings him to me, or John Briggs at Falmouth, or secures him in any county gaol so that I may get him again, shall have five pounds reward, paid by me or John Briggs.

Andrew Burd.

N.B. As he is a very good scholar, it is imagined he will forge a pass.

Virginia *Historical Register,* vol. vi, 96–97, advertisements reprinted from the Virginia *Gazette* (Williamsburg), 1736–1737.

Ran away lately from the Bristol Company's Iron Works, in King George County, a servant man named James Summers, a West Country [i.e. Cornish] Man, and speaks thick, he is a short thick fellow, with short black hair and a ruddy complexion. Whoever secures the said servant and brings him to the said Iron Works, or to the Hon. John Taylor, Esq., in Richmond County, or gives notice of him, so as he may be had again, shall be well rewarded besides what the law allows.

Nansemond, July 14, 1737.

Ran away some time in June last, from William Pierce of Nansemond County, near Mr. Theophilus Pugh's Merchant: a convict servant woman named Winifred Thomas. She is Welsh woman, short black Hair'd and young; mark'd on the Inside of her Right Arm with Gunpowder W. T. and the Date of the Year underneath. She knits and spins, and is supposed to be gone into North Carolina by the way of Cureatuck and Roanoke Inlet. Whoever brings her to her master shall be paid a Pistole besides what the law allows, paid by

William Pierce.

South Carolina *Gazette* (Charleston), June 16 to 23, 1739. Advertisement.

Savannah, May 7, 1739.

Run away on the 5th Instant from Robert William's Plantation in Georgia, 3 Men Servants, one named James Powell, is a Bricklayer by Trade about Five Feet 9 inches high, a strong made man, born in Wiltshire, talks broad, and when he went away he wore his own short hair, with a White cap: Among his comrades he was call'd Alderman.

Another named Charles Gastril did formerly belong to the Pilot Boat at Pill near Bristol, is by Trade a Sawyer, about 5 feet 10 Inches high, of a thin spare make, raw boned, and has a Scar somewhere on his upper Lip, aged about 25.

The 3rd named Jenkin James, a lusty young fellow, about the same Height as Gastrill, has a good fresh complection, bred by trade a Taylor, but of late has been used to Sawing, talks very much Welshly, and had on when he went away a coarse red coat and waistcoat, the Buttons and Button holes of the Coat black.

Any person or Persons who apprehend them, or either of them, and bring them to Mr. Thomas Jenys in Charleston, or to the said Mr. Robert Williams in Savannah shall receive 10 l. Currency of South Carolina for each.

Robert Williams.

Besides the above mentioned Reward, there is a considerable sum allow'd by the Trustees [of the colony of Georgia] for taking run away Servants.

N.B. About a Fortnight ago, three other of the said Robert William's Servants run away, who are already advertized.

5

Black Slavery

Slavery was about as old as the English experience in North America. In fact, only a dozen years after Jamestown was settled, the first Africans were purchased as slaves. But it was not until after 1700 that slavery began to displace white servitude as the most significant form of forced labor. Gradually—first in Virginia and then in other colonies, both North and South—the legal status of slave was defined. Especially in the Southern colonies where large-scale commercial agriculture was the way of life, slaves became *the* work force on many plantations. Almost before the English colonies realized it, they had built a society that was profoundly dependent on human bondage. By 1750, the largest single stream of immigration into British North America was composed of black slaves from Africa.

Shocking as this development may seem from a twentieth-century perspective—and even more shocking as it was to those Africans who found themselves caught in the slave trade—it shocked very few English colonists at the time. Like many other momentous human decisions, it was not made by any single individual or government. Slavery happened, and it happened as a gradual result of innumerable small choices.

To understand this development, it is necessary to realize that North America was always on the fringes of the immense slave trade that developed between West Africa and tropical America. The Spanish colonies and Portuguese Brazil began importing slaves in the early 1500s, and by the time Jamestown was settled in 1607 some 250,000 African slaves had been brought to the New World. It was primarily the need for labor on the sugar plantations of Brazil and the Caribbean that stimulated the growth of the Atlantic slave trade after 1700. As that trade skyrocketed, the number of slave ships that wandered as far north as Virginia also increased. Yet of the 6 million slaves who survived the Atlantic voyages between 1700 and 1810,

94

less than 6 percent ended up in what is now the United States. So the growth of slavery in the thirteen colonies was only a small part of the growth of slavery in the New World.

It is also necessary to realize that very few people in colonial times had any qualms about slavery. Human bondage had been considered a part of the natural scheme of things since ancient times— and except for a few Quakers and kindred German sects, colonists everywhere accepted slavery as "normal." Even churches owned slaves. Indeed, the pious often bequeathed slaves to their ministers as tokens of affection. When the Reverend Cotton Mather, one of the leading New England ministers of his day, was honored with the gift of a slave, he recorded the event in his diary as "a smile from Heaven."

Interpretive Essay

Daniel P. Mannix and Malcolm Cowley

The Middle Passage

Slavery had many ugly features, but perhaps the ugliest was the slave trade between Africa and the New World. Both Africans and Europeans participated in the trade, and both societies were deeply influenced by it. But it was such a dirty business that it later became an unmentionable subject, a blot on a nation's good name. Thus, most national histories have treated it as something peripheral to their country's social and political development. It was anything but peripheral, however, to the development of colonial America and to the millions of Africans who were wrenched from their villages, driven in chains to the coast, and transported across the Atlantic in the foul holds of slave ships. In the following selection, literary critic Malcolm Cowley and historian Daniel P. Mannix combine their talents to describe this experience.

From Daniel P. Mannix and Malcolm Cowley, "Middle Passage," *American Heritage,* Vol. 13, No. 2 (February 1962): 22–25, 103–107. © 1962 by Daniel Mannix and Malcolm Cowley. Reprinted by permission of the Harold Matson Company, Inc.

Long before Europeans appeared on the African coast, the merchants of Timbuktu were exporting slaves to the Moorish kingdoms north of the Sahara. Even the transatlantic slave trade had a long history. There were Negroes in Santo Domingo as early as 1503, and the first twenty slaves were sold in Jamestown, Virginia, about the last week of August, 1619, only twelve years after the colony was founded. But the flush days of the trade were in the eighteenth century, when vast supplies of labor were needed for the sugar plantations in the West Indies and the tobacco and rice plantations on the mainland. From 1700 to 1807, when the trade was legally abolished by Great Britain and the United States, more than seventy thousand Negroes were carried across the Atlantic in any normal year. The trade was interrupted by wars, notably by the American Revolution, but the total New World importation for the century may have amounted to five million enslaved persons.

Most of the slaves were carried on shipboard at some point along the four thousand miles of West African coastline that extend in a dog's leg from the Sahara on the north to the southern desert. Known as the Guinea Coast, it was feared by eighteenth-century mariners, who died there by hundreds and thousands every year.

Contrary to popular opinion, very few of the slaves—possibly one or two out of a hundred—were free Africans kidnapped by Europeans. The slaving captains had, as a rule, no moral prejudice against man-stealing, but they usually refrained from it on the ground of its being a dangerous business practice. A vessel suspected of man-stealing might be "cut off" by the natives, its crew killed, and its cargo of slaves offered for sale to other vessels.

The vast majority of the Negroes brought to America had been enslaved and sold to the whites by other Africans. There were coastal tribes and states, like the Efik kingdom of Calabar, that based their whole economy on the slave trade. The slaves might be prisoners of war, they might have been kidnapped by gangs of black marauders, or they might have been sold with their whole families for such high crimes as adultery, impiety, or, as in one instance, stealing a tobacco pipe. Intertribal wars, the principal source of slaves, were in many cases no more than large-scale kidnapping expeditions. Often they were fomented by Europeans, who supplied both sides with muskets and gunpowder—so many muskets or so much powder for each slave that they promised to deliver on shipboard.

The ships were English, French, Dutch, Danish, Portuguese, or American. London, Bristol, and finally Liverpool were the great English slaving ports. By 1790 Liverpool had engrossed five eighths of the English trade and three sevenths of the slave trade of all Europe. Its French rival, Nantes, would soon be ruined by the Napoleonic wars. During the last years of legal slaving, Liverpool's only serious competitors were the Yankee captains of Newport and Bristol, Rhode Island.

Profits from a slaving voyage, which averaged nine or ten months, were reckoned at thirty per cent, after deducting sales commissions, insurance premiums, and all other expenses. The Liverpool merchants became so rich from the slave trade that they invested heavily in mills, factories, mines, canals, and railways. That process was repeated in New England, and the slave trade provided much of the capital that was needed for the industrial revolution.

A slaving voyage was triangular. English textiles, notions, cutlery, and firearms were carried to the Guinea Coast, where they were exchanged for slaves. These were sold in America or the West Indies, and part of the proceeds was invested in colonial products, notably sugar and rice, which were carried back to England on the third leg of the voyage. If the vessel sailed from a New England port, its usual cargo was casks of rum from a Massachusetts distillery. The rum was exchanged in Africa for slaves—often at the rate of two hundred gallons per man—and the slaves were exchanged in the West Indies for molasses, which was carried back to New England to be distilled into rum. A slave ship or Guineaman was expected to show a profit for each leg of its triangular course. But the base of the triangle, the so-called Middle Passage from Africa to the New World with a black cargo, was the most profitable part of the voyage, at the highest cost in human suffering. Let us see what happened in the passage during the flush days of the slave trade.

As soon as the assortment of naked slaves was carried aboard a Guinea-man, the men were shackled two by two, the right wrist and ankle of one to the left wrist and ankle of another; then they were sent below. The women—usually regarded as fair prey for the sailors—were allowed to wander by day almost anywhere on the vessel, though they spent the night between decks, in a space partitioned off from that of the men. All the slaves were forced to sleep without covering on bare wooden floors, which were often constructed of unplaned boards. In a stormy passage the skin over their elbows might be worn away to the bare bones.

William Bosman says, writing in 1701, "You would really wonder to see how these slaves live on board; for though their number sometimes amounts to six or seven hundred, yet by the careful management of our masters of ships"—the Dutch masters, in this case—"they are so regulated that it seems incredible: And in this particular our nation exceeds all other Europeans; for as the French, Portuguese and English slave-ships, are always foul and stinking; on the contrary ours are for the most part clean and neat."

Slavers of every nation insisted that their own vessels were the best in the trade. Thus, James Barbot, Jr., who sailed on an English ship to the Congo in 1700, was highly critical of the Portuguese. He admits that they made a great point of baptizing the slaves before taking them on board, but then, "It is pitiful," he says, "to see how they crowd those poor wretches, six hundred and fifty or seven hundred in a ship, the men standing in the hold ty'd to stakes, the women between decks and those that are with child in the great cabin and the children in the steeridge which in that hot climate occasions an intolerable stench." Barbot adds, however, that the Portuguese provided the slaves with coarse thick mats, which were "softer for the poor wretches to lie upon than the bare decks . . . and it would be prudent to imitate the Portuguese in this point." The English, however, did not display that sort of prudence.

There were two schools of thought among the English slaving captains, the "loose-packers" and the "tight-packers." The former argued that by giving the slaves a little more room, better food, and a certain amount of liberty, they reduced the death rate and received a better price for each slave in the West Indies. The tight-packers answered that although the loss of life might be greater on each of their voyages, so too were the net receipts from a larger cargo. If many of the survivors were weak and emaciated, as was often the case, they could be fattened up in a West Indian slave yard before being offered for sale.

The argument between the two schools continued as long as the trade itself, but for many years after 1750 the tight-packers were in the ascendant. So great was the profit on each slave landed alive that hardly a captain refrained from loading his vessel to its utmost capacity. Says the Reverend John New-ton, who was a slaving captain before he became a clergyman:

> The cargo of a vessel of a hundred tons or a little more is calculated to purchase from 220 to 250 slaves. Their lodging rooms below the deck which are three (for the men, the boys, and the women) besides a place for the sick, are sometimes more than five feet high and sometimes less; and this height is divided toward the middle for the slaves to lie in two rows, one above the other, on each side of the ship, close to each other like books upon a shelf. I have known them so close that the shelf would not easily contain one more.
>
> The poor creatures, thus cramped, are likewise in irons for the most part which makes it difficult for them to turn or move or attempt to rise or to lie down without hurting themselves or each other. Every morning, perhaps, more instances than one are found of the living and the dead fastened together.

Newton was writing in 1788, shortly before a famous parliamentary investigation of the slave trade that lasted four years. One among hundreds of witnesses was Dr. Alexander Falconbridge, who had made four slaving voyages as a surgeon. Falconbridge testified that "he made the most of the room," in stowing the slaves, "and wedged them in. They had not so much room as a man in his coffin either in length or breadth. When he had to enter the slave deck, he took off his shoes to avoid crushing the slaves as he was forced to crawl over them." Falconbridge "had the marks on his feet where the slaves bit and pinched him."

Captain Parrey of the Royal Navy was sent to measure the slave ships at Liverpool and make a report to the House of Commons. That was also in 1788. Parrey discovered that the captains of many slavers possessed a chart showing the dimensions of the half deck, lower deck, hold, platforms, gun-room, orlop, and great cabin, in fact of every crevice into which slaves might be wedged. Miniature black figures were drawn on some of the charts to illustrate the most effective method of packing in the cargo.

On the *Brookes,* which Parrey considered to be typical, every man was allowed a space six feet long by sixteen inches wide (and usually about two feet seven inches high); every woman, a space five feet ten inches long by sixteen inches wide; every boy, five feet by fourteen inches; every girl, four feet six inches by twelve inches. The *Brookes* was a vessel of 320 tons. By a new law passed in 1788 it was permitted to carry 454 slaves, and the chart, which later became famous, showed where 451 of them could be stowed away. Parrey failed to see how the captain could find room for three more. Nevertheless, Parliament was told by reliable witnesses, including Dr. Thomas Trotter, formerly surgeon of the *Brookes,* that before the new law she had carried 600 slaves on one voyage and 609 on another.

Taking on slaves was a process that might be completed in a month or two by vessels trading in Lower Guinea, east and south of the Niger delta. In Upper Guinea, west and north of the delta, the process was longer. It might last from six months to a year or more on the Gold Coast, which supplied the slaves most in demand by the English colonies. Meanwhile the captain was buying Negroes, sometimes one or two a day, sometimes a hundred or more in a single lot, while haggling over each purchase.

Those months when a slaver lay at anchor off the malarial coastline were the most dangerous part of her voyage. Not only was her crew exposed to African fevers and the revenge of angry natives; not only was there the chance of her being taken by pirates or by a hostile man-of-war; but there was also the constant threat of a slave mutiny. Captain Thomas Phillips says, in his account of a voyage made in 1693–94:

> When our slaves are aboard we shackle the men two and two, while we lie in port, and in sight of their own country, for 'tis then they attempt to make their escape, and mutiny; to prevent which we always keep centinels upon the hatchways, and have a chest full of small arms, ready loaden and prim'd, constantly lying at hand upon the quarter-deck, together with some granada shells; and two of our quarterdeck guns, pointing on the deck thence, and two more out of the steerage, the door of which is always kept shut, and well barr'd; they are fed twice a day, at 10 in the morning, and 4 in the evening, which is the time they are aptest to mutiny, being all upon the deck; therefore all that time, what of our men are not employ'd in distributing their victuals to them, and settling them, stand to their arms; and some with lighted matches at the great guns that yaun upon them, loaden with partridge, till they have done and gone down to their kennels between decks.

In spite of such precautions, mutinies were frequent on the Coast, and some of them were successful. Even a mutiny that failed might lead to heavy losses among the slaves and the sailors. Thus, we read in the Newport, Rhode Island, *Mercury* of November 18, 1765:

> By letters from Capt. Hopkins in a Brig belonging to Providence arrived here from Antigua from the Coast of Africa we learn That soon after he left the Coast, the number of his Men being reduced by Sickness, he was obliged to

permit some of the Slaves to come upon Deck to assist the People: These Slaves contrived to release the others, and the whole rose upon the People, and endeavoured to get Possession of the Vessel; but was happily prevented by the Captain and his Men, who killed, wounded and forced overboard, Eighty of them, which obliged the rest to submit.

There are scores of similar items in the colonial newspapers.

William Richardson, a young sailor who shipped on an English Guineaman in 1790, tells of going to the help of a French vessel on which the slaves had risen while it was at anchor. The English seamen jumped into the boats and pulled hard for the Frenchman, but by the time they reached it there were "a hundred slaves in possession of the deck and others tumbling up from below." The slaves put up a desperate resistance. "I could not but admire," Richardson says, "the courage of a fine young black who, though his partner in irons lay dead at his feet, would not surrender but fought with his billet of wood until a ball finished his existence. The others fought as well as they could but what could they do against fire-arms?"

There are fairly detailed accounts of fifty-five mutinies on slavers from 1699 to 1845, not to mention passing references to more than a hundred others. The list of ships "cut off" by the natives—often in revenge for the kidnapping of free Africans—is almost as long. On the record it does not seem that Africans submitted tamely to being carried across the Atlantic like chained beasts. Edward Long, the Jamaica planter and historian, justified the cruel punishments inflicted on slaves by saying, "The many acts of violence they have committed by murdering whole crews and destroying ships when they had it in their power to do so have made these rigors wholly chargeable on their own bloody and malicious disposition which calls for the same confinement as if they were wolves or wild boars." For "wolves or wild boars" a modern reader might substitute "men who would rather die than be enslaved."

With the loading of the slaves, the captain, for his part, had finished what he regarded as the most difficult part of his voyage. Now he had to face only the ordinary perils of the sea, most of which were covered by his owners' insurance against fire, shipwreck, pirates and rovers, letters of mart and counter-mart, barratry, jettison, and foreign men-of-war. Among the risks not covered by insurance, the greatest was that of the cargo's being swept away by disease. The underwriters refused to issue such policies, arguing that they would expose the captain to an unholy temptation. If insured against disease among his slaves, he might take no precautions against it and might try to make his profit out of the insurance.

The more days at sea, the more deaths among his cargo, and so the captain tried to cut short the next leg of his voyage. If he had shipped his slaves at Bonny, Old Calabar, or any port to the southward, he might call at one of the Portuguese islands in the Gulf of Guinea for an additional supply of food and fresh water, usually enough, with what he had already, to last for three months. If he had traded to the northward, he made straight for the West Indies. Usually he had from four to five thousand nautical miles to sail—or even more, if the passage was from Angola to Virginia. The shortest passage—that from the Gambia River to Barbados—might be made in as little as three weeks, with favoring winds. If the course was much longer, and if the ship was becalmed in the doldrums or driven back by storms, the voyage might take more than three months, and slaves and sailors would be put on short rations long before the end of the Middle Passage.

On a canvas of heroic size, Thomas Stothard, Esquire, of the Royal Academy, depicted *The Voyage of the Sable Venus from Angola to the West Indies*. His painting is handsomely reproduced in the second volume of Bryan Edwards' *History of the British Colonies in the West Indies* (1793), where it appears beside a poem on the same allegorical subject by an unnamed Jamaican author, perhaps Edwards himself.

The joint message of the poem and the painting is simple to the point of coarseness: that slave women are preferable to English girls at night, being passionate and accessible; but the message is embellished with classical details, to show the painter's learning.

Meanwhile the Sable Venus, if she was a living woman carried from Angola to the West Indies, was roaming the deck of a ship that stank of excrement; as was said of any slaver, "You could smell it five miles down wind." She had been torn from her husband and her children, she had been branded on the left buttock, and she had been carried to the ship bound hand and foot, lying in the bilge at the bottom of a dugout canoe. Now she was the prey of the ship's officers.

Here is how she and her shipmates spent the day.

If the weather was clear, they were brought on deck at eight o'clock in the morning. The men were attached by their leg irons to the great chain that ran along the bulwarks on both sides of the ship; the women and half-grown boys were allowed to wander at will. About nine o'clock the slaves were served their first meal of the day. If they were from the Windward Coast—roughly, the shoreline of present-day Liberia and Sierra Leone—the fare was boiled rice, millet, or corn meal, sometimes cooked with a few lumps of salt beef abstracted from the sailor's rations. If they were from the Bight of Biafra, at the east end of the Gulf of Guinea, they were fed stewed yams, but the Congos and the Angolas preferred manioc or plantains. With the food they were all given half a pint of water, served out in a pannikin.

After the morning meal came a joyless ceremony called "dancing the slaves." "Those who were in irons," says Dr. Thomas Trotter, surgeon of the *Brookes* in 1783, "were ordered to stand up and make what motions they could, leaving a passage for such as were out of irons to dance around the deck." Dancing was prescribed as a therapeutic measure, a specific against suicidal melancholy, and also against scurvy—although in the latter case it was a useless torture for men with swollen limbs. While sailors paraded the deck, each with a cat-o'-nine-tails in his right hand, the men slaves "jumped in their irons" until their ankles were bleeding flesh. Music was provided by a slave thumping on a broken drum or an upturned kettle, or by an

African banjo, if there was one aboard, or perhaps by a sailor with a bagpipe or a fiddle. Slaving captains sometimes advertised for "A person that can play on the Bagpipes, for a Guinea ship." The slaves were also told to sing. Said Dr. Claxton after his voyage in the *Young Hero,* "They sing, but not for their amusement. The captain ordered them to sing, and they sang songs of sorrow. Their sickness, fear of being beaten, their hunger, and the memory of their country, etc., are the usual subjects."

While some of the sailors were dancing the slaves, others were sent below to scrape and swab out the sleeping rooms. It was a sickening task, and it was not well performed unless the captain imposed an iron discipline. James Barbot, Sr., was proud of the discipline maintained on the *Albion-Frigate*. "We were very nice," he says, "in keeping the places where the slaves lay clean and neat, appointing some of the ship's crew to do that office constantly and thrice a week we perfumed betwixt decks with a quantity of good vinegar in pails, and red-hot iron bullets in them, to expel the bad air, after the place had been well washed and scrubbed with brooms." Captain Hugh Crow, the last legal English slaver, was famous for his housekeeping. "I always took great pains," he says, "to promote the health and comfort of all on board, by proper diet, regularity, exercise, and cleanliness, for I considered that on keeping the ship clean and orderly, which was always my hobby, the success of our voyage mainly depended." Certainly he lost fewer slaves in the Middle Passage than the other captains, some of whom had the filth in the hold cleaned out only once a week.

At three or four in the afternoon the slaves were fed their second meal, often a repetition of the first. Sometimes, instead of African food, they were given horse beans, the cheapest provender from Europe. The beans were boiled to a pulp, then covered with a mixture of palm oil, flour, water, and red pepper, which the sailors called "slabber sauce." Most of the slaves detested horse beans, especially if they were used to eating yams or manioc. Instead of eating the pulp, they would, unless carefully watched, pick it up by handfuls and throw it in each other's faces.

That second meal was the end of their day. As soon as it was finished they were sent below, under the guard of sailors charged with stowing them away on their bare floors and platforms. The tallest men were placed amidships, where the vessel was widest; the shorter ones were tumbled into the stern. Usually there was only room for them to sleep on their sides, "spoon fashion." Captain William Littleton told Parliament that slaves in the ships on which he sailed might lie on their backs if they wished—"though perhaps," he conceded, "it might be difficult all at the same time."

After stowing their cargo, the sailors climbed out of the hatchway, each clutching his cat-o'-nine-tails; then the hatchway gratings were closed and barred. Sometimes in the night, as the sailors lay on deck and tried to sleep, they heard from below "an howling melancholy noise, expressive of extreme anguish." When Dr. Trotter told his interpreter, a slave woman, to inquire about the cause of the noise, "she discovered it to be owing to their having dreamt they were in their own country, and finding themselves when awake, in the hold of a slave ship."

More often the noise heard by the sailors was that of quarreling among the slaves. The usual occasion for quarrels was their problem of reaching the latrines. These were inadequate in size and number, and hard to find in the darkness of the crowded hold, especially by men who were ironed together in pairs.

In squalls or rainy weather, the slaves were never brought on deck. They were served their two meals in the hold, where the air became too thick and poisonous to breathe. Dr. Falconbridge writes:

> For the purpose of admitting fresh air, most of the ships in the slave-trade are provided, between the decks, with five or six airports on each side of the ship, of about six inches in length and four in breadth; in addition to which, some few ships, but not one in twenty, have what they denominate wind-sails [funnels made of canvas and so placed as to direct a current of air into the hold]. But whenever the sea is rough and the rain heavy, it becomes necessary to shut these and every other conveyance by which the air is admitted. . . . The negroes' rooms very soon become intolerably hot. The confined air, rendered noxious by the effluvia exhaled from their bodies and by being repeatedly breathed, soon produces fevers and fluxes which generally carry off great numbers of them.

Dr. Trotter says that when tarpaulins were thrown over the gratings, the slaves would cry, "Kickeraboo, kickeraboo, we are dying, we are dying." Falconbridge gives one instance of their sufferings:

> Some wet and blowing weather having occasioned the portholes to be shut and the grating to be covered, fluxes and fevers among the negroes ensued. While they were in this situation, I frequently went down among them till at length their rooms became so extremely hot as to be only bearable for a very short time. But the excessive heat was not the only thing that rendered their situation intolerable. The deck, that is, the floor of their rooms, was so covered with the blood and mucus which had proceeded from them in consequence of the flux, that it resembled a slaughter-house.

While the slaves were on deck they had to be watched at all times to keep them from committing suicide. Says Captain Phillips of the *Hannibal,* "We had about 12 negroes did wilfully drown themselves, and others starv'd themselves to death; for," he explained, " 'tis their belief that when they die they return home to their own country and friends again."

This belief was reported from various regions, at various periods of the trade, but it seems to have been especially strong among the Ibos of eastern Nigeria. In 1788, nearly a hundred years after the *Hannibal's* voyage, Dr. Ecroide Claxton was the surgeon who attended a shipload of Ibos. Some, he testified, wished to die on an idea that they should then get back to their own country. The captain in order to obviate this idea, thought of an expedient viz. to cut off the heads of those who died intimating to them that if determined to go, they must return without heads. The slaves were accordingly brought up to witness the operation. One of them by a violent exertion got loose and flying to the place where the nettings had been unloosed in order to empty the tubs, he darted overboard. The ship brought to, a man was placed in the main chains to catch him which he perceiving, made signs which words cannot express expressive of his happiness in escaping. He then went down and was seen no more.

Dr. Isaac Wilson, a surgeon in the Royal Navy, made a Guinea voyage on the *Elizabeth,* captain John Smith, who was said to be very humane. Nevertheless, Wilson was assigned the duty of flogging the slaves. "Even in the act of chastisement," Wilson says, "I have seen them look up at me with a smile, and, in their own language, say 'presently we shall be no more.'" One woman on the *Elizabeth* found some rope yarn which she tied to the armorer's vise; she fastened the other end round her neck and was found dead in the morning.

On the *Brookes* when Thomas Trotter was her surgeon, there was a man who, after being accused of witchcraft, had been sold into slavery with all his family. During the first night on shipboard he tried to cut his throat. Dr. Trotter sewed up the wound, but on the following night the man not only tore out the stitches but tried to cut his throat on the other side. From the ragged edges of the wound and the blood on his fingers, he seemed to have used his nails as the only available instrument. His hands were then tied together, but he refused all food, and he died of hunger in eight or ten days.

Besides the propensity for suicide, another deadly scourge of the Guinea cargoes was a phenomenon called "fixed melancholy." Even slaves who were well fed, treated with kindness, and kept under relatively sanitary conditions would often die, one after another, for no apparent reason; they had simply lost the will to live. Dr. Wilson believed that fixed melancholy was responsible for the loss of two thirds of the slaves who died on the *Elizabeth*. "No one who had it was ever cured," he says, "whereas those who had it not and yet were ill, recovered. The symptoms are a lowness of spirits and despondency. Hence they refuse food. This only increases the symptoms. The stomach afterwards got weak. Hence the belly ached, fluxes ensued, and they were carried off." But in spite of the real losses from despair, the high death rate on Guineamen was due to somatic more than to psychic afflictions.

Along with their human cargoes, crowded, filthy, undernourished, and terrified out of the wish to live, the ships also carried an invisible cargo of microbes, bacilli, spirochetes, viruses, and intestinal worms from one continent to another; the Middle Passage was a crossroad and market place of diseases. From Europe came smallpox, measles (somewhat less deadly to Africans than to American Indians), gonorrhea, and syphilis (which last Columbus' sailors had carried from America to Europe). The African diseases were yellow fever (to which the natives were resistant), dengue, blackwater fever, and malaria (which was not specifically African, but which most of the slaves carried in their blood streams). If anopheles mosquitoes were present, malaria spread from the slaves through any new territories to which they were carried. Other African diseases were amoebic and bacillary dysentery (known as "the bloody flux"), Guinea worms, hookworm (possibly African in origin, but soon endemic in the warmer parts of the New World), yaws, elephantiasis, and leprosy.

The particular affliction of the white sailors after escaping from the fevers of the Guinea Coast was scurvy, a deficiency disease to which they were exposed by their monotonous rations of salt beef and sea biscuits. The daily tot of lime juice (originally lemon juice) that prevented scurvy was almost never served on merchantmen during the days of the legal slave trade, and in fact was not prescribed in the Royal Navy until 1795. Although the slaves were also subject to scurvy, they fared better in this respect than the sailors, partly because they made only one leg of the triangular voyage and partly because their rough diet was sometimes richer in vitamins. But sailors and slaves alike were swept away by smallpox and "the bloody flux," and sometimes whole shiploads went blind from what seems to have been trachoma.

Smallpox was feared more than other diseases, since the surgeons had no way of curing it. One man with smallpox infected a whole vessel, unless— as sometimes happened—he was tossed overboard when the first scabs appeared. Captain Wilson of the *Briton* lost more than half his cargo of 375 slaves by not listening to his surgeon. It was the last slave on board who had the disease, says Henry Ellison, who made the voyage. "The doctor told Mr. Wilson it was the small-pox," Ellison continues. "He would not believe it, but said he would keep him, as he was a fine man. It soon broke out amongst the slaves. I have seen the platform one continued scab. We hauled up eight or ten slaves dead of a morning. The flesh and skin peeled off their wrists when taken hold of, being entirely mortified."

But dysentery, though not so much feared, probably caused more deaths in the aggregate. Ellison testified that he made two voyages on the *Nightingale*. On the first voyage the slaves were so crowded that thirty boys "messed and slept in the long boat all through the Middle Passage, there being no room below"; and still the vessel lost only five or six slaves in all, out of a cargo of 270. On the second voyage, however, the *Nightingale* buried "about 150, chiefly of fevers and flux. We had 250 when we left the coast."

The average mortality in the Middle Passage is impossible to state accurately from the surviving records. Some famous voyages were made without the loss of a single slave. On one group of nine voyages between 1766 and 1780, selected at random, the vessels carried 2,362 slaves and there were no epidemics of disease. The total loss of slaves was 154, or about six and one-half per cent. That figure is to be compared with the losses on a list of twenty voyages compiled by Thomas Clarkson, the abolitionist, in which the vessels carried 7,904 slaves with a mortality of 2,053, or twenty-six per cent. Balancing high and low figures together, the English Privy Council in 1789 arrived at an estimate of twelve and one-half per cent for the average mortality among slaves in the Middle Passage. To this figure it added four and one-half per cent for the deaths of slaves in harbors before they were sold, and thirty-three per cent for deaths in the so-called "seasoning" or acclimatizing process, making a total of fifty per cent. If these figures are correct, only one slave was added to the New World labor force for every two purchased on the Guinea Coast.

To keep the figures in perspective, it might be said that the mortality among slaves in the Middle Passage was possibly no greater than that of white indentured servants or even of free Irish, Scottish, and German immigrants in the North Atlantic crossing. On the better-commanded Guineamen it was probably less, and for a simple economic reason. There was no profit on a slaving voyage until the Negroes were landed alive and sold; therefore the better captains took care of their cargoes. It was different on the North Atlantic crossing, where even the hold and steerage passengers paid their fares before coming aboard, and where the captain cared little whether they lived or died.

After leaving the Portuguese island of São Tomé—if he had watered there—a slaving captain bore westward along the equator for a thousand miles, and then northwestward toward the Cape Verde Islands. This was the tedious part of the Middle Passage. "On leaving the Gulf of Guinea," says the author of a *Universal Geography* published in the early nineteenth century, ". . . that part of the ocean must be traversed, so fatal to navigators, where long calms detain the ships under a sky charged with electric clouds, pouring down by torrents of rain and of fire. This *sea of thunder,* being a focus of mortal diseases, is avoided as much as possible, both in approaching the coasts of Africa and those of America." It was not until reaching the latitude of the Cape Verde Islands that the vessel fell in with the northeast trades and was able to make a swift passage to the West Indies.

Dr. Claxton's ship, the *Young Hero,* was one of those delayed for weeks before reaching the trade winds. "We were so streightened for provisions," he testified, "that if we had been ten more days at sea, we must either have eaten the slaves that died, or have made the living slaves *walk the plank,*" a term, he explained, that was widely used by Guinea captains. There are no authenticated records of cannibalism in the Middle Passage, but there are many accounts of slaves killed for various reasons. English captains believed that French vessels carried poison in their medicine chests, "with which they can destroy their negroes in a calm, contagious sickness, or short provisions." They told the story of a Frenchman from Brest who had a long passage and had to poison his slaves; only twenty of them reached Haiti out of five hundred. Even the cruelest English captains regarded this practice as Latin, depraved, and uncovered by their insurance policies. In an emergency they simply jettisoned part of their cargo.

Often a slave ship came to grief in the last few days of the Middle Passage. It might be taken by a French privateer out of Martinique, or it might disappear in a tropical hurricane, or it might be wrecked on a shoal almost in sight of its harbor. On a few ships there was an epidemic of suicide at the last moment.

These, however, were exceptional disasters, recounted as horror stories in the newspapers of the time. Usually the last two or three days of the passage were a comparatively happy period. All the slaves, or all but a few, might be released from their irons. When there was a remaining stock of provisions, the slaves were given bigger meals—to fatten them for market— and as much water as they could drink. Sometimes on the last day—if the ship was commanded by an easygoing captain—there was a sort of costume party on deck, with the women slaves dancing in the sailors' castoff clothing. Then the captain was rowed ashore, to arrange for the disposition of his cargo.

This was a problem solved in various fashions. In Virginia, if the vessel was small, it might sail up and down the tidal rivers, bartering slaves for tobacco at private wharves. There were also public auctions of newly imported slaves, usually at Hampton, Yorktown, or Bermuda Hundred. In South Carolina, which was the great mainland slave market, the cargo was usually consigned to a commission merchant, who disposed of the slaves at auction, then had the vessel loaded with rice or indigo for its voyage back to England.

In the smaller West Indian islands, the captain sometimes took charge of selling his own slaves. In this case he ferried them ashore, had them drawn up in a ragged line of march, and paraded them through town with bagpipes playing, before exposing them to buyers in the public square. In the larger islands, commission merchants took charge of the cargo, and the usual method of selling the slaves at retail was a combination of the "scramble"—to be described in a moment—with the vendue or public auction "by inch of candle."

First the captain, with the commission merchant at his side, went over the cargo and picked out the slaves who were maimed or diseased. These were carried to a tavern and auctioned off, with a lighted candle before the auctioneer; bids were received until an inch of candle had burned. The price of so-called "refuse" slaves sold at auction was usually less than half of that paid for a healthy Negro. "I was informed by a mulatto woman," Dr. Falconbridge says, "that she purchased a sick slave at Grenada, upon speculation, for the small sum of one dollar, as the poor wretch was apparently dying of the flux." There were some slaves so diseased and emaciated that they could not be sold for even a dollar, and these might be left to die on the wharves.

The healthy slaves remaining after the auction were sold by "scramble," that is, at standard prices for each man, each woman, each boy, and each girl in the cargo. The prices were agreed upon with the purchasers, who then scrambled for their pick of the slaves. During his four voyages Falconbridge was present at a number of scrambles. "In the *Emilia*," he says,

> at Jamaica, the ship was darkened with sails, and covered round. The men slaves were placed on the main deck, and the women on the quarter deck. The purchasers

on shore were informed a gun would be fired when they were ready to open
the sale. A great number of people came on board with tallies or cards in their
hands, with their own names upon them, and rushed through the barricado
door with the ferocity of brutes. Some had three or four handkerchiefs tied
together, to encircle as many as they thought fit for their purposes.

For the slaves, many of whom believed that they were about to be eaten, it
was the terrifying climax of a terrifying voyage.

The parliamentary investigations of 1788–1791 presented a complete picture of the Middle Passage, with testimony from everyone concerned except
the slaves, and it horrified the English public. Powerful interests in Parliament,
especially those representing the Liverpool merchants and the West Indian
planters, prevented the passage of restrictive legislation at that time. But the
Middle Passage was not forgotten, and in 1807 Parliament passed a law forbidding any slaver to sail from a British port after May 1 of that year. At
about the same time, Congress prohibited the importation of slaves into American territory from and after January 1, 1808. All the countries of Europe
followed the British and American example, if with some delay. During the
next half century, however, reformers would learn that the trade was difficult
to abolish in fact as well as in law, and that illegal slaving would continue
as long as slavery itself was allowed to flourish.

Sources

Portraits of Slavery

**What follows is a collection of pictures representing the institution of
black slavery, from its beginnings in Africa, through the horrors of
the "middle passage," to life and suffering in the New World. As
you examine the pictures, look for evidence that supports or seems
to question Mannix and Cowley's interpretation. What does the engraving of the slave being whipped suggest about the ways whites
were able to keep discipline in the system? The slave ship shown is
the infamous "negrier" (as it was called in French) *La Vigilante de
Nantes.* Do you think that spending weeks in such a suffocating
prison would break down the human cargo psychologically, or
would they be able to maintain a hold on sanity and on their cultural
identity? Does the advertisement for a slave sale in South Carolina
suggest that the owners of the cargo would be ruthless or careless
with their human commodity, or would they have reason to guard
their investment against spoilage? Finally, remember that all these
pictures were produced by white men. Can you imagine how pictures left by the slaves themselves would have looked?**

Africans were smuggled into the United States between 1808 and 1860 in violation of a congressional act prohibiting new slaves. Here, they cram the upper decks of the bark *Wildfire.* *Culver Pictures.*

Bartering for Slaves on the Gold Coast. *Wilberforce Museum and Georgian Houses, Hull.*

Engraving by Alexander Anderson in Volume 2 of his scrapbooks. *Prints Division/New York Public Library.*

Shock of Enslavement. *The Granger Collection.*

This is a diagram of the slave ship *La Vigilante de Nantes*, showing how 400 slaves could be crammed into a hold 36 feet in length and 3½ feet in height.
New York Public Library at Lincoln Center.

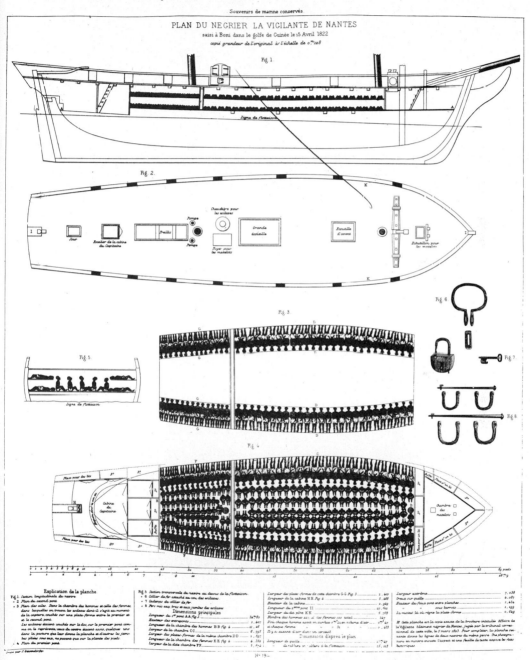

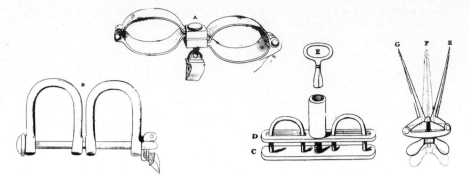

Standard Equipment for the Middle Passage. *A* **is a pair of iron handcuffs by which one slave was padlocked to another.** *B* **is a pair of leg irons, also for two slaves.** *C, D, E* **is the thumbscrew, an instrument of torture;** *F, G, H* **is the mouth opener for slaves who refused to eat.** The History of the Abolition of the African Slave Trade *by Thomas Clarkson.*

Advertisement in a Charleston, S.C., newspaper, 1766. Slaves from the Windward Coast were highly valued for their knowledge of growing rice. The Laurens of the commission merchants was Henry Laurens, later president of the Continental Congress. *Library of Congress.*

Wanted: Runaway Slaves

Angry masters advertised for runaway slaves just as they did for runaway indentured servants. The following notices, published in
Southern newspapers between 1767 and 1808, contain some of our
most detailed descriptions and accounts of slaves. They also reveal
much of the masters' attitudes toward their "property" and their
general insensitivity toward pain and brutality. What do these advertisements mean, really? Do they suggest that slaves were, on the
whole, so broken by their experience that they became submissive?
Can you generalize about the kinds of backgrounds the runaways
had? Is John Brown interested only in getting his property back, or
does he want punishment too? Notice that the last document in the
set is signed with a famous name—Andrew Jackson, who was soon to
become one of the nation's most popular presidents. Notice the reward offered and the additional payment Jackson offered to anyone
who could whip this slave. Do these documents throw any additional
light on the slave community? How do you think the owners could
guess where the slaves might run to?

Advertisement from the Virginia *Gazette* (Williamsburg), March 26, 1767.

Run away about the 15th of December last, a small yellow Negro wench
named Hannah, about 35 years of age; had on when she went away a green
plains petticoat, and sundry other clothes, but what sort I do not know, as
she stole many from the other Negroes. She has remarkable long hair, or
wool, is much scarified under the throat from one ear to the other, and has
many scars on her back, occasioned by whipping. She pretends much to the
religion the Negroes of late have practised, and may probably endeavour to
pass for a free woman, as I understand she intended when she went away,
by the Negroes in the neighbourhood. She is supposed to have made for
Carolina. Whoever takes up the said slave, and secures her so that I get her
again, shall be rewarded according to their trouble, by

Stephen Dence.

Advertisement from the Virginia *Gazette* (Williamsburg), April 23, 1767.
Bounty on the head of an outlawed slave.

Run Away from the subscriber in Norfolk, about the 20th of October
last, two young Negro fellows, viz. Will, about 5 feet 8 inches high, middling

black, well made, is an outlandish fellow, and when he is surprised the white of his eye turns red; I bought him of Mr. Moss, about 8 miles below York, and imagine he is gone that way, or some where between York and Williamsburg. Peter, about 5 feet 9 inches high, a very black slim fellow, has a wife at Little Town, and a father at Mr. Philip Burt's quarter, near the half-way house between Williamsburg and York, he formerly belonged to Parson Fontaine, and I bough him of Doctor James Carter. They are both outlawed; and Ten Pounds a piece offered to any person that will kill the said Negroes, and bring me their heads, or Thirty Shillings for each if brought home alive.

John Brown.

Advertisement from the Virginia *Gazette* (Williamsburg), Nov. 5, 1767.

Taken up on the 26th of July last, and now in Newbern gaol, North Carolina, Two New Negro Men, the one named Joe, about 45 years of age, about 5 feet 6 inches high, much wrinkled in the face, and speaks bad English. The other is a young fellow, about 5 feet 10 inches high, speaks English better than Joe, who he says is his father, has a large scar on the fleshy part of his left arm, and says they belong to Joseph Morse, but can give no account where he lives. They have nothing with them but an old Negro cloth jacket, and an old blue sailors jacket without sleeves. Also on the 21st of September was committed to the said gaol a Negro man named Jack, about 23 years of age, about 5 feet 4 inches high, of a thin visage, blear eyed, his teeth and mouth stand very much out, has six rings of his country marks round his neck, his ears full of holes, and cannot tell his master's name. And on the 27th of September two other Negro men, one named Sampson, about 5 feet 10 inches high, about 25 years of age, well made, very black, and is much marked on his body and arms with his country marks. The other named Will, about 5 feet 4 inches high, about 22 years of age, and marked on the chin with his country marks[*]; they speak bad English, and cannot tell their masters names. Whoever own the said Negroes are desired to come and pay the fees and take them away.

Richard Blackledge, Sheriff.

Advertisement from the Virginia *Gazette* (Williamsburg), Jan. 13, 1774.

Twenty Pounds Reward. Run away from Subscriber, a Mullatto Man named Abel, about forty Years old, near six Feet high, has lost several of his Teeth, large Eyebrows, a Scar or two on some Part of his Face, occasioned by a Brick thrown at him by a Negro, is very apt to stroke his Hand over

---

[*] "Country marks" were the scars, tattooing, boring of ears, filing of teeth, etc., by which the Africans of certain tribes were accustomed to mark their persons.—Ed.

his Chin, and plays on the Violin. He is well known as a Pilot for York River and the Bay. As I have whipped him twice for his bad Behaviour, I believe Scars may be seen upon his Body. He can write so as to be understood, and once wrote a Pass for a Negro belonging to the Honourable Colonel Corbin, wherein he said the Fellow had served his Time honestly and truly. He has been to England, but the Captain he went with took Care to bring him back, and since his Return from that Country is very fond of Liquor. He is gone off in a Boat with two Masts, Schooner rigged, once a Pilot Boat, but now the Property of the Magdalen Schooner of War, and was seen, I am told, fifty or sixty Leagues to the southward of Cape Henry, from which it is expected he intends for one of the Carolinas. He is a very great Rogue, and is so instructed by several Persons not far from Wormeley's Creek, York River; one of whom, he told me, said I was not worthy to be his Master. He had some Cash of my Son's, and an Order drawn by Captain Punderson on Richard Corbin, Esq; payable to Ralph G. Meredith or myself. A White Lad went off with him, whom I cannot describe, never having seen him to my Knowledge. Whoever secures said Servant, so that I might get him again, shall have the above Reward.

Samuel Meredith, Senior.

King and Queen, November 16, 1773.

Advertisement from the Virginia *Gazette,* April 21, 1774.
A talented and wily mulatto.

Run away from the Neabsco Furnace, on the 16th of last Month, a light coloured Mulatto Man named Billy or Will, the Property of the Honourable John Taylor, Esquire. When I tell the Publick that he is the same Boy who, for many Years, used to wait on me in my Travels through this and the neighbouring Province, and, by his Pertness, or rather Impudence, was well known to almost all my Acquaintances, there is the less Occasion for a particular Description of him. However, as he is now grown to the Size of a Man, and has not attended me for some Time past, I think it not amiss to say that he is a very likely young Fellow, about twenty Years old, five Feet nine Inches high, stout and strong made, has a remarkable Swing in his Walk, but is much more so by a surprising Knack he has of gaining the good Graces of almost every Body who will listen to his bewitching and deceitful Tongue, which seldom or ever speaks the Truth; has a small Scar on the right Side of his Forehead, and the little Finger of his right Hand is quite straight by a Hurt he got when a Child. He had on when he went away a blue Fearnaught and an under Jacket of green Baize, Cotton Breeches, Osnabrug Shirt, a mixed Blue Pair of Stockings, a pair of Country made Shoes, and yellow Buckles. From his Ingenuity, he is capable of doing almost any Sort of Business, and for some Years past has been chiefly employed as a Founder, a Stone Mason, and a Miller, as Occasion required; one of which Trades, I imagine, he will, in the Character of a Freeman, profess. I have some Reason to suspect his travelling towards James River, under the Pretence of being sent by me on Business. Whoever apprehends the said Mulatto Slave, and brings him to me, or his Master, the Honourable John Taylor of Mount Airy, or secures him so as to be had again, shall have double what the Law allows, and all reasonable Charges paid by

                                                              Thomas Lawson.

Neabsco Furnace, April 1, 1774.

Advertisement from the Georgia *Express* (Athens), Dec. 17, 1808.

Runaway from the subscriber living in Jackson county, on the Oconee river near Clarkesborough, on Sunday night the 13th of November last a mulatto man of the name of Joe. He is a very bright mulatto, almost white, about six feet high, tolerably well made, yellow gray eyes and yellow hair. He is branded on each cheek with the letter R, one of his upper fore teeth out, and, on examining under one of his arms there will be found a scar. He carried off with him clothes of different kinds, among them is a blue regimental coat turned up with red. He likewise took away with him a smooth bored gun. I suspect he will attempt to pass for a free man, and no doubt will aim northwardly or for the Indian Nation. Any person who will apprehend the above described negro, deliver him to me or confine him in jail shall be handsomely compensated.

                                                              Richard Thurmond.

Advertisement from the Tennessee *Gazette & Mero District Advertiser* (Nashville), Nov. 7, 1804.
Andrew Jackson's way.

STOP THE RUNAWAY. FIFTY DOLLARS REWARD. Eloped from the subscriber, living near Nashville on the 25th of June last, a Mulatto Man Slave, about thirty years old, five feet and an inch high, stout made and active, talks sensible, stoops in his walk, and has a remarkably large foot, broad across the root of the toes—will pass for a free man, as I am informed he has obtained by some means, certificates as such—took with him a drab great-coat, dark mixed body coat, a ruffled shirt, cotton home spun shirts and overalls. He will make for Detroit, through the states of Kentucky and Ohio, or the upper part of Louisiana. The above reward will be given any person that will take him and deliver him to me or secure him in jail so that I can get him. If taken out of the state, the above reward, and all reasonable expenses paid—and ten dollars extra for every hundred lashes any person will give him to the amount of three hundred.

                                                              Andrew Jackson,
                                                    near Nashville, State of Tennessee.

6

Toward Revolution

To Englishmen and colonists alike, the year 1763 was a great one. For almost a hundred years, the British had carried on an intense struggle with the French for the control of North America. For the colonists, this had meant involvement in one war after another, with Indians and their French allies sweeping down from Canada in raids on the New England and New York frontiers. Now, after the bloodiest of those wars, the French were finally beaten. Canada was British. In London and in all British North America, the loyal subjects of the now mighty British Empire ought to be able to look forward to peace and prosperity. Small wonder that proud colonists toasted the British monarch, George III, and swore their undying allegiance to king and Parliament. Small wonder, too, that authorities in London now saw a chance to put their governmental house in order and to extend a more efficient administration to their growing colonies across the Atlantic.

Twelve years later, the same loyal colonists were at war with the same authorities in England. Twelve years later, the names of George III and even of Parliament were cursed all up and down the North American seaboard.

This astonishing turn of events had its seeds in the situation of 1763. The British government came out of its long series of wars with France with a large debt. And the wish to extend efficient government across the Atlantic was in part a wish to make the colonies profitable through taxes—primarily taxes on trade, on the goods the colonists shipped to Europe and the manufactured items they imported. Parliament began to add to the list of taxes and duties the colonists were supposed to pay, and to send over officials to administer the duties and collect the taxes. The colonists, who had been virtually untaxed, responded vigorously and angrily. They began to boycott English goods, mob Crown officers, quarrel relentlessly with their royal governors, and destroy British property. The out-

117

come of a succession of crises and protests was open rebellion, followed by a full-scale war for independence.

Who rebelled and why? Historians have been grappling with
these related questions ever since the Revolution began in 1775. The
only thing we know for certain is that there are no simple and easy
answers. A number of general guesses have been proposed over the
years. One takes the colonists more or less at their word and suggests that the cause of the rebellion was the attempt of the British to
undercut some of the "liberties" the colonists had enjoyed as "free-
born" Englishmen. Another kind of answer has been that the colonists were reacting basically to their economic interests, trying to
protect a trading position that was vulnerable to British attempts to
regulate commerce. Still others have argued that the issue was not
the relationship between the home country and the colonies at all,
but within the *colonies,* and that the Revolution was an *internal* revolution in which "radicals" in the colonies seized power from colonial
elites who were dependent on their connection with authority in
London. And within such general arguments, there are specific questions that still are unanswered. How much attention should be paid,
for example, to the efforts of leading agitators like Sam Adams or
Tom Paine? How important were the blundering shifts in policy in
London, or the incompetence of British officials in the colonies?

Questions like these have made the interpretation of the American Revolution one of the most complicated and interesting of our
historical problems. Underneath all the interpretations and disagreements lies a profoundly important question: Should the Revolution
be seen as an anticipation of modern political and social history, or
as an event rooted in local quarrels and the concerns of British and
American politicians at the time? Was it a violent family squabble, or
was it, as Ralph Waldo Emerson called it, the "shot heard round the
world"? Or was it somehow and mysteriously *both?*

Interpretive Essay

Carl Becker

The Spirit of '76

Some of the best work on the coming of the Revolution was done by Carl Becker, who was a professor of history at Cornell University from 1917 until his death in 1945. Becker insisted that one must look at the prerevolutionary period through the eyes of different social groups, and that one must realize that there were at least two issues at stake. "The first was the question of home rule; the second was the question of who should rule at home." An imaginative scholar, Becker once used two fictional characters, Jeremiah Wynkoop and his father-in-law, Nicholas Van Schoickendinck, to explain the break with England. Here is that classic essay.

Last October Mr. Lyon asked me to come down to the Brookings School and tell you about the Spirit of '76. I suspected that he hadn't any clear notion of what was meant by the phrase "Spirit of '76," and I was positive I hadn't. I was therefore about to decline the invitation when, rummaging among my papers, I came upon an old and imperfect manuscript which seemed providentially designed to throw some light on this obscure subject. The manuscript bore the date of 1792, but who may have written it I was unable to determine. There are obviously some pages missing, and the tale ends suddenly as if never quite finished. But such as it is I have transcribed it, and I give it to you for what it may be worth. The title of the manuscript is "Jeremiah Wynkoop."

Jeremiah Wynkoop

During the war of independence I not infrequently heard zealous patriots say that Mr. Wynkoop was not as warm in the cause as he should be. The charge has lately been revived by those who had no great liking for Mr. Wynkoop's Federalist principles. Mr. Wynkoop was of course not alone in being thus distinguished. It is now said of many men who were never suspected of being Tory that they look back with regret to the old days before the breach with Britain. It is said of them, to employ a phrase now becoming current, that they were never really inspired by the true spirit of '76. For my part, I suspect that, in recalling the desperate days of the war, we are likely to invest the so-called spirit of '76 with a glamor which it did not have at the time. Be that as it may, I knew Jeremiah Wynkoop as an honest man and a genuine patriot. I was his closest friend, intimate enough to know better than most the difficulties that confronted him and the sentiments that determined his conduct. And so I think it worth while, now that the man is dead, to set down a plain tale of his activities and opinions from the beginning of the quarrel in 1763 to the final breach in 1776. This I do, not only for old friendship's sake and as a justification of Mr. Wynkoop, but as a contribution to the history of those troubled times; for Jeremiah Wynkoop was fairly representative, both in his station in life and in his opinions, of that considerable class of substantial men who did as much as any other class, and I think more than any other class, to enable these states to maintain their liberties against British tyranny.

Born of rich middle class parents of genuine Dutch-American stock, Jeremiah was educated at Kings College, then recently established. In fact we both entered the College the year it was founded, and graduated with the first class in 1758. Jeremiah then spent two years in the office of William Moore reading law, a profession which he nevertheless abandoned for the trade. Taking over a profitable business upon the sudden death of his father, he rapidly achieved a notable success in commerce, chiefly in West Indian ventures, and was already known, in 1765, as a leading merchant in New York, where he had offices near the wharves, and a town house, inherited from his father, on the Bowling Green. But Jeremiah, being much given to study and the reading of books, preferred to live away from the distractions of the city, and had in fact for some years resided in the country, out Greenwich Village way, where he possessed a fine estate which had come to him as part of the generous dowry of his wife, the daughter of old Nicholas Van Schoickendinck, a great landowner in the province.

Mr. Wynkoop was much given to the reading of books, as I have said; and it is necessary to dwell on this matter a little since it helps to explain his opinions and conduct. Of all books, histories of the ancient and the modern times were his favorite study. It was an interest which he acquired in college, and never afterward lost. In college of course we all read the standard Greek and Roman writers, and acquired the usual knowledge of classical history. To admire the classical poets and essayists was nothing out of the way for young men in college, but the ancient civilization fascinated Jeremiah more than most of us, and I recall that he devoured every book on that subject which the college afforded, and many others which he bought or borrowed. The Parallel Lives of Plutarch he knew almost by heart, and was never weary of discanting on the austere morality and virtuous republicanism of those heroic times. For Jeremiah a kind of golden age was pictured there, a lost world which forever disappeared when Caesar crossed the Rubicon. The later Roman times never interested him much—"five hundred years," he used to say, "in which the civilized world groaned under the heavy hands of tyrants, relieved only by the reigns of five good emperors." Still less was he interested in the Dark Ages, when the light of learning and the spirit of liberty were submerged by feudal anarchy and ecclesiastical superstition. But the story of modern times fascinated Jeremiah as much as the story of the ancient world because all its significance seemed to lie in the slow and painful emergence from that long mediaeval night, through the recovery of the wisdom of the ancients, the progress of natural philosophy, and the struggle for political liberty.

All these matters I recall we used to discuss at great length, so that I was perfectly familiar with Jeremiah's reflections on history. At that time his ideas seemed to me wonderfully novel and interesting, but I have since thought them, in a vague general way at least, those of most cultivated Americans. Be that as it may, all the significance of history appeared to Mr. Wynkoop to lie in the age-long conflict between Truth and Error, between Freedom and Oppression. And for this reason he opined that the central event of modern times was the struggle of the last century between the English people and the Stuart kings. With the history of that heroic time he was entirely familiar, and in a less degree I was too. Our heroes were Pym and Eliot, and John Hampden, imprisoned for refusing to pay a twenty shilling tax. Cromwell we admired as the man of iron who had forever laid the ghost of the Divine Right doctrine, and whose mistakes were later corrected by the liberal Whigs who called in Dutch William to replace the last of the Stuarts. We knew the great charters of liberty—the Magna Charta, the Petition of Right and the Bill of Rights. We knew our Milton, the man who defended the authority of elected magistrates, and erected an impregnable bulwark against the denial of free speech. We knew our Grotius, who had discovered in right reason the foundation of civil and international society. Above all we knew our Locke, and especially his second discourse on Civil Government, in which he so eloquently defended the Revolution of '88 as an act of reasonable men defending their natural rights against the usurping king who had broken the original compact.

Much as Jeremiah admired England as the home of political liberty, he was thoroughly American, and it was always his idea that America had played a most notable part in the great modern struggle against the oppression of Church and State. He used to find great satisfaction in recalling that our ancestors, at the hazard of their lives and fortunes, had braved the terrors of the new world in pursuit of religious and political liberty; that they had persisted, often at the point of failure, in the desperate determination to transform the inhospitable wilderness into a land fit for human habitation; and he would point out that they had succeeded beyond any reasonable expectation, so much so that these thirteen colonies were now the most fortunate and the freest countries in the world—thirteen communities living in peace and content, happily without kings, neither burdened with an idle aristocracy nor menaced by a depraved populace, with a press uncensored, and many religious faiths deprived of the power of persecution and long habituated to the spirit of toleration. For my part I used to complain sometimes that after all we were only "provincials," remote from the center of things. I used to express the wish that fate had set us down in London, nearer Piccadilly and the Beefsteak Club. But Jeremiah would have none of such repining. Provincials we might be in a geographical sense, he would say, but spiritually we were at "the center of the world, in the direct line of those heroes and martyrs who since the beginning of time have done battle for the dignity and happiness of mankind against the leagued assailants of both."

Here some pages are missing in the manuscript. It goes on as follows.

". . . are become so populous and wealthy that we are as indispensable to Britain as Britain is to us. The time is surely approaching when this vast country will be the center of power and wealth of the Empire. We are now freed from the French menace. The peace will be an enduring one, and the two branches of the English race will continue in the future as in the past to exemplify to the world those incomparable blessings that are the prerogatives of free peoples."

Such was Jeremiah Wynkoop's conception of history in general and of the part which Britain and America had played in the story of human progress. With him it was a kind of philosophy, a religion indeed, the only religion really that he had. I don't mean that he was of the atheistical school of thought. He believed indeed in the existence of the Deity as the First Cause and Original Contriver of the universe; and this was in fact the very reason why he found so much delight in the study of history. History was God's revelation of the meaning of life and of human destiny on earth, making plain the gradual progress and the ultimate triumph of Truth and Freedom. And this I think was the secret of his profound loyalty to both Britain and America; these were in his view the promised lands, the homes of the chosen peoples whose mission it was to lead mankind toward the final goal.

Nothing at all events was farther from his thought in 1763 than that there could be any serious differences between the two peoples who were so bound together by ties of blood and affection, by mutual respect, and by the common tradition of . . .

Another break in the manuscript here.

In the year 1765 Mr. Wynkoop shared the general feeling of apprehension which for two years had been steadily increasing on account of the measures, as unprecedented as they were unfortunate, of the king's minister, Mr. George Grenville. The chief of these measures were undoubtedly the Sugar Act of the last, and the Stamp Act of the then present year. On the nature and effects of these measures Mr. Wynkoop had read and reflected as much as a busy man well could do. The Sugar Act, obviously designed to placate the British West Indian sugar planters, was certain, as indeed it was intended, to put obstacles in the way of the island trade with New York and New England. In that trade Mr. Wynkoop was personally interested. It is true, as indeed he was careful to tell me, that his profits for the last year were much as usual; but it had been abundantly demonstrated in pamphlets that the Sugar duties were bound to have a disastrous effect on American trade in general; would, for example, undermine the New England rum industry and thereby depress the fisheries and the African trade; would diminish the exports of lumber and grain from New York and Pennsylvania; would above all, since the new duties were to be paid in silver, drain the colonies of their small store of hard money and thereby make it difficult for American merchants to settle their balances due in London on account of imported British manufactures.

No one doubted, at least no one in America, that the Sugar Act was unwise in point of policy, calculated to defeat the very end intended. Yet there it was, an act of Parliament imposing duties for the regulation of trade, and we could not deny that Parliament had long exercised without opposition the right to regulate trade. But I recall Mr. Wynkoop's pointing out to me one novel feature of the act, which was the declared purpose, expressed in the preamble, of raising a revenue in "his Majesty's dominions in America, for defraying the expenses of defending, protecting, and securing the same." For some reason Mr. Wynkoop disliked the term "dominions," always preferring the term "colonies." But he disliked still more the term "securing." For two years ministers had been prone to talk of laying restrictions on his Majesty's dominions for their better security. This idea Mr. Wynkoop disliked extremely. I remember his saying that the term "free-born Englishmen" had always given him great satisfaction, that he had always supposed that Americans were possessed of all the rights of Englishmen born within the realm; and indeed I knew him well enough to know that he harbored the firm conviction that Americans were not only as free as Englishmen but even a little freer, a degree less subservient to aristocrats and kings, a degree more emancipated from custom and the dead hand of the past. I often heard him compare the Assembly of New York, chosen by the free suffrages of the people, with the British Parliament in which so often the members were chosen by irresponsible Peers and Borough-mongers—compare them of course to the disadvantage of the latter. To suppose that Parliament was now bent upon restricting the dearly bought and well deserved liberties of America was to Jeremiah, as indeed it was to all of us, an alien and distressing thought.

We could scarcely therefore avoid asking the question: "What constitutional right has the British Parliament to legislate in restraint of American liberties?" We never doubted that we were possessed of liberties, and no American, certainly no American as well informed as Mr. Wynkoop, needed to be told that there was a British Constitution which guaranteed the rights of Englishmen. Yet, as I recall those early years, I must confess that we were somewhat perplexed, had a little the air of groping about in the dark for the precise provisions of the British Constitution. The spirit of the British Constitution we knew was to be found in the Magna Charta and the Bill of Rights. Rights were indeed of its very essence; and to Mr. Wynkoop at least it was incredible that there was not to be found in it an adequate guarantee of the rights which Americans ought to enjoy. I remember his reading to me certain passages from the pamphlets of Stephen Hopkins and Governor

Hutchinson—pamphlets which he thought expressed the American view very adequately. "What motive," Mr. Hopkins asked, "can remain to induce the Parliament to hedge the principles and lessen the rights of the most dutiful and loyal subjects—subjects justly entitled to ample freedom, who have long enjoyed and not abused, their liberties?" This passage I think expressed Mr. Wynkoop's state of mind very well in the year of the Sugar Act. His state of mind was one of amazement, the state of mind of a man who is still at the point of asking questions—Why? For what reason?

Meantime the Stamp Act, presenting the question more clearly, did much to clarify our ideas on the matter of American taxation; and certainly Mr. Wynkoop was never in doubt as to the unconstitutionality of that famous measure. In those days I was much at Mr. Wynkoop's house, and I remember one day in November, 1765, sitting with him and his father-in-law, old Nicholas Van Schoickendinck, discussing the state of the nation. Even old Nicholas had been startled out of his customary complacency by the furious excitement occasioned by the Stamp Act.

"The Act is unconstitutional, sir," Mr. Wynkoop had just declared, somewhat dogmatically it must be confessed, and for perhaps the third time. "There can be no question about that I think. It is not only contrary to precedent, but is destructive of British liberty, the fundamental principle of which is that Englishmen may not be taxed without their own consent. We certainly never gave our assent to the Stamp Act."

"I won't say no to that," old Nicholas remarked. "And if we had done no more than to protest the measure I should be well content."

"Little good protests would have done, sir. We protested before the bill was passed, and without effect. Mr. Grenville would not hear our protests, and now he finds the act virtually nullified. I can't say I regret it."

"Nullified!" Old Nicholas exclaimed with some asperity. "A soft word for a nasty business. Mr. Grenville finds his law 'nullified,' you say. But in getting the law nullified we get half the windows of the Broad Way smashed too, and Governor Colden gets his chariot burned. For my part I don't know what Mr. Colden's chariot had to do with the devilish stamps—it wasn't designed to carry them."

"Very true, sir, I admit. And regrettable enough, all this parading and disturbance. But if Ministers will play with oppression the people will play with violence. Similar incidents occurred in England itself in the last century. Let Mr. Grenville beware of playing the role of Strafford. God knows I am no friend of rioting. I have windows too. But a little rioting may be necessary on occasion to warn ministers that legislative lawlessness is likely to be met by popular violence."

Mr. Wynkoop had perhaps a little the air of talking to convince himself rather than old Nicholas. Old Nicholas at least was not convinced.

"Tush!" he exclaimed irritably. "That's a new word, 'popular.' You young fellows have picked up a lot of precious democratical phrases, I must say. Who are 'the people' you talk so loosely about? Another word for 'populace' or I miss my guess. Don't delude yourself by supposing that it was hatred of the Stamps that made them break Mr. Livingston's windows and burn Mr. Colden's chariot. They hate Mr. Livingston and Mr. Colden because they are men of substance and standing. It is not windows they aim at but class privileges, the privileges of my class and yours, the class that always has, and I trust always will, govern this province. The bald fact is that a mob of mechanics and ne'er-do-wells, led by obscure fellows like John Lamb and Isaac Sears who have hitherto doffed their caps and known their places, are now aiming to control the city through their self constituted committees. Sons of Liberty, they call themselves; sons of anarchy, in fact. I wish as much as you to preserve our liberties. But I warn you that liberty is a sword that cuts two ways, and if you can't defend your rights against ministerial oppression without stirring the 'people,' you will soon be confronted with the necessity of defending your privileges against the encroachments of the mob on the Bowling Green."

Old Nicholas stopped to light his pipe, and after a few puffs added:

"You don't associate with *Mr.* John Lamb, do you? You ain't one of the Liberty Boys who erect poles and break windows, I hope."

Mr. Wynkoop laughed off the sarcasm.

"Certainly not, sir. I don't know the fellow Lamb, never saw him in fact, although I am told, and believe, that he is an honest, worthy man. The danger you mention has of course occurred to me, but I think you probably exaggerate it. Let Britain repeal the Stamp Act, as she must do, and the populace will be quiet enough."

We sat until a late hour. I took but little part in the discussion, enjoying nothing better than to listen to the good natured wrangling of these two friends. During the course of the evening each repeated, many times over, his former argument, all without rancor, but all equally without effect. Except in opinion, they were not divided; and at last, pledging one another courteously in a glass of stiff toddy, we separated for the night.

During the following months Mr. Wynkoop continued firm in the defense of American rights. He agreed, as all the substantial merchants did, not to use the stamps, which was indeed not possible since none were to be had. Yet he would do no business without them. Let the courts close, he said. Let his ships stand idle in harbor, a year, two years, let them rot there rather than submit to an unconstitutional measure. So I often heard him declare roundly, sitting at dinner sipping his madeira. . . .

Again something missing from the manuscript.

. . . secret misgivings, during the long cold winter, by the continued disturbances in the streets, and by the clamor of those, mostly of the common sort, who demanded that the courts should open and denounced the merchants for timidly refusing to do business without stamps. The Sons of Liberty were saying that the stopping of business was all very well for gentlemen of fortune, but that it was ruining the people who must starve unless business went on as usual. The Sons of Liberty were grown more hostile to the merchants than they were to ministers, and they even hinted that the better sort were by their timidity betraying the cause. Meantime Old Nicholas appeared to enjoy the situation, and never lost an opportunity of asking him, Jeremiah Wynkoop, whether he hadn't yet joined the Liberty Boys, and why after all he didn't send his ships out, clearance papers or no clearance papers.

Mr. Wynkoop was therefore immensely relieved when the British Parliament finally repealed the hateful measure, thus at once justifying his conduct and restoring his confidence in the essential justice of Britain. He had now, I recall, rather the better of the argument with Old Nicholas (the two were forever disputing) and pointed out to him ever so often that a little firmness on America's part was all that was needful to the preservation of her liberties. For two years he went about his business and pleasure with immense content. I dare say he easily forgot, as men will do, the distasteful incidents of the Stamp Act struggle, and allowed his mind to dwell chiefly on its satisfactions. He often spoke of the principle, "No taxation without representation," as being now fully established; often expressed his gratification that, by taking a firm and sensible stand, he and his substantial friends had brought Britain to recognize this principle; so that by the mere passing of time as it were these ideas acquired for Jeremiah a certain axiomatic character. I was never so sure of all this, and sometimes called his attention to the Declaratory Act as evidence that Britain still claimed the right of binding the colonies in all matters whatsoever. Needless to say, old Nicholas called his attention to the Declaratory Act oftener than I did. But Mr. Wynkoop would not take the Declaratory Act seriously. It was, he said, no more than a bravely flying banner designed to cover a dignified retreat from an untenable position; and he had no fear that Britain, having confessed its error by repealing the Stamp Act, would ever again repeat it.

It presently appeared that the British government could commit errors without repeating itself. In 1767, following the mysterious retirement and delphic silences of Mr. Pitt, Mr. Charles Townshend had come forward, no one knew on whose authority, and promised the House to obtain a revenue from America without doing violence to her alleged rights. The Americans, he said, had drawn a distinction between "internal" and "external" taxes, denying the former but admitting the latter. This distinction Mr. Townshend thought "perfect nonsense," but was willing to humor Americans in it; which he would do by laying an external tax on the importation of glass, lead, paper, and tea. These duties, which would bring into the Exchequer about £40,000, the Americans must on their own principles, Mr. Townshend thought, admit to be constitutional.

It may strike my readers as odd that any one could have been surprised by anything Mr. Townshend took a notion to; but we were indeed not then as well aware of the man's essential frivolity as we have since become. I recall at all events that Mr. Wynkoop followed the proceedings in the House with amazement; and when we learned, one day in 1768, that Mr. Townshend had actually blarneyed the House into passing the Tea Act, the whole business struck Jeremiah as preposterous—"doubtless one of those deplorable jokes,"

I remember his saying, "which Mr. Townshend is fond of perpetrating when half drunk." I had some recollection that in the time of the Stamp Act troubles certain writers had hinted at a distinction between "internal" and "external" taxes; and Mr. Wynkoop admitted that some such distinction may have been made. But he said that for his part he thought little of such subtle distinctions, agreeing rather with Mr. Pitt that the real question was whether Parliament could "take money out of our pockets without our consent" by any tax whatsoever. There was, however, a difficulty in taking so advanced a position at that time, and as usual it was old Nicholas, always quick to perceive difficulties, who pointed it out.

"I fancy," Old Nicholas had said, "that every act in regulation of trade takes money out of our pockets, but I don't imagine you have yet become so ardent a Son of Liberty as to deny Parliament the right of regulating our trade."

At that time we were all reading Mr. Dickinson's Letters of A Pennsylvania Farmer, and Mr. Wynkoop, who read everything, was able to meet that objection.

"The essential question," he said, "is whether an act of Parliament is laid primarily for the regulation of trade or for the raising of a revenue. If for the latter, it is a tax. The intention of the framers must decide, and there can be no question that the Tea Act is a tax since the framers expressly declare its purpose to be the raising of a revenue."

"A fine distinction, that! But it would be easy for the framers of an act to levy duties on imports with the real intention of raising a revenue, all the while professing loudly their intention of regulating trade. What then?"

"Americans would not be so easily deceived, sir. The nature of the Act would reveal the real intention clearly enough."

"Ha! You would determine the nature of an act by the intention of the framers, and the intention of the framers by the nature of the act. Excellent! That is the logic of your Pennsylvania Farmer. The New Englanders are still more advanced, I see. They are now saying that our rights are founded on a law of Nature, and God only knows what that is. God and Mr. Adams— it's the same thing, I dare say."

"The New Englanders are likely to be a little rash, sir, I think," Mr. Wynkoop admitted. "The argument of their Mr. Adams is complicated, and I fear too subtle to be easily followed. I'm not sure I understand it."

"Well, never mind. You will all understand it soon enough. First you say that Britain has no right to lay internal taxes. Then that she has no right to levy taxes of any sort. Next you will be saying that Parliament has no right of legislation for the colonies on any matter whatsoever. And as you can't derive that from precedent you will derive it from the law of nature."

Mr. Wynkoop smiled at this outburst.

"I have no fear of its coming to that," he said. "The Tea Act is not really an act of Britain; it is Mr. Townshend's foolish hobby. A firm and sensible resistance on our part will effect its repeal. But if one could conceive Britain to be so blind as to push matters to extremes—well, I don't know.

If it were really a choice between admitting that Parliament has a right of making all laws for us or denying that she has a right of making any laws for us, it would be a hard choice, but should we not be forced to choose the latter alternative? What other answer could we make?"

"You may well ask! What answer will you make when your precious Adams comes out with a declaration of independency from Great Britain?"

"Independence!" Mr. Wynkoop exclaimed. "Good God, sir, what an idea!"

And indeed, at that time, the idea of separation from Great Britain struck us all as fantastic.

A firm and sensible resistance, Jeremiah had maintained, would bring a repeal of the Townshend duties, as it had formerly brought a repeal of the Stamp Act. When it was learned that Lord North, on March 5, 1770, had moved the repeal of all the Townshend duties save that on tea, Mr. Wynkoop could with some reason say, and did say, that events had proved the justice of his view. And Mr. Wynkoop felt, rightly enough, although he modestly refrained from boasting of it, that he had contributed to this happy result. With no more than the grudging consent of old Nicholas, he had taken a leading part in organizing the Merchant's Association—an agreement not to import any goods from Great Britain so long as the Townshend duties should be in force. That Association had been faithfully kept by the New York merchants of substance and standing. Mr. Wynkoop had himself kept it to the letter, and had sacrificed much in doing so. He told me that his enlarged stock of goods, ordered in anticipation of the agreement, had soon been sold out—at high prices indeed, but not sufficiently high to recoup him for his subsequent losses. For four months last past business had been dull beyond all precedent—scarcely a ship moving; debts not to be collected; money hardly to be had at any price; and the poorer sort of people in dire need for want of employment.

There were indeed plenty of unscrupulous men who had done well enough, who had even profited while pretending to defend their country's rights. The Boston and Philadelphia merchants, as was definitely known in New York, had observed the Association none too well; and even in New York men of no standing had done a thriving business in the smuggling way, especially in Holland tea. Obviously the longer the Association was maintained by honest merchants, the more unscrupulous smugglers would profit by it. We were therefore somewhat surprised to learn that the Boston merchants were in favor of maintaining the Association in full vigor, in spite of Lord North's concessions, so long as the 3d duty on tea was retained. This policy was also advocated by the dishonest beneficiaries of the system in New York, who made use of agitators like Mr. MacDougall to stir up the Mechanics Association and the populace generally against the Merchants, their argument being that our liberties were as much endangered by the 3d duty on tea as they had been by all the Townshend duties.

I am not so sure now that they were wrong, but at that time all of the substantial merchants of New York were strong for a modification of the

Association. Mr. Wynkoop, I recall, took a leading part in the affair. He was much irritated with the Boston merchants whom he described as being more active in "resolving what to do than in doing what they had resolved." His opinion was that the Association no longer served any "purpose other than to tie the hands of honest men to let rogues, smugglers, and men of no character plunder their country." Besides, he was much gratified, as all the merchants were, by the recent act of the British government permitting the issue in New York of a paper currency, which was so essential to business prosperity. And therefore, in view of the fact that Britain had taken the first step by repealing the major part of the Townshend duties, it seemed to him the part of wisdom for the colonies to make some concession on their part. The New York merchants of standing were I think generally of Mr. Wynkoop's opinion; and at all events, after taking a canvass of the city, they resolved to abandon the old Association, agreeing for the future to import all commodities, "except teas and other articles that are or may be subject to an importation duty." Some were apprehensive lest New York might find itself alone in this action, and thereby suffer the stigma of having deserted the cause. But in the event it proved otherwise, as Mr. Wynkoop had anticipated. In spite of protests from Boston and Philadelphia, the merchants of those cities followed the lead of New York. Demonstrations in the streets soon subsided, importation became general, business revived, and the controversy with Britain seemed definitely closed.

The years of '71 and '72 were quiet years—ominously so as it proved. But in those days we all nourished the conviction that the controversy with Britain was definitely closed. Nothing occurred to remind us of it even, unless it would be the annual celebrations of the repeal of the Stamp Act, or the faint reverberations, always to be heard in any case, of political squabbles in the Massachusetts Bay. Then, out of a clear sky as it seemed, the storm burst—the landing of the tea ships, the destruction of the tea in Boston harbor, and the subsequent meeting of the Philadelphia Congress. These events, all occurring in rapid succession, seemed to fall like so many blows on Mr. Wynkoop's head, and I recall his saying to me . . .

Here the manuscript breaks off again, and there are evidently some pages missing.

. . . return from Philadelphia, I met him at his father's house where we were to take dinner, as often happened. Arriving early, we had a long talk while waiting for old Nicholas to come down. I found Mr. Wynkoop in low spirits, an unusual thing for him. It may have been no more than a natural weakness after the excitement of attending the Congress, but to my accustomed eyes his low spirits seemed rather due to the uncomfortable feeling that he had been elbowed by circumstances into a position which he never intended to occupy. I was eager for the details of the Congress, but he seemed unwilling to talk of that, preferring rather to dwell upon the events leading up to it—matters which we had threshed out many times before. It was as if Mr. Wynkoop wished to revive the events of the last year and his own part in them, as if, feeling that he might and perhaps should have followed a different line of conduct, his mind was eagerly engaged in finding some good reasons for the line of conduct which he had followed in fact. What first gave me this notion was his saying, *apropos* of nothing:

"I will confess to you, what I would not to another, that if I could twelve months ago have foreseen the present situation I should probably not have attended the Congress."

The remark alarmed me. Mr. Wynkoop's admiration for Britain and his faith in her essential justice were always stronger than mine. For my part I doubted not, from the moment of the passing of the Coercive Acts, that we were in for it, that Britain would not back down again, and that we must either break with her or submit to her demands. My decision was made. I would go with America when the time came for the final breach, I knew that; and above all things I wished Mr. Wynkoop, who was my closest friend, to throw the weight of his powerful interest on the side of my country. But I knew him well enough to be sure that if he now convinced himself that it would come to a breach with Britain he would probably wash his hands of the whole business. What I counted on was a certain capacity in the man, I won't say for deceiving himself, but for convincing himself that what he strongly desired would somehow come to pass. I therefore did what I could to convince him, or rather to help him convince himself, that his past and present conduct was that of a wise and prudent man.

"No man can foresee the future," I remarked, somewhat sententiously.

"That is true," he said. "And even could I have foreseen the future, I fail to see how I could have acted differently, at least not honorably and with any satisfaction to myself. It is past a doubt that Britain, in authorizing the India Company to sell its teas in America, deliberately sought to raise the issue with America once more. It was a challenge, and so insidiously contrived that America had no choice but submission or a resort to a certain amount of violence. Once landed the teas were bound to be sold, since even with the 3d duty they were offered at a less price than the Holland teas. The issue could not be met by commercial agreements, still less by argument. Well, we sent the teas back to London. The Massachusetts people threw theirs into the harbor. Violence, undoubtedly. I had no part in it, but what could be done? Who after all was responsible for the violence? Let ministers who revived an issue happily settled answer that."

"There is no doubt in my mind," I said, "that Britain welcomed the violence in Boston harbor as a pretext for strong measures."

"It seems incredible," Mr. Wynkoop resumed, "but what else can we think? Hitherto it might be said of ministers that they blundered, that they did not know the consequences of their acts. But not on this occasion. They knew perfectly the temper of America; and in any case the destruction of a little tea was surely a mild offense compared with the abrogation of the Massa-chusetts Charter and the closing of Boston harbor. To subject a loyal province to military despotism, and then deliberately to set about starving the people into submission reveals a vindictiveness foreign to the British character. I can't think the Coercive Acts represent the will of the English people, and I am confident, always have been, that the sober second thought of the nation will repudiate these acts of ministerial despotism."

It was not the first time I had heard Mr. Wynkoop express that sentiment.

"I trust it may prove so," I said. "At least we have done our part. No one can say that the Congress has countenanced rash measures. It has merely adopted a commercial agreement, a measure which we have frequently resorted to before. I don't see how it could have done less."

Mr. Wynkoop seemed a little uncertain of that

"Yes," he said. "I suppose we could not have done less; Heaven knows we have shown a proper restraint. And I may say that what little influence I have had has always been exerted to that end."

I knew well enough what he was thinking of. After the tea episode there were rash spirits who talked of resort to arms, and even hinted at independence. There were such men even in New York. They had formed the Committee of 25, but fortunately the more moderate minded had got the committee enlarged to 51; and Mr. Wynkoop, together with Mr. Jay and Mr. Alsop and other men of substance, had consented to serve on the Committee of 51 in order to prevent the firebrands from carrying the province into violent measures. Old Nicholas had advised against it.

"Beware of meddling with treason," I recall hearing him say to Mr. Wynkoop at that time.

"Precisely my idea," Mr. Wynkoop had replied, with the smile he always had for old Nicholas' penchant for using stronger terms than the occasion warranted. "I wish to steer clear of treason, or anything remotely approaching it. But it is plain to be seen that New York will support Boston in some fashion, plain to be seen that she will send delegates to Philadelphia. Suppose I and all moderate men follow your advice and wash our hands of the affair? What then? Then the Mechanics will take the lead and send MacDougall and Sears and men of their kidney to Philadelphia, with instructions for vigorous measures. Vigorous measures! God only knows what measures they may be for!"

It was to keep New York from violent measures of all sorts that Mr. Wynkoop had consented to serve on the Committee of 51; it was for that reason he had gone to Philadelphia. I knew that better than most, and I knew that that was what he was now thinking of.

"I am very glad you went to Philadelphia," I said.

"What else could I have done?" he exclaimed. "I have asked myself that a dozen times without finding any answer. But about the Association I don't know. You say it is a moderate measure, but after all it was the measure of the New Englanders, and among the moderates of Philadelphia it was commonly thought to be perhaps too vigorous. I was opposed to it. I voted against it. And having done so perhaps I was ill advised to sign it. I don't know."

I was about to make some reply, when old Nicholas came into the room, and I fancied I could see Mr. Wynkoop stiffen to defend his conduct against inevitable sarcasms.

"Fine doings!" Old Nicholas growled. "The New Englanders had their way, as I expected. I warned you against meddling with treason."

"Treason's a strong word, sir."

"The Association smells of it."

"I cannot think so, sir. The Association is a voluntary agreement not to do certain things; not to import or to export certain goods after a certain date. No law that I know of compels me to import or to export."

"No law requires you to import or to export, very true. But does any law require *me* not to import or export? Certainly no law of the British Parliament or of New York Province obliges me. But suppose I exercise my lawful privilege of importing after the date fixed? What then? Will not your Association compel me not to import, or try to do so? Are not your committees pledged to inspect the customs, to seize my goods, and to sell them at public auction for the benefit of the starving mechanics of Boston? I tell you your Association erects a government unknown to the law; a government which aims to exert compulsion on all citizens. When I am given a coat of tar for violating the Association, will you still say it is a *voluntary* Association?"

"I think little compulsion will be necessary," Mr. Wynkoop replied. "The continent is united as never before; and when the British people realize that, and when British merchants find markets wanting, ministers will be made to see reason."

"You signed the Association, I hear."

"I did, sir. I was opposed to it as Mr. Jay was, but when it was finally carried we both signed it. Once adopted as expressing the policy of Congress, it seemed useless to advertise our divisions, and so weaken the effect of the measures taken. Congress has decided. The important thing now is not what policy Congress should have adopted; the important thing now is for all to unite in support of the policy which it has in fact adopted. If the Colonies present a united front to Britain, as they will do, Britain must yield."

"My advice," old Nicholas said as we went into dinner, "is to drop it. And don't say I didn't warn you."

Over our after dinner wine the matter was gone into at greater length. I said but little, no more than to throw in a remark now and then to keep the argument alive; for I felt that the opposition of old Nicholas would do more to keep Mr. Wynkoop in the right frame of mind than anything I could say. Be that as it may, I left the house well satisfied; for whether it was the dinner, or the wine, or the truculent arguments of old Nicholas, or all of these combined, I felt sure that the total effect of the evening had been to confirm Mr. Wynkoop in the conviction that the Association was a wise measure, well calculated to bring Britain to terms.

As Mr. Wynkoop had anticipated, little compulsion was necessary to secure the observance of the Association; the threat of confiscation, on the authority of the Committee of 60, of which Mr. Wynkoop was a member, was quite sufficient, save in the case of certain obstinate but negligible traders. And at first it seemed to many that the measures taken would produce the desired effect, for in February Lord North introduced his famous Resolution on Conciliation. I thought the Resolution signified little or nothing, and when in April the news came from Lexington I was not much surprised. It meant war to a certainty, and my first thought was to learn what Mr. Wynkoop would make of it. Curiously enough, with that faculty he had for moulding the world close to the heart's desire, Mr. Wynkoop found some satisfaction in this untoward event. War with Great Britain—no, he would not pronounce the word prematurely. He spoke of the Lexington affair as a repetition of the Boston Massacre, seemingly more serious only because America was now prepared to defend its liberties with arms in its hands. I was delighted that he could take it so; for it convinced me that we might still carry him along with us. The Assembly of New York was too lukewarm to be depended on, half the members or more being frankly Tory, so that we found it convenient to organize a Provincial Congress, composed of delegates elected under the supervision of the Committees, in order to take charge of affairs and keep New York in line with the continent. The most advanced party was already suspicious of Mr. Wynkoop's loyalty; but the moderate men saw the wisdom of winning his support if possible. Mr. Jay and Mr. Alsop were especially keen to have Mr. Wynkoop serve in the Provincial Congress, and they asked me to do what I could to obtain his consent to stand as a candidate.

I did what I could, and I flatter myself that my representations had some influence with him. Knowing his admiration for Mr. Jay, I put it to him as a thing strongly urged by that gentleman.

"Mr. Jay thinks it the more necessary," I said to Mr. Wynkoop, "for men of your sound and moderate views to serve, since the Mechanics are every day gaining headway, and at the same time many men of standing are withdrawing altogether. There is a two-fold danger to meet; we must keep the province loyal to the cause, and we must prevent the levelling ideas of the New Englanders from gaining the ascendancy here. If men of your standing refuse to direct the affairs of the colony in these crucial times we shall surely succumb to one or the other of these evils."

"I understand that very well," Mr. Wynkoop replied, "but the decision is not, as you know, an easy one for me."

"Your difficulties are appreciated, and by no one more than by Mr. Jay and all his friends. But it is precisely for that reason, as they point out, that we need your support. Old Nicholas is known to be Tory, and it is much commented on that the Van Schoickendinck Interest is largely lukewarm if not actually hostile. The family Interest is a powerful one, and if you are cordially with us it will do much to bring over many who are hesitating. Your responsibility is the greater, as Mr. Jay rightly says, because of the fact that you will carry with you, one way or another, a great number."

"It is very flattering of Mr. Jay to say so."

Mr. Wynkoop had a great respect for Mr. Jay's judgment—had always had. He consented to stand, and was elected. Throughout the summer of 1775 he attended the sessions of the Provincial Congress faithfully, giving his support to those who were endeavoring to hold the province to a sane middle course—enforcing the Association; raising a militia for defense; keeping the door carefully open for conciliation. Old Nicholas charged him with being too much led about by Mr. Jay. Mr. Wynkoop naturally replied that the notion was ridiculous. What kept him to the mark I feel sure was the feeling that his views and his conduct had been hitherto justified by events, and were now justified by Lord North's Resolution on Conciliation. On this he placed all his hopes. Unacceptable Lord North's Resolution was, he told me on one occasion; but he regretted that the Congress at Philadelphia had seen fit to pronounce it "unseasonable and insidious." When bargains are to be struck, Mr. Wynkoop said, politicians do not offer everything at the first approach. The Resolution proved, he thought, that Lord North was preparing to retreat, as gracefully as possible no doubt. Meantime the policy adopted by the Philadelphia Congress Mr. Wynkoop thought eminently satisfactory; the Resolution on Taking up Arms was admirably phrased to convince Britain that America would defend her rights; the Petition to the King admirably phrased to prove her loyalty. Throughout the summer and autumn Mr. Wynkoop therefore held the same language to men of extreme views—to the over timid and to the over zealous: the Petition's the thing, he said; it will surely effect the end desired.

Hope delayed makes the heart sick, it has been said. But I think this was not the effect on Mr. Wynkoop. On the contrary, I am sure that for four months he found peace of mind by looking forward to the happy day when the king would graciously make concessions. I had little expectation of any concessions, and it was no great shock to me when the news arrived in November that the king had not even deigned to receive the Petition, much less to answer it. But I knew it would be a heavy blow to Mr. Wynkoop; and when the British government, placing an embargo on American trade, proclaimed America to be in a state of rebellion, it is not too much to say that Mr. Wynkoop's little world of opinion and conduct, held together by recollection of the past and hope for the future, was completely shattered. For a month I saw him scarcely at all. He rarely went abroad, even to attend the Provincial Congress. He must have sat at home in seclusion, endeavoring to adjust his thought to the grim reality, gathering together as best he could the scattered fragments of a broken faith.

During the winter of '76 I saw him more frequently. We often discussed the situation at length. The time for discussion, for discussion of the past that is, seemed to me to be over. But Mr. Wynkoop was seemingly more interested in discussing what had happened than in discussing what ought now to be done. At first this puzzled me; but I soon found the explanation, which was that he knew very well what had to be done; or at least what he had to do, and was only engaged in convincing himself that it had been from the first inevitable, that the situation that now confronted him was not of his making. His one aim from the first, he said, and he said it many times, was to prevent the calamity now impending. I know not how many times he reviewed his past conduct. Short of tamely submitting to the domination of Parliament, he was forever asking, what other course could America have followed but the one she had followed? What other course could he have followed? If America had appealed, not to force but to reason, was this not due to the efforts of men of substance and standing, men of Mr. Wynkoop's class? If Mr. Wynkoop and all his kind had washed their hands of the affair, would not the populace and their hot headed leaders long since have rushed America into violence, and so have given Britain's measures the very justification which they now lacked?

In all this I quite agreed with Mr. Wynkoop. I assured him that his conduct had always been that of a wise and prudent man, and that if events had disappointed the expectations of prudent men, the fault was clearly not his. Responsibility lay with the British government, with those mad or unscrupulous ministers who, wittingly or unwittingly, were betraying the nation by doing the will of a stubborn king. Mr. Wynkoop found consolation in the thought that since ministers had appealed to the sword, the decision must be by the sword. Fight or submit, they had said. The alternative was not of America's choosing, nor of Mr. Wynkoop's choosing. Could America submit now? Could Mr. Wynkoop submit now? Whatever he might have done a year ago, two years ago, could he now tamely submit, bowing the head like a scared school boy, renouncing the convictions of a lifetime, advising the friends with whom he had been associated on committees and congresses to eat their words, to cry out for mercy, saying that they did not mean what they said, saying that it was only a game they were playing. "I have made commitments," Mr. Wynkoop often said to me. "I have given hostages." This was true, and this I think was the consideration of greatest weight with him; he could not deny his words and renounce his friends without losing his self respect.

War with Great Britain! Mr. Wynkoop was forced to pronounce the word at last. But independence! That was the hardest word of all. Yet the word was in the air, passing from mouth to mouth behind closed doors and in the open streets. I had long since accustomed myself to the idea, but Mr. Wynkoop hated the thought of it, said he had never desired it, did not now desire it—"unless," he admitted as a kind of after thought, "the Britain I have always been loyal to proves an illusion." It was this notion, I think, that enabled Mr. Wynkoop to reconcile himself to the policy of separation. The Britain of his dreams was an illusion. The Britain he had known did not exist. In those days we were all reading the fiery papers of Mr. Paine entitled *Common Sense*. I know that Mr. Wynkoop read them, and I fancy that they helped him to see Britain in her true colors.

"I like neither the impudence of the man's manner nor the uncompromising harshness of his matter," Mr. Wynkoop once said to me. "Yet it seems that events give only too much foundation for his assertion that we have deluded ourselves in proclaiming the advantages of the connection with Britain. I can't agree with him that the loyal and respectful tone of our pamphlets and petitions is no more than mawkish sentiment; but I do wonder if the alleged benefits of the union with Britain are but figments of the imagination. It is hard to think so. And yet what now are those benefits? We must surely ask that."

Thus in the long winter of '76 Mr. Wynkoop repaired the illusions by which he lived, reconciling himself to the inevitable step. At this time he saw little of Mr. Van Schoickendinck—it was too painful for both of them, I dare say. At least their last conversation I know (it was by Jeremiah's express invitation that I was present) was a trying one. It was on the 30th of May that we found old Nicholas in the hall of his house, standing, leaning on his cane, evidently much moved.

"I asked you to come," old Nicholas said after greeting us a little stiffly, "because I must know what you purpose to do. General Howe is about to take New York. The Philadelphia Congress is about to declare a separation from Great Britain. The so-called Provincial Congress of New York will hesitate, but it will probably support the measure. Am I to understand that you will burn your bridges and side with the rebels?"

With great seriousness and gravity, Mr. Wynkoop replied:

"I wish you to believe, sir, that I have given the matter every consideration in my power; and it seems to me that I can't do other than go with America. America is my country, and yours too, sir."

"America *is* my country." The voice of old Nicholas was shrill. "I have no great love for Britishers, as you know. Damn them all, I say! But I am too old to meddle with treason. Especially when it can't come to any good. Either we shall be crushed, in which case our last state will be worse than our first; or we shall succeed, in which case we shall be ruled by the mob. Which is better, God knows. What I can't see is why you have allowed the fanatics to run away with the cart. Fight if you must, but why close the door to reconciliation by declaring an independency?"

"We can't fight without it, sir. That's the whole truth of the matter. I was much against it, and so were most. But the necessity is clear. First we refused to trade, hoping that Britain would make terms as she had formerly done. Instead of making terms Britain closed our ports and prepared to make war. To fight we must have supplies and munitions. We must have money. We can get none of these things without reviving trade; and to revive trade we must have allies, we must have the support of France. But will France aid us so long as we profess our loyalty to Britain? France will give money and troops to disrupt the British empire, but none to consolidate it. The act of separation will be the price of a French alliance."

"Am I to understand that the act of separation is not to be seriously made, except to buy French assistance? That you will let France go by the board as soon as Britain is willing to negotiate?"

Mr. Wynkoop did not at once reply. After a moment he said,

"No, I would not say that, sir. The act of separation is intended for Britain's benefit too. It will make it plain that we mean what we say—that we mean to defend our liberties to the last ditch if necessary. Yet I hope, and believe, in spite of all, that it will not come to that."

For a long moment old Nicholas stood stiff and silent. Suddenly extending his hand, but turning his face away, he said,

"Well, good bye. Our ways part then."

"Don't say that, sir."

"I must say it. I must remain as I began—a loyal British subject. You have ceased to be one. I am sorry to have seen this day. But I must submit to necessity, and you must too."

Slowly old Nicholas ascended the stairs, tapping each tread with his cane. Half way up, he cried out, as if in anger,

"Good bye, I say!"

"God keep you, sir," was all Mr. Wynkoop could find to reply.

Mr. Wynkoop afterwards told me that he spent a sleepless night in his half-abandoned house. In anticipation of General Howe's arrival he had already begun to move his effects out of the city, into Westchester County, near White Plains, where the Provincial Congress was adjourned to meet on July 2. With the business of settling his personal affairs to the best advantage he was so fully occupied that he did not attend the Congress on the opening days. But on the afternoon of the 9th of July he took his place, a little late. Slipping quietly into a vacant chair just in front of me, he was handed a copy of "A Declaration by the Representatives of the United States of America, in Congress Assembled." The chairman of a committee, appointed to report on the validity of the reasons given for separation from Great Britain, was reading the document. We listened to the felicitous and now familiar phrases—"hold these truths to be self-evident"—"just powers from the consent of the governed"—"right of the people to alter or abolish it"—

"Who are the people?" I heard Mr. Wynkoop murmur to his neighbor.

His neighbor, not hearing or not understanding him, whispered behind his hand,

"This is not an easy time for you, I dare say. Mr. Van Schoickendinck can't be induced to join us." The last a statement rather than a question.

"No," Mr. Wynkoop said. "He will go Tory. He will not oppose us. His sympathies are with us really, I think. He is thoroughly American, with no great love for Britain. But he is old—he will go Tory."

"The Declaration will carry, I think."

"Yes."

"It seems well phrased. Jefferson's pen, I understand."

Presently the chairman, having finished the reading of the Declaration, read the report of the committee. "While we lament the cruel necessity which has made that measure unavoidable, we approve the same, and will, at the risk of our lives and fortunes, join with the other colonies in supporting it."

The report of the committee was carried, unanimously, a bare majority being present.

Whereupon a member begged leave, before proceeding to other routine business, to make a few remarks. Permission being granted, the member spoke of the decisive step which had just been taken; of the solemn crisis which confronted all America; of the duty of meeting that crisis with high courage, with the indomitable perseverance of freemen fighting for their liberties. "The time for discussion is over," he said. "The time for action has come. Once thoroughly united, we cannot fail, and if we triumph, as we shall, a grateful posterity will recall these days, and do honor to the patriotic men whose conduct was inspired by the spirit of freedom. God grant we may so act that the spirit of freedom will ever be synonymous with the spirit of '76!"

In the perfunctory applause which greeted these remarks, Mr. Wynkoop joined, as heartily I think, as . . .

Here, most unfortunately, the manuscript ends. What the conclusion of the story may have been, if indeed it ever was concluded, will probably never be known.

Sources

George III

The American Revolution had many victims—the dead and wounded, the loyalists who went into exile, and a host of others. But perhaps the most dramatic victim (though the loss was bloodless) was the habitual reverence the king's loyal subjects felt for His Majesty. In fact, it was only at the moment of revolution that Americans could bring themselves to stop complaining about Parliament, or the Board of Trade, and to address their complaints directly to their revered monarch, George III. You can gather something about the completeness of the shift by comparing these two illustrations. The first is a woodcut that appeared in a schoolbook published in America in 1770. The second shows a mob attacking a statue of the same king just five years later. Do the two pictures seem to you to have implications about social class as well as politics? How would you characterize the dress and expression attributed to George III in the first picture? What generalization can you make about the dress and manner of the mob in the second picture? Do the pictures add anything to Becker's essay on Jeremiah Wynkoop? Do they challenge his interpretation?

**Woodcut Frontispiece
to Watt's *Speller*, 1770.**
The Granger Collection.

GEORGE III. by the Grace of
G O D, of GREAT-BRITAIN,
FRANCE and IRELAND, King,
Defender of the Faith.

In ev'ry Stroke, in ev'ry Line,
Does fome exalted Virtue fhine ;
And *Albion*'s Happinefs we trace,
In every Feature of his Face.

**Pulling Down the
Statue of George III.**
Prints Division/New York Public Library.

Thomas Paine

Common Sense, 1776

**No one who wrote about the Revolution had an influence even re-
motely comparable to that of Thomas Paine, an English radical who
had come to Philadelphia only in 1774. Paine's pamphlet *Common
Sense*, published in 1776, was quickly an astonishing success. Within
months, it had sold 150,000 copies. Paine's success was a result, in
part, of his rhetorical skills. He was simply a master propagandist.
But *Common Sense* was significant for another reason, too: Paine realized before many of his countrymen that the time for reason had
passed. And so had the time for emotional appeals to British sentiment. The colonies were at war, and *Common Sense* was a war document that intended to fasten words like "brute" and "savage" on the
enemy. Whom do you think Paine thought he was writing for? Englishmen or Americans? Or was he addressing what he called "Mankind"? How did Jeremiah Wynkoop react to *Common Sense*?**

. . . Volumes have been written on the subject of the struggle between
England and America. . . . but all have been ineffectual, and the period of
debate is closed. Arms, as the last resource, decide the contest; the appeal
was the choice of the king, and the continent hath accepted the challenge. . . .

I have heard it asserted by some, that as America hath flourished under
her former connexion with Great-Britain, that the same connexion is necessary
towards her future happiness. . . . Nothing can be more fallacious than this
kind of argument. We may as well assert that because a child has thrived
upon milk, that it is never to have meat, or that the first twenty years of
our lives is to become a precedent for the next twenty. But even this is
admitting more than is true, for I answer roundly, that America would have
flourished as much, and probably much more, had no European power had
any thing to do with her. The commerce, by which she hath enriched herself,
are the necessaries of life, and will always have a market while eating is the
custom of Europe.

But she has protected us, say some. . . .

Alas, we have been long led away by ancient prejudices, and made large
sacrifices to superstition. We have boasted the protection of Great-Britain,
without considering, that her motive was *interest* not *attachment*; that she did
not protect us from *our enemies* on *our account*, but from *her enemies* on *her
own account*, from those who had no quarrel with us on any *other account*,
and who will always be our enemies on the *same account*. Let Britain wave
her pretensions to the continent, or the continent throw off the dependance,

From Thomas Paine, *Common Sense* (1776) in Moncure Daniel Conway, ed., *The Writings of
Thomas Paine* (New York: Putnam, 1894), Vol. I, pp. 67–120.

and we should be at peace with France and Spain were they at war with Britain. . . .

But Britain is the parent country, say some. Then the more shame upon her conduct. Even brutes do not devour their young, nor savages make war upon their families; . . . but it happens not to be true, or only partly so. . . . Europe, and not England, is the parent country of America. This new world hath been the asylum for the persecuted lovers of civil and religious liberty from *every part* of Europe. Hither have they fled, not from the tender embraces of the mother, but from the cruelty of the monster; and it is so far true of England, that the same tyranny which drove the first emigrants from home, pursues their descendants still. . . .

But admitting, that we were all of English descent, what does it amount to? Nothing. Britain, being now an open enemy, extinguishes every other name and title: And to say that reconciliation is our duty, is truly farcical. The first king of England, of the present line (William the Conqueror) was a Frenchman, and half the Peers of England are descendants from the same country; wherefore, by the same method of reasoning, England ought to be governed by France. . . .

I challenge the warmest advocate for reconciliation, to shew, a single advantage that this continent can reap, by being connected with Great-Britain. I repeat the challenge, not a single advantage is derived. Our corn will fetch its price in any market in Europe, and our imported goods must be paid for buy them where we will.

But . . . any submission to, or dependance on Great-Britain, tends directly to involve this continent in European wars and quarrels; and sets us at variance with nations, who would otherwise seek our friendship, and against whom, we have neither anger nor complaint. As Europe is our market for trade, we ought to form no partial connection with any part of it. It is the true interest of America to steer clear of European contentions, which she never can do, while by her dependance on Britain, she is made the make-weight in the scale of British politics.

Europe is too thickly planted with kingdoms to be long at peace, and whenever a war breaks out between England and any foreign power, the trade of America goes to ruin, *because of her connection with Britain*. The next war may not turn out like the last, and should it not, the advocates for reconciliation now, will be wishing for separation then, because, neutrality in that case, would be a safer convoy than a man of war. Every thing that is right or natural pleads for separation. The blood of the slain, the weeping voice of nature cries, 'TIS TIME TO PART. Even the distance at which the Almighty hath placed England and America, is a strong and natural proof, that the authority of the one, over the other, was never the design of Heaven. The time likewise at which the continent was discovered, adds weight to the argument, and the manner in which it was peopled encreases the force of it. The reformation was preceded by the discovery of America, as if the Almighty graciously meant to open a sanctuary to the persecuted in future years, when home should afford neither friendship nor safety.

The authority of Great-Britain over this continent, is a form of government, which sooner or later must have an end: And a serious mind can draw no true pleasure by looking forward, under the painful and positive conviction, that what he calls "the present constitution" is merely temporary. . . .

As to government matters, it is not in the power of Britain to do this continent justice: The business of it will soon be too weighty, and intricate, to be managed with any tolerable degree of convenience, by a power so distant from us, and so very ignorant of us; for if they cannot conquer us, they cannot govern us. To be always running three or four thousand miles with a tale or a petition, waiting four or five months for an answer, which when obtained requires five or six more to explain it in, will in a few years be looked upon as folly and childishness—There was a time when it was proper, and there is a proper time for it to cease.

Small islands not capable of protecting themselves, are the proper objects for kingdoms to take under their care; but there is something very absurd, in supposing a continent to be perpetually governed by an island. In no instance hath nature made the satellite larger than its primary planet, and as England and America, with respect to each other, reverses the common order of nature, it is evident they belong to different systems; England to Europe, America to itself. . . .

But admitting that matters were now made up, what would be the event? I answer, the ruin of the continent. And that for several reasons.

First. The powers of governing still remaining in the hands of the king, he will have a negative over the whole legislation of this continent. And as he hath shewn himself such an inveterate enemy to liberty, and discovered such a thirst for arbitrary power; is he, or is he not, a proper man to say to these colonies, "*You shall make no laws but what I please.*" And is there any inhabitant in America so ignorant, as not to know, that according to what is called the *present constitution,* that this continent can make no laws but what the king gives leave to; and is there any man so unwise, as not to see, that (considering what has happened) he will suffer no law to be made here, but such as suit *his* purpose. We may be as effectually enslaved by the want of laws in America, as by submitting to laws made for us in England. After matters are made up (as it is called) can there be any doubt, but the whole power of the crown will be exerted, to keep this continent as low and humble as possible? Instead of going forward we shall go backward, or be perpetually quarrelling or ridiculously petitioning.—We are already greater than the king wishes us to be, and will he not hereafter endeavour to make us less? To bring the matter to one point. Is the power who is jealous of our prosperity, a proper power to govern us? Whoever says No to this question, is an *independant,* for independancy means no more, than, whether we shall make our own laws, or whether the king, the greatest enemy this continent hath, or can have, shall tell us "*there shall be no laws but such as I like.*"

But the king you will say has a negative in England; the people there can make no laws without his consent. In point of right and good order, there is something very ridiculous, that a youth of twenty-one (which hath often happened) shall say to several millions of people, older and wiser than himself, I forbid this or that act of yours to be law. But in this place I decline this sort of reply, though I will never cease to expose the absurdity of it, and only answer, that England being the King's residence, and America not so, makes quite another case. The king's negative *here* is ten times more dangerous and fatal than it can be in England, for *there* he will scarcely refuse his consent to a bill for putting England into as strong a state of defence as possible, and in America he would never suffer such a bill to be passed. . . .

Secondly. That as even the best terms, which we can expect to obtain, can amount to no more than a temporary expedient, or a kind of government by guardianship, which can last no longer than till the colonies come of age, so the general face and state of things, in the interim, will be unsettled and unpromising. Emigrants of property will not choose to come to a country whose form of government hangs but by a thread, and who is every day tottering on the brink of commotion and disturbance; and numbers of the present inhabitants would lay hold of the interval, to dispose of their effects, and quit the continent.

But the most powerful of all arguments, is, that nothing but independance, i.e. a continental form of government, can keep the peace of the continent and preserve it inviolate from civil wars. I dread the event of a reconciliation with Britain now, as it is more than probable, that it will be followed by a revolt somewhere or other, the consequences of which may be far more fatal than all the malice of Britain.

Thousands are already ruined by British barbarity; (thousands more will probably suffer the same fate) Those men have other feelings than us who have nothing suffered. All they *now* possess is liberty, what they before enjoyed is sacrificed to its service, and having nothing more to lose, they disdain submission. . . .

But where, says some, is the King of America? I'll tell you. Friend, he reigns above, and doth not make havoc of mankind like the Royal Brute of Britain. Yet that we may not appear to be defective even in earthly honors, let a day be solemnly set apart for proclaiming the charter; let it be brought forth placed on the divine law, the word of God; let a crown be placed thereon, by which the world may know, that so far we approve of monarchy, that in America THE LAW IS KING. For as in absolute governments the King is law, so in free countries the law *ought* to be King; and there ought to be no other. But lest any ill use should afterwards arise, let the crown at the conclusion of the ceremony, be demolished, and scattered among the people whose right it is.

A government of our own is our natural right: And when a man seriously reflects on the precariousness of human affairs, he will become convinced, that it is infinitely wiser and safer, to form a constitution of our own in a cool deliberate manner, while we have it in our power, than to trust such an interesting event to time and chance. . . .

Ye that tell us of harmony and reconciliation, can ye restore to us the time that is past? Can ye give to prostitution its former innocence? Neither can ye reconcile Britain and America. The last cord now is broken, the people of England are presenting addresses against us. There are injuries which nature cannot forgive; she would cease to be nature if she did. As well can the lover forgive the ravisher of his mistress, as the continent forgive the murders of Britain. The Almighty hath implanted in us these unextinguishable feelings for good and wise purposes. They are the guardians of his image in our hearts. They distinguish us from the herd of common animals. The social compact would dissolve, and justice be extirpated from the earth, or have only a casual existence were we callous to the touches of affection. The robber, and the murderer, would often escape unpunished, did not the injuries which our tempers sustain, provoke us into justice.

O ye that love mankind! Ye that dare oppose, not only the tyranny, but the tyrant, stand forth! Every spot of the old world is overrun with oppression. Freedom hath been hunted round the globe. Asia, and Africa, have long expelled her—Europe regards her like a stranger, and England hath given her warning to depart. O! receive the fugitive, and prepare in time an asylum for mankind. . . .

7

The
American Revolution

After festering for a decade or more, discontent in the American colonies erupted in violence on April 19, 1775, at Lexington and Concord. Months later, when news of the Battle of Bunker Hill reached London, George III and his advisers decided that they had no alternative but to use force to put down the insurrection. The king was confident that the insurrection would be quickly over "when once these rebels have felt a smart blow." Britain, after all, was the greatest empire since Rome, and the colonial militia were "raw, undisciplined, cowardly men."

There was good reason for the confidence of George III and his advisers. So far as they knew, violent resistance to British authority had been confined to the area around Boston. No doubt the colonies to the south would behave as they had in the past and place their own local interests above those of any neighbor. And surely, even in Boston, the rebellion had been the work of a minority of citizens, led astray by a few agitators. It would be easy for the British army and its navy, the most powerful in the world, to occupy strategic centers like Boston and New York, Philadelphia and Charleston. And since the colonists depended economically on trade with Europe, whoever held those trading centers would control the fate of North America.

The king, in his determination and optimism, obviously overlooked some formidable problems. Surpassing all others, perhaps, was the immense distance between England and the rebellious colonies. Every musket and every soldier had to be shipped across 3,000 miles of Atlantic. At least 10 percent of the soldiers, and perhaps a higher percentage of animals, died on these crossings. And beyond the water lay the vast American wilderness, which only the best axmen in the world could conquer. The British soldier was no match for the American with an ax. There was, moreover, no chance of striking a single crushing blow. All the major seats of government—Boston, New York, and Philadelphia—were held at one time or another by British troops without much damage to the rebel cause. There was simply no great political center in America like Paris or London, whose loss might have been totally demoralizing to Americans. And even if Washington's Continental Army was totally crushed, that alone would not guarantee victory. For there was always the chance that Washington, or some other rebel, could raise another army among the thousands of guerrillas that swarmed the countryside.

In retrospect, the outcome may seem almost inevitable. But it did not appear very likely in 1775, either in London or to those Americans who understood fully that they were committing treason and, if they lost, would have nothing to look forward to but the noose.

What stood between the leaders of the Revolution and the gallows was a process that we could call today mobilization. The Spirit of '76 was a necessary ingredient, and so were the words of men like Franklin and Paine presented in the preceding chapter. But the spirit and the words would count for nothing if they could not be backed up with a mobilized population.

Mobilization had three phases. The first, and most obvious, was raising and supplying an army in the field to resist the introduction of British troops all along the seaboard. The second was the enforcement of discipline and revolutionary order in the great stretches of land the British did not occupy—a task that was partly political, partly military. The third was the repression of dissent, the silencing and driving out of those called Tories, who remained loyal to the Crown.

The material in this chapter bears on all these phases of mobilization. You may find it useful to think of them as an examination of the ways the Spirit of '76 had to be given meaning amid the Realities of '78 or '80.

Interpretive Essay

John Shy

Mobilizing Armed Force in the American Revolution

What kind of men could Washington count on? Fourth of July orators would have us believe that the woods and fields were swarming with "minutemen" who were willing and able to bear arms against the redcoats. True enough, perhaps, for the short haul, for an engagement at Lexington or Concord, or on Bunker Hill—then home to the farm. But what of the long run? Who was willing to shoulder a musket, camp in the snows of Valley Forge, and face death month in and month out to "secure these liberties"? In the following essay, John Shy tries to come to terms with that question. In so doing, he tells us much about the character of the American Revolution. As you read the essay, pay particular attention to the distinctions Shy makes between the types of men who served year after year in the regular army and the others who served from time to time in the militia. You should note, too, the ways that social class was reflected in the military experience of Americans. What place does Shy give to ideology—to belief, political theory, philosophical attitudes? What is your guess about what, in the long run, motivated "Long Bill" Scott? Can you make any connection between his career and, say, the excerpt from *Common Sense* in the preceding chapter? If you cannot, is the problem yours, or is it Shy's? Or was it Long Bill's?

Armed force, and nothing else, decided the outcome of the American Revolution. Without armed force mobilized on a decisive scale, there would not today be a subject for discussion; shorn even of its name, the Revolution would shrink to a mere rebellion—an interesting episode perhaps, but like dozens of others in the modern history of Western societies. Crude, obvious, and unappealing as this truism may be, it is still true. And its truth needs to be probed and understood if we are to understand the Revolution, because that revolution overcame the armed resistance of one of the two militarily strongest powers in the eighteenth-century world.

If the subject of mobilizing armed force in the American Revolution is important, it is also an exceptionally difficult one. Violence, with all its ramifi-

From John Shy, "Mobilizing Armed Force in the American Revolution," in John Parker and Carol Urness, eds., *The American Revolution: A Heritage of Change* (Minneapolis: Associates of the James Ford Bell Library, 1975), pp. 96–106. Reprinted by permission.

cations, remains a great mystery for students of human life, while the deeper motivational sources of human behavior—particularly behavior under conditions of stress—are almost equally mysterious. When these two mysteries come together, as they do in wars and revolutions, then the historian faces a problem full of traps and snares for the unwary, a problem that challenges his ability to know *anything* about the past. A certain humility is obviously in order. Any of us who are tempted not to be humble might recall how recently intelligent, well-informed American leaders spoke glibly about winning the "hearts and minds" of another few million people caught up by war and revolution. That is our subject: the hearts and minds of Americans whose willingness to engage in violence, two centuries ago, fundamentally changed the course of history.

Ideas on our subject, as opposed to analysis based solidly on evidence, come cheap. Writing about an earlier revolutionary war, Thomas Hobbes expressed a cynical view of the relationship between armed force and mere public opinion—like that in the Declaration of Independence—when he said that "covenants without swords are but words." But a century later David Hume tempered Hobbes' cynicism with realism: "As Force is always on the side of the governed," Hume wrote, "the governors have nothing to support them but opinion." Perhaps Hume's view has lost some of its validity in our own time, when technology vastly multiplies the amount of force that a few people can wield, but it certainly held good for the eighteenth century, when even the best weapons were still relatively primitive and widely available. If Hobbes—like all his fellow cynics down through history—is right in believing that public opinion is a fairly fragile flower which can seldom survive the hot wind of violence, Hume reminds us that no one uses force without being moved to do so. John Adams put his finger on this matter of motivation when he said that the real American Revolution, the revolution that estranged American hearts from old British loyalties and readied American minds to use (and to withstand) massive violence, was over before the war began. Adams also opined that a third of the American people supported the revolutionary cause, another third remained more or less loyal to Britain, and that the rest were neutral or apathetic. Clearly, even Adams conceded that not all hearts and minds had been affected in the same way. Many British observers thought that the real American revolutionaries were the religious dissenters, Congregationalists and Presbyterians who had always been secretly disloyal to the Crown because they rejected the whole Anglican Establishment, whose head was the king; and that these revolutionaries persuaded poor Irishmen, who had poured into the American colonies in great numbers during the middle third of the eighteenth century, to do most of the dirty business of actual fighting. American observers, on the other hand, generally assumed that all decent, sane people supported the Revolution, and that those who did not could be categorized as timid, vicious, corrupt, or deluded. Each of these ideas on our subject contains a measure of truth; but they seem to contradict one another, and they do not carry us very far toward understanding.

Like these stock ideas, we have two standard images of the popular response to revolutionary war. One is of whole towns springing to arms as Paul Revere carries his warning to them in the spring of 1775. The other is of a tiny, frozen, naked band of men at Valley Forge, all that are left when everyone else went home in the winter of 1778. Which is the true picture? Both, evidently. But that answer is of no use at all when we ask whether the Revolution succeeded only by the persistence of a very small group of people, the intervention of France, and great good luck; or whether the Revolution was—or became—unbeatable because the mass of the population simply would not give up the struggle, and the British simply could not muster the force and the resolution to kill them all or break their will or sit on all, or even any large proportion, of them. Who actually took up arms and why? How strong was the motivation to serve, and to keep serving in spite of defeat and other adversities? What was the intricate interplay and feedback between attitude and behavior, events and attitude? Did people get war-weary and discouraged, or did they become adamant toward British efforts to coerce them? If we could answer these questions with confidence, not only would we know why the rebels won and the government lost, but we would also know important things about the American society that emerged from seven years of armed conflict.

A suitably humble approach to these staggering questions lies readily to hand in a book written by Peter Oliver, who watched the Revolution explode in Boston. Oliver descended from some of the oldest families of Massachusetts Bay, he was a distinguished merchant and public official, and he became a bitter Tory. His book, *The Origin and Progress of the American Rebellion,* not published until 1961 and recently out in paperback, is a fascinatingly unsympathetic version of the Revolution, and in it Oliver makes an attempt to answer some of our questions. Using the technique, perfected by S. L. A. Marshall during the Second World War, of the after-action interview, Oliver asked a wounded American lieutenant, who had been captured at Bunker Hill, how he had come to be a rebel. The American officer allegedly replied as follows:

> The case was this Sir! I lived in a Country Town; I was a Shoemaker, & got my Living by my Labor. When this Rebellion came on, I saw some of my Neighbors get into Commission, who were no better than myself. I was very ambitious, & did not like to see those Men above me. I was asked to enlist, as a private Soldier. My Ambition was too great for so low a Rank; I offered to enlist upon having a Lieutenants Commission; which was granted. I imagined myself now in a way of Promotion: if I was killed in Battle, there would be an end of me, but if my Captain was killed, I should rise in Rank, & should still have a Chance to rise higher. These Sir! were the only Motives of my entering into the Service; for as to the Dispute between great Britain & the Colonies, I know nothing of it; neither am I capable of judging whether it is right or wrong.

Those who have read U.S. Government publications over the last decade will find this POW interrogation familiar; during the Vietnam war, the State and Defense Department published many like it, and more than one Vietcong prisoner is said to have spoken in the vein of the wounded American lieutenant so long ago.

Now the lieutenant was not a figment of Oliver's embittered imagination. His name is given by Oliver as Scott, and American records show that a Lieutenant William Scott, of Colonel Paul Sargent's regiment, was indeed wounded and captured at the Battle of Bunker Hill. Scott turns out, upon investigation, to have been an interesting character. Perhaps the first thing to be said about him is that nothing in the record of his life down to 1775 contradicts anything in Oliver's account of the interview. Scott came from Peterborough, New Hampshire, a town settled in the 1730s by Irish Presbyterians. Scott's father had served in the famous Rogers' Rangers during the French and Indian War. At the news of the outbreak of fighting in 1775, a cousin who kept the store in Peterborough recruited a company of local men to fight the British. Apparently the cousin tried to enlist our William Scott—known to his neighbors as "Long Bill," thus distinguishing him from the cousin, "Short Bill." But "Long Bill"—our Bill—seems to have declined serving as a private, and insisted on being a lieutenant if cousin "Short Bill" was going to be a captain. "Short Bill" agreed. So far the stories as told by Oliver and as revealed in the New Hampshire records check perfectly. Nor is there any reason to think that "Long Bill" had a deeper understanding of the causes of the Revolution than appear in Oliver's version of the interview.

What Peter Oliver never knew was the subsequent life history of this battered yokel, whose view of the American rebellion seemed so pitifully naive. When the British evacuated Boston, they took Scott and other American prisoners to Halifax, Nova Scotia. There, after more than a year in captivity, Scott somehow managed to escape, to find a boat, and to make his way back to the American army just in time for the fighting around New York City in 1776. Captured again in November, when Fort Washington and its garrison fell to a surprise British assault, Scott escaped almost immediately, this time by swimming the Hudson River at night—according to a newspaper account—with his sword tied around his neck and his watch pinned to his hat. He returned to New Hampshire during the winter of 1777 to recruit a company of his own; there, he enlisted his two oldest sons for three years or the duration of the war. Stationed in the Boston area, he marched against Burgoyne's invading army from Canada, and led a detachment that cut off the last retreat just before the surrender near Saratoga. Scott later took part in the fighting around Newport, Rhode Island. But when his light infantry company was ordered to Virginia under Lafayette in early 1781, to counter the raiding expedition led by Benedict Arnold, Scott's health broke down; long marches and hot weather made the old Bunker Hill wounds ache, and he was permitted to resign from the army. After only a few months of recuperation, however, he seems to have grown restless, for we find him during the last year of the war serving as a volunteer on a navy frigate.

What would Scott have said if Oliver had been able to interview him again, after the war? We can only guess. Probably he would have told Oliver that his oldest son had died in the army, not gloriously, but of camp fever, after six years of service. Scott might have said that in 1777 he had sold his Peterborough farm in order to meet expenses, but that the note which he took in exchange turned into a scrap of paper when the dollar of 1777 became worth less than two cents by 1780. He might also have said that another farm, in Groton, Massachusetts, slipped away from him, along with a down payment that he had made on it, when his military pay depreciated rapidly to a fraction of its nominal value. He might not have been willing to admit that when his wife died he simply turned their younger children over to his surviving elder son, and then set off to beg a pension or a job from the government. Almost certainly he would not have told Oliver that when the son—himself sick, his corn crop killed by a late frost, and saddled with three little brothers and sisters—begged his father for help, our hero told him that, if all else failed, he might hand the children over to the selectmen of Peterborough.

In 1792, "Long Bill" Scott once more made the newspapers: he rescued eight people from drowning when their small boat capsized in New York harbor. But heroism did not pay very well. At last, in 1794, Secretary of War Henry Knox made Scott deputy storekeeper at West Point; and a year later General Benjamin Lincoln took Scott with him to the Ohio country, where they were to negotiate with the Indians and survey the land opened up by Anthony Wayne's victory at Fallen Timbers. At last he had a respectable job, and even a small pension for his nine wounds; but Lincoln's group caught something called "lake fever" while surveying on the Black River, near Sandusky. Scott, ill himself, guided part of the group back to Fort Stanwix, New York, then returned for the others. It was his last heroic act. A few days after his second trip, he died, on September 16, 1796.

Anecdotes, even good ones like the touching saga of "Long Bill" Scott, do not make history. But neither can a subject like ours be treated in terms of what Professor Jesse Lemisch has referred to as the lives of Great White Men—Washington, Adams, Jefferson, Hamilton, and the handful like them. Scott's life, in itself, may tell us little about how armed force and public opinion were mobilized in the Revolution; yet the story of his life leads us directly—and at the level of ordinary people—toward crucial features of the process.

Peterborough, New Hampshire, in 1775 had a population of 549. Town, State and Federal records show that about 170 men were credited to Peterborough as performing some military service during the Revolution. In other words, almost every adult male, at one time or another, carried a gun in the war. Of these 170 participants, less than a third performed really extensive service; that is, service ranging from over a year up to the whole eight years of the war. Only a fraction of these—less than two dozen—served as long as Bill Scott. In Scott we are not seeing a typical participant, but one of a small "hard core" of revolutionary fighters—men who stayed in the army for more than a few months or a single campaign. As we look down the list of long-service soldiers from Peterborough, they seem indeed to be untypical people. A few, like Scott and his cousin "Short Bill" and James Taggert and Josiah Munroe, became officers or at least sergeants, and thereby acquired status and perhaps some personal satisfaction from their prolonged military service. But most of the hard core remained privates, and they were an unusually poor, obscure group of men, even by the rustic standards of Peterborough. Many—like John Alexander, Robert Cunningham, William Ducannon, Joseph Henderson, Richard Richardson, John Wallace, and Thomas Williamson— were recruited from outside the town, from among men who never really lived in Peterborough. Whether they lived *anywhere*—in the strict legal sense— is a question. Two men—Zaccheus Brooks and John Miller—are simply noted as "transients." At least two—James Hackley and Randall McAllister—were deserters from the British army. At least two others—Samuel Weir and Titus Wilson—were black men, Wilson dying as a prisoner of war. A few, like Michael Silk, simply appear to join the army, then vanish without a documentary trace. Many more reveal themselves as near the bottom of the socioeconomic ladder: Hackley, Benjamin Allds, Isaac Mitchell, Ebenezer Perkins, Amos Spofford, Jonathan Wheelock, and Charles White were legal paupers after the Revolution; Joseph Henderson was a landless day-laborer; Samuel Spear was jailed for debt; and John Millet was mentally deranged.

We can look at the whole Peterborough contingent in another way, in terms of those in it who were, or later became, prominent or at least solid citizens of the town. With a few exceptions like "Short Bill" Scott and "Long Bill's" son John, who survived frost-killed corn and a parcel of unwanted siblings to become a selectman and a leader of the town, these prominent men and solid citizens had served in the war for only short periods—a few months in 1775, a month or two in the Burgoyne emergency of 1777, maybe a month in Rhode Island or a month late in the war to bolster the key garrison of West Point. The pattern is clear, and it is a pattern that reappears wherever the surviving evidence has permitted a similar kind of inquiry. Lynn, Massachusetts; Berks County, Pennsylvania; Colonel Smallwood's recruits from Maryland in 1782; several regiments of the Massachusetts Line; a sampling of pension applicants from Virginia—all show that the hard core of Continental soldiers, the Bill Scotts who could not wangle commissions, the soldiers at Valley Forge, the men who shouldered the heaviest military burden, were something less than average colonial Americans. As a group, they were poorer, more marginal, less well anchored in the society. Perhaps we should not be surprised; it is easy to imagine men like these actually being attracted by the relative affluence, comfort, security, prestige, and even the chance for satisfying human relationships offered by the Continental army. Revolutionary America may have been a middle-class society, happier and more prosperous than any other in its time, but it contained a large and growing number of fairly poor people, and many of them did much of the actual fighting and suffering between 1775 and 1783: A very old story.

The large proportion of men, from Peterborough and other communities, who served only briefly might thus seem far less important to our subject than the disadvantaged minority who did such a large part of the heavy work of revolution. This militarily less active majority were of course the militiamen. One could compile a large volume of pithy observations, beginning with a few dozen from Washington himself, in which the value of the militia was called into question. The nub of the critique was that these part-time soldiers were untrained, undisciplined, undependable, and very expensive, consuming pay, rations, clothing, and weapons at a great rate in return for short periods of active service. By the end of the war, the tendency of many Continental officers, like Colonel Alexander Hamilton, to disparage openly the military performance of the militia was exacerbating already strained relations between State and Continental authorities. And indeed there were a number of cases in which the failure of militia to arrive in time, to stand under fire, or to remain when they were needed, either contributed to American difficulties or prevented the exploitation of American success. But the revolutionary role of the men from Peterborough and elsewhere who did *not* serve as did Bill Scott, but whose active military service was rather a sometime thing, is easily misunderstood and underestimated if we look at it only in terms of traditional military strategy and set-piece battles.

To understand the revolutionary militia and its role, we must go back to the year before the outbreak of fighting at Lexington and Concord. Each colony, except Pennsylvania, had traditionally required every free white adult male, with a few minor occupational exceptions, to be inscribed in a militia unit, and to take part in training several times a year. These militia units seldom achieved any degree of military proficiency, nor were they expected to serve as actual fighting formations. Their real function might be described as a hybrid of draft board and modern reserve unit—a modicum of military training combined with a mechanism to find and enlist individuals when they were needed. But the colonial militia did not simply slide smoothly into the Revolution. Militia officers, even where they were elected, held royal commissions, and a significant number of them were not enthusiastic about rebellion. Purging and restructuring the militia was an important step toward revolution, one that deserves more attention than it has had.

When in early 1774, the news reached America that Parliament would take a very hard line in response to the Boston Tea Party, and in particular had passed a law that could destroy economically and politically the town of Boston, the reaction in the colonies was stronger and more nearly unanimous than at any time since the Stamp Act. No one could defend the Boston Port Act; it was an unprecedented, draconian law the possible consequences of which seemed staggering. Radicals, like Sam Adams, demanded an immediate and complete break in commercial relations with the rest of the empire. Boycotts had worked effectively in the past, and they were an obvious response to the British hard line. More moderate leaders, however, dreaded a hasty confrontation that might quickly escalate beyond their control, and they used democratic theory to argue that nothing ought to be done without a full and proper consultation of the popular will. Like the boycott, the consultative congress had a respectable pedigree, and the moderates won the argument. When the Continental Congress met in September, 1774, there were general expectations in both Britain and America that it would cool and seek to compromise the situation.

Exactly what happened to disappoint those expectations is even now not wholly clear; our own sense that Congress was heading straight toward revolution and independence distorts a complex moment in history, when uncertainty about both ends and means deeply troubled the minds of most decisionmakers. Congress had hardly convened when it heard that the British had bombarded Boston. For a few days men from different colonies, normally suspicious of one another, were swept together by a wave of common fear and apprehension. Though the report was quickly proved false, these hours of mutual panic seem to have altered the emotional economy of the Congress. Soon afterward it passed without any serious dissent a resolution in favor of the long-advocated boycott, to be known as the Association. Local committees were to gather signatures for the Association, and were to take necessary steps to enforce its provisions. The Association was the vital link in transforming the colonial militia into a revolutionary organization.

For more than a year, a tenuous line of authority ran directly from the Continental Congress to the grass roots of American society. The traditional, intermediate levels of government, if they did not cooperate fully, were bypassed. Committees formed everywhere to enforce the Association, and sympathetic men volunteered to assist in its enforcement. In some places, like Peterborough, the same men who were enrolled in the militia became the strong right arm of the local committee; reluctant militia officers were ignored because, after all, not the militia as such but a voluntary association of militia members was taking the action. In other places, like parts of the Hudson valley and Long Island, reluctance was so widespread that men opposed to the Association actually tried to take over the committee system in order to kill it; when meetings were called to form the new armed organization of Associators, loyal militiamen packed the meetings and re-elected the old, royally commissioned lieutenants and captains. But even where the Association encountered heavy opposition, it effectively dissolved the old military structure and created a new one based on consent, and whose chief purpose was to engineer consent, by force if necessary. The new revolutionary militia might look very much like the old colonial militia, but it was, in its origins, less a draft board and a reserve training unit than a police force and an instrument of political surveillance. Although the boycott could be defended to moderate men as a constitutional, non-violent technique, its implementation had radical consequences. Adoption by Congress gave it a legitimacy and a unity that it could have gained in no other way. Ordinary men were forced to make public choices, and thus to identify themselves with one side or the other. Not until the Declaration of Independence clarified the hazy status of the traditional levels of government did the local committees, acting through the new militia, relinquish some of their truly revolutionary power.

It is difficult to overestimate the importance of what happened in 1775 to engage mass participation on the side of the Revolution. The new militia, which was repeatedly denying that it was in rebellion and proclaimed its loyalty to the Crown, enforced a boycott intended to make Britain back down; Britain did not back down, but the attempt drew virtually everyone into the realm of politics. Enlistment, training, and occasional emergencies were the means whereby dissenters were identified, isolated, and dealt with. Where the new militia had trouble getting organized, there revolutionary activists could see that forceful intervention from outside might be needed. Connecticut units moved into the New York City area; Virginia troops moved into the Delmarva peninsula; in Pennsylvania, men from Reading and Lancaster marched into Bucks County. Once established, the militia became the infrastructure of revolutionary government. It controlled its community, whether through indoctrination or intimidation; it provided on short notice large numbers of armed men for brief periods of emergency service; and it found and persuaded, drafted or bribed, the smaller number of men needed each year to keep the Continental army alive. After the first months of the war, popular enthusiasm and spontaneity could not have sustained the struggle; only a pervasive armed organization, in which almost everyone took some part, kept people constantly, year after year, at the hard task of revolution. While Scott and his sons, the indigent, the blacks, and the otherwise socially expendable men fought the British, James and Samuel Cunningham, Henry Ferguson, John Gray, William McNee, Benjamin Mitchell, Robert Morison, Alexander and William Robbe, Robert Swan, Robert Wilson, and four or five men named Smith—all militiamen, but whose combined active service hardly equalled that of "Long Bill" Scott alone—ran Peterborough, expelling a few Tories, scraping up enough recruits for the Continental army to meet the town's quota every spring, taking time out to help John Stark destroy the Germans at the battle of Bennington.

The mention of Tories brings us, briefly, to the last aspect of our subject. Peterborough had little trouble with Tories; the most sensational case occurred when the Presbyterian minister, the Reverend John Morrison, who had been having trouble with his congregation, deserted his post as chaplain to the Peterborough troops and entered British lines at Boston in June, 1775. But an informed estimate is that about a half million Americans, about a fifth of the population, can be counted as loyal to Britain. Looking at the absence of serious Loyalism in Peterborough, we might conclude that Scotch-Irish Presbyterians almost never were Tories. That, however, would be an error of fact, and we are impelled to seek further for an explanation. What appears as we look at places, like Peterborough, where Tories are hardly visible, and at other places where Toryism was rampant, is a pattern—not so much an ethnic, religious, or ideological pattern, but a pattern of raw power. Wherever the British and their allies were strong enough to penetrate in force— along the seacoast, in the Hudson, Mohawk and lower Delaware valleys, in Georgia, the Carolinas, and the transappalachian west—there Toryism flourished. But geographically less exposed areas, if population density made self-defense feasible—most of New England, the Pennsylvania hinterland, and piedmont Virginia—where the enemy hardly appeared or not at all, there Tories either ran away, kept quiet, even serving in the rebel armies, or occasionally took a brave but hopeless stand against revolutionary committees and their gunmen. After the war, of course, men remembered their parts in the successful revolution in ways that make it difficult for the historian to reconstruct accurately the relationship between what they thought and what they did.

The view which I have presented of how armed force and public opinion were mobilized may seem a bit cynical—a reversion to Thomas Hobbes. True, it gives little weight to ideology, to perceptions and principles, to grievances and aspirations, to the more admirable side of the emergent American character. Perhaps that is a weakness; perhaps I have failed to grasp what really drove Bill Scott. But what strikes me most forcibly in studying this part of the Revolution is how much in essential agreement almost all Americans were in 1774, both in their views of British measures and in their feelings about them. What then is puzzling, and thus needs explaining, is why so many of these people behaved in anomalous and in different ways. Why did so many, who did not intend a civil war or political independence, get so inextricably involved in the organization and use of armed force? Why did relatively few do most of the actual fighting? Why was a dissenting fifth of the population so politically and militarily impotent, so little able to affect the outcome of the struggle? Answers to these questions cannot be found in the life of one obscure man, or in the history of one backwoods town. But microscopic study does emphasize certain features of the Revolution: the political structuring of resistance to Britain, the play of social and economic factors in carrying on that resistance by armed force, and the brutally direct effects on behavior, if not on opinions, of military power.

Sources

A Spy's View of Washington's Army, 1775

What do contemporary sources tell us about Washington's army? What follows is an eyewitness version—written by a spy. He was a New Englander named Benjamin Thompson, in the pay of the British. He was, in other words, a British patriot, who later moved to Europe, where he became famous as a scientist and philosopher known to the world as Count Rumford. As you read, note that Rumford's observations were made at about the same time that Peter Oliver interviewed William Scott (see p. 149). Do Rumford's observations seem believable to you? What do you think his attitude toward "lower-class" soldiers was? Would it surprise you to know that Washington might have agreed with most of what Rumford says? What do you think lies behind Rumford's attempt to puncture the myth of the deadly accuracy of American riflemen? It might all be

simply true, of course. But could it also reflect his desire to cause the British officials to be confident in their capacity to defeat the Americans militarily? Or could this opinion have something to do with social class? What would you suppose was the class status of the riflemen? Of Rumford?

Observations by Benjamin Thompson

Boston, November 4, 1775

. . . The army in general is not very badly accoutered, but most wretchedly clothed, and as dirty a set of mortals as ever disgraced the name of a soldier. They have had no clothes of any sort provided for them by the Congress (except the detachment of 1,133 that are gone to Canada under Col. Arnold, who had each of them a new coat and a linen frock served out to them before they set out), tho' the army in general, and the Massachusetts forces in particular, had encouragement of having coats given them by way of bounty for inlisting. And the neglect of the Congress to fulfill their promise in this respect has been the source of not a little uneasiness among the soldiers.

They have no women in the camp to do washing for the men, and they in general not being used to doing things of this sort, and thinking it rather a disparagement to them, choose rather to let their linen, etc., rot upon their backs than to be at the trouble of cleaning 'em themselves. And to this nasty way of life, and to the change of their diet from milk, vegetables, etc., to living almost intirely upon flesh, must be attributed those putrid, malignant and infectious disorders which broke out among them soon after their taking the field, and which have prevailed with unabating fury during the whole summer.

The leading men among them (with their usual art and cunning) have been indefatigable in their endeavors to conceal the real state of the army in this respect, and to convince the world that the soldiers were tolerably healthy. But the contrary has been apparent, even to a demonstration, to every person that had but the smallest acquaintance with their camp. And so great was the prevalence of these disorders in the month of July that out of 4,207 men who were stationed upon Prospect Hill no more than 2,227 were returned fit for duty.

The mortality among them must have been very great, and to this in a great measure must be attributed the present weakness of their regiments; many of which were much stronger when they came into the field. But the number of soldiers that have died in the camp is comparatively small to

From "Miscellaneous Observations upon the State of the Rebel Army," in Great Britain Historical Manuscripts Commission, Report on the Manuscripts of Mrs. Stopford-Sackville, 2 vols. (London: H. M. Stationery Office, by Mackie, 1904–1910), Vol. II, pp. 15–18.

those vast numbers that have gone off in the interior parts of the country. For immediately upon being taken down with these disorders they have in general been carried back into the country to their own homes, where they have not only died themselves, but by spreading the infection among their relatives and friends have introduced such a general mortality throughout New England as was never known since its first planting. Great numbers have been carried off in all parts of the country. Some towns 'tis said have lost near one-third of their inhabitants; and there is scarce a village but has suffered more or less from the raging virulence of these dreadful disorders. . . .

The soldiers in general are most heartily sick of the service, and I believe it would be with the utmost difficulty that they could be prevailed upon to serve another campaign. The Continental Congress are very sensible of this, and have lately sent a committee to the camp to consult with the general officers upon some method of raising the necessary forces to serve during the winter season, as the greatest part of the army that is now in the field is to be disbanded upon the last day of December.

Whether they will be successful in their endeavours to persuade the soldiers to re-inlist or not, I cannot say, but am rather inclined to think that they will. For as they are men possessed of every species of cunning and artifice, and as their political existence depends upon the existence of the army, they will leave no stone unturned to accomplish their designs.

Notwithstanding the indefatigable endeavours of Mr. Washington and the other generals, and particularly of Adjutant General Gates, to arrange and discipline the army, yet any tolerable degree of order and subordination is what they are totally unacquainted with in the rebel camp. And the doctrines of independence and levellism have been so effectually sown throughout the country, and so universally imbibed by all ranks of men, that I apprehend it will be with the greatest difficulty that the inferior officers and soldiers will be ever brought to any tolerable degree of subjection to the commands of their superiors.

Many of their leading men are not insensible of this, and I have often heard them lament that the existence of that very spirit which induced the common people to take up arms and resist the authority of Great Britain, should induce them to resist the authority of their own officers, and by that means effectually prevent their ever making good soldiers.

Another great reason why it is impossible to introduce a proper degree of subordination in the rebel army is the great degree of equality as to birth, fortune and education that universally prevails among them. For men cannot bear to be commanded by others that are their superiors in nothing but in having had the good fortune to get a superior commission, for which perhaps they stood equally fair. And in addition to this, the officers and men are not only in general very nearly upon a par as to birth, fortune, etc., but in particular regiments are most commonly neighbours and acquaintances, and as such can with less patience submit to that degree of absolute submission and subordination which is necessary to form a well-disciplined corps.

Another reason why the army can never be well united and regulated is the disagreement and jealousies between the different troops from the different Colonies; which must never fail to create disaffection and uneasiness among them. The Massachusetts forces already complain very loudly of the partiality of the General to the Virginians, and have even gone so far as to tax him with taking pleasure in bringing their officers to court martials, and having them cashiered that he may fill their places with his friends from that quarter. The gentlemen from the Southern Colonies, in their turn, complain of the enormous proportion of New England officers in the army, and particularly of those belonging to the province of Massachusetts Bay, and say, as the cause is now become a common one, and the experience is general, they ought to have an equal chance for command with their neighbours.

Thus have these jealousies and uneasiness already begun which I think cannot fail to increase and grow every day more and more interesting, and if they do not finally destroy the very existence of the army (which I think they bid very fair to do), yet must unavoidably render it much less formidable than it otherways might have been.

Of all useless sets of men that ever incumbered an army, surely the boasted riflemen are certainly the most so. When they came to the camp they had every liberty and indulgence allowed them that they could possibly wish for. They had more pay than any other soldiers; did no duty; were under no restraint from the commands of their officers, but went when and where they pleased, without being subject to be stopped or examined by any one, and did almost intirely as they pleased in every respect whatever. But they have not answered the end for which they were designed in any one article whatever. For instead of being the best marksmen in the world, and picking off every regular that was to be seen, there is scarsely a regiment in camp but can produce men that can beat them at shooting, and the army is now universally convinced that the continual fire which they kept up by the week and month together has had no other effect than to waste their ammunition and convince the King's troops that they are not really so formidable adversaries as they would wish to be thought. . . .

Three Views of the American Soldier

Here are three representations of the American soldier. The first is an English caricature. The second is a painting by Charles Willson Peale (a soldier himself) that shows the highest ideal the Americans had of soldierly appearance and conduct, George Washington. The Marquis de Lafayette is the center figure, and to the right is Washington's aide, General Tench Tilghman. The third is a French painting show-

ing two infantrymen, a rifleman, and an artilleryman. (Each is wearing a different uniform, not just because they serve in different branches of the army, but because they come from different colonies.)

As you examine these three pictures, keep these points and questions in mind. Patrick Henry's famous remark, "Give me liberty or give me death," is mocked in the British picture. But what is the effect of reversing the order of the words? Notice the clothing, stance, and the facial expression of Washington. What kinds of class values and attitudes do you think Peale is trying to depict here? In the French picture, do the soldiers look "American" at all, or do they conform more to your image of a typical European soldier of the Napoleonic period? Or is there a mixture?

British Caricature.
Metropolitan Museum of Art. Bequest of Charles Allen Munn, 1924.

Washington, with the Marquis de Lafayette. By the American artist Charles Willson Peale. *M. E. Warren Photography/Photo Researchers.*

A Contemporary French Painting. *Anne S. K. Brown Military Collection/Brown University Library.*

Silencing the Tories

The following documents tell us something about the American treatment of Tories, who probably constituted about 20 percent of the population—potentially a powerful and dangerous force. The first is a cartoon drawn in London mocking the way the rebels treated John Malcomb, a Crown official who had tried to collect the tea tax in Boston in 1774. What do the clothes tell you about the kinds of people the British thought were in rebellion? Look at the facial features. How does the cartoonist try to convince us that John Malcomb is made of finer stuff than the men who have tarred and feathered him?

The second document is part of the letter from a Tory woman, Ann Hulton, a Bostonian, about another 1774 tarring and feathering; the third is a rebel description of a similar event in New York about a year later. Which document do you find more convincing? Taken together, do they support Shy's point about the importance of using military and quasi-military force to keep revolutionary order? Or do they hint at a rabble acting in undisciplined anger?

The BOSTONIAN'S Paying the EXCISE-MAN, or TARRING & FEATHERING

Library of Congress.

Ann Hulton to Mrs. Lightbody.

Boston, January 31, 1774

. . . But the most shocking cruelty was exercised a few nights ago, upon a poor old man, a tidesman, one Malcolm. He is reckoned creasy, a quarrel was picked with him, he was afterward taken and tarred and feathered. Theres no law that knows a punishment for the greatest crimes beyond what this is of cruel torture. And this instance exceeds any other before it. He was stript stark naked, one of the severest cold nights this winter, his body covered all over with tar, then with feathers, his arm dislocated in tearing off his cloaths. He was dragged in a cart with thousands attending, some beating him with clubs and knocking him out of the cart, then in again. They gave him several severe whippings, at different parts of the town. This spectacle of horror and sportive cruelty was exhibited for about five hours.

The unhappy wretch they say behaved with the greatest intrepidity and fortitude all the while. Before he was taken, [he] defended himself a long time against numbers, and afterwards when under torture they demanded of him to curse his masters, the King, Governor, etc., which they could not make him do, but he still cried, "Curse all traitors!" They brought him to the gallows and put a rope about his neck, saying they would hang him. He said he wished they would, but that they could not, for God was above the Devil. The doctors say that it is impossible this poor creature can live. They say his flesh comes off his back in stakes.

It is the second time he has been tarred and feathered and this is looked upon more to intimidate the judges and others than a spite to the unhappy victim tho' they owe him a grudge for some things particularly. He was with Govr. Tryon in the battle with the Regulators and the Governor has declared that he was of great servise to him in that affair, by his undaunted spirit encountering the greatest dangers.

Govr. Tryon had sent him a gift of ten guineas just before this inhuman treatment. He has a wife and family and an aged father and mother who, they say, saw the spectacle which no indifferent person can mention without horror.

These few instances amongst many serve to shew the abject state of government and the licentiousness and barbarism of the times. There's no majestrate that dare or will act to suppress the outrages. No person is secure. There are many objects pointed at, at this time, and when once marked out for vengeance, their ruin is certain.

The judges have only a weeks time allowed them to consider whether they will take the salaries from the Crown or no. Govr. Hutchinson is going to England as soon as the season will permit.

We are under no apprehension at present on our own account but we can't look upon our safety secure for long.

From Ann Hulton, *Letters of a Loyalist Lady . . . 1767–1776* (Cambridge, Mass., 1927), pp. 70–72.

From the records of the Committee of Safety.

New York, December 28, 1775

The 6th of December, at Quibbletown, Middlesex County, Piscataway Township, New-Jersey, Thomas Randolph, cooper, who had publickly proved himself an enemy to his country, by reviling and using his utmost endeavours to oppose the proceedings of the Continental and Provincial Conventions and Committees, in defence of their rights and liberties; and he, being judged a person of not consequence enough for a severer punishment, was ordered to be stripped naked, well coated with tar and feathers, and carried in a wagon publickly round the town; which punishment was accordingly inflicted. And as he soon became duly sensible of his offence, for which he earnestly begged pardon, and promised to atone, as far as he was able, by a contrary behaviour for the future, he was released, and suffered to return to his house in less than half an hour. The whole was conducted with that regularity and decorum that ought to be observed in all publick punishments.

From Peter Force, ed., *American Archives: Fourth Series,* 6 vols. (Washington, D.C.: M. St. Clair Clarke and Peter Force, 1837–1846), Vol. IV, p. 203.

8

Creating the Constitution

The new nation brought into being by the Revolution stretched from the Atlantic to the Mississippi. It was a huge wilderness by European standards, six times the size of England and Wales combined, but thinly populated. Although most of the 3 million inhabitants lived near the Atlantic, the population had begun to move into the forests beyond the seaboard, farther and farther away from the centers of communication. So poor were communications and so rudimentary were transportation facilities that the country was little more than a collection of isolated communities. There were only six cities with over 8,000 inhabitants. The largest was Philadelphia, with some 40,000, followed by New York, Boston, Charleston, Baltimore, and Salem. Ninety-five percent of the population lived elsewhere, on isolated farms or in small villages, scattered from Maine to Georgia.

How could 3 million people, dispersed over a vast wilderness, be governed? That question was faced by every state in the revolutionary period, and also by the new nation. But it was never really resolved. Laws were passed and orders were given, but there was simply no way that a handful of government officials could force a scattered—and somewhat unruly—population to obey the law. And few officials were foolish enough to try.

Instead, America's leaders were content to fashion a new system of government. And that, to them, was exciting. They saw themselves as daring innovators, creating a republic in a world of monarchies, establishing a new government not only for themselves but "for millions yet unborn." Wrote John Adams in 1776: "You and I, my dear friend, have been sent into life at a time when the greatest lawgivers of antiquity would have wished to live. How few of the human race have enjoyed an opportunity of making an election of government for themselves or their children.''

It would be foolish to ignore this self-perception. But it would be equally foolish to forget that nine-tenths of those who had the chance to mold the new government were men of property, members of the colonial elite, old hands at government. Clearly, their vision of the new order was tempered by experience. But was it also tempered by self-interest? That question has been raised particularly in regard to the men who met in Philadelphia in 1787, destroyed the first system of federal government, and established the present system.

Interpretive Essay

John C. Miller

The Creation of a More Perfect Union

The modern debate over the nature of the Constitutional Convention has been dominated by two opinions. One is that the Founding Fathers were men of detached and lofty perceptions, men of principle who tried to embody those principles in a frame of government they hoped would endure for generations. The other is that the members of the convention were men of property whose actions were tied directly to their own economic stake in the outcome. In the following selection, John C. Miller takes the middle ground. He sees the framers of the Constitution as neither modern saints nor eighteenth-century sinners, but as an assembly of "notables" who represented primarily the interests of southern planters and northern merchants, yet who also wanted to stand in history as the able and farsighted creators of a "more perfect Union." As you read, try to determine who gained the most from their efforts. Southern planters? Northern merchants? Western farmers? Or future generations?

The men who assembled in Philadelphia in May 1787 were compared by contemporaries with the Assembly of Notables then meeting in Paris.

From John C. Miller, *The Emergence of the Nation, 1783–1815* (Glenview, Ill.: Scott, Foresman, 1972), pp. 35–45.

But the American notables came to terminate a revolution and to consolidate its gains, whereas the French Notables, although they were unaware of it, had come to start a revolution.

Certainly the members of the Constitutional Convention were entitled to the designations of notables. In general the states vied with each other in sending their most eminent citizens to Philadelphia. John Adams and Thomas Jefferson were not present because they were serving the United States in London and Paris respectively, and Patrick Henry declined to attend because, he said, he "smelled a rat." George Washington presided over the meeting as president; Benjamin Franklin was a delegate from Pennsylvania; and James Madison assumed from the start the role of philosopher and guide to the convention. Among the delegates were signers of the Declaration of Independence, past and present members of the Continental Congress, state governors, judges, lawyers, and planters. Without exception, the delegates came from the long settled eastern part of the country. The West, as a section, had no representatives. Nor were any yeomen farmers present; the agricultural interest being represented mainly by the southern planters.

The Decision to Make the Government National

Patrick Henry's rat, by which he meant a consolidated government, immediately revealed itself. Despite the directives of the Continental Congress and several states that the delegates confine their work to drafting amendments to the Articles, it soon became evident that the most influential members of the convention did not consider themselves bound by any restrictions whatever. On May 30, almost before the delegates had warmed their seats, Edmund Randolph, the governor of Virginia, proposed a plan of government drawn up by James Madison. The Madison-Randolph or Virginia Plan proposed a radically new approach to the problem of creating a more cohesive union and a stronger central government.

The Virginia Plan

Randolph told the delegates that the only hope of preserving the Union lay in virtually annihilating the power of the states and in giving the national government—he freely used the word *national,* seldom heard during the period of the Articles of Confederation—power to tax, legislate for, and if necessary coerce the people of the United States. The national government, as envisaged by the Virginia Plan, was to be divided into three distinct branches, and the legislature was to be divided into a house and senate. A powerful executive was to replace the President of Congress, and a hierarchy of federal courts was to provide for the first time direct enforcement of the laws of the union. By a system of checks and balances, each branch was to be kept within the bounds assigned it by the Constitution.

Finally, to ensure that the authority of the national government should permeate the Union, the Virginia Plan empowered the national legislature to negate any state law which in its opinion was contrary to the national interest. This provision would give the national government supreme and unrestricted powers and, as Randolph admitted, would leave the states with hardly a shred of the sovereign power they had enjoyed under the Articles of Confederation.

While the delegates agreed that the country was ailing, the Virginia Plan struck many of them as stronger medicine than the patient would tolerate. On the other hand, Alexander Hamilton thought that the Virginia Plan did not go far enough toward concentrating power in the general government. Hamilton, who was a West Indian by birth and therefore lacked strong state attachments, favored melting down all the states to form a consolidated union to be animated by an all-powerful central government. Hamilton dismissed the Virginia Plan as "the same pork" as the Articles of Confederation with a little change of the sauce. He made clear that his dish was an approximation of the British constitution with a president and senate elected for life. But, as several delegates were quick to point out, this was building castles in the air, whereas the task of the convention was to erect a government upon the solid bedrock of reality. Above all, the convention had to be guided by what was practicable, and the principal criterion of practicability was what the American people, acting in separate state units, would approve.

The most explosive idea Randolph introduced was his suggestion that state equality be abolished by instituting proportional representation in both houses of Congress, which would mean that the large states, by virtue of their population, would dominate the government. By this provision, Madison hoped to redress the wrong done the large states in 1777 when state equality was written into the Articles of Confederation. Here Madison struck the small states in their most sensitive spot. For they conceived of the state as the primary unit and felt that their existence depended upon the principle of one state, one vote. Deprived of equality, they feared that they would lose their influence in the general government and that the large states would preempt the national revenue and enact tariff and tonnage laws to the disadvantage of the small, noncommercial states. Some spokesmen of the small states even professed to fear that they would ultimately be absorbed by their larger neighbors.

The New Jersey Plan

Speaking on behalf of the small states, William Paterson of New Jersey put forward the New Jersey or Small State Plan as a substitute for the Virginia Plan. Essentially, Paterson proposed a revision of the Articles of Confederation and thereby put himself in accord with the expectations of the American people and with the directive of the Continental Congress. Even though drastically limited in the changes which it proposed, the New Jersey Plan would have given Congress the impost and control over commerce and would have established a system of federal courts.

So inflamed were the passions raised by the issue of state equality versus proportional representation that for several weeks the convention seemed on the verge of dissolution. The American people knew nothing of this crisis. The convention met in the utmost secrecy, and the delegates were forbidden to inform any outsider of what was transpiring inside the Pennsylvania State House where the convention met.

The Connecticut Compromise

The impasse was finally resolved by the appointment of a committee consisting of one member from each state. On July 5, 1787, this committee reported the Great or Connecticut Compromise, sponsored by Roger Sherman of Connecticut, in which state equality was perpetuated in the Senate while proportional representation prevailed in the House of Representatives. This compromise was accepted by the convention by the margin of five states to four, Virginia voting in the negative. Only after the House had been given the exclusive right to originate money bills which could, however, be amended by the Senate were the large states reconciled to the Connecticut Compromise.

By admitting state equality in the Senate, the Constitution gave the states a foothold within the very citadel of the general government. Nevertheless, one of the features of the Confederation most objectionable to nationalists was eliminated: no longer did an entire delegation cast one vote for the state as a unit. Instead, senators voted as individuals rather than as ambassadors whose duty was to register the will of sovereign states. Moreover, since congressmen's salaries were to be paid by the federal government, they were made financially independent of the states.

The Issues of Slavery and Sectionalism

The real gainers by the Connecticut Compromise were not the small states. They were never in danger of being absorbed by the large states. The South and later the West were the real beneficiaries, although not the advocates, of this arrangement. In American history, states' rights have been the mask assumed by sectionalism, and as a minority section the ante bellum South found that equality in the Senate was its shield and buckler against northern oppression. This was especially true since the southern states contained, on the average, smaller white populations than the northern states. In 1860, for example, the state of New York, with a population of four million, was represented by two senators, whereas the fifteen slaveholding states, with a population of eight million free people, sent thirty senators to Washington.

An attempt to create a more cohesive union was bound to occasion a dispute over slavery. Even though slavery was not yet the "peculiar institution" of the South, it was already beginning to make trouble between the two sections. Under the Articles of Confederation when requisitions were laid by the Continental Congress, the sum was determined by the population of the state. The question had arisen in the Continental Congress whether slaves were to be counted along with whites. Southerners insisted that slaves were not persons but property. As such, they ought not to be counted any more than should sheep, cattle, and horses. To which Benjamin Franklin drily remarked that there was an important difference between sheep and slaves: "Sheep," he said, "will never make any insurrections."

The Three-fifths and Fugitive Slave Clauses

Here the practice of the Continental Congress under the Articles of Confederation proved useful. In apportioning requisitions, the old Congress had counted three fifths of the slaves. Since the new Constitution provided that representation in the House of Representatives and votes in the electoral college were to be determined by population, southerners insisted upon incorporating the three-fifths rule into the new frame of government as a basis for counting population. Therefore, over weak northern opposition, southerners wrote this clause into the Constitution. It was not the result of a compromise: the North received no *quid pro quo* except that three fifths of the slaves would also be counted for the purposes of direct taxation. Gouverneur Morris of Pennsylvania, who opposed the three-fifths clause, said that because of southern intransigence on this issue he was "reduced to the dilemma of doing justice to the Southern states or to human nature, and must therefore do it to the former."

The three-fifths clause proved to be the greatest concession made by either section to secure the adoption of the Constitution. In 1790 as a result of it, Virginia, with a smaller free population than Massachusetts, sent five more representatives to Congress and therefore possessed five more votes in the electoral college than did the Bay State. Without benefit of the three-fifths clause, Thomas Jefferson would not have been elected President of the United States in 1800. Finally, the three-fifths clause gave slavery a privileged and virtually indestructible position in the federal government. The Constitution makes clear that property could consist of human beings.

The framers of the Constitution were obviously embarrassed by the existence of slavery in a society which purported to be a model for mankind. Most of them sincerely hoped that slavery would die of its own accord. Only one speech in praise of slavery was made in the Constitutional Convention. The members could not bring themselves to use the word *slave* or even *bondservant*. Instead the slaves were covered by the euphemistic phrase "persons held to Service or Labor" which in 1787 included white indentured servants as well as black slaves. To placate the slaveowners, the Constitution provided that fugitives should be "delivered up on Claim of the Party to whom such Service or Labor may be due." Although the framers obviously intended that the rendition of fugitive slaves should be primarily a state responsibility, this clause of the Constitution became the basis for a Fugitive Slave Act in 1793 which obligated the federal government to aid in returning runaways to their masters.

The circumlocution with which the delegates approached the subject of slavery indicated both their aversion to the institution and their awareness of the disruptive potential of the slavery question. The convention realized that it could not take an unequivocal position either for or against slavery *per se* without imposing an intolerable strain upon the fragile bonds of union.

Economic Aspects of Sectionalism

Once the issue between the large and small states had been settled, the sectional division reflected in the three-fifths clause provided the focal point for conflicts of interest within the convention. The main struggle was between the commercial and shipping northern states and the agricultural, staple-producing, exporting states of the South. At first, victory clearly inclined to the South. Northerners demanded that Congress be permitted by a mere majority vote to lay a tax upon exports and to enact a tariff and navigation system, by which was meant discriminatory tonnage rates designed to benefit American shipping. By acting as a unit, the southern states, with the aid of some of the agricultural northern states, were able to block this demand and to insert into the Constitution not only an outright prohibition of taxes on exports but also a requirement that navigation laws be enacted by a two-thirds majority of Congress.

The African Slave Trade

But after this success, the South failed to maintain the united front to which it owed its influence. When the convention came to consider the African slave trade, fundamental differences among the southern states were brought to light. Virginia, having a surplus of slaves, competed with Africa in supplying the plantations of South Carolina and Georgia. As domestic producers of slaves and, in some instances, as idealists, the Virginians were determined to protect their market against foreign competition and to remove the blot of the African trade from the United States. Accordingly, they favored giving Congress power to stop this trade at any time after the establishment of the new government. The South Carolinians and Georgians, on the other hand, opposed giving Congress any power whatever over the trade. Charles Pinckney of South Carolina delivered an encomium upon slavery and the slave trade, and he served notice upon the convention that his state would not accept any frame of government which gave the general government power to prevent the free importation of blacks from Africa. The delegations from Georgia and South Carolina backed up this speech by threatening to walk out of the convention.

As was its settled practice, the convention appointed a committee to find a way out of the impasse. Such a way opened when South Carolina and Georgia, resentful of Virginia's treachery, decided to enter into a bargain with certain northern delegates whereby these two slave-hungry states agreed to vote in favor of empowering Congress to enact navigation acts by a simple majority in exchange for a vote by the northern commercial states in favor of a provision which would forbid any federal interference with the slave trade until 1808. It was now the Virginians' turn to cry treachery, but the bargain was consummated in spite of the objections of the Old Dominion.

By thus delaying for twenty years the national prohibition of the African slave trade, the proponents of the trade hoped to stock southern plantations with blacks from the slave barracoons of Africa. In actuality, however, there was opposition to the trade not only on moral grounds but also because slave purchases drained the money supply. For these reasons, the trade was prohibited by all the states except Georgia and South Carolina, and in the latter state it was open only between 1804–1808. Yet during this period of grace for American slave traders, fifty thousand or more human beings suffered the ordeal of the middle passage and a lifetime of slavery in order to make possible the more perfect union of white Americans.

The Broad Agreement on the Constitution

While many compromises went into the making of the Constitution, the drafting of a frame of government in 1787 was made possible only by the existence of a broad agreement upon fundamentals and the determination of the delegates to establish an efficient central government capable of upholding the credit, dignity, and rights of the United States.

The Federal System

Instead of creating a unitary government along the lines sketched by the Virginia Plan, in which the states would hardly have been more than administrative agents of the central authority, the Constitution effected a division of sovereignty between the states and the general government. Each exercised sovereignty within a sphere defined by the Constitution. Some functions, especially those regarded as common to the entire country, were assigned to the general government; other functions were placed exclusively in the hands of the states; and a third area was shared by the two jurisdictions concurrently. Because the states and the general government coexist within the same territory, the United States has diverse systems of law, an entire galaxy of taxing powers, and dual police and armed forces. Both the state and federal governments operate directly upon the people. In the United States, each citizen is subject to two governments.

Although the Constitution did not establish the "high toned" central government envisaged by the Virginia Plan, it contained several clauses which, as Alexander Hamilton perceived, might later be used to achieve a vast extension of federal powers. These were the commerce clause, the necessary and proper clause, and the general welfare clause. Although some of these phrases were derived from the Articles of Confederation, in the context of the document of 1787, they assumed new and far-reaching implications. They helped make possible the broad interpretation of national powers. In short, unlike the Articles, the Constitution created a government capable of meeting changing circumstances by invoking flexible powers which the courts, Congress, and the President found implied or inherent in the language of the instrument.

A Government with Power

Under the Articles of Confederation, it had been difficult to carry on interstate business or, indeed, business of any kind. The Constitution remedied this defect by making possible a single, integrated monetary system, which, however, was long delayed; by prohibiting the states from laying tariff and tonnage duties without the consent of Congress; by directing that all federal duties, imposts, and excises be uniform throughout the United States; by requiring that "the citizens of each state shall be entitled to all the privileges and immunities of Citizens in the several states"; and by giving the federal government exclusive power to regulate interstate trade and to prescribe a common standard of weights and measures.

Thus, as regards the relative positions of the general government and the states, the Constitution brought about a change almost as revolutionary as that of 1776. From a position of humiliating impotence, the general government acquired powers by which it gradually became dominant. Instead of being dependent upon the states for its very existence, the general government, under the Constitution, became independent of the states, leaving the latter no means short of nullification and secession for regaining their lost preeminence. As events proved, although it took a long time before the implications of federal power were fully realized, the Constitution made the sphere of federal power potentially much greater than the sphere allotted to the states. The general government was given unlimited powers of taxation, although the United States Supreme Court later decided that an income tax was unconstitutional; the states were prohibited from making paper money legal tender or impairing the obligation of contracts, a reaction against the paper money and debtor-relief laws enacted by the states; and the national government was enabled to enforce its decrees through a federal system of courts. No longer were the states to enjoy the position of intermediaries between the general government and the people. Finally, the state governments were effectively isolated from each other by the provision that "no state shall, without the consent of Congress . . . enter into any general agreement or compact with another state." The tables, it appeared, were to be turned completely: the federal government became the guarantor of a republican form of government in the states.

Within the definition accepted in 1787, this kind of government was not federal. The Constitutional Convention had in fact created a new synthesis. While the frame of government it devised was in some respects federal, since it made the states autonomous in some matters, in other and equally important respects it was national and made the central government autonomous in other areas. Nevertheless, the supporters of the new Constitution took the name *Federalist,* leaving to its opponents the invidious, but wholly unwarranted, name of Antifederalists. Thus the advocates of the Constitution won the first battle in the campaign for ratification: they routed their opponents upon the field of semantics.

The Governmental Mechanism

As for the central government itself, it was characterized by a system of checks and balances between its three branches. The executive, legislature, and judiciary were each provided with the constitutional means of defending their own powers against the encroachments of the other branches. Hamilton thought that this system of "power as a rival of power" would be so effective that it would be "next to impossible that impolitic or wicked measures should pass the great scrutiny." Yet the framers did not intend to divide the government into rigid, compartmentalized, autonomous branches. The doctrine of the separation of powers was certainly given application, but each branch shared in functions that were not strictly within its province. The President could exercise legislative as well as executive powers, for instance, by issuing administrative orders. Congress could perform executive functions, such as approving appointments, and the federal courts, by construing the meaning of statutes, could exercise a legislative role. This role has sometimes been extended so broadly as to incur charges of usurpation of legislative powers.

Was the Constitution Democratic?

All this was accomplished without impairment to the democratic gains of the American Revolution. Indeed, in several areas, the federal Constitution appeared more democratic than the state constitutions. Unlike the states, the federal government required no property qualifications for holding office, and it implemented the principle of religious freedom by dispensing altogether with religious tests. The federal Constitution did not disbar Jews, Roman Catholics, or even nonbelievers from any public office, although some state constitutions did. The federal Constitution was a great experiment in religious as well as political liberalism.

Unless liberty was identified with states' rights, the American people were not the losers by this shift of power from the states to the general government. In fact by the adoption of the Constitution, the people stood to gain a large measure of control over the central government, a privilege they had certainly not enjoyed under the Articles of Confederation. They were now promised the right to elect directly members of the House of Representatives. In some states, and ultimately in all, they gained the right to elect presidential electors.

On the other hand, the framers clearly did not intend to establish the kind of government in which the popular will prevailed at all times without let or hindrance. The immediate concern of most of the members of the convention was to protect the "opulent minority" from expropriation by democratic majorities. The government of the United States, in consequence, is not based upon the principle that the majority have the right to govern arbitrarily, nor does it contemplate a government in which the people govern in the usual sense of that word. The people merely decide who shall govern and, broadly speaking, to what ends. Although the people are declared to be sovereign, there are things which even a majority cannot do. The Constitution itself, for example, cannot be amended except with the approval of three fourths of the states. The Constitution, which is the supreme law of the land, created a system which comes closer to being a government of laws rather than of men than any other country has been able to devise.

The Break with the Confederation

The framers of the federal Constitution proposed not only to effect a revolution in the relations between the states and the general government. They also recognized that it was necessary to make a sharp break with the law of the land in order to carry their plan into execution. The Articles of Confederation, which in 1787 were still in force, required that any changes in the fundamental law be approved by all thirteen state legislatures. Every previous effort to amend the Articles had been frustrated by this rule of unanimity. It was a foregone conclusion that if the proposed Constitution were subjected to the same rule it would suffer the fate of the impost. Rhode Island, the erring sister of the Confederation, had not even recognized the existence of the Constitutional Convention. In New York Governor Clinton, whose forces had defeated the effort to strengthen the commercial powers of Congress, was known to be hostile to the Constitution.

Faced with the certainty of having its work blocked by one or more of the state governments, the Constitutional Convention decided to break the rule of unanimity. It decreed that the proposed frame of government was to be submitted not to state legislatures but to popularly elected conventions and that it should go into effect after nine states, not thirteen, had ratified it.

These changes were more democratic than the procedures ordained by the Articles of Confederation. By appealing directly to the people to sanction its handiwork, the Constitutional Convention applied the doctrine of the sovereignty of the people to the process of constitution-making. Consequently, the Constitution of the United States, if adopted, could be regarded as the creation of "We, the People" of the United States, even though they acted severally by states rather than collectively as one people.

The Constitution Viewed Pragmatically

None of the framers was prepared to pronounce the result of the labors of the Philadelphia convention as the best of all possible constitutions. Most of the delegates agreed with James Madison's observation that it was the best constitution that could be wrung from the jarring sectional, state, and personal interests. Nevertheless, the Constitution bore the signatures of thirty-nine members. At various times during the proceedings, fifty-five men attended the convention, but of this number sixteen had left Philadelphia before the convention completed its work. Of these sixteen, four disapproved of the finished Constitution. Of even greater concern to the framers was the fact that despite Benjamin Franklin's plea for unanimity, three of the delegates still in attendance—Elbridge Gerry of Massachusetts, and George Mason and Edmund Randolph of Virginia—refused to sign the Constitution.

The Controversy Around the Constitution

Obviously, the framers of the Constitution could not afford to neglect any circumstance which might favor ratification. For the American people were being called upon to embrace ideas which seemed to be at variance with some of the basic teachings of the colonial and revolutionary experience. Americans had learned to fear centralized government, to cherish local liberty, and to believe that that government was best which governed least. In 1787–1788 they were asked to recast their thinking and to look upon an energetic central government as the guardian of their property and of republican government itself.

The traditional distrust of power, derived from the colonial and revolutionary periods, was widespread in 1787–1788. This feeling was given expression by the Antifederalists, the most articulate of whom were Richard Henry Lee, George Mason, and Patrick Henry of Virginia; Luther Martin of Maryland; and Governor George Clinton of New York. These men held the view later enunciated by Lord Acton, the nineteenth-century British historian, that while all power corrupts, absolute power corrupts absolutely. From their viewpoint, the United States was too large, its economy too diverse, and its mode of life too varied from one region to another for it to be ruled as a whole by any government except an absolute and despotic one. If the United States fell under the sway of a centralized government, they feared that the "overbearing insolence of office," the lust for power, and the arrogance of wealth would lead to the subversion of all liberty. Liberty and strong, coercive government, they pessimistically believed, could not be reconciled.

. . . Suspicious of government and of the officials who administered it, the Antifederalist spokesmen lacked any compensating faith in the wisdom of the people and in the people's ability to prevent the encroachments of power. In effect, they insisted that the prevention of any effective exercise of power on a national scale was the only reliable guarantee of liberty. Their solution to the dilemma of power was to protect the minority by making it impossible for the majority to rule. In the name of liberty, they were prepared to negate the idea of popular government not, it is true, as regards the states but certainly as regards the general government. In their view, the only true security for liberty was a weak central government constitutionally debarred from interfering in the internal affairs of the states. . . .

. . . Although some of the Antifederalist leaders were themselves men of wealth, they attacked the proposed Constitution as the culmination of a long-standing plot to destroy republican government and to establish an aristocracy and perhaps even a monarchy in the United States. As they pictured it, the advocates of the Constitution were "partisans of arbitrary power" who moved toward their objective by means of "dark, secret and profound intrigues."

Obviously, the Antifederalist leaders were aware that nothing was more calculated to prejudice the American people against the proposed frame of government than the charge that it was an aristocratic plot. Even though the Antifederalists did not succeed in 1787–1788 in convincing a majority of the electorate that this was true, their propaganda later had a profound effect upon a whole generation of American historians.

Sources

Ratification

There was considerable agreement on at least the major point among
the members of the Constitutional Convention: a stronger central
government was needed to replace the Confederation of the States.
But when the Constitution was sent out to the country, not even this
initial assumption was widely shared. The result was that after sailing through four or five state ratifying conventions with ease, the
Constitution ran into bitter opposition in such key states as Massachusetts, Virginia, and New York. In those states the supporters of
the Constitution, who were called Federalists, were able to win majorities only by promising a host of amendments to the Constitution.
The most exciting fight was in New York, where the Constitution
squeaked through by a mere three votes. The map on page 180, and
the table giving the order of ratification, will give you some idea of
how the Constitution fared from state to state. Do you see any patterns in the vote? Is it fair to say that the seaboard was for the Constitution and the back country was generally against it? What would
have happened if New York, Virginia, or Massachusetts had gone the
other way? It took only nine states to ratify the Constitution, but
could the new government have survived without one of these key
states?

Order of Ratification

State	Date	Vote in Convention	Rank in Population	1790 Population
1. Delaware	Dec. 7, 1787	Unanimous	13	59,096
2. Pennsylvania	Dec. 12, 1787	46 to 23	3	433,611
3. New Jersey	Dec. 18, 1787	Unanimous	9	184,139
4. Georgia	Jan. 2, 1788	Unanimous	11	82,548
5. Connecticut	Jan. 9, 1788	128 to 40	8	237,655
6. Massachusetts (incl. Maine)	Feb. 7, 1788	187 to 168	2	475,199
7. Maryland	Apr. 28, 1788	63 to 11	6	319,728
8. South Carolina	May 23, 1788	149 to 73	7	249,073
9. New Hampshire	June 21, 1788	57 to 46	10	141,899
10. Virginia	June 26, 1788	89 to 79	1	747,610
11. New York	July 26, 1788	30 to 27	5	340,241
12. North Carolina	Nov. 21, 1789	195 to 77	4	395,005
13. Rhode Island	May 29, 1790	34 to 32	12	69,112

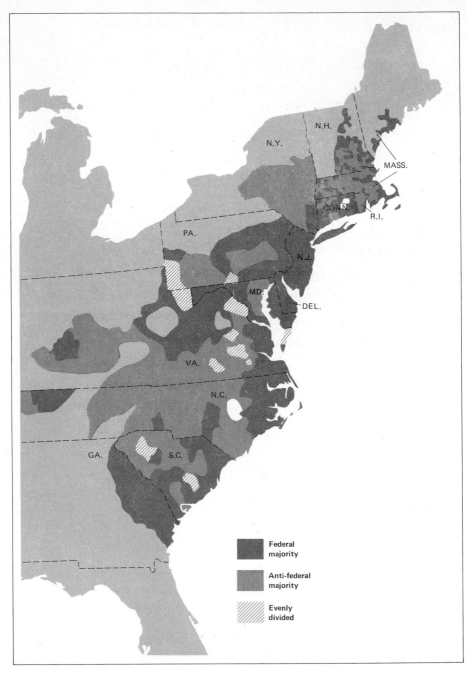

Voting for Ratification.

The Virginia Debates

Proud Virginia, the biggest and most populous state, was sharply divided over the Constitution. Only by promising a Bill of Rights, and by making good use of the knowledge that Washington would undoubtedly be the first president, were the supporters of the Constitution able to win by an 89 to 79 vote.

Here are some selections from one of the significant debates in Virginia. What opinions divided the proponents of the Constitution (who seized the name Federalists for themselves) from its opponents (who seem to have been left with the uninspired title of anti-Federalists)?

Some historians, notably Charles Beard early in the twentieth century, have argued that the Constitution was a political maneuver by the elite designed to protect their economic position and interests. Other historians have disagreed and have seen the Constitution as an able response to a political, not an economic or social, problem. What evidence can you find in the following debate to support either point of view?

Many years later, Abraham Lincoln argued that the nation had been conceived in liberty and dedicated to the proposition that all men are created equal. Which of these two values, liberty or equality, can you find expressed in the debate between Mason and Pendleton?

Mr. George Mason. Mr. Chairman, whether the Constitution be good or bad, the present clause clearly discovers that it is a national government, and no longer a Confederation. I mean that clause which gives the first hint of the general government laying direct taxes. The assumption of this power of laying direct taxes does, of itself, entirely change the confederation of the states into one consolidated government. This power, being at discretion, unconfined, and without any kind of control, must carry every thing before it. The very idea of converting what was formerly a confederation to a consolidated government, is totally subversive of every principle which has hitherto governed us. This power is calculated to annihilate totally the state governments. Will the people of this great community submit to be individually taxed by two different and distinct powers? Will they suffer themselves to be doubly harassed? These two concurrent powers cannot exist long together; the one will destroy the other: the general government being paramount to, and in every respect more powerful than the state governments, the latter must give way to the former. . . . Was there ever an instance of a general national government extending over so extensive a country, abounding in such a variety of climates, &c., where the people retained their liberty? I

From Jonathan Elliott, ed., *The Debates in the Several State Conventions on the Adoption of the Federal Constitution* (Washington, D.C.: Jonathan Elliott, 1836), Vol. 3, pp. 29–38, 80–84.

solemnly declare that no man is a greater friend to a firm union of the American states than I am; but, sir, if this great end can be obtained without hazarding the rights of the people, why should we recur to such dangerous principles? . . .

The mode of levying taxes is of the utmost consequence; and yet here it is to be determined by those who have neither knowledge of our situation, nor a common interest with us, nor a fellow-feeling for us.

Why should we give up this dangerous power of individual taxation? Why leave the manner of laying taxes to those who, in the nature of things, cannot be acquainted with the situation of those on whom they are to impose them, when it can be done by those who are well acquainted with it? . . .

. . . There is one thing in it which I conceive to be extremely dangerous. Gentlemen may talk of public virtue and confidence; we shall be told that the House of Representatives will consist of the most virtuous men on the continent, and that in their hands we may trust our dearest rights. This, like all other assemblies, will be composed of some bad and some good men; and, considering the natural lust of power so inherent in man, I fear the thirst of power will prevail to oppress the people.

But my principal objection is, that the Confederation is converted to one general consolidated government, which, from my best judgment of it, (and which perhaps will be shown, in the course of this discussion, to be really well founded,) is one of the worst curses that can possibly befall a nation. Does any man suppose that one general national government can exist in so extensive a country as this? I hope that a government may be framed which may suit us, by drawing a line between the general and state governments, and prevent that dangerous clashing of interest and power, which must, as it now stands, terminate in the destruction of one or the other. When we come to the judiciary, we shall be more convinced that this government will terminate in the annihilation of the state governments: the question then will be, whether a consolidated government can preserve the freedom and secure the rights of the people.

Mr. Pendleton. Mr. Chairman, my worthy friend has expressed great uneasiness in his mind, and informed us that a great many of our citizens are also extremely uneasy, at the proposal of changing our government; but that, a year ago, before this fatal system was thought of, the public mind was at perfect repose. It is necessary to inquire whether the public mind was at ease on the subject, and if it be since disturbed, what was the cause. What was the situation of this country before the meeting of the federal Convention? Our general government was totally inadequate to the purpose of its institution; our commerce decayed; our finances deranged; public and private credit destroyed: these and many other national evils rendered necessary the meeting of that Convention. If the public mind was then at ease, it did not result from a conviction of being in a happy and easy situation: it must have been an inactive, unaccountable stupor. The federal Convention devised the paper on your table as a remedy to remove our political diseases.

What has created the public uneasiness since? Not public reports, which are not to be depended upon; but mistaken apprehensions of danger, drawn from observations on government which do not apply to us. When we come to inquire into the origin of most governments of the world, we shall find that they are generally dictated by a conqueror, at the point of the sword, or are the offspring of confusion, when a great popular leader, taking advantage of circumstances, if not producing them, restores order at the expense of liberty, and becomes the tyrant over the people. It may well be supposed that, in forming a government of this sort, it will not be favorable to liberty: the conqueror will take care of his own emoluments, and have little concern for the interest of the people. In either case, the interest and ambition of a despot, and not the good of the people, have given the tone to the government. A government thus formed must necessarily create a continual war between the governors and governed.

Writers consider the two parties (the people and tyrants) as in a state of perpetual warfare, and sound the alarm to the people. But what is our case? We are perfectly free from sedition and war: we are not yet in confusion: we are left to consider our real happiness and security: we want to secure these objects: we know they cannot be attained without government. Is there a single man, in this committee, of a contrary opinion? What was it that brought us from a state of nature of society, but to secure happiness? And can society be formed without government? Personify government: apply to it as a friend to assist you, and it will grant your request. This is the only government founded in real compact. There is no quarrel between government and liberty; the former is the shield and protector of the latter. The war is between government and licentiousness, faction, turbulence, and other violations of the rules of society, to preserve liberty. Where is the cause of alarm? We, the people, possessing all power, form a government, such as we think will secure happiness: and suppose, in adopting this plan, we should be mistaken in the end; where is the cause of alarm on that quarter? . . .

But an objection is made to the form: the expression, We, the people, is thought improper. Permit me to ask the gentlemen who made this objection, who but the people can delegate powers? Who but the people have a right to form government? The expression is a common one, and a favorite one with me. The representatives of the people, by their authority, is a mode wholly inessential. If the objection be, that the Union ought to be not of the people, but of the state governments, then I think the choice of the former very happy and proper. What have the state governments to do with it? Were they to determine, the people would not, in that case, be the judges upon what terms it was adopted.

But the power of the Convention is doubted. What is the power? To propose, not to determine. This power of proposing was very broad; it extended to remove all defects in government: the members of that Convention, who were to consider all the defects in our general government, were not confined to any particular plan. Were they deceived? This is the proper question here. Then the question must be between this government and the Confederation. The latter is no government at all. It has been said that it has carried us, through a dangerous war, to a happy issue. Not that Confederation, but common danger, and the spirit of America, were bonds of our union: union and unanimity, and not that insignificant paper, carried us through that dangerous war. "United, we stand; divided, we fall!" echoed and reëchoed through America—from Congress to the drunken carpenter—was effectual, and procured the end of our wishes, though now forgotten by gentlemen, if such there be, who incline to let go this stronghold, to catch at feathers; for such all substituted projects may prove.

Mr. Madison then arose. . . .

Before I proceed to make some additions to the reasons which have been adduced by my honorable friend over the way, I must take the liberty to make some observations on what was said by another gentleman, (Mr. Patrick Henry.) He told us that this Constitution ought to be rejected because it endangered the public liberty, in his opinion, in many instances. Give me leave to make one answer to that observation: Let the dangers which this system is supposed to be replete with be clearly pointed out: if any dangerous and unnecessary powers be given to the general legislature, let them be plainly demonstrated; and let us not rest satisfied with general assertions of danger, without examination. If powers be necessary, apparent danger is not a sufficient reason against conceding them. He has suggested that licentiousness has seldom produced the loss of liberty; but that the tyranny of rulers has almost always effected it. Since the general civilization of mankind, I believe there are more instances of the abridgment of the freedom of the people by gradual and silent encroachments of those in power, than by violent and sudden usurpations; but, on a candid examination of history, we shall find that turbulence, violence, and abuse of power, by the majority trampling on the rights of the minority, have produced factions and commotions, which, in republics, have, more frequently than any other cause, produced despotism. If we go over the whole history of ancient and modern republics, we shall find their destruction to have generally resulted from those causes. If we consider the peculiar situation of the United States, and what are the sources of that diversity of sentiment which pervades its inhabitants, we shall find great danger to fear that the same causes may terminate here in the same fatal effects which they produced in those republics. This danger ought to be wisely guarded against. Perhaps, in the progress of this discussion it will appear that the only possible remedy for those evils, and means of preserving and protecting the principles of republicanism, will be found in that very system which is now exclaimed against as the parent of oppression.

I must confess I have not been able to find his usual consistency in the gentleman's argument on this occasion. He informs us that the people of the country are at perfect repose—that is, every man enjoys the fruits of his labor peaceably and securely, and that every thing is in perfect tranquillity and safety. I wish sincerely, sir, this were true. If this be their happy situation, why has every state acknowledged the contrary? Why were deputies from all the states sent to the general Convention? Why have complaints of national and individual distresses been echoed and reechoed throughout the continent? Why has our general government been so shamefully disgraced, and our Constitution violated? Wherefore have laws been made to authorize a change, and wherefore are we now assembled here? A federal government is formed for the protection of its individual members. Ours has attacked itself with impunity. Its authority has been disobeyed and despised. I think I perceive a glaring inconsistency in another of his arguments. He complains of this Constitution, because it requires the consent of at least three fourths of the states to introduce amendments which shall be necessary for the happiness of the people. The assent of so many he urges as too great an obstacle to the admission of salutary amendments, which, he strongly insists, ought to be at the will of a bare majority. We hear this argument, at the very moment we are called upon to assign reasons for proposing a constitution which puts it in the power of nine states to abolish the present inadequate, unsafe, and pernicious Confederation! In the first case, he asserts that a majority ought to have the power of altering the government, when found to be inadequate to the security of public happiness. In the last case, he affirms that even three fourths of the community have not a right to alter a government which experience has proved to be subversive of national felicity! nay, that the most necessary and urgent alterations cannot be made without the absolute unanimity of all the states! Does not the thirteenth article of the Confederation expressly require that no alteration shall be made without the unanimous consent of all the states? Could any thing in theory be more perniciously improvident and injudicious than this submission of the will of the majority to the most trifling minority? Have not experience and practice actually manifested this theoretical inconvenience to be extremely impolitic? Let me mention one fact, which I conceive must carry conviction to the mind of any one: the smallest state in the Union has obstructed every attempt to reform the government; that little member has repeatedly disobeyed and counteracted the general authority; nay, has even supplied the enemies of its country with provisions. Twelve states had agreed to certain improvements which were proposed, being thought absolutely necessary to preserve the existence of the general government; but as these improvements, though really indispensable, could not, by the Confederation, be introduced into it without the consent of every state, the refractory dissent of that little state prevented their adoption. The inconveniences resulting from this requisition, of unanimous concurrence in alterations in the Confederation, must be known to every member in this Convention; it is therefore needless to remind them of them. Is it not self-evident that a trifling minority ought not to bind the majority? Would not foreign influence be exerted with facility over a small minority? Would the honorable gentleman agree to continue the most radical defects in the old system, because the petty state of Rhode Island would not agree to remove them? . . .

Charles Cotesworth Pinckney
and James Wilson

The Meaning of the Slave Trade Provision

One of Miller's arguments is that the Founding Fathers were canny politicians who knew the hopes and fears of their constituents. The following speeches were made by two members of the 1787 convention, in defense of the same clause of the Constitution—the provision that Congress could not prohibit the international slave trade until after 1808. In the first speech, Charles Cotesworth Pinckney defends the clause to a pro-slavery audience in his home state of South Carolina. In the second, Pennsylvanian James Wilson tells his audience why they should accept the provision. As you read the two speeches, note the extent to which each man defends the clause as the best compromise that could be achieved in the circumstances. Does this seem consistent with Miller's way of characterizing the convention? If you thought the Constitution was a bundle of just such compromises, would you still regard it as a great document?

South Carolina

Gen. Charles Cotesworth Pinckney . . . then said he would make a few observations on the objections which the gentleman had thrown out on the restrictions that might be laid on the African trade after the year 1808. On this point your delegates had to contend with the religious and political prejudices of the Eastern and Middle States, and with the interested and inconsistent opinion of Virginia, who was warmly opposed to our importing more slaves. I am of the same opinion now as I was two years ago, when I used the expressions the gentleman has quoted—that, while there remained one acre of swamp-land uncleared of South Carolina, I would raise my voice against restricting the importation of negroes. I am as thoroughly convinced as that gentleman is, that the nature of our climate, and the flat, swampy situation of our country, obliges us to cultivate our lands with negroes, and that without them South Carolina would soon be a desert waste.

You have so frequently heard my sentiments on this subject, that I need

From Jonathan Elliott, ed., *The Debates in the Several State Conventions on the Adoption of the Federal Constitution* (Washington, D.C.: Jonathan Elliott, 1836), Vol. 2, p. 452; Vol. 4, pp. 285–286.

not now repeat them. It was alleged, by some of the members who opposed an unlimited importation, that slaves increased the weakness of any state who admitted them; that they were a dangerous species of property, which an invading enemy could easily turn against ourselves and the neighboring states; and that, as we were allowed a representation for them in the House of Representatives, our influence in government would be increased in proportion as we were less able to defend ourselves. "Show some period," said the members from the Eastern States, "when it may be in our power to put a stop, if we please, to the importation of this weakness, and we will endeavor, for your convenience, to restrain the religious and political prejudices of our people on this subject." The Middle States and Virginia made us no such proposition; they were for an immediate and total prohibition. We endeavored to obviate the objections that were made in the best manner we could, and assigned reasons for our insisting on the importation, which there is no occasion to repeat, as they must occur to every gentleman in the house: a committee of the states was appointed in order to accommodate this matter, and, after a great deal of difficulty, it was settled on the footing recited in the Constitution.

By this settlement we have secured an unlimited importation of negroes for twenty years. Nor is it declared that the importation shall be then stopped; it may be continued. We have a security that the general government can never emancipate them, for no such authority is granted; and it is admitted, on all hands, that the general government has no powers but what are expressly granted by the Constitution, and that all rights not expressed were reserved by the several states. We have obtained a right to recover our slaves in whatever part of America they may take refuge, which is a right we had not before. In short, considering all circumstances, we have made the best terms for the security of this species of property it was in our power to make. We would have made better if we could; but, on the whole, I do not think them bad.

Pennsylvania

Mr. JAMES WILSON. . . . With respect to the clause restricting Congress from prohibiting the *migration or importation of such persons* as any of the states now existing shall think proper to admit, prior to the year 1808, the honorable gentleman says that this clause is not only dark, but intended to grant to Congress, for that time, the power to admit the importation of *slaves.* No such thing was intended. But I will tell you what was done, and it gives me high pleasure that so much was done. Under the present Confederation, the states may admit the importation of slaves as long as they please; but by this article, after the year 1808, the Congress will have power to prohibit such importation, notwithstanding the disposition of any state to the contrary. I consider this as laying the foundation for banishing slavery out of this country; and though the period is more distant than I could wish, yet it will produce the same kind, gradual change, which was pursued in Pennsylvania. It is with much satisfaction I view this power in the general government, whereby they may lay an interdiction on this reproachful trade: but an immediate advantage is also obtained; for a tax or duty may be imposed on such importation, not exceeding ten dollars for each person; and this, sir, operates as a partial prohibition; it was all that could be obtained. I am sorry it was no more; but from this I think there is reason to hope, that yet a few years and it will be prohibited altogether; and in the mean time, the *new* states which are to be formed will be under the control of Congress in this particular, and slaves will never be introduced amongst them. . . .

Designing the Nation's Capitol

Once the Constitution was ratified, the creative effort was not over with. It was followed by another bold plan, the creation of the city of rulers that the world today knows as Washington. Within four years of the ratification of the Constitution, the leaders of the new government, who met first at New York and then at Philadelphia, made plans to turn wetlands along the Potomac into the nation's capital. The plans were no less detailed than the Constitution, and they provide eloquent testimony about the kind of government that many of the Founding Fathers envisaged.

Consider, for example, the Capitol building, the home of the Senate and the House of Representatives, and until 1935 of the Supreme Court. In 1791 George Washington and other political leaders agreed with the French architect Pierre Charles L'Enfant that the Capitol should be located at the crest of Jenkins' Hill, the highest point in the envisioned city. And in 1792 the government offered a prize of $500 and a piece of property in the District of Columbia to whomever submitted the best design.

Below are some of the designs that were offered. You will notice that the designers, most of whom were rank amateurs, emphasized symmetry, domes, monumentality. Why do you think they did that? And why do you think the nation's leaders chose William Thornton's design as best suited for a community of republican rulers? Etienne Hallet's plan as second best? What do the winning plans tell you about the kind of government that the Founding Fathers envisaged?

This design, submitted by Samuel Dobie, included three enormous statues on the building's roof. *Library of Congress.*

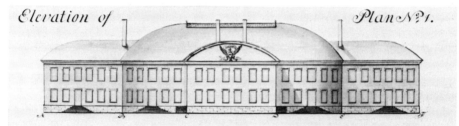

Contemporaries felt that the design submitted by Charles Wintersmith lacked elegance. *The Maryland Historical Society.*

Étienne Hallet's plan placed second in the competition, but he was chosen to supervise the actual construction according to Thornton's design. *Library of Congress.*

James Diamond capped his building with an enormous weathercock. *Library of Congress.*

William Thornton's design was praised by President Washington for its "Grandeur, Simplicity and Convenience." It called for a central rotunda flanked by two identical wings, one for the Senate and the other for the House of Representatives. The above drawing is a slightly revised version of his first plan, which has been lost. *Library of Congress.*

William Thornton. *Library of Congress.*

9

Federalists and Republicans

The Constitution created only the framework of the new government. The details still had to be worked out. At first the Federalists, under Presidents George Washington and John Adams, tried to build a consolidated and aristocratic nation. They were convinced that the fear of disunity and anarchy was so great that Americans would accept almost any sort of strong national government. They were dead wrong. Their goals ran against the grain of the revolutionary impulse. Indeed, they were so out of touch with the realities of American life that they came close to provoking a second revolution. Only the electoral victory of the Republican opposition in 1800 ended this threat.

The very existence of a Republican opposition pointed to a serious problem on which the Constitution had been totally silent: the problem of political parties. To the men who wrote the Constitution, the idea of parties and factions was an evil one—as evil as the idea of democracy. Their conception of a successful government was one in which there *were* no factions. To a few sophisticated men, especially to James Madison, faction seemed to be an inevitable feature of human society. But, Madison believed, a well-framed government was one in which faction could *not* express itself in party.

The problem with political parties, of course, was that they led to disunity and disruption. They fed the ambitions of unscrupulous men. They gave demagogues a chance to excite the masses, and so led toward mob rule and an anarchic democracy. Madison, in a famous paper in the series known as *The Federalist,* had even argued that the republic ought to be large, so that no faction could easily seize control of it. In short, the leaders of the first period of American history were still committed to the idea of a society in which status and deference were more fundamental than ideology or faction.

In his famous Farewell Address, Washington spent much more time warning against the spirit of faction and party than he did trying to persuade his fellow citizens not to become involved in entangling alliances with European powers. And the warning was well taken. Washington, during his second administration especially, had watched while a faction developed into a party, a party of opposition to the very policies that he and his successor, John Adams, pursued.

The opposition leader was Thomas Jefferson. He has been portrayed most vividly as an ideologist who feared both national and presidential power; who believed that states' rights should be predominant; that the small farmer was the foundation of the good society; that the threat to American life was the growth of big cities, industrialization, national banking, an urban proletariat, and a consolidated national government; that the best governments were those that governed least. He has also been portrayed as a revolutionary dreamer who made radical statements such as this about the need for revolutions every twenty years or so: "The tree of liberty must be refreshed from time to time with the blood of patriots and tyrants. It is its natural manure."

Interpretive Essay

James MacGregor Burns

Jefferson and the Strategy of Parties

There was another side to Jefferson. And that was Jefferson the clever politician who first won a seat in the Virginia House of Burgesses at age twenty-six and then went on to serve in one office after another—including governor of Virginia, secretary of state, vice president, and president. And it is this side of Jefferson that James MacGregor Burns, a professor of political science at Williams College, emphasizes in the following selection. According to Burns, Jefferson not only created the first national party, but also used it to overturn the system of checks and balances that his friend James Madison had written into the Constitution. Instead of weakening presidential power, which he preached, he actually strengthened it

and dominated Congress through his control of the first Republican party.

How does a great party get started? Some historians have pictured the founding of the first Republican party as a stroke of genius on Jefferson's part. Like a commander surveying the battlefield, it is said, he rallied people and politicians behind him, built a mighty national machine, and swept on to win the presidential battle of 1800. What really happened was more complicated but no less instructive for understanding American politics, nor less testimonial to Jefferson's key role. Actually, the first Republican party grew out of a series of gropings and blunderings, small ambitions and great issues, petty politics and superb national leadership. And it originally grew up in Congress, not around the Presidency.

Most Americans in the early 1790's did not want parties. Not only the exalted George Washington, who was trying to be President of all the people, but Jefferson, Hamilton, and Madison railed against the spirit of party. "If I could not go to heaven but with a party," Jefferson exclaimed, "I would not go there at all." An anonymous Philadelphian spoke for many Americans when he wrote in a local paper: "We want no *Ticket Mongers:* let every citizen exercise his own judgment, and we shall have a good representation—intrigue, favoritism, cabal and party will be at rest." Party stood for selfish faction and petty maneuver. But the impulse toward political organization was inexorable. As Madison said, men tend to be selfish and aggressive; they attach themselves to one another and to ambitious leaders; and they find plenty of things to quarrel about, sensible and silly. Factions spring up behind leaders contending for place and power. Much of the fighting occurs on a darkling plain of ignorance, but not all is confusion. What gives order to the combat is the structure of political and governmental offices. Around every desired position, administrative, legislative, judicial, develop little clusters of aspirants and their circles of supporters.

Since the Constitution of 1787 set up a new system of national offices—President, Senator, and so on—it might be expected that the first tendencies toward national parties would focus on contests for national offices, especially for Congress and the Presidency. Such was the case. But since Washington was "above politics," the first national party contests revolved around battles for seats in the House and Senate. During most of Washington's first term, congressional politics was personal, fluid, placid on the surface, and sometimes vicious underneath. Politicians ran for Congress and voted in Congress on their own. Such a wholly individualistic politics could not last; inevitably politicians would join forces with like-minded men in order to concert and broaden their power. The only question was when and how.

The man who unwittingly threw down the gage of party battle was

Washington's Secretary of the Treasury, Alexander Hamilton. While his chief denounced politics, Hamilton went about the tricky business of organizing congressional support for the Administration's measures—for the national bank, assumption of state debts by the national government, federal subsidies, and the other parts of Hamilton's famous "system." For the New Yorker saw that his program could not be enacted without pressure and persuasion and hard bargaining from the top. If Washington would not provide political leadership, Hamilton would. He forced through his program, but only at the price of uniting the opposition.

The heart of that opposition was the Virginia delegation in Congress, and the head of it was James Madison. As Washington's first term came to an end, the alert Virginian was busy converting the anti-Federalist irregulars in Congress into an organized phalanx. People even spoke of the "Madison party." The anti-Federalists were not content simply to oppose Hamilton's measures. They organized forays against his position in the Administration. They set up a Ways and Means committee in the House to clip his financial powers. They backed Jefferson's successful effort to have the Mint shifted from Hamilton's department to his own. They swore they would topple Hamilton from his "fiscal throne."

Foreign affairs widened the breach. During the mid-1790's Americans were taking sides over the French Revolution. The fall of the Bastille set off a wave of sympathy in revolution-minded America, checked later by news of the execution of Louis XVI and of other excesses. As hostilities flared up between Paris and London, Republicans tended to attach themselves to the French cause, Federalists to the English. And both domestic and foreign conflicts were interlaced with disputes over the very style of government. Republicans charged their foes with secretly wanting monarchy under Washington and Adams; Federalists denounced the Republicans for seeking to subordinate the executive to a radical legislature.

Soon the political winds were full of epithets. The Republicans charged that the Federalists were not really Federalists but Monarchists (or Monocrats), Tories, Royalists, aristocrats, the British party. Federalists countered that Republicans were not really Republicans but Democrats, Jacobins, and Frenchified. By early 1797, when Washington gave his farewell speech against parties, the language of party dialogue was complete.

It was a time of numerous newspapers—Philadelphia alone had twelve—and many of these threw themselves into the party battle. Some were the kept organs of a party leader. Hamilton gave printing patronage to the Federalist *Gazette of the United States* and loaned money to its editor, John Fenno. Disgusted by the "hymns & lauds chanted" by this "paper of pure Toryism," Jefferson, with Madison's help, asked a New York journalist, Philip Freneau, to set up a Republican newspaper in Philadelphia. Jefferson sweetened his bid with the offer of a clerkship for Freneau, official advertising for the paper, and inside information from the State Department. Soon the *National Gazette* was fulminating against Hamilton, who complained indignantly to Washington about Jefferson's hireling.

Alarmed at Hamilton's influence, tired by political abuse and squabbles, Jefferson quit Washington's cabinet at the end of 1793 and returned to the tranquillity of Monticello. He left Madison in full command of the Republican party in Congress. During the mid-nineties, with the expected departure of the nonpartisan Washington from the presidency and the likelihood of a party fight over the succession, the Republicans in Congress were becoming more organized. Although party unity was still rough, party lines were tightening in Senate and House. "No disciplined Prussians or enthusiastic French, adhere more firmly to their ranks than the differing members of Congress to their respective standards," a South Carolinian complained, with some exaggeration. Madison was a brilliant congressional tactician, keeping in touch with Jefferson and other Republican leaders outside Congress, planning parliamentary strategy, holding his ranks firm through persuasion and bargaining, occasionally calling his men into caucus.

But the Republican party was not just a group in Congress; gradually during the 1790's it built electoral strength in the states and districts. Earlier members of Congress had won office through small, informal groups of friends and neighbors, with no extensive organization in the modern sense. As the party cleavage widened, members of Congress sent out increasingly partisan circulars to their constituents. In 1796 congressmen in several states campaigned on party tickets. Sometimes the tickets bore partisan labels, sometimes not, but the party groupings behind the ticket were made clear to all. Madison gave some direction to the effort; one of his best grass-roots organizers and reporters was House Clerk John Beckley (who was promptly sacked when the Federalists regained control of the House). Even more, the Republican party in Congress dominated the party's presidential effort in 1796. Meeting in informal caucus, its leaders easily agreed on Jefferson as their presidential nominee. The sage of Monticello was not consulted.

By the end of Washington's second term, in short, America had its first national party in the Republicans. Significantly, it was a congressional party, organized in Congress, around members of Congress and candidates for Congress, with rough party discipline, and reaching out to embrace networks of followers in the constituencies. The Federalists had identity and some organization too, but it was limited; the Federalists were more likely to assume their right to office and less inclined to hustle at the polls. (After the fatal Federalist setback of 1800 Hamilton proposed that the party organize local clubs, debate issues, and set up real party machinery, all under national party control, but by then it was too late for both Hamilton and the Federalists.) It was the Republican party in Congress under Madison that pioneered in America's early experiments in nationwide organization.

At this point Jefferson's role was uncertain. As Secretary of State he had quietly led the Republican cause: not only had he got the *National Gazette* started under Freneau, but he had encouraged Republican politicians to seek office; he had stimulated Republican pamphleteering against Hamilton; and on his own he had disseminated Republican philosophy and policies. But when he quit Washington's cabinet in 1793 he also quit his role as party chieftain and left everything to Madison. He wanted Madison to run for President in 1796; Republicans feared, however, that their congressional leader could not carry the crucial mid-Atlantic states. So they ran a reluctant Jefferson who, after sitting the campaign out at Monticello, came in second to John Adams and hence became the new Vice-President. The congressional Republicans were not yet strong enough to elect a President.

Like vice-presidents ever since, Jefferson found his position an awkward one for directing a national party. But now he was back in the swirl of politics, and he could not escape the rising political temper. "Men who have been intimate all their lives," he noticed, "cross the streets to avoid meeting, and turn their heads another way, lest they should be obliged to touch their hats." Madison had retired from Congress, so political intelligence between the two men ran in the opposite direction. In Philadelphia Jefferson led the Republican congressional opposition to Adams and tried to get a new paper started; in Monticello he talked with state politicos that passed by, and corresponded with others.

That Jefferson still had no clear idea where he and his party were headed, however, was shown by a sharp change in his political strategy in 1798. This was his leadership in drafting the Virginia and Kentucky resolutions. A protest against Adams' alien and sedition laws, these resolutions by state legislatures declared the Federalist measures unconstitutional and—far more important—affirmed the right of states to judge for themselves the constitutionality of acts of Congress. There was even the hint of a right of secession. The resolutions failed; to most informed Americans they were a long step backward toward the weak Articles of Confederation that the Virginians had taken the lead in abandoning. They were the Madisonian formula but carried to such an extreme as to be a caricature. They were the reverse of the strategy of party opposition, which assumed that the way to overcome a bad national administration is not to play the politics of Chinese warlords and pull out but to win enough votes at the next election to drive the administration out of power.

The Jeffersonians were still floundering. It was not conscious political planning but the election of 1800 that impelled them to create a great national party.

Jefferson Builds a Party

When Jefferson returned to Philadelphia shortly before New Year's, 1800, he was already planning to run for President. Gone were the doubts and vacillations of earlier days. Bombarded by the Republicans and undermined by Hamilton and his anti-Adams guerrillas, the Adams administration was an easy target. But to Jefferson the Federalists still seemed formidable. To be sure, he considered them inferior in numbers, comprising mainly, he said, "old refugees & tories," British and American merchants, speculators in public funds, federal jobholders, a "numerous and noisy tribe" of office hunters, and "nervous persons, whose languid fibres have more analage with a passive than active state of things." But the Federalists, he noted, were concentrated in the cities and hence could influence government in a way that the Republicans, dispersed in the back country, could not easily overcome.

Jefferson did not campaign across the country, as presidential candidates do today. Stumping was against his nature, and against the custom of the day. Indeed, the masses of voters often did not need to be approached directly, for in some states the presidential electors were not chosen directly by the voters, as they are today, but by state legislatures. Jefferson's presidential campaign was in large part an effort to elect state legislators who would choose the right electors to pick the right man for President.

During 1800 Jefferson decisively asserted control over the Republican party. He had already drawn up a set of party policies—frugal government, reduced national debt, smaller national defense, "free commerce with all nations" but "political connections with none," freedom of religion, press, and speech—and during the year his followers used these policies as a rough party platform in their own campaigns. Jefferson did not answer Federalist charges, however, "for while I would be engaged with one," he said, "they would publish twenty new ones." His tactic was to out-organize the Federalists, not merely out-debate them.

Jefferson's main strategy, however, was simply being Jefferson—Jefferson the revolutionary, the framer of the Declaration of Independence, the author of the Virginia statute for religious freedom, the intellectual leader and symbol of the Virginia Republicans, the great successor to Franklin in Paris, the Secretary of State, the philosopher and politician. Actually Jefferson was a complicated man, so mixed and shifting in his point of view as to appear irresolute to his friends, arrantly hypocritical to his foes, and a puzzle to later historians. But at the time the Jefferson image was glowingly clear, especially to the back-country people living in a long crooked swath from the interior of Maine through the Green Mountains and the Berkshires down the long uplands to his own Virginia country and then on to the inland South and the Southwest.

But Jefferson realized—and this was his supreme achievement as a party leader—that it was not enough to solicit the old centers of Republican support. He must broaden his appeal in order to reach into the cities. He played down his earlier warnings about the city mobs, while his Republican supporters in the cities played up his opposition to speculation, high taxes, usury, British seizure of American ships, and similar matters that vexed mechanics, sailors, and other city dwellers.

Indeed, the first great election test, according to Jefferson's calculations, would come in the nation's largest city, New York. At the end of April 1800, New York state would elect its legislature, which in turn would choose a slate of electors that might hold the balance of power between Jefferson and Adams in the electoral college. Sizing up the political terrain, Jefferson sounded much like any political analyst a century and a half later: "If the city election of New York is in favor of the Republican ticket," he wrote

Madison, "the issue will be Republican; if the federal ticket for the city of New York prevails, the probabilities will be in favor of a federal issue because it would then require a Republican vote both from New Jersey and Pennsylvania to preponderate against New York, on which we could not count with any confidence." In charge of the Republican group in Manhattan was Aaron Burr. Jefferson had always been a bit dubious about the slick New Yorker, but this was no time for squeamishness. During the winter Burr made a quick trip to Philadelphia and the two men discussed strategy.

In the next three months Burr staged a masterly political campaign. He faced severe odds, for the Federalists were ably led by his old adversary, Alexander Hamilton, who had won the previous election decisively, and the Republicans were divided. Burr quietly persuaded the older party leaders to unite on one ticket of eminent local Republicans; shrewdly waited to announce his ticket until after Hamilton had pieced together an inferior one (Hamilton had shortsightedly chosen his own satellites instead of eminent Adams supporters); organized his lieutenants solidly on a ward-by-ward basis; card-indexed the voters, their political history, attitudes, and how to get them to the polls; set up committees to canvass for funds from house to house; put the heat on wealthy Republicans for bigger donations; organized rallies; enlisted in his cause the members of the Tammany Society, then a struggling fraternal group; debated publicly with Hamilton; and spent ten hours straight at the polls on the last day of the three-day election.

A superb local tactician behind a great strategic leader—Burr could hardly fail. The entire Republican ticket for the assembly carried by an average of almost 500 votes, and there was a good deal of straight-ticket voting. Word was dispatched to Jefferson in Philadelphia: "We have completely and triumphantly succeeded." Such a hubbub rose in the Senate that it had to adjourn. Federalists were downcast; Republicans exclaimed that the New York returns presaged Jefferson's success nationally.

They were right. During the summer Republican candidates for state legislature and the electoral college toured their districts and talked to crowds wherever they could find them—even "at a horse race—a cock fight—or a Methodist quarterly meeting." The Federalists, solidly based in New England, fought hard to retain the balance-of-power states, but in vain. Although nowhere else did the Republicans have an organization rivalling New York's, the backwoods seemed alive with Jeffersonian politicians who were acting with unprecedented unity and who seemed to have a bottomless supply of pamphlets and printed lists of nominees.

It was well for the Republicans that they fought as hard as they did, for in the end they gained only a narrow victory over the divided Federalists: Jefferson and Burr both won 73 electoral votes, Adams 65, General Charles Pinckney 64, and Jay one. The Jeffersonians' elation was dimmed by the tie vote between their leader and Burr. They had produced party regularity in the elections without really understanding it; now party regularity was playing a mean trick on them. The election was thrown into the strongly Federalist lameduck Congress. For thirty-five ballots the House was stalemated. Only because the Congressional Republicans stuck together while the Federalists were divided, and because Burr dared not connive with the Federalists, while Jefferson (evidently) indicated through intermediaries that he would carry on certain Federalist policies, was the Virginian able to win out on February 17, 1801.

So Jefferson was President. But would he really be *President?* He had made the Republican party into a tool for winning a presidential election. Could he continue to run the party, or would the party run him? Everything seemed to point to a period of executive weakness. No one had preached with more unction than Jefferson about the sanctity of the separation of powers and checks and balances. He had seemingly looked on his party as something to win through, rather than as something to rule through. And now he faced the Republican majority in Congress, enlarged by the election, prepared to carry out their doctrines of congressional supremacy in a weak national government. Independent, divided, jealous of their legislative powers, the congressional Republicans, after years of carping at Washington, Hamilton, and Adams, had now come into their own.

So they thought. But they underrated the steel in Jefferson's gangling frame and his knack for overlooking general principles when faced with practical politics. "What is practicable must often control what is pure theory," he said blithely, "and the habits of the governed determine in a great degree what is practicable." Not only did Jefferson accept much of the Federalist policy, such as the Bank. He went far beyond Federalists in broadening executive power. And in the Louisiana Purchase he took a step that he considered unconstitutional, telling Congress that it must ratify the agreement with Napoleon, "casting behind them Metaphysical subtleties," and throw themselves on the country for approval of the step at the next election.

What astonishing doctrine! Here was the first Republican President saying in effect that his party should support his unconstitutional act because the voters would sustain the party at the next election. It was a daring move, and wholly successful. Not only was the Louisiana Purchase magnificently vindicated in history, but Jefferson was vindicated in the presidential election of 1804, winning by 162 electoral votes to 14, while the congressional Republicans enlarged their already big majority.

Above all, it was in his leadership of Congress that Jefferson upset old Republican notions of the executive-legislative balance. Considering himself the national head of the party, he gave close and constant leadership to his forces in Congress; he personally drafted bills and had them introduced into Congress; saw to it that the men he wanted took the leadership posts in Congress; induced men he favored to run for Congress by holding out promises of advancement; made the Speaker and the floor leader of the House his personal lieutenants; changed the leadership as he saw fit; used Ways and Means and other committees as instruments of presidential control; dominated the Republican caucus in the House. In short, he took the machinery that the congressional Republicans had built up against Federalist Presidents and turned it to his own uses.

Some Republicans complained bitterly, but they were helpless. Jefferson followed every measure with a hawk's eye, applied pressure where necessary, wined and dined the legislators, and used his Cabinet members and other subordinates as his agents on the Hill. He did not crack the whip publicly, nor did he need to. He simply threw into the balance every ounce of his political, administrative, and moral power—power all the greater because Jefferson had created the electoral foundations of the party.

And he knew how to deal with his enemies, by attacking them from the rear, on their own ground. One of his foes—or so Jefferson thought— was his Vice-President, Aaron Burr. Jefferson not only denied patronage to Burr and his friends; he set out deliberately to destroy the dapper little New Yorker's power in his home state by giving patronage to Burr's adversaries there. Then Jefferson denied him re-nomination for the Vice-Presidency, completing Burr's isolation and helping, in the end, to make an adventurer out of him. John Randolph was another Republican run over by Jefferson's party machine. At first a rising star, a parliamentary leader and chairman of the potent Ways and Means Committee, the stormy young Virginian turned against the President. At the right moment Jefferson simply eased him out of the chairmanship, and then out of the leadership. A few years later Jefferson's lieutenant and son-in-law, John W. Eppes, took up residence in Randolph's district and defeated him for Congress; whether Jefferson's fine hand was behind this *coup de grâce* is for once hard to say.

There were, of course, limits to Jefferson's power. Before leaving office John Adams had carefully packed the judicial branch with staunch Federalists. The enemy had taken refuge in the courts, Republicans noted, but how much power would they have? The right of judicial review had not yet been established in the national government; if the courts tried to invalidate good Jeffersonian measures, Republicans calculated, the President would simply defy the Federalist judges. But the Republicans underestimated the new Federalist Chief Justice, John Marshall—surprisingly, since he was a Virginian. In the famous case *Marbury* v. *Madison,* he invalidated not a great Republican measure but a minor part of a bill that had given certain technical powers to the Supreme Court. It was a brilliant stroke, for Marshall set forth the vital precedent of judicial review, but in such a way that Jefferson could not retaliate, for there was not even a specific court order that he could refuse to obey. The President had no better luck in his impeachment of Supreme Court Justice Samuel Chase, an intemperate Federalist propagandist. Conviction of Chase would have prepared the way for an attack upon Marshall, but the Senate Republicans could not muster the necessary two-thirds vote to convict Chase.

Marshall himself had astutely predicted at the outset that Jefferson would repudiate old Republican principles of congressional supremacy. "Mr. Jefferson appears to me to be a man," Marshall wrote Hamilton, "who will embody himself with the House of Representatives . . . and become the leader of that party which is about to constitute itself the majority of the legislature." What Marshall did not see was that in doing so Jefferson would augment rather than weaken the Presidency. Because Jefferson repudiated the anti-national ideas of the old guard of the Republican party, because he adopted the strong legislative methods of the "presidential" Federalists, because he built a new Republican party to win a presidential election and then governed through it—because of all this Jefferson was the father of the first truly national Republican party, as Madison had been of the Constitution, and again like Madison, one of the grand strategists of American politics.

The Theory of Majority Rule

Timid ladies in Boston, so it is said, had hid their Bibles under their beds on the eve of Jefferson's Inauguration. They had been frightened by Federalist alarms that March 4, 1801, would usher in a hideous new revolution with "the loathesome steam of human victims" offered in sacrifice to a new Goddess of Reason. As steady a man as the new Chief Justice, John Marshall, had written on Inauguration morning that the democrats were divided into "speculative theorists & absolute terrorists," and he was not sure in which class to put the new President. But Marshall, unlike the ladies in Boston, would attend the Inaugural, since he had to administer the oath. By the afternoon of March 4 he was feeling much relieved, for the Inaugural speech had struck him as judicious and conciliatory.

Despite the fierceness of the election contest, Jefferson had told the crowd, all would now abide the result. "All, too, will bear in mind this sacred principle, that though the will of the majority is in all cases to prevail, that will to be rightful must be reasonable; that the minority possess their equal rights, which equal law must protect, and to violate would be oppression. . . ." Events abroad had divided Americans, he granted. "But every difference of opinion is not a difference of principle. We have called by different names brethren of the same principle. We are all Republicans, we are all Federalists. If there be any among us who would wish to dissolve this Union or to change its republican form, let them stand undisturbed as monuments of the safety with which error of opinion may be tolerated when reason is left free to combat it."

"We are all Republicans, we are all Federalists"—these words must have fallen like soothing music on Marshall's ear. And ever since, the famous phrase has been quoted as a lofty and patriotic expression of nonpartisanship. Actually, Jefferson was making a partisan gambit. Recognizing that his election majority had been perilously thin, he saw that he must detach moderate Federalists from the extremists, keep the support of his own party, and thus consolidate his position. He was not pretending that he would follow Federalist principles or even neutral ones; most of his speech called for good Republican measures. He was arguing that no deep division of principle separated him from moderate Federalists.

The Inaugural speech was, indeed, an almost perfect expression of the practical operation of majority rule. The will of the majority must always prevail, Jefferson said, but it must be and would be reasonable. The Republicans would not press extreme party doctrines. Opponents—even those preaching disunion—would be left free. Jefferson was implying that in order to hold and expand his majority, he must embrace policies so broad and so moderate that no minority party or group would be imperiled. We do not need to infer Jefferson's strategy only from his public speeches. In letter after letter he made his plan crystal clear—to bring over moderate Federalists into the Republican camp and thus to create an invincible majority behind the new Administration. Jefferson had an ingenious nomenclature for this strategy. Moderate Federalists he termed "Republican Federalists," and the radicals in his own party he called "Sweeping Republicans." Jefferson served as umpire, connector, and ultimately as unifier of the two groups, as the 1804 triumph proved.

It was Jefferson's actions, however, more than his words, that revealed the anatomy of majority rule. On the one hand he carried on many of the more moderate Federalist policies; and despite Republican grumbling he left in office Federalists who were not extremely partisan or "monarchical." On the other hand, he put good Republican measures through Congress and saw to it that his own loyal followers were rewarded as much as possible. But the high point of Jefferson's majoritarianism, as we have seen, came in the Louisiana Purchase. When the chips were down, when a great decision had to be made and pressed quickly, Jefferson violated congressional rights, by-passed accepted constitutional processes, refused to go through the long process of a constitutional amendment, and threw himself and his party on the mercy of the new popular majority that he was building up. . . .

To operate properly majority rule required a reliable mechanism: a vigorous, competitive party, under strong leadership. To be sure, majority rule in one sense is not the same as a strong two-party system; the liquid, ever-changing majorities, embracing different coalitions, that form and re-form in a New England town meeting, a city council, or the French Assembly, can do so apart from durable party lines. But effective majority rule on a national scale in a continental nation demands a durable popular majority organized by a leader who can depend on his following in moments of need, as in Jefferson's case. This makes the national majority something more than a mere expedient, a mere holding company for a collection of minorities. Moreover, the majority party—and the opposition that hopes to supplant it—must be competitive; if either one forsakes victory in order to stick to principle, as the Federalists did after the turn of the century, it threatens the whole mechanism of majority rule. Majoritarian strategy assumes that in the end politicians will rise above principle in order to win an election.

Madison's system demanded a reliable mechanism too: interlocking gears of government, each one responding to different thrusts originating in different groups of the electorate. To get the gears to mesh demanded endless bargaining and adjusting among the groups who had their hands on the gears—and hence demanded high-level negotiators who could deal with group leaders. It also meant that government action could be feeble and halting, as agreements among hostile groups might be overly compromised and meaningless. Madison's formula, like Jefferson's, could be abused—especially if one group became so adamant and rigid that it refused to bargain.

So much—for the moment—for the competing formulas. The important point is that by the end of Jefferson's second term the nation was trying to operate both systems. Would such a hybrid work?

The Checking and Balancing of James Madison

James Madison succeeded Jefferson as President in March 1809 and promptly ran into trouble. The big Republican majority in Congress, which Jefferson had barely been able to hold together at the end, now began to get out of hand. The machinery that Jefferson had used to control Congress—the Speakership, floor leadership, caucus, committees—was now used by the congressional party to thwart and sometimes to control the President.

Madison was not allowed even to construct a Cabinet of his own choosing. He wanted to appoint the talented Albert Gallatin, Jefferson's Secretary of the Treasury, as Secretary of State, but congressional Republicans compelled him to keep Gallatin where he was and to select as ranking Secretary the incompetent brother of an influential Senator. Four years later the same faction forced Gallatin out of the Treasury against Madison's will. The power of the Senate to ratify executive appointments—a power that the Father of the Constitution had once seen as a check against presidential oppression—was now being used against Madison himself.

Soon Jefferson's whole system of legislative leadership was crumbling under his successor. During Madison's first two years no Republican group in Congress was able to dominate legislation; rather the old Jeffersonian majority fell into factions strong enough only to defeat Administration measures. Madison's Vice-President, George Clinton, was unfriendly to him; James Monroe had wanted the Presidency and was still sulking; John Randolph returned to the House to head a faction of Old Guard Republicans, the Quids. Gleefully—and correctly—a Federalist predicted that "though there may not be a Federal majority in the House against (Madison), there will be one composed of Federalists, Monroeites and Clintonians. And the D—l would be in it, if we could not handle Mr. Madison then." Within a few months Madison was complaining to Jefferson that Congress was in an "unhinged state."

Madison's great failing was that he refused to be the hinge. When the recharter of the National Bank came up, he let Gallatin support it but refused himself to put pressure on Congress or even take a public stand. The Senate split evenly on the bill, and Vice-President Clinton cast the deciding ballot against the Administration. Heartsick, Gallatin submitted his resignation to the President in a letter that deserves extensive quotation, for it described many Administrations yet to come:

". . . In a government organized like that of the United States, a govern-

ment not too strong for affecting its principal object,—the protection of national rights against foreign aggressions . . . ,—it appears to me that not
only capacity and talents in the Administration, but also a perfect heartfelt
cordiality among its members, are essentially necessary to command the public
confidence and to produce the requisite union of views and action between
the several branches of government. In at least one of these points your
present Administration is defective, and the effects, already sensibly felt, become every day more extensive and fatal. New subdivisions and personal
factions, equally hostile to yourself and to the general welfare, daily acquire
additional strength. Measures of vital importance have been and are defeated;
every operation . . . is prevented or impeded; the embarrassments of government, great as from foreign causes they already are, are unnecessarily increased;
public confidence in the public councils and in the Executive is impaired,
and every day seems to increase every one of these evils." Madison was
able to keep Gallatin in the Treasury for another two years, but the latter's
fears for the "administration party," as the Madison faction of Republicans
was called, were soon vindicated.

The midterm congressional elections in 1810 produced a tidal wave of
new Congressmen, many of them Westerners bent on a tougher policy toward
England. Their leader was Henry Clay of Kentucky, whom they promptly
chose as Speaker of the House. Clay was a new breed in the Speaker's chair:
young, independent, militant, and commanding. At the rostrum he was not
merely an umpire; he was a political leader who took clear positions on
questions before the House, voted even when there was not a tie and manipu-
lated the rules to suit his needs; managed the debate; incessantly pressured
the members on and off the floor; and organized committees as he wished,
not as the President wished. This dazzling new chief of the congressional
Republicans simply supplied from the rostrum the leadership that Madison
would not provide from the White House. Soon he had wrested the initiative
from the President.

The judgment of history is harsh. Madison "could write a constitution
of divided powers," Herbert Agar has summed it up, "but he could not
administer one."

Why could not Madison duplicate Jefferson's success? Was it because he
was weak, soft, just a "withered little apple-john," as his enemies said? But
this was the same Madison who had tenaciously steered his measures through
earlier legislatures, who had impressed the "demi-Gods" of Philadelphia (as
Jefferson called them) with the strength of his ideas, who had a rare understanding of politicians' ambitions and passions. Was it lack of political skill?
Evidently not; Madison was a resourceful legislative politician who knew all
the tactics of parliamentary chieftains. The reasons lie deeper and bring us
back to the competing strategies of politics.

For one thing, Madison wanted less from the national government than
Jefferson finally did. Logically, one can believe in a relatively strong President
while opposing a strong national government. Practically, the two go together;
an active Presidency has always meant an expansion of national power. Jeffer-

son, above all a pragmatist, was willing to forsake his old preference for checks and balances in order to do what must be done. Madison, a supreme theorist, was not willing to forsake his basic principles in order to do what he was not sure had to be done.

Secondly, the different careers of the two men influenced their presidential effectiveness. While Madison may not have been politically inept, his earlier political influence had been largely legislative. Jefferson's had been mainly executive; as governor of Virginia he had had a particularly harrowing time with the state legislature. He had learned what an executive must do to protect himself. Without drawing the line too sharp, we can say that Jefferson's instinct as President was to master the legislators, using both the carrot and the stick. Madison was a negotiator and bargainer, a behind-the-scenes manipulator— qualities necessary but not adequate for the Presidency. He demonstrated early that congressional experience does not guarantee that a President will know how to master Congress.

Finally, Madison's political situation was different from Jefferson's. He inherited his predecessor's mantle but not the power relationships that Jefferson had developed. Jefferson had built a "presidential" party rooted in the elector- ate; he could deal with Congressmen on superior terms because he had a political base in their own states that rivaled theirs. Hence he was able to curb men like Burr and Randolph, for he had the kind of power that politicians most respect—power in the electorate. Madison had been a good congressional leader but his strength rested on his ability to negotiate with independent men. And of course he lacked the older man's vast moral authority and nationwide appeal.

The whole story offers many ironies: the Republicans denouncing the Federalist methods of executive influence and then taking them over; Jefferson, whose theories of limited government are still quoted in behalf of every cause, repudiating them in the face of necessity; the Federalists, in opposition, turning to states' rights, congressional supremacy, and other governmental checks that once they had spurned; Madison finally checkmated by his own formulas. But the supreme irony, for our purposes, was that the Madisonian system, which above all aimed at balance, moderation, adjustment, and a harmony of interests, was soon to be perverted by extremists into a caricature of itself, and to help produce a tragic disruption of government and breaking of the nation.

But we must not dismiss Madison too cavalierly. He was no less a great theoretician for having been a second-rate President. To be sure, Jefferson turned his system upside down, but not for many years, if ever, would any other President prove as effective as the great Virginian in organizing his party and Congress in defiance of the Madisonian formula. And even Jefferson, after all, had failed to take control of the judiciary—the final barricade erected by the Madisonian system against majority rule. In the years ahead the country would try to manage a strange hybrid of both majority rule and checks and balances, but Madisonian theory much more than Jeffersonian practice would dominate the strategy of American politics.

Sources

Roughhouse Politics

On all sides, Americans were apparently convinced that party politics mobilized the worst passions of men. And it did seem to be true. In the early years of the republic, party politics was a roughhouse affair. Gentlemen fought in the streets, in taverns, and even in Congress itself. Here is a cartoon lampooning a famous brawl in the House of Representatives in February, 1798. In the chair, wearing the silliest possible grin, is Speaker of the House Jonathan Dayton. The principals are, on the left, Republican Matthew Lyon, and, suitably on the right, Federalist representative Roger Griswold. What is the clerk at the lower left doing? Does any member have dignity, or are all shown as either involved or behaving almost as absurdly as Lyon and Griswold? Compare this picture with the Peale painting of Washington in Chapter 7 (p. 161). If the clothing of the members of Congress shown here identifies them with Washington as members of the republic's elite, what sets them apart? How have they failed? What connection can you draw between this cartoon and Jefferson's famous remark, after his victory in 1800, "We are all Republicans—we are all Federalists"?

Picture Collection/New York Public Library.

He in a trice struck Lyon thrice
Upon his head, enraged sir.

Who seized the tongs to ease his wrongs,
And Griswold thus engaged, sir.

Truth versus Treason

American politics eventually was founded on the assumption that contests between major political parties are not struggles for control of the nation, but are contests between two groups, *both* legitimate and loyal, *both* with valid programs, *both* with patriotic voter support. In the early stages, however, this was not the assumption at all. The governing idea was simple: one party represented the real interests of the nation, the other was so misguided as to be downright treasonable. The following documents illustrate the point nicely. In the first, Washington is leading an army to put down a rebellion in Pennsylvania—the so-called Whiskey Rebellion of 1794–1795. He is, in short, saving the country. But in this Federalist depiction, Jefferson is shown to be giving traitorous aid and comfort to the enemy. In fact, he is made to speak in pidgin French: "Stop de wheels of de gouvernement," thus supporting the Federalist opinion that Jefferson was little better than an American agent of the French Revolution. On the other hand, the Republican handbills of 1804 and 1807 depict the Federalists as *British* agents, the servants of George III, and as men who would undo the hard-won triumphs of the Revolution.

New-York Historical Society.

REPUBLICANS

Turn out, turn out and save your Country from ruin !

From an *Emperor*—from a *King*—from the iron grasp of a *British Tory Faction*—an unprincipled banditti of British speculators.   The hireling tools and emissaries of his majesty king George the 3d have thronged our city and diffused the poison of principles among us.

DOWN WITH THE TORIES, DOWN WITH THE BRITISH FACTION,

Before they have it in their power to enslave you, and reduce your families to distress by heavy taxation. Republicans want no Tribute-liars—they want no ship Ocean-liars—they want no Rufus King's for Lords —they want no Varick to lord it over them—they want no Jones for senator, who fought with the British against the Americans in time of the war.—But they want in their places such men as

Jefferson & Clinton,

who fought their Country's Battles in the year '76

New-York Historical Society.

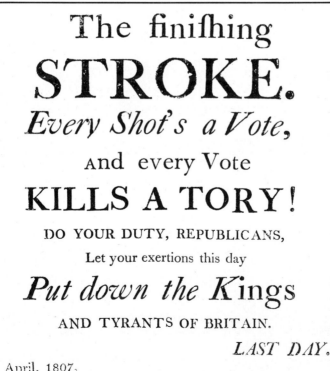

New-York Historical Society.

The finifhing
STROKE.
Every Shot's a Vote,
And every Vote
KILLS A TORY !
DO YOUR DUTY, REPUBLICANS,
Let your exertions this day
Put down the Kings
AND TYRANTS OF BRITAIN.
LAST DAY.

April, 1807.

Thomas Jefferson
and John Adams

The Nature of American Aristocracy, 1813

When John Adams lost the presidency to Jefferson in the "revolution" of 1800, he was so embittered that he refused to stay in Washington to see Jefferson inaugurated. But many years later, after Jefferson had also retired from the presidency, the two men began corresponding. The letters that follow are part of their exchange on the nature of American government, and particularly on the relationship between the idea of popular government and the equally attractive idea of aristocracy. Both men believe that aristocracy is "natural." But how does each one think that this fact ought to be reflected in government? What do you think Jefferson means by the phrase "pseudo-aristocracy"? Adams by "artificial aristocracy"? Are they talking about the same thing? If so, how do they think the republic can best be protected?

Jefferson to Adams, October 28, 1813

. . . I agree with you that there is a natural aristocracy among men. The grounds of this are virtue and talents. Formerly, bodily powers gave place among the aristoi. But since the invention of gunpowder has armed the weak as well as the strong with missile death, bodily strength, like beauty, good humor, politeness and other accomplishments, has become but an auxiliary ground of distinction. There is also an artificial aristocracy, founded on wealth and birth, without either virtue or talents; for with these it would belong to the first class. The natural aristocracy I consider as the most precious gift of nature, for the instruction, the trusts, and government of society. And indeed, it would have been inconsistent in creation to have formed man for the social state, and not to have provided virtue and wisdom enough to manage the concerns of the society. May we not even say, that that form of government is the best, which provides the most effectually for a pure selection of these natural aristoi into the offices of government? The artificial aristocracy is a mischievous ingredient in government, and provision should be made to prevent its ascendency. On the question, what is the best provision, you and I differ; but we differ as rational friends, using the free exercise of our own reason, and mutually indulging its errors. You think it best to put the

The texts of both letters are taken from Andrew A. Lipscomb and Albert E. Bergh, eds., *The Writings of Thomas Jefferson*, 20 vols. (Washington, D.C., 1905), Vol. 13, pp. 394–403; Vol. 14, pp. 1–10.

pseudo-aristoi into a separate chamber of legislation, where they may be hindered from doing mischief by their co-ordinate branches, and where, also, they may be a protection to wealth against the agrarian and plundering enterprises of the majority of the people. I think that to give them power in order to prevent them from doing mischief, is arming them for it, and increasing instead of remedying the evil. For if the co-ordinate branches can arrest their action, so may they that of the co-ordinates. Mischief may be done negatively as well as positively. Of this, a cabal in the Senate of the United States has furnished many proofs. Nor do I believe them necessary to protect the wealthy; because enough of these will find their way into every branch of the legislation, to protect themselves. From fifteen to twenty legislatures of our own, in action for thirty years past, have proved that no fears of an equalization of property are to be apprehended from them. I think the best remedy is exactly that provided by all our constitutions, to leave to the citizens the free election and separation of the aristoi from the pseudo-aristoi, of the wheat from the chaff. In general they will elect the really good and wise. In some instances, wealth may corrupt, and birth blind them; but not in sufficient degree to endanger the society.

It is probable that our difference of opinion may, in some measure, be produced by a difference of character in those among whom we live. From what I have seen of Massachusetts and Connecticut myself, and still more from what I have heard, and the character given of the former by yourself, who know them so much better, there seems to be in those two States a traditionary reverence for certain families, which has rendered the offices of the government nearly hereditary in those families. I presume that from an early period of your history, members of those families happening to possess virtue and talents, have honestly exercised them for the good of the people, and by their services have endeared their names to them. In coupling Connecticut with you, I mean it politically only, not morally. For having made the Bible the common law of their land, they seem to have modeled their morality on the story of Jacob and Laban. But although this hereditary succession to office with you, may, in some degree, be founded in real family merit, yet in a much higher degree, it has proceeded from your strict alliance of Church and State. These families are canonized in the eyes of the people on common principles, "you tickle me, and I will tickle you." In Virginia we have nothing of this. Our clergy, before the revolution, having been secured against rivalship by fixed salaries, did not give themselves the trouble of acquiring influence over the people. Of wealth, there were great accumulations in particular families, handed down from generation to generation, under the English law of entails. But the only object of ambition for the wealthy was a seat in the King's Council. All their court then was paid to the crown and its creatures. . . . Hence they were unpopular; and that unpopularity continues attached to their names. A Randolph, a Carter, or a Burwell must have great personal superiority over a common competitor to be elected by the people even at this day. At the first session of our legislature after the Declaration of Independence, we passed a law abolishing entails. And this was followed by one abolishing the privilege of primogeniture, and dividing the lands of intestates equally among all their children, or other representatives. These laws, drawn by myself, laid the axe to the foot of pseudo-aristocracy. And had another which I prepared been adopted by the legislature, our work would have been complete. It was a bill for the more general diffusion of learning. This proposed to divide every county into wards of five or six miles square, like your townships; to establish in each ward a free school for reading, writing and common arithmetic; to provide for the annual selection of the best subjects from these schools, who might receive, at the public expense, a higher degree of education at a district school; and from these district schools to select a certain number of the most promising subjects, to be completed at an university, where all the useful sciences should be taught. Worth and genius would thus have been sought out from every condition of life, and completely prepared by education for defeating the competition of wealth and birth for public trusts. . . .

With respect to aristocracy, we should further consider, that before the establishment of the American States, nothing was known to history but the man of the old world, crowded within limits either small or overcharged, and steeped in the vices which that situation generates. A government adapted to such men would be one thing; but a very different one, that for the man of these States. Here every one may have land to labor for himself, if he chooses; or, preferring the exercise of any other industry, may exact for it such compensation as not only to afford a comfortable subsistence, but wherewith to provide for a cessation from labor in old age. Every one, by his property, or by his satisfactory situation, is interested in the support of law and order. And such men may safely and advantageously reserve to themselves a wholesome control over their public affairs, and a degree of freedom, which, in the hands of the *canaille* of the cities of Europe, would be instantly perverted to the demolition and destruction of everything public and private. The history of the last twenty-five years of France, and of the last forty years in America, nay of its last two hundred years, proves the truth of both parts of this observation.

But even in Europe a change has sensibly taken place in the mind of man. Science had liberated the ideas of those who read and reflect, and the American example had kindled feelings of right in the people. An insurrection has consequently begun, of science, talents, and courage, against rank and birth, which have fallen into contempt. It has failed in its first effort, because the mobs of the cities, the instrument used for its accomplishment, debased by ignorance, poverty, and vice, could not be restrained to rational action. But the world will recover from the panic of this first catastrophe. Science is progressive, and talents and enterprise on the alert. Resort may be had to the people of the country, a more governable power from their principles and subordination; and rank, and birth, and tinsel-aristocracy will finally shrink into insignificance, even there. This, however, we have no right to meddle with. It suffices for us, if the moral and physical condition of our own citizens qualifies them to select the able and good for the direction of their government, with a recurrence of elections at such short periods as will enable them to displace an unfaithful servant, before the mischief he mediates may be irremediable. . . .

Adams to Jefferson, November 15, 1813

. . . We are now explicitly agreed upon one important point, viz., that there is a natural aristocracy among men, the grounds of which are virtue and talents. . . . But though we have agreed in one point, in words, it is not yet certain that we are perfectly agreed in sense. Fashion has introduced an indeterminate use of the word talents. Education, wealth, strength, beauty, stature, birth, marriage, graceful attitudes and motions, gait, air, complexion, physiognomy, are talents, as well as genius, science, and learning. Any one of these talents that in fact commands or influences two votes in society, gives to the man who possesses it the character of an aristocrat, in my sense of the word. Pick up the first hundred men you meet, and make a republic. Every man will have an equal vote; but when deliberations and discussions are opened, it will be found that twenty-five, by their talents, virtues being equal, will be able to carry fifty votes. Every one of these twenty-five is an aristocrat in my sense of the word; whether he obtains his one vote in addition to his own, by his birth, fortune, figure, eloquence, science, learning, craft, cunning, or even his character for good fellowship, and a *bon vivant*.

. . . Your distinction between natural and artificial aristocracy, does not appear to me founded. Birth and weight are conferred upon some men as imperiously by nature as genius, strength, or beauty. The heir to honors, and riches, and power, has often no more merit in procuring these advantages, than he has in obtaining a handsome face, or an elegant figure. When aristocracies are established by human laws, and honor, wealth and power are made hereditary by municipal laws and political institutions, then I acknowledge artificial aristocracy to commence; but this never commences till corruption in elections becomes dominant and uncontrollable. But this artificial aristocracy can never last. The ever-lasting envies, jealousies, rivalries, and quarrels among them; their cruel rapacity upon the poor ignorant people, their followers, compel them to set up Caesar, a demagogue, to be a monarch, a master; *pour mettre chacun à sa place*. Here you have the origin of all artificial aristocracy, which is the origin of all monarchies. And both artificial aristocracy and monarchy, and civil, military, political, and hierarchical despotism, have all grown out of the natural aristocracy of virtues and talents. We, to be sure, are far remote from this. Many hundred years must roll away before we shall be corrupted. Our pure, virtuous, public-spirited, federative republic will last forever, govern the globe, and introduce the perfection of man; his perfectibility being already proved by Price, Priestley, Condorcet, Rousseau, Diderot, and Godwin. Mischief has been done by the Senate of the United States. I have known and felt more of this mischief, than Washington, Jefferson, and Madison all together. But this has been all caused by the constitutional power of the Senate, in executive business, which ought to be immediately, totally, and essentially abolished. Your distinction between the aristoi and pseudo aristoi will not help the matter. I would trust one as well as the other with unlimited power. The law wisely refuses an oath as a witness in his own case, to the saint as well as the sinner. No romance would be more amusing than the history of your Virginian and our New England aristocratical families. Yet even in Rhode Island there has been no clergy, no church, and I had almost said no State, and some people say no religion. There has been a constant respect for certain old families. Fifty-seven or fifty-eight years ago, in company with Colonel, Counsellor, Judge, John Chandler, whom I have quoted before, a newspaper was brought in. The old sage asked me to look for the news from Rhode Island, and see how the elections had gone there. I read the list of Wantons, Watsons, Greens, Whipples, Malbones, etc. "I expected as much," said the aged gentleman, "for I have always been of opinion that in the most popular governments, the elections will generally go in favor of the most ancient families.". . .

You suppose a difference of opinion between you and me on the subject of aristocracy. I can find none. I dislike and detest hereditary honors, offices, emoluments, established by law. So do you. I am for excluding legal, hereditary distinctions from the United States as long as possible. So are you. I only say that mankind have not yet discovered any remedy against irresistible corruption in elections to offices of great power and profit, but making them hereditary.

But will you say our elections are pure? Be it so, upon the whole; but do you recollect in history a more corrupt election than that of Aaron Burr to be President, or that of De Witt Clinton last year? By corruption here, I mean a sacrifice of every national interest and honor to private and party objects. I see the same spirit in Virginia that you and I see in Rhode Island and the rest of New England. In New York it is a struggle of family feuds— a feudal aristocracy. Pennsylvania is a contest between German, Irish and Old England families. When Germans and Irish unite they give 30,000 majorities. There is virtually a white rose and a red rose, a Caesar and a Pompey, in every State in this Union, and contests and dissensions will be as lasting. The rivalry of Bourbons and Noailleses produced the French Revolution, and a similar competition for consideration and influence exists and prevails in every village in the world. Where will terminate the *rabies agri?* The continent will be scattered over with manors much larger than Livingston's, Van Rensselaer's or Philips's; even our Deacon Strong will have a principality among you southern folk. What inequality of talents will be produced by these land jobbers. Where tends the mania of banks? At my table in Philadelphia, I once proposed to you to unite in endeavors to obtain an amendment of the Constitution prohibiting to the separate States the power of creating banks; but giving Congress authority to establish one bank with a branch in each State, the whole limited to ten millions of dollars. Whether this project was wise or unwise, I know not, for I had deliberated little on it then, and have never thought it worth thinking of since. But you spurned the proposition from you with disdain. This system of banks, begotten, brooded and hatched by Duer, Robert and Gouverneur Morris, Hamilton and Washington, I have always considered as a system of national injustice. A sacrifice of public and private interest to a few aristocratical friends and favorites. My scheme could have had no such effect. Verres plundered temples, and robbed a few rich men, but he never made such ravages among private property in general, nor swindled so much out of the pockets of the poor, and middle class of people, as these banks have done. No people but this would have borne the imposition so long. . . .

10

The Transformation
of Northern Society

Thomas Jefferson wanted America to remain a nation of farmers.
Identifying corruption and vice with the "dark satanic mills" of
Europe, he hoped that America would never have an industrial revolution. There was a need, he acknowledged, for small rural mills to
provide useful employment for "a few women, children and inva-
lids, who could do little on the farm." But large industrial cities
would destroy the moral fiber of the American people. Farming had
to remain the basis of American life.

The South remained true to Jefferson's vision much longer than
the North. Even though Southerners moved west and turned to cotton as their cash crop, the basic structure of Southern society
changed very little after Jefferson's death in 1826. The South continued to be an agrarian society with few industries of its own and a
small urban population. And, as always, the great planters ran
things. In contrast the North—and particularly the Northeast—un-
derwent something of a metamorphosis. New York became a huge
city. Factories sprang up throughout New England, New York,
Pennsylvania. Boatloads of Irish and German workers descended
upon Boston, New York, Philadelphia, and other port cities. And
between 1800 and 1850 the portion of the Northern labor force in
agriculture declined from 70 percent to 40 percent.

Our own society is so much a product of the industrial revolution that we sometimes find it difficult to appreciate just how deep
the transformation went, just how disconcerting and exciting the
process of "modernization" really was. Much of what a modern society is we take for granted and treat almost as "natural" or "human." But, though much lingered on from the past, the society that
Americans were building in the first half of the nineteenth century
was fundamentally new. And the newness reached into every detail

of life. The ways Americans dressed and the ways they decorated
their houses changed. So too did their ideas about childrearing and
education, domestic architecture and even diet. The nature and pace
of work were altered in ways everyone knew about, but few understood.

Amid all the excitement about "progress" and "growth," there
was a good deal of fear. Many Americans responded to change by
trying to find ways to hold on to old values and habits. Religious revivalism, which swept across the nation in the period, was one way
of trying to preserve inherited values. So was a rash of reform
movements. But even the attempt to resist change employed the
methods of modernity. Revivalists and reformers appealed to mass
constituencies through the most modern means of communication.
And they organized themselves in ways that paralleled the ways the
new corporations were discovering to reach their markets.

All in all, the society that Lincoln would later look back on
across his "four-score and seven years" was a society in which little
or nothing stood still. The South might still exhibit many eighteenth-century features, and might dress itself out as a kind of feudal
scene of romance, but the reality was one of transformation.

Interpretive Essay

John F. Kasson

Civilizing the Machine

Today, we normally think of cities when we think of factories; but
in the early nineteenth century water power dictated the location of
factories and hence factories were often located in rural areas. This
was especially true of New England, where almost overnight cow
pastures were turned into mill towns. Of these the most famous was
Lowell, Massachusetts, which grew from nothing to 28,000 in just
two decades. Founded by rich Boston merchants, it was purposely
laid out to take advantage of the peaceful rural setting as well as the
water power of the Merrimack River. The town, in fact, became
something of a tourist attraction, and everybody of importance—
from Charles Dickens to the legendary Davy Crockett—came to see
the "factory girls of Lowell."

Here is a modern account of the famous Lowell "system." It
was written by John F. Kasson, a historian who is primarily inter-

ested in the question of whether it was possible to have industrial cities and still maintain the values of Jefferson's America.

The question of what social environment American manufacturers would create went to the heart of the republican venture. The introduction of new manufacturing centers portended dramatic changes in the structure of society. Their impact upon the character of American life was an issue of national concern. Could a system of manufactures be established that would nurture and protect the health, intelligence, independence, and virtue of their operatives, qualities essential to a republic? Or would factories breed disease, ignorance, dependence, and corruption? Would industrialization provide new prosperity and comfort for all levels of society? Or would industrialization prove an instrument of economic and political repression and social cleavage? In short, was the Revolutionary ideal of a republican civilization compatible with rapid industrial development? On the answer to these questions much of the nation's future depended.

Americans in the early nineteenth century united in admiration of English machine technology; smuggling British industrial secrets and mechanics was the sincerest form of flattery. However, there was considerably less enthusiasm for the social consequences of the English factory system. Jefferson found cause to revise his earlier opposition to the promotion of domestic manufactures, but not his horror of the "mobs" of workmen in European cities. In the late eighteenth and early nineteenth centuries, factory towns sprang up in England at unprecedented rates, stimulated by the colossal expansion in cotton manufactures in Lancashire. The capital of the cotton industry, Manchester, expanded from an ancient town of 17,000 people in 1770 to over 70,000 by 1801, 142,000 in 1831, and over 250,000 by midcentury, with more than an additional 150,000 in the sprawling towns that surrounded it. It stood as the "shock city" of the age, attracting numerous visitors both from England and abroad anxious to confront the symbol and embodiment of the new industrial order. Manchester's contrasts both fascinated and repelled: the advanced technology and immense productivity of its factories; the unbelievably primitive, cramped, and diseased hovels; the vitality of its magnates; the feebleness and despair of its workers. Wrestling with its conflicting characteristics during a visit in 1835, the astute social critic Alexis de Tocqueville concluded: "From this foul drain the greatest stream of human industry flows out to fertilise the whole world. From this filthy sewer pure gold flows. Here humanity attains its most complete development and its most brutish; here civilisation works its miracles, and civilised man is turned back almost into a savage.". . .

From John F. Kasson, *Civilizing the Machine: Technology and Republican Values in America, 1776–1900* (New York: Grossman Publishers, 1976), pp. 55–56, 61–62, 64–79, 82–84, 85, 86–87, 93–100, 103–104, 105–106. Copyright © 1976 by John F. Kasson. Reprinted by permission of Viking Penguin, Inc.

Such reports confirmed the popular American image of English factory towns in the first half of the nineteenth century as centers of advanced technology and productivity but also as cancers against both nature and society, producing an oppressed, ignorant, and debauched working class and threatening the civilization as a whole. Could the United States develop a system of manufactures that would avoid a similar fate? If American technology could indeed, as its proponents from Coxe to Everett claimed, integrate the country socially and politically and buttress its republican virtue, it would have to prove it first at the local level in the nation's new manufacturing towns. Here more than anywhere else would be the testing ground of the new republican industrial order.

No one was more aware of this challenge than American manufacturers themselves. The merchant-entrepreneurs who created the leading industrial towns of the nineteenth century shared their fathers' sense of republican mission and distrust of aristocratic Europe. Though some advocates of manufactures took heart in reports that pauperism pervaded England's agricultural counties to a much greater extent than her manufacturing ones, they were not generally inclined to dispute the sordid reputation of English factory towns. Many of them had observed firsthand what Nathan Appleton called the "misery and poverty" of English industrial workers, and they resolved that American manufactures must never be allowed to take a similar course. Manufacturing itself need not be debilitating, they reasoned. Many of the social and moral evils of the English system, they believed, stemmed from the establishment of factories in large cities, in which vice thrived unchecked and a debased proletariat perpetuated itself. They shared the faith of some of the earliest American planners of industrial towns, including Tench Coxe and Alexander Hamilton, that by locating American manufactures in the countryside and instituting a strict system of moral supervision, the health and virtue of operatives would be protected. Thus situated, manufactures would harmoniously complement agricultural life, and the nation's agrarian character would remain undisturbed.

However, the leading American factory towns of the first half of the nineteenth century were shaped not only in response to the English factory system but to events in America as well. As we have seen, technology was absorbed into a conservative ideology of republicanism as early as the 1780s in part as an instrument of social order and control against both the insidious influences of European manufactures and symptoms of social discord and rebellion at home. As Americans advanced into the nineteenth century, pressures on a deferential society continued and the problems of republican order increased. The whole country surged with dramatic volatility and energy. The nation's population, which had more than doubled every twenty-five years in the eighteenth century, continued to grow at the same phenomenal rate through the first half of the nineteenth. People migrated restlessly not only along the vast new frontier but within the rapidly mushrooming urban centers as well. And the concept of republicanism, instead of controlling and containing this expansion, became in the hands of new egalitarian forces a weapon with which to challenge established authority in politics, religion, law, commerce—virtually every aspect of society. Social conservatives rubbed their eyes to see a reversion in American life from civilization to barbarism as the whole social order upon which the republican experiment was premised appeared to be collapsing around them. Some recent scholars, including Stanley Elkins and David Donald, have in effect supported their perception, arguing that ante-bellum America suffered from a general "institutional breakdown" and "an excess of democracy" which ultimately paved the way for Civil War. . . .

To the total institution, then, turned a group of merchants known as the Boston associates, who would become America's leading manufacturers before the Civil War, as they sought an alternative to the poverty and neglect of English industrial conditions and a safeguard against the fluidity and potential corruption of an expanding American society. Beginning in Waltham, Massachusetts, in 1815, they established a successful pattern of textile manufactures and extended it rapidly. By 1850 the Boston associates controlled mills in operation in Chicopee, Taunton, and Lawrence, Massachusetts; Manchester, Dover, Somersworth, and Nashua, New Hampshire; and Saco and Biddeford, Maine; and were making active preparations for new mills in Holyoke, Massachusetts. But the queen city of their system and the leading producer of cotton goods, the nation's largest industry before the Civil War, was Lowell, Massachusetts. Lowell's fame rested not only on its industrial capacity but even more on its reputed social achievement. One of the most important and influential of all total institutions of republican reform in the ante-bellum period, Lowell promised to resolve the social conflict between the desire for industrial progress and the fear of a debased and disorderly proletariat. Its founding sprang from the conviction that, given the proper institutional environment, a factory town need not be a byword for vice and poverty, but might stand as a model of enlightened republican community in a restless and dynamic nation. Lowell offers a dramatic example of the effort to put this conservative faith into practice. Its story is particularly interesting because within a few years of its founding, the basic assumptions of the Lowell factory system and its conception of republican community were challenged both on ideological and institutional grounds by the working class and their spokesmen. Branding Lowell's directors as a repressive new aristocracy, dissident workers increasingly rejected what they regarded as a manipulative social structure and an exploitative industrial capitalism. Against the conservative view of republicanism of Lowell's directors, protesting workers interpreted the American Revolution as the beginning of a continuing struggle toward a radical egalitarianism. The early history of Lowell thus provides an encapsulated version of the debate over the meaning of republicanism in an industrial society and the attempt to give that meaning institutional shape.

Lowell was conceived in the second decade of the nineteenth century by a trio of innovative and energetic young Boston merchants: Francis Cabot Lowell, Nathan Appleton, and Patrick Tracy Jackson. Touring Great Britain in 1810 and 1811 for his health, F. C. Lowell visited a large iron works in Edinburgh and grew excited over the enormous possibilities such large-scale manufacturing had for America. While in Edinburgh, he also met Nathan Appleton, his friend and fourth cousin, and the merchants discussed the idea of establishing cotton manufacture employing English technology in the United States. At the same time Lowell was corresponding on the subject with his business partner and brother-in-law, P. T. Jackson, and he determined, before his return to America, to study thoroughly the cotton mills at Manchester and Birmingham. He spent weeks in these factories, applying his keen mathematical and mechanical skill and questioning engineers eager to accommodate a wealthy potential customer. Thus Lowell circumvented stringent regulations against the exportation of English machinery or mechanical drawings and smuggled into America valuable mental baggage. His contemporaries would later acclaim him a hero and a genius, who had performed an act of patriotic espionage to rank with Samuel Slater's a generation earlier.

Shortly after Lowell's return from Europe, he and Jackson bought a water-power site in Waltham, obtained a charter of incorporation from the Massachusetts legislature for their new Boston Manufacturing Company, and sought investors for the enterprise within their circle of friends and relatives among Boston's merchants. Some of Lowell's relations, including the Cabots whose pioneering 1787 cotton factory at Beverly had failed, attempted to dissuade him from what they considered "a visionary and dangerous scheme, and thought him mad." Nathan Appleton himself warily agreed to invest only five thousand dollars, half the amount Lowell and Jackson requested, "in order to see the experiment fairly tried." The two merchants also enlisted the financial support of Patrick Jackson's brothers; Israel Thorndike and his son; Uriah Cotting; James Lloyd; and two of Lowell's brothers-in-law, Benjamin Gorham and Warren Dutton.

Lowell hired a talented engineer, Paul Moody, and quickly set about a series of reinventions based upon his observations of English machinery and contemporary American developments. Of these the most important was the power loom, which promised to free American mills from dependence on neighborhood weavers and to permit the organization of all manufacturing processes from raw cotton to finished cloth within a single integrated mill complex. When Nathan Appleton first saw Lowell's loom in 1814, he was stupefied by its significance and, in a "state of admiration and satisfaction," sat with Lowell "by the hour, watching the beautiful movement of this new and wonderful machine, destined as it evidently was, to change the character of all textile industry." To exploit the capacity of large-scale mechanized production to its fullest extent while relying on unskilled labor, Lowell decided to concentrate production on standardized inexpensive cotton cloths, sheetings, and shirtings. Later, as new corporations arose at the town of Lowell and elsewhere, each manufactured a different type of cotton goods to avoid duplication and competition with fellow companies. Mills were designed to facilitate the flow of materials from one stage of processing to the next. Cotton was carded on the first floor, spun on the second, woven on the third and fourth, while machine shops resided in the basement. In the next fifteen years New England inventors would build upon this structure and introduce a series of labor-saving technological innovations which equaled or excelled British methods and machinery and mechanized all the basic processes of cloth manufacturing except spooling and warping. Even before some of these refinements, however, Lowell's system achieved dramatic gains in production. According to one technological historian, from its first years of operation the Waltham mill could with the same number of employees produce three and a half times as much as other American factories still operating according to pre-1812 methods. The achievement of Lowell and his colleagues, sometimes known as the "Massachusetts system," thus marked a significant stage in the development of modern mass production.

As a final stroke in his grand design, Lowell turned his attention to politics. Competition with British textiles had in the past been the bane of the American industry. Thus when Congress began deliberations over a new tariff measure in 1816, Lowell rushed to Washington to lobby for his cause. He adroitly steered through Congress a minimum valuation tariff which helped to establish the principle of protection to American industry and sheltered his own company's products from foreign competition, while leaving exposed rival manufacturers of more expensive cotton goods. Lowell made a powerful impression even on opponents of the protective tariffs, such as Daniel Webster, then a representative from New Hampshire. Only two years earlier, discussing another tariff measure Webster had declared he was "not in haste to see Sheffields and Birminghams in America." The grim image of English industrial towns dominated his thinking on the subject, and he gestured with foreboding toward the day "when the young men of the country shall be obliged to shut their eyes upon external nature, upon the heavens and the earth, and immerse themselves in close and unwholesome workshops; when they shall be obliged to shut their ears to the bleating of their own flocks, upon their own hills, and to the voice of the lark that cheers them at the plough, that they may open them in dust, and smoke, and steam, to the perpetual whirl of spools and spindles, and the grating of rasps and saws." Lowell helped Webster to change his opinion and to convert him gradually to the protectionist position. Webster's ambition was outgrowing New Hampshire, and he soon moved to Boston, where Lowell supplied him with letters of introduction. Such ministrations, including a later offer to obtain stock in the Boston associates' new enterprise at the town of Lowell, ultimately won Webster's services as a major apologist for American industrial interests.

In the eyes of his contemporaries, however, Lowell's greatest achievement lay in neither his technological success, nor his political skill, nor his business acumen. The special reverence with which his name was spoken in the period before the Civil War emerged from the sense that he had conceived a manufacturing system that concerned itself as much with the health, character, and well-being of its operatives as it did with profits. By allegedly protecting the integrity of America's workers, he had in important measure safeguarded the character of the republic itself. From the beginning, Lowell and his associates were mindful of the condition of European workers and particularly concerned to avoid a similar fate here. As Appleton recalled their earnest discussions, "The operatives in the manufacturing cities of Europe, were notoriously of the lowest character, for intelligence and morals. The question therefore arose, and was deeply considered, whether this degradation was the result of the peculiar occupation, or of other and distinct causes. We could not perceive why this peculiar description of labor should vary in its effects upon character from all other occupation."

Their solution was to organize the factory as a total institution, so that the company might exercise exclusive control over the environment. Unlike most English cotton factories of this time, which were powered by steam, American mills depended upon water power; and the necessity to locate the plant near an important rapids further insured that the community would be placed in the country, apart from urban contamination. But where Lowell's plan differed radically from both earlier English and American factory settlements was in his decision to establish a community with a rotating rather than a permanent population; this was central to the conception. Previous American factory settlements had retained the English system of hiring whole families, often including school-aged children. Lowell and his associates opposed the idea of a long-term residential force that might lead to an entrenched proletariat. They planned to hire as their main working force young, single women from the surrounding area for a few years apiece. For a rotating work force such women were an obvious choice. Able-bodied men could be attracted from farming only with difficulty, and their hiring would raise fears that the nation might lose her agrarian character and promote resistance to manufactures. Women, on the other hand, had traditionally served as spinners and weavers when textiles had been produced in the home, and they constituted an important part of the family economy. However, imports of European manufactured fabrics were eroding American household industry. At the same time, southern New England farmers were gradually shifting from subsistence to commercial agriculture. By employing young farm women in American factories on a relatively short-term basis, the Lowell system in effect extended and preserved the family economy while at the same time avoiding incorporation into the factory of the family as a whole. Factory work, then, would not become a lifetime vocation or mark of caste, passed on from parent to child in the omnipresent shadow of the mill. Rather it might form an honorable stage in a young woman's maturation, allowing her to supplement her family's income or earn a dowry, before assuming what the founders regarded as "the higher and more appropriate responsibilities of her sex" in a domestic capacity. Her factory experience would be a moral as well as an economic boon, numerous spokesmen for American manufactures maintained, rescuing her from idleness, and vice, pauperism, possibly even confinement in an almshouse or penitentiary. Instead, in the cotton mill, under the watchful eyes of supervisors, she would receive a republican education, inbibing "habits of order, regularity and industry, which lay a broad and deep foundation of public and private future usefulness." During her term at Lowell, the worker would be protected *in loco parentis* by strict corporate supervision, lodged in company boardinghouses kept by upright matrons, and provided compulsory religious services. Such stringent standards of moral scrutiny and company control would serve a treble purpose: to attract young women and overcome the reluctance of their parents, most of them farmers; to provide optimal factory discipline and management control of the operatives; and to maintain an intelligent, honorable, and exemplary republican work force. Though Lowell's founders never regarded their efforts as utopian, they aimed to establish an ideal New England community, which would stand not as a blight but a beacon of republican prosperity and purity upon the American landscape.

Recently, however, some scholars have questioned the extent to which the Lowell system actually stemmed from any grand social vision or solicitude in behalf of the workers. How much choice, they ask, did Lowell's founders really have in developing their vaunted system? According to the economist Howard M. Gitelman, the complexity of the early power-driven machinery employed at Lowell and elsewhere made child labor unfeasible, and thus the economies of a family labor system were not a viable option for the founders. Moreover, he contends, the rural location of Waltham, Lowell, and similar mill towns was dictated mainly by considerations of available water power; company housing then had to be provided in order to staff the mills. Concerned parents and an aroused community, Gitelman speculates, would in any case have insisted upon supervised company housing and a strict system of rules and regulations for the operatives. Economic necessity, not employer magnanimity, so the argument runs, compelled the shape of Lowell.

But to conclude that because the Boston associates were not altruistic reformers, they were therefore simply capitalists following the line of least economic resistance clearly ignores a broad middle ground. A fuller, more satisfactory explanation of the founding of Lowell would recognize *both* commercial and social and ideological motives. For the Boston associates and many of their colleagues were in fact both capitalists and concerned citizens, hard-dealing merchants and public-spirited philanthropists, entrepreneurs and ideologues. Even as they helped to transform New England's economy, they sought to preserve a cohesive social order by adhering tenaciously to a rigorous code of ethics and responsibility. They took seriously their role as republican leaders, and the public turned to them for leadership. The Unitarian reformer Theodore Parker expressed the sense of gratitude of many when he praised the development of manufactures and improvements in transportation as helping to "civilize, educate, and refine men." "These are men," he concluded, "to whom the public owes a debt which no money could pay, for it is a debt of life." Whether it was sufficient payment or not, obviously these manufacturers received a great deal of money for their services. Nevertheless, they insisted both publicly and privately that wealth was not their goal. "My mind has always been devoted to many other things rather than money-making," Nathan Appleton declared toward the end of his life. "Accident, and not effort, has made me a rich man." Amos Lawrence, who with his brother Abbott joined forces with Lowell's investors in 1830, filled his diary and letters with reminders of the stewardship and public trust which wealth entailed. From 1829 through 1852 he personally and meticulously made charitable gifts of $639,000 in cash, as well as clothing, food, books, and other articles. He once wrote a factory agent, "We must make a good thing out of this establishment, unless you ruin us by working on Sundays. Nothing but works of necessity should be done in holy time." Boston's leading merchants generally scorned a narrowly acquisitive view of their role and participated in a wide variety of public affairs. They were active and influential in Federalist and later Whig politics and held important offices on both state and national levels. Their contributions to numerous charities and philanthropies, including hospitals, orphanages, and asylums, as well as libraries, historical societies, schools and colleges, helped to make Boston a center of social and cultural institutions in the nineteenth century. Such enterprises, they believed, were essential to the solidity and progress of society. As Francis Cabot Lowell's son John Lowell declared in establishing a series of public lectures, the Lowell Institute, in 1835, "The prosperity of my native land, New England, which is sterile and unproductive, must depend . . . 1st on the moral qualities and 2dly on the intelligence and information of its inhabitants."

Concern with the social consequences of Lowell, Massachusetts, as a tight-knit, carefully regulated republican community, then, was certainly consistent with the values and activities of the founders and their associates in a variety of other fields. Moreover, their philanthropic and industrial pursuits were related both historically and institutionally. Nineteenth-century textile mills were direct descendants of the manufacturing societies formed in various American colonies in the eighteenth century and more distant relatives of the work houses of the seventeenth century. Institutions such as the Boston Society for Encouraging Industry and Employing the Poor, established in 1751 and one of the colonies' most important pre-Revolutionary factories, had, as its name indicates, a dual purpose: not only to stimulate American manufactures but to provide work for the destitute; to encourage industry in both senses of the word, under official supervision. Undoubtedly, with increased mechanization in the textile industry, commercial motives were uppermost in the establishment of Lowell and other mill towns in the nineteenth century, but at the same time one should not lose sight of the social vision that accompanied them. Of course Lowell's founders and directors were not always as idealistic as they professed. But in instituting their factory system, they did not have to choose between their ethical and ideological convictions and their economic advantage as entrepreneurs—not in the beginning at least. The Lowell system united advanced technology, factory discipline, and conservative republicanism; and when it was eventually challenged, protest came on both economic and ideological grounds.

F. C. Lowell lived only until 1817, long enough to see the success of his Waltham experiment but before practical plans for the city that would bear his name had begun. Yet despite his premature death, he remained, in Nathan Appleton's words, "the informing soul, which gave direction and form to the whole proceeding." To carry on his work, Appleton and Jackson selected as agent Kirk Boott, a trained engineer with an autocratic personality who had perhaps acquired his rigorous standards of discipline and strong class-consciousness in his service in the British army under the Duke of Wellington. They purchased the Pawtucket canal on the Merrimack in what was then the town of Chelmsford, together with four hundred acres of farmland, in the fall of 1821. Boott quickly set about the planning and construction of the industrial town according to F. C. Lowell's general conception, opening the first factory complex, the Merrimack Manufacturing Company, for production in September 1823. The company's six factory buildings were grouped in a spacious quadrangle bordering the river and landscaped with flowers, trees, and shrubs. They were dominated by a central mill, crowned with a Georgian cupola. Made of brick, with flat, plain walls, and white granite lintels above each window space, the factories presented a neat, orderly, and efficient appearance, which symbolized the institution's goals and would be emulated by many of the penitentiaries, insane asylums, orphanages, and reformatories of the period. Beyond the counting house at the entrance to the mill yard stretched the company dormitories. Their arrangement reflected a Federalist image of proper social structure. The factory population of Lowell was rigidly defined into four groups and their hierarchy immutably preserved in the town's architecture. As chief agent for the corporation, most of whose stockholders resided in Boston, Boott and the other company agents formed the unquestioned aristocracy of the community; a Georgian mansion with an imposing Ionic portico just below the original factory in Lowell powerfully symbolized Boott's authority. Beneath this class stood the overseers, who lived in simple yet substantial quarters at the ends of the rows of boarding-houses where the operatives resided, thus providing a secondary measure of surveillance. In the boardinghouses themselves lived the female workers, who outnumbered male employees roughly three to one. Originally these apartments were constructed in rows of double houses, at least thirty girls to a unit, with intervening strips of lawn. Later, in the 1830s, as companies expanded and proliferated, the houses were strung together, blocking both light and air. These quarters were intended to serve essentially as dormitories and offered few amenities beyond dining rooms and bedrooms, each of the latter shared by as many as six or eight girls, two to a bed. Boardinghouse keepers were responsible for both the efficient administration of the buildings and for enforcing company regulations as to the conduct of the workers. Similar tenements were provided for male mechanics and their families. At the bottom of this hierarchy were the Irish day laborers, who built the canals and mills and made possible the continuing expansion of Lowell. Significantly, no housing had been planned for this group, and they lived in hundreds of little shanties next to a small Catholic church in an area called "New Dublin" and the "Acre." This early corporate insensitivity to the needs of the immigrant presaged Lowell's response to the great mass of immigrants later on.

The adjustment of workers to factory life marked a critical juncture in America's transition to a mature industrial society. Many of Lowell's operatives had known long hours and hard tasks before in farms or shops; but the regularity and discipline of factory work were altogether new. They no longer labored at their own speeds in completing of a task, but to the clock at the pace of the machine. The employer aimed to standardize irregular labor rhythms and to make time the measurement of work. Thus the cupolas which crowned Lowell mills were not simply ornamental; their bells insistently reminded workers that time was money. Operatives worked a six-day week, approximately twelve hours a day, and bells tolled them awake and to their jobs (lateness was severely punished), to and from meals, curfew, and bed. Other factory owners also demanded long hours, even while they simultaneously claimed that the factory system had in large measure repealed the primeval curse "In the sweat of thy face shalt thou eat bread." In the hands of their operatives, they believed, leisure meant mischief; idleness at best; at worst vicious amusements, drink, gambling, and riot. Hence the resistance to shorter working hours throughout the nineteenth century and into the twentieth; work was a form of social control. Lowell's managers shared this perception and wove it into the entire social order. They established an elaborate structure of social deterrents and incentives, insisting at all times upon "respectability" and defining it to suit their needs. Here the heritage of the Puritan ethic served employers especially well. Many Lowell women had been raised in a strongly evangelical atmosphere which placed heavy emphasis upon personal discipline and restraint. Injunctions to industry and the redemption of time pervaded their home communities, and their reading of popular didactic literature, from Isaac Watts's "How doth the little busy Bee," and Poor Richard's *Way to Wealth,* to the writings of Hannah More, reinforced these teachings. Company officials appropriated these values and adapted them to the imperatives of industrial capitalism. The Lawrence Company regulations, for example, stipulated that all employees "must devote themselves assiduously to their duty during working hours" and "on all occasions, both in their words and in their actions, show they are penetrated by a laudable love of temperance and virtue, and animated by a sense of their moral and social obligations."

A policy of strict social control, implicit in the residential architecture, enforced this code of factory discipline. The factory as a whole was governed by the superintendent, his office strategically placed between the boardinghouses and the mills at the entrance to the mill yard. From this point, as one spokesman enthusiastically reported, his "mind regulates all; his character inspires all; his plans, matured and decided by the directors of the company, who visit him every week, control all." Beneath his watchful eye in each room of the factory, an overseer stood responsible for the work, conduct, and proper management of the operatives therein. Should he choose to exercise it, an overseer possessed formidable power. The various mill towns of New England participated in a "black list" system. A worker who bridled at employers' demands was charged with an offense of character, such as "insubordination," "profanity," or "improper conduct." Issued a "dishonorable discharge," she would be unable to find similar work elsewhere. Supervision was thus constant. If the lines of social division occasionally relaxed on special occasions, it was only because the hierarchical authority of the community, which formed the basis of factory discipline, remained so indisputable.

In addition to these powerful institutional controls, corporate authorities relied upon the factory girls to act as moral police over one another. The ideal, as described by an unofficial spokesman of the corporation, represented a tyranny of the majority that would have made Tocqueville shudder. Declared the Rev. Henry A. Miles of Lowell, "Among the virtuous and high-minded young women, who feel that they have the keeping of their characters and that any stain upon their associates brings reproach upon themselves, the power of opinion becomes an ever-present, and ever-active restraint. A girl, *suspected* of immoralities, or serious improprieties of conduct, at once loses caste." As Miles approvingly described the ostracism, the girl's fellow-boarders would threaten to leave the house unless the housekeeper dismissed the offender. They would shun her on the street, refuse to work with her, and point her out to their companions. "From their power of opinion, there is no appeal." Eventually the outcast would submit to her punishment and leave the community. Even if, as one suspects, Miles overestimated the moral severity of Lowell women, his description nevertheless represented the official standard of behavior. On no account did employers wish to encourage independence of character, for it threatened the stability of the entire factory system.

During its first two decades of operation, Lowell's reputation as a model factory town, offering economic opportunity in a wholesome moral and intellectual atmosphere, proved notably successful in attracting labor. Eager and intelligent young women flocked to the city, mostly from farms in New Hampshire, Vermont, Massachusetts, and Maine. Though their pay was not great and declined relative to the general economy over the years, manufacturing initially offered the greatest income of any occupation open to women at the time; domestic service in particular suffered as a result. Women came for manifold reasons: for money to assist their families, to support a brother's education, or to earn a dowry, and in some cases to gain independence from family life. Often Lowell women offered more romantic explanations as well: a failed family fortune, infidel parents, a cruel mistress, a lover's absence. As Lowell operatives reported their experiences and the community's reputation spread, many came for an informal education and the stimulation of their peers in an urban setting. In addition, company recruiters traveled through New England painting glowing pictures of the life and wages to be enjoyed at Lowell and collecting a commission for each young woman they persuaded. With the construction of new factories and the rise of a middle class in the town to serve the needs of the enterprise, Lowell's population expanded rapidly: From roughly 200 in 1820, it climbed to 6477 in 1830, 21,000 in 1840, and over 33,000 in 1850. For many young women away from home and family for the first time, the factory town appeared overwhelming at first, though most soon adapted to the new industrial environment and institutional life. Some even found the community rather snug and reassuring. With memories tinged by the nostalgia of old age, Harriet Robinson described the early days of Lowell as a life of "almost Arcadian simplicity," and Lucy Larcom recalled "a frank friendliness and sincerity in the social atmosphere," a purposefulness and zest for life which contrasted warmly with her early days as a child on the Massachusetts seacoast. Despite Lowell's swelling population and the lack of public parks until the mid-1840s, the town retained at least suggestions of a rural life. House plants in windows often gave corners of the mills the effect of a bower, and some of the overseers cultivated flower gardens behind the factories as well. According to Miss Larcom, "Nature came very close to the mill gates . . . in those days. There was green grass all around them; violets and wild geraniums grew by the canals; and long stretches of open land between the corporation buildings and the street made the town seem countrylike."

Gradually, most of these young women adjusted to the demands of factory life. Probably the greatest challenge confronting them was the machinery itself. "The buzzing and hissing and whizzing of pulleys and rollers and spindles and flyers"—as one ex-worker described them—often proved bewildering and oppressive for people completely unaccustomed to such devices. As they mastered their machines' intricacies, they learned to defy the noise and tedium by distancing themselves from their work through private thoughts and daydreams. Furthermore, before operatives were given more looms to attend and the machines speeded up in the mid-1840s, they often had long periods of idleness between catching broken threads. Regulations prohibited books in the mill, but women frequently cut out pages or clippings from the newspaper and evaded the edict. Others worked on compositions in their spare moments or spent the time lost in contemplation. Thus they attempted to give meaning to the time that their work denied and to cultivate a mental separation from their activities and surroundings.

In the two or three hours they had remaining at the end of a long working day, and on Sundays, many Lowell women relentlessly pursued an education. They borrowed books from lending libraries, attended the lyceum at which Edward Everett, John Quincy Adams, and Ralph Waldo Emerson spoke, met in church groups, and organized a number of "Improvement Circles," two of which produced their own periodicals, the *Operatives' Magazine* (1841–42) and, most famous, the *Lowell Offering* (1840–45), and its successor, the *New England Offering* (1848–50). Writers in these journals were self-conscious of their position as "factory girls" and eager to vindicate their reputations. As they endeavored "to remove unjust prejudice—to prove that the female operatives of Lowell were, as a class, intelligent and virtuous"—they offered impressive support for the Lowell system as a model republican community. Factory life at Lowell, a number of writers maintained, did not injure their health or degrade their morals. On the contrary, they asserted, the conscientious worker's "intellect is strengthened, her moral sense quickened, her manners refined, her whole character elevated and improved, by the privileges and discipline of her factory life." To those who chafed against this regimen and thought of returning to the country, various authors replied that Lowell presented the most stimulating moral and intellectual climate, the most authentic republican community, in the land. Declared one woman in the *Lowell Offering:* "I believe there is no place where there are so many advantages within the reach of the laboring class of people, as exist here; where there is so much equality, so few aristocratic distinctions, and such good fellowship, as may be found in this community." A contributor to the *Operatives' Magazine* agreed: "We are, in fact, a truly republican community, or rather we have among us the only aristocracy which an intelligent people should sanction— an aristocracy of worth." While the stress of these remarks was more egalitarian than the conception of Lowell's founders, they effectively supported the existing system. The icon of the *Lowell Offering*'s title page depicted the symbolic landscape in which the operative stood: "the school girl, near her cottage home, with a bee-hive, as emblematical of industry and intelligence, and, in the background, the Yankee school-house, church and factory." With school and church, the factory thus formed a triad of republican instruction and uplift.

As Lowell's fame spread in the 1830s, '40s, and '50s, countless visitors made the pilgrimage to the town, were conducted through its factories by representatives of the corporations, and emerged awe-stricken by its technological splendor and moral sublimity. Their rhapsodic testimonies overwhelmingly endorsed the policies of F. C. Lowell, his associates, and successors. Not only did the town appear to sustain the nation's highest standards of health, intellect, prosperity, and character; its success was such that in many respects it presented a model for American communities. . . .

American enthusiasm over Lowell was eminently shared by European visitors. The town quickly emerged as the celestial countertype to infernal Manchester. By the 1830s it had become an obligatory stop on foreign itineraries, as distinctively a republican innovation as the American penitentiary, as established a landmark as Niagara Falls. Despite Lowell's international reputation, each traveler retained a European conception of factory towns which left him unprepared for what he saw. The dramatic natural setting along the banks of the Merrimack, nestled in the hills, with views reputedly as far as the White Mountains, no less than the crisp, clean aspect of the town itself, gave Lowell an air of "rural freshness" which dazzled foreign guests. As a result, each took his first glimpse of Lowell in amazement, even an air of disbelief. Viewing the city from a hilltop one winter evening, the Swedish novelist Fredrika Bremer compared it to "a magic castle on the snow-covered earth." Upon closer inspection she exclaimed, "To think and to know that these lights were not *ignes fatui,* not merely pomp and show, but that they were actually symbols of a healthful and hopeful life." Alexander Mackay found himself searching in vain for "the tall chimneys and the thick volumes of black smoke" that characterized English manufacturing towns. Lowell's appearance of newness overwhelmed Charles Dickens in the early 1840s, so that it seemed to him created only yesterday. And the perspicacious French engineer Michel Chevalier, who had earlier experienced "the delusive splendor" of the great Manchester mills, approached Lowell warily. His sense of pleasure at the town, "new and fresh like an opera scene," warred with his fear of its eventual decline, causing him to ponder, "Will this become like Lancashire?" Only gradually, watching Lowell operatives passing neatly through the streets and learning of their wages, did he wholly credit the enormous gulf between Lowell and Manchester. . . .

Lowell's planners and directors might thus have felt deservedly proud of their accomplishment. For in Lowell and its sister cities—Chicopee, Holyoke, Lawrence, Manchester, Saco, and the rest—they had apparently built a productive, cohesive, and harmonious community based upon the earlier ideological fusion of technology and republicanism. Lowell promised not to compromise the nation's agrarian commitment, but rather to supplement it, to strengthen the country economically, socially, and morally. The factory town ostensibly reconciled the myth of the American garden with a new myth of the machine. Safely removed from Boston yet connected by the railroad, Lowell represented in the public mind a region in the middle distance, between city and wilderness. In this setting among the hills and on the banks of the Merrimack River, the town at once partook of the purifying influences of nature, yet—unwilling totally to submit to its siren song and reel as debauchees of dew—retained the beneficial discipline of the factory. The flowers in factory windows, so often noted by visitors, provided a fitting token of the community's premise, that an oasis of harmony and joy was attainable only through the maintenance of rigid moral standards and the fulfillment of hard work. One may protest that this represented a vitiated pastoralism, hardly worthy of the name; but this mythic fusion reconfirmed America's self-image as a natural yet disciplined republic and a land of abundance and opportunity. Prosperity and republicanism, the directors might have congratulated one another, had—despite John Adams's anguished cry—indeed been reconciled in a temperate and industrious community: This was the stunning achievement of Lowell. But was it?

Alongside the proud affirmations of company officials, the hosannas of industrial spokesmen and technological enthusiasts, and the admiring testimonies of European visitors, the 1830s and 1840s saw an insurgent attack upon the basic assumptions of the Lowell factory system and its conception of republican community. This assault was launched by members of the working class and their spokesmen, who, with the emergence of the labor movement, protested their oppressive working conditions and the hierarchical conception of society which sustained them. Probably their sentiments were not shared by the preponderance of Lowell workers, many of whom shunned political opinions of any sort. But if these dissidents were a minority, they were nonetheless significant. Their very existence contradicted Lowell's image as a uniquely happy and harmonious community, and their arguments brought a radically different perspective to the institutionalization of the Lowell ideology and to the course of American technological development. Instead of remaining content in their station and allowing the social machinery to run smoothly, these workers rejected the notion that they shared a community of interests with mill-owners and called for the secret class war which was being waged against them to be fought in the open. The contrast between American and English factory systems did not appear to them so impressively distinct, and they were hardly inclined to join Whig politicians like Edward Everett in proclaiming Lowell as the fulfillment of the American Revolution and a model of republicanism. Quite the reverse; the more extreme among them charged that the manufacturing elite had betrayed everything the Revolution stood for and were following in the footsteps of the luxury-loving and tyrannical British. Under the guise of humanitarian concern for the republic, they contended, Lowell's supporters were busily erecting a repressive new aristocracy. . . .

The attack against the Lowell factory system gained momentum . . . as Lowell women began to demonstrate on behalf of reform. In 1834 they participated in their first "turn-out," a demonstration and short-lived strike. Their numbers were estimated from "nearly eight hundred" (*Lowell Journal*) to two thousand (*The Man*), varying with the sympathies of newspaper reporters. The workers issued a proclamation asking the support of all "who imbibe the spirit of our patriotic ancestors," and ending with the verse:

> Let oppression shrug her shoulders,
>   And a haughty tyrant frown,
> And little upstart Ignorance
>   In mockery look down.
> Yet I value not the feeble threats
>   Of Tories in disguise,
> While the flag of Independence
>   O'er our noble nation flies.

The immediate occasion of the "turn-out" was the announcement of a 15 per cent reduction in wages, but it represented as well a protest against Lowell's paternalism as unrepublican. As one of the demonstrators announced, "We do not estimate our liberty by dollars and cents; consequently it was not the reduction of wages alone which caused the excitement, but that haughty, overbearing disposition, that purse-proud insolence, which was becoming more and more apparent." Two and a half years later, in October 1836, Lowell women struck against an increase in the price of board in company houses, amounting to a one-eighth cut in wages. Again they fortified their resolution by reminding one another of the Revolutionary struggle against tyranny: "As our fathers resisted unto blood the lordly avarice of the British ministry," they declared, "so we, their daughters, never will wear the yoke which has been prepared for us."

Thus, despite the founders' best efforts and most stringent regulations, the radical, egalitarian strain of republicanism they had hoped to suppress broke out within the fortress of Lowell itself. Like other dissident workers throughout the nineteenth century, Lowell operatives returned repeatedly to the American Revolution and particularly to the Declaration of Independence to fortify and articulate their protest against what they regarded as a repressive social and industrial system. They insisted that since they were "created with certain unalienable rights," their labor could not simply be reduced to a commodity of which they were denied the fruits; human rights, "life, liberty, and the pursuit of happiness," took precedence over property rights. Lowell's leading investors were also acutely conscious of the Revolution. Though Amos Lawrence, for example, was not born until 1786, so steeped was he in stories of that event that he felt himself "an actor in the scenes described," and a simple incident like the sound of a gunshot in 1843 instantly transported him back to the battles of Lexington and Concord in 1775. But the moral he and other manufacturers drew from the Revolution was very different from the workers'. As his biographer Freeman Hunt wrote shortly after Lawrence's death, "In all [the Revolution's] phases it was of a conservative character, aiming to maintain what was, and not seeking the development of fanciful theories. Our ancestors had no projects for the colonization of Utopia. The revolutionists were all on the other side." So the revolutionists must have seemed again in the 1830s and '40s. Lowell's directors and other manufacturers were not about to surrender to these dangerous new visionaries. Prior to 1860 in Massachusetts not a single strike ended in victory for the workers or checked the reduction of wages.

The workers were handicapped not only in the lack of union organization; the very institutional character of the Lowell factory system placed immense obstacles in the way of labor resistance. As George Fredrickson and Christopher Lasch have observed in considering the problem of resistance against another total institution, plantation slavery, "all total institutions are set up in such a way as to preclude any form of politics based on consent." In such a situation the conditions for organized and sustained resistance were meager. The authority of Lowell's staff was directed not just at the workers' productive performance but their private activities and feelings as well; and traditional moral values were appropriated to reinforce the purposes and perspective of the institution. Political agitation not only smacked of "insubordination," but was also considered "unladylike" in the dominant culture. In this respect, extremely valuable allies to company management in quelling dissent were the much publicized journals that Lowell women produced themselves. The *Lowell Offering,* the *Operatives' Magazine,* and the *New England Offering,* though all nominally independent, served in effect as house organs, expressing solidarity between workers and management, and they were covertly encouraged by Lowell's directors. Wishing to elevate the reputation of the factory girl and to prove her virtue and intelligence, these periodicals rigidly excluded criticism of factory conditions or management policies and resolutely presented cheerful expressions to the public. Occasionally, an editor would sharply rebuke those who violated their decorous image. "Constant abuse of those from whom one is voluntarily receiving the means of subsistence," Harriet Farley lectured dissident workers, was "something more than bad taste." If an operative really wished to improve her condition, Miss Farley suggested, she should leave the mills altogether. A character in Lucy Larcom's poem *An Idyl of Work* supported this point of view when she asked:

> Why should we,
> Battling oppression, tyrants be ourselves,
> Forcing mere brief concession to our wish?
> Are not employers human as employed?
> Are not our interests common? If they grind
> And cheat as brethren should not, let us go
> Back to the music of the spinning-wheel,
> And clothe ourselves at hand-looms of our own,
> As did our grandmothers.

This theme that rather than protest, the dissatisfied worker should go elsewhere and seek a separate peace recurred in the pages of the *Offering*. If wages should finally drop too sharply, another young woman grandiloquently declared, "I fear not for the crust of black bread, the suppliant voice, and bended knee; for then the inducement to remain will be withdrawn. Our broad and beautiful country will long present her spreading prairies, verdant hills, and smiling vales, to all who would rather work than starve." In the last analysis, this supposedly "voluntary" character of Lowell and the fact that employment was temporary by design, encouraged cooperation between workers and management and mitigated against the formation of a class consciousness. High job turnover rates alone would have inhibited the development of a sense of solidarity among workers and of united opposition to their employers. In addition, as women who regarded their work in the mills as transient rather than a career, most Lowell workers were not disposed toward collective solutions to factory abuses.

Other obstacles also stood in the way of Lowell's protesting workers. The Panic of 1837 and subsequent depressions threw an estimated one-third of American laborers out of work and seriously damaged the union movement. With jobs scarce, workingmen's organizations came to regard the system of female labor as doubly pernicious; not only did it harm the women themselves, it brought women in competition with men, thereby either throwing the latter out of work or reducing their wages. In light of this situation, the National Trades' Union suggested in 1839 that the solution to the female labor problem might be to keep women at home where they belonged. Women operatives, clearly, could no longer depend upon male labor spokesmen always to uphold their position.

In spite of these impediments, however, resistance to the Lowell factory system gradually increased. By December 1844 Lowell's dissident workers, led by the redoubtable Sarah Bagley, had achieved sufficient strength to form an organization of their own, the Lowell Female Labor Reform Association. Its ranks swelled quickly: within three months it numbered three hundred members and by the end of 1845 it claimed six hundred workers in Lowell alone, plus branches in all major New England textile centers. Now workers were able to establish connections outside Lowell to the labor movement and hence to some degree to subvert institutional pressures. Immediately, they formed their own journal, *Factory Tracts,* and soon formed an alliance with the *Voice of Industry,* a new labor weekly newspaper, and brought it to Lowell. Denouncing the *Lowell Offering* as a "mouthpiece of the corporations," these dissident workers powerfully inveighed against the oppressive character of factory life. Like Luther and Douglas, they pointed with horror to the specter of a degenerate race, spawned in the mills to serve as slaves to a manufacturing aristocracy. And as in earlier appeals to labor, they attempted to rally and organize workers by applying the language and lessons of 1776 to their own times. "Is not," the *Voice of Industry* asked, "the same secret fawning, devouring monster, wilely [sic] drawing his fatal folds around us as a nation which has crushed the freedom, prosperity and existence of other republics whose sad fate, history long ago recorded. . . . ?" In such conspiracies, the paper charged, industrious and virtuous labor was inevitably targeted as the first victim. Every year its burdens grew more grievous, and the *Voice of Industry* demanded for all workingmen their God-given right to " 'life, liberty, and the pursuit of happiness.' " The fact that conditions of European operatives might be even worse, the paper argued, was essentially irrelevant: "The American workingmen and women, will not long suffer this gradual system of *republican* encroachment, which is fast reducing them to dependence, vassalage and slavery; because the English, Irish or French operatives are greater slaves, their condition more deplorable or English capitalists and task masters have the power to be more tyrannical and oppressive." An article in *Factory Tracts* similarly appealed to America's true nobility, its workers, to cast off the yoke of tyranny from about their necks before their country became "one great hospital, filled with worn out operatives and colored slaves!" It closed defiantly, "EQUAL RIGHTS, or death to the corporations."

Such rhetoric reasserted the radical egalitarianism of the republican message which conservatives had been struggling to contain ever since the Revolution. References to the possibility of violent revolution formed a recurrent theme in the writings of Luther, Douglas, and other labor spokesmen of the period; now such phrases were being shouted outside the very mills of Lowell. How seriously is one to take them? Certainly no laborers were stockpiling arms and actively preparing for an insurrection. But neither should one dismiss such talk as a kind of verbal spice utterly without significance. In part, of course, it was intended to goad manufacturers toward reforms. Yet one cannot help but feel that it had an opposite effect: that such language only reconfirmed in Lowell's managers and stockholders their sense of the violence and chaos that would erupt should their institutional controls be removed. Of equal if not greater significance, this rhetorical violence also represented tacit admission of the immense gulf between labor reformers' vision of life in an ideal technological society, freed from the exigencies of industrial capitalism, and the formidable obstacles they encountered even to such minimal reforms as the ten-hour day. Indeed, the primacy of the ten-hour movement, as one historian has suggested, only reflects the extent to which workers accepted and fought within their employers' categories of time and work discipline. From this point of view, one might speculate that the apocalyptic rhetoric of dissident laborers and other ante-bellum reformers signaled, not the weakness of American institutions, but their strength and the difficulty of gaining any real leverage for resistance. While continuing to affirm their faith in the ballot box, they summoned forth the image of revolution not only because it made another link in the carefully elaborated analogy between nineteenth-century workers and the American revolutionists, but because it provided a vague yet powerful metaphor by which the bleak conditions of the present might suddenly be wrenched to their conception of the future.

Whatever efficacy the workers' protests had, then, was as symbolic rather than instrumental action; whatever gains they achieved were expressive rather than substantial. Efforts at specific reforms encountered powerful resistance. Workers from several mill towns had petitioned the Massachusetts legislature for establishment of a ten-hour day and other factory reforms as early as 1842, with no response. The petition of 1600 workers from Lowell and elsewhere the next year met a similar fate. In 1844 a third petition was tabled until the next session; so that at last in 1845 a legislative committee held hearings on labor conditions for the first time. In the absence of an existing labor committee, the task was assigned to William Schouler, publisher of the *Lowell Courier* and a staunch supporter of the corporations. Sarah Bagley and the Lowell Female Labor Reform Committee feverishly circulated new petitions to support the ten-hour cause and gained over two thousand signatures, half of them from Lowell. Two conflicting groups of witnesses then paraded before the committee. Spokesmen for the employers defended the healthful environment of the mills, while Miss Bagley and a group of operatives personally testified that Lowell workers endured overlong work days for insufficient pay to the detriment of health, mind, and spirit. To examine conditions firsthand, a portion of the committee went to Lowell, and they returned substantially impressed. Of their visit to the Massachusetts and Boott Mills, they reported, "The rooms are large and well-lighted, the temperature, comfortable, and in most of the window sills were numerous shrubs and plants, such as geraniums, roses, and numerous varieties of the cactus. These were the pets of the factory girls, and they were to the Committee convincing evidence of the elevated moral tone and refined taste of the operatives." Thus Lowell's technological version of pastoral proved remarkably resilient; even in the midst of protest, legislators found confirmation of the essential rightness of the enterprise in a single whiff of a potted flower.

The committee as a whole affirmed the healthfulness of existing conditions and further shied away from a ten-hour law as jeopardizing Massachusetts' industry with respect to its neighbors. Paying left-handed tribute to Lowell's petitioners, the committee declared, "Labor is intelligent enough to make its own bargains, and look out for its own interests without any interference from us." While it acknowledged that hours should be lessened, mealtimes extended, ventilation improved, and other reforms instituted, the committee contended, "the remedy is not with us. We look for it in the progressive improvement in art and science, in a higher appreciation of man's destiny, in a less love for money, and a more ardent love for social happiness and intellectual superiority." The *Lowell Offering* could not have put it better. Protesting workers did gain official support in Dr. Josiah Curtis's report on public hygiene for 1849 and the minority report of the legislature's special committee on labor for 1850. Finally, the Lowell corporation voluntarily shortened the work day to eleven hours in 1853. But no ten-hour legislation was passed in Massachusetts until 1874. . . .

. . . The failure of the ten-hour movement added to discontent. When profits declined and new wage-cuts were announced in 1848, the turnover of operatives rose sharply; at one of the most prosperous companies, the Merrimack, average workers' tenure dropped to nine months. In the past, the city's mystique had proved a powerful agent of employee recruitment. Now, as mechanization spread to other industries, such as boots and clothing, and other employment opportunities rivaled the textile mills, Lowell's companies appeared in danger of losing their command over their labor force.

Nevertheless, when the Lowell factory system was suddenly transformed in the late 1840s and 1850s, it was from quite another source than capitulation to workers' demands. At just the moment when company control of its traditional labor pool was growing shaky, Ireland's terrible potato famine that had begun in 1845 and the subsequent eviction of Irish peasants by their landlords triggered a massive immigration to America, over one and a half million people before the Civil War. As a major ship and railroad terminus, Boston received tens of thousands of these Irish immigrants. Upon arriving, however, they encountered a constricted social and economic life with little receptivity to foreigners. Nativist prejudice combined with the newcomers' lack of training and capital to shut them out of all but unskilled occupations. In such a position, Irish immigrants offered textile factories at Lowell and neighboring mill towns a ready and abundant supply of labor, and the incentive to accommodate demands of native workers diminished. Almost immediately, Irish began to take the places of departing New Englanders in the mills; once established, their presence further hastened the flow of native workers to other jobs and discouraged the entrance of other New England women into the industry. Only 7 per cent of the operatives in Lowell mills were Irish in 1845, but by the early 1850s their proportion was estimated as one half, and it grew still higher year by year. Later in the century, the labor force would be supplemented by French-Canadians and other immigrant groups. Instead of predominantly single women, the Irish came as families. As adult males were discriminated against, Irish women and, increasingly, children went to the mills, the last receiving lower wages than ever. High turnover rates thus persisted. But if the work force was not immobile, neither was the work force in Britain; it was certainly not the kind of circulatory labor force able to enter and leave the industrial economy at will with which the Lowell system had begun. Most lived not in company boardinghouses to be supervised by alien authority, but with family or friends in the town at large. With a different culture, training, aspirations, and status from earlier Lowell workers, the Irish obviously did not immerse themselves in improvement circles and literary magazines. And the Lowell mills, which had eagerly received credit for the talents and accomplishments of earlier operatives, now found themselves without their trophies. In less than a decade Lowell lost its prized population of well-educated and temporary New England women and with it the factory system's very rationale. Suddenly the basis that Lowell's founders and most ardent defenders had insisted constituted the principal difference between this city and English manufacturing towns and upon which its welfare would stand or fall—its lack of an established proletariat—was totally overthrown. . . .

The early history of Lowell, like that of other institutional innovations during this period, thus revealed complexities far beyond the shaping powers or expectations of its confident founders. The factory system they established, no matter how benign in intention, was still based upon a hierarchical and manipulative model in which workers were passive agents, tied to the demands of machine production and industrial capitalism as a whole. Ironically, Lowell's very success in attracting educated and independent New England women meant that at least an outspoken minority would refuse to accept the management's conception of "republicanism," inherent in its strict factory discipline, and insist upon a true egalitarian order. Reliance upon temporary workers, in any case, only postponed the question of what accommodations industry should make for a permanent labor force. But the arrival of the Irish triggered not a new concern upon the part of corporate officials and a reexamination of their conception of republican community, but, on the contrary, increased apathy. . . .

By the 1850s the possibility of an integrated and harmonious republican community seemed further off than ever. Even while Lowell's praises echoed, its founders' optimistic vision lay tarnished, and its most ardent defenders were forced on the defensive. The problems of urban and industrial growth and social disorder which Lowell was established to correct had spread to the community itself.

Sources

Henry A. Miles

Lowell: As It Was and As It Is, 1845

Once the owners of Lowell came under attack, they took pains to refute the charges made against them. Beginning in the 1840s they published articles, pamphlets, and books that defended Lowell's leading investors and company officials. Of these one of the most important was *Lowell, As It Was and As It Is* by Henry A. Miles, a Unitarian minister at Lowell. Do you think he succeeded in convincing his fellow citizens that he was an impartial observer? That the influences going forth from Lowell were not "pernicious"?

Lowell has been highly commended by some, as a model community, for its good order, industry, and general freedom from vice. It has been strongly condemned, by others, as a hotbed of corruption, tainting the whole land. We all, in New England, have an interest in knowing what are the exact facts of the case. We are destined to be a great manufacturing people. The influences that go forth from Lowell will go forth from many other manufacturing villages and cities. If these influences are pernicious, we have a great calamity impending over us. Rather than endure it, we should prefer to have every factory destroyed.

If, on the other hand, a system has been introduced, carefully provided with checks and safeguards, and strong moral and conservative influences, it is our duty to see that this system be faithfully carried out, so as to prevent the disastrous results which have developed themselves in the manufacturing towns of other countries. Hence the topics assume the importance of the highest moral questions. The author writes after a nine years' residence in this city, during which he has closely observed the working of the factory system, and has gathered a great amount of statistical facts which have a bearing upon this subject. He believes himself to be unaffected by any partisan views, as he stands wholly aside from the sphere of any interested motives.

From Henry A. Miles, *Lowell, As It Was and As It Is* (Lowell: Powers and Bagley, 1845), pp. 62–63, 66–67, 100–103, 128–135, 140–147.

A Lowell Boardinghouse

Each of the long blocks of boardinghouses is divided into six or eight tenements, and are generally three stories high. These tenements are finished off in a style much above the common farmhouses of the country, and more nearly resemble the abodes of respectable mechanics in rural villages. These are constantly kept clean, the buildings well painted, and the premises thoroughly whitewashed every spring, at the corporation's expense.

As one important feature in the management of these houses, it deserves to be named that male operatives and female operatives do not board in the same tenement; and the following regulations, printed by one of the companies, and given to each keeper of their houses, are here subjoined, as a simple statement of the rules generally observed by all the corporations.

Regulations to be observed by persons occupying the boardinghouses belonging to the Merrimack Manufacturing Company.

They must not board any persons not employed by the company, unless by special permission.

No disorderly or improper conduct must be allowed in the houses.

The doors must be closed at ten o'clock in the evening.

Those who keep the houses, when required, must give an account of the number, names, and employment of their boarders; also with regard to their general conduct, and whether they are in the habit of attending public worship.

The buildings, both inside and out, and the yards about them, must be kept clean, and in good order.

The hours of taking meals in these houses are uniform throughout all the corporations in the city. The time allowed for each meal is thirty minutes for breakfast, when that meal is taken after beginning work; for dinner, thirty minutes.

The food that is furnished in these houses is of a substantial and wholesome kind, is neatly served, and in sufficient abundance. Operatives are under no compulsion to board in one tenement rather than another. And then, as to the character of these boardinghouse keepers themselves, on no point is the superintendent more particular than on this. Applications for these situations are very numerous. The rents of the company's houses are purposely low, averaging only from one-third to one-half of what similar houses rent for in the city. There is no intention on the part of the corporation to make any revenue from these houses. They are a great source of annual expense. But the advantages of supervision are more than an equivalent for this.

The influence which this system of boardinghouses has exerted upon the good order and good morals of the place, has been vast and beneficent. To a very great degree the future condition of Lowell is dependent upon a faithful adhesion to this system.

The following table shows the average hours per day of running the mills, throughout the year, on all the corporations in Lowell.

Hours of Labor

	H.	M.		H.	M.
January	11	24	July	12	45
February	12	00	August	12	45
March	11	52	September	12	23
April	13	31	October	12	10
May	12	45	November	11	56
June	12	45	December	11	24

In addition to the above, it should be stated that lamps are never lighted on Saturday evening, and that four holidays are followed in the year, viz. Fast Day, Fourth of July, Thanksgiving Day, and Christmas Day.

The average daily time of running the mills is twelve hours and ten minutes. Arguments are not needed to prove that toil, if it be continued for this length of time, each day, month after month, and year after year, is excessive, and too much for the tender frames of young women to bear. No one can more sincerely desire than the writer of this book, that they had more leisure time for mental improvement and social enjoyment. It must be remembered, however, that their work is comparatively light. All the hard processes, not conducted by men, are performed by machines, the movements of which female operatives are required merely to oversee and adjust.

Moral Police of the Corporations

The productiveness of these works depends upon one primary and indispensable condition—the existence of an industrious, sober, orderly, and moral class of operatives. Without this, the mills in Lowell would be worthless. Profits would be absorbed by cases of irregularity, carelessness, and neglect; while the existence of any great moral exposure in Lowell would cut off the supply of help from the virtuous homesteads of the country. Public morals and private interests, identical in all places, are here seen to be linked together in an indissoluble connection. Accordingly, the sagacity of self-interest, as well as more disinterested considerations, has led to the adoption of a strict system of moral police.

The female operatives in Lowell do not work, on an average, more than four and a half years in the factories. They then return to their homes, and their places are taken by their sisters, or by other female friends from their neighborhood.

To obtain this constant importation of female hands from the country, it is necessary to secure *the moral protection of their characters while they are resident in Lowell.* This, therefore, is the chief object of that moral police.

No persons are employed on the corporations who are addicted to intemperance, or who are known to be guilty of any immoralities of conduct. As the parent of all other vices, intemperance is most carefully excluded.

In respect to discharged operatives, there is a system observed. Any person wishing to leave a mill is at liberty to do so, at any time, after giving a fortnight's notice. The operative so leaving, if of good character, and having worked a year, is entitled, as a matter of right, to an honorable discharge.

That form is as follows:

Mr. or Miss _____, has been employed by the _____ Manufacturing Company, in a _____ room, _____ years _____ months, and is honorably discharged.

_____, *Superintendent.*

Lowell, _____ _____

This discharge is a letter of recommendation to any other mill in the city, and not without its influence in procuring employment in any other mill in New England. Those dishonorable have another treatment. The names of all persons dismissed for bad conduct, or who leave the mill irregularly, are also entered in a book, and these names are sent to all the counting rooms of the city. *Such persons obtain no more employment throughout the city.*

Any description of the moral care, studied by the corporations, would be defective if it omitted a reference to the overseers. Every room in every mill has its first and second overseer. At his small desk, near the door, where he can see all who go out or come in, the overseer may generally be found, and he is held responsible for the good order, and attention to business, of the operatives of that room. Hence, this is a post of much importance. It is for this reason that peculiar care is exercised in their appointment. The overseers are almost universally married men, with families; and as a body, numbering about one hundred and eighty in all, are among the most permanent residents, and most trustworthy and valuable citizens of the place. The guiding and salutary influence which they exert over the operatives is one of the most essential parts of the moral machinery of the mills.

It may not be out of place to present here the regulations, which are observed alike on all the corporations, which are given to the operatives when they are first employed, and are posted up conspicuously in all the mills. They are as follows:

Regulations to be observed by all persons employed by the Manufacturing Company, in the factories.
Every overseer is required to be punctual himself, and to see that those employed under him are so.

The overseers may, at their discretion, grant leave of absence to those employed under them, when there are sufficient spare hands in the room to supply their place; but when there are not sufficient spare hands, they are not allowed to grant leave of absence unless in cases of absolute necessity.

All persons are required to observe the regulations of the room in which they are employed. They are not allowed to be absent from their work without the consent of their overseer, except in case of sickness, and then they are required to send him word of the cause of their absence.

All persons are required to board in one of the boardinghouses belonging to the company, and conform to the regulations of the house in which they board.

All persons are required to be constant in attendance on public worship, at one of the regular places of worship in this place.

Persons who do not comply with the above regulations will not be employed by the company.

Persons entering the employment of the company are considered as engaging to work one year.

All persons intending to leave the employment of the company are required to give notice of the same to their overseer, at least two weeks previous to the time of leaving.

Anyone who shall take from the mills, or the yard, any yarn, cloth, or other article belonging to the company will be considered guilty of *stealing*—and prosecuted accordingly.

The above regulations are considered part of the contract with all persons entering the employment of the _____ Manufacturing Company. All persons who shall have complied with them, on leaving the employment of the company, shall be entitled to an honorable discharge, which will serve as a recommendation to any of the factories in Lowell. No one who shall not have complied with them will be entitled to such a discharge.

_____ _____, Agent.

Portraits of Industrialism

The following documents illustrate some important features of the mental picture of industrialism that Americans began to form around the Lowell experience. The first is an engraving, a "View of Lowell." The second is the title page of the *Lowell Offering* of 1845, a collection of the writings of some of the young women who worked in the textile mill there. The third is an engraving by the famous painter Winslow Homer of workers in the nearby mill town of Lawrence. And the last is an artist's sketch of one of the most famous strikes of the century, the strike of 800 women shoemakers of Lynn, Massachusetts, in 1860. As you look at the pictures, think about the ways in which the artists have tried to resolve any potential contradiction between industry and nature, between industry and ordinary community life, between industry and femininity. Have the mills intruded on the landscape in its greenery, or do the artists create the impression that factories and trees can be integral parts of one harmonious landscape? What kind of relationship is suggested between the new factories and the traditional high points of a New England skyline, the church steeples? And what kind of relationship is suggested between the workers and the communities in which they lived? Notice the sign in the strike picture, comparing workers with

slaves. Notice also that the Lynn City Guards, the local militia, preceded the striking women. What do you think middle-class women would have said upon seeing this picture?

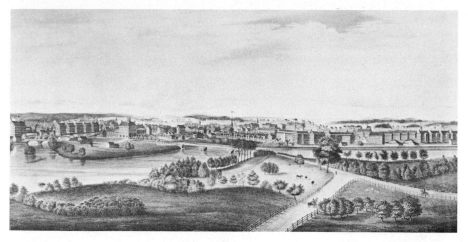

View of Lowell, Massachusetts. *Prints Division/New York Public Library.*

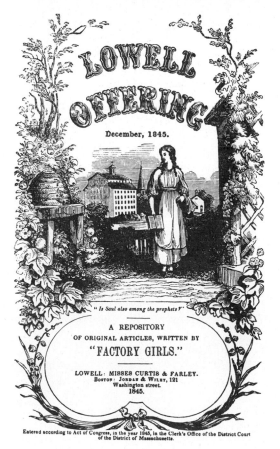

The Title Page of the *Lowell Offering.* *The Bettmann Archive.*

Textile Workers of Lawrence, Massachusetts. Engraving by Winslow Homer. *Culver Pictures*.

Striking Women and Local Militia. *Culver Pictures*.

11

Jacksonian Democracy

The dramatic changes that took place in the Northern economy after the War of 1812 were accompanied by equally dramatic changes in national politics. Under President James Monroe (1817–1825) the party system that Jefferson helped to fashion fell apart. The Federalists dropped out of presidential politics after losing to Monroe in the election of 1816. The victorious Jeffersonian Republicans split into warring factions. Party leaders lost control of the political arena, and suddenly the most divisive issues of the day—slavery and Southern power—came to dominate congressional debate when Missouri in 1819 asked to be admitted to the Union as a slave state. By 1824 Jefferson's party was in hopeless disarray. Instead of running one man for president, the party was unable to make a binding nomination, and four men—all calling themselves Jeffersonian Republicans—ran for the presidency. None of the four received the necessary majority of electoral votes, and hence the election went to the House of Representatives. There, after much wheeling and dealing, Andrew Jackson lost the presidency to John Quincy Adams. The outcome, said Jackson, was due to "bargain and corruption."

Along with the old party system went the old style of politics. James Monroe was the last president to dress like an aristocrat, powder his hair, and wear the knee-length pantaloons and white-topped boots of Washington's day. His successor, John Quincy Adams, wore long pants and was the least ostentatious of our early presidents. But he too was identified with the old style of politics in which ordinary citizens were expected to defer to their "betters." However, a new style was developing in which politicians sang the praises of "democracy," lauded the natural instincts of the ordinary white man, and even pretended to be just common folk. The new style came to be identified with General Andrew Jackson, the hero of the Battle of New Orleans, who defeated Adams in the election of 1828.

Historians have debated the meaning of Jacksonian democracy almost as vigorously as they have the American Revolution or the Civil War. The Jacksonian movement has seemed to some the expression of the spirit of the rise of democracy along the frontier, North and South. To others, the new democracy has appeared to be something even newer and more remarkable: the politics of a new urban working class in the North. Others, content enough with the label "Jacksonian," have doubted the element of democracy. To them, Jackson was a conservative who might manipulate the rhetoric of the "common man," but a conservative nonetheless, a slaveholder with all the political instincts of a member of the Southern elite.

Interpretive Essay

Leonard L. Richards

Jacksonian Democracy

The following essay, by Leonard Richards, deals with the relationship between sectionalism and the Jacksonian movement. It raises this issue: if the vote for Jackson was overwhelming in one section of the country; if the vote against him was just as overwhelming in another; and if real two-party politics was evident in only a few states between, what becomes of the notion of *democracy* in the phrase "Jacksonian democracy"?

Of the various forces that arose after the War of 1812 to shape the destiny of the nation, none had commanded more attention than the advent of democracy. Historians almost universally use the expression "Jacksonian Democracy," and a few minutes' browsing in almost any library will reveal scores of books with chapters entitled "Jacksonian Democracy."

But what does it mean? For Frederick Jackson Turner and his followers, it meant the triumph of western egalitarianism over eastern conservatism. Democracy, according to Turner, was the result of the frontier's continuous impact on American society, and with the election of Jackson, the western democrat, the long process of democratization finally triumphed. Not so, argued Arthur Schlesinger, Jr., whose *Age of Jackson* won the Pulitzer prize

From Leonard L. Richards, *The Advent of American Democracy, 1815–1848* (Glenview, Ill.: Scott, Foresman, 1977), pp. 121–127, 131–133. Copyright © 1977 by Scott, Foresman and Company. Reprinted by permission.

in 1945 and set off a historical debate that waxed hot and heavy for twenty years. Democracy triumphed with the election of Jackson, but the democratic upsurge came more from the urban masses than Turner's frontier; it was linked closely with the eastern workingmen's "enduring struggle" against the privileged, class-conscious capitalist elite. Not so, said many of Schlesinger's critics. The basic struggle was not between noncapitalists and capitalists, but rather between one set of capitalists and another; "men on the make," rather than hard-fisted workingmen, rode to power on the shoulders of Old Hickory and democratic dogma. And so it goes: in one book, the typical democrats are the urban masses; in another, simple farming folk and restless pioneers; in another, expectant capitalists; and in still another, a motley assortment of all three.

The Politics of Being Democratic

To avoid hopeless confusion, the discerning student should recognize that from the beginning two distinct phenomena—the triumph of Andrew Jackson and the growth of democracy—have been linked together. Were they inseparable developments? Not necessarily! Historians have linked the two so often that it has become habit—and habit probably has kept the two phenomena together as much as anything else.

Jackson, it is true, differed from his predecessors. Savage in his hatreds, no one ever forgot his numerous duels, stabbings, and other frays:

> He's none of your old New England stock,
> Or your gentry-proud Virginians,
> But a regular Western fighting-cock
> With Tennessee opinions.

He was the first President from west of the Appalachians, and he was the first President since Washington who was not a college graduate. Born in a Carolina cabin and orphaned as a teenager, he became a rich Tennessee planter, acquired all the social graces of a southern gentleman, and lived in one of the finest mansions in America, the Hermitage. Yet he never completely shed his past. Like many plain citizens, he never came close to mastering spelling and on occasion could misspell the same word in two different ways in the same letter. More important, Jackson was undoubtedly the most forceful and dramatic political figure between the Battle of New Orleans and the Civil War, the period when democracy became dogma. His followers, moreover, shrewdly called themselves Democrats.

But such facts hardly provide solid ground for the common notion that the rise of Jackson and the advent of democracy went hand in hand. Actually, in his home state of Tennessee, Jackson was hardly the champion of the "common man." When the Panic of 1819 set class against class, he was clearly on the side of the well-to-do. He pushed his own debtors to the wall, sued

129 of them in one lawsuit, and protested vehemently against the state's "relief" program. In 1821, when General William Carroll ran for governor on a popular program of democratic economic reform, Old Hickory campaigned vigorously for Carroll's opponent, Colonel Edward Ward, who was generally regarded to be an "aristocrat," a rich, college-educated planter "who despised the poor." Carroll won a smashing victory, and became invincible in Tennessee politics as the people's candidate, putting through a program of tax revision, constitutional reform, educational and penal improvement. None of this had any effect at all on national politics: the democrats of Tennessee, along with the conservatives, joined the Jackson party almost to a man.

White Man's Democracy.

Actually, the Jackson party as a whole developed in a political atmosphere where politicians of all stripes tried to outdo one another in proclaiming the virtue of white man's democracy. And it was strictly white man's democracy! There was no place in it for women family heads who once had the vote in New Jersey and lost it, and there was no place in it for black men who gradually lost the right to vote in many northern states, as well as in Maryland, Tennessee, and North Carolina. Yet, even with these limitations, it was radical by the world's standards, and white Americans were extremely self-conscious about being ahead—or out of step—when hordes of European travelers descended upon them to take a close look at "the great experiment in popular government."

Advocates of white man's democracy suffered a smashing defeat in Jefferson's Virginia, ran into trouble where Federalist conservatism still lingered on, and railed constantly against the evil machinations of insidious aristocrats. But generally most politicians, rich and poor alike, sang the praises of the ordinary white man. In this atmosphere the future supporters of Jackson sometimes damned the aristocrats and celebrated the virtues of the common man with a bit more zeal than the supporters of Clay and Adams. At times, however, they lagged behind and suffered the consequences. For the democratic dogma came out of many streams and took some striking twists and turns.

The Case of New York.

For a better understanding of the whole process, let us look at some of the twists and turns that enlivened New York politics. There was, first of all, a concerted drive after the War of 1812 to get rid of the state constitution of 1777. It had long been regarded as a backward and aristocratic document. Under it there were two classes of voters: the governor and state senators were elected by well-to-do townsmen and the farmers of the state, "free and independent lords of the soil," who were worth at least $250 in freehold estate; the assemblymen were chosen by freeholders who had land worth at least $50, and renters who paid $5 or more yearly. As a result, about 40 percent of the adult male population could vote for governor, and 70 percent for assemblymen. Also under this document, the governor and leading judges, sitting as the Council of Revision, had veto power over all legislation and the judges could only be removed by impeachment. Finally, the governor and four senators, sitting as the Council of Appointment, controlled all kinds of local offices; they appointed officers of the militia, local judges, district attorneys, sheriffs, coroners, mayors, and so forth; altogether, they controlled fifteen thousand jobs. So power was concentrated in the hands of a few men who were completely beyond the control of ordinary citizens.

By 1815 the old constitution had few defenders, and the swarms of Yankees who had come into the state since the Revolution never tired of pointing out its defects. "Only drunken Dutchmen," so the Yankee saying went, "would consent to live under such tyranny." Then in 1818 Connecticut revised its constitution, and Yankee pressure for change became intense. At the same time, Martin Van Buren and his followers decided to jump on the bandwagon and use the popular demand for constitutional reform to rout Governor De-Witt Clinton and the Clintonians. They forced upon the reluctant governor and the Council of Revision legislation calling for revision of the state constitution.

When the constitutional convention met in 1821, Van Buren had little trouble with the conservatives, who were outnumbered by at least five to one. His problem was General Erastus Root and his radical followers, who were generally Yankee farmers—and not lawyers. They trusted only "the majesty of democracy." They wanted universal white manhood suffrage, "emancipation of the state from judicial thralldom," which included the elimination of some courts and legislative power to fire judges at will, plus an assortment of measures to curb the governor's power. Take away the governor's appointive power, strip him of his veto and pardoning powers, subject him to annual elections, and the people would be safe from tyranny. So said the radicals.

Van Buren preferred to think of the radicals as "Mad-caps . . . old democrats, who think nothing wise that is not violent and flatter themselves that they merit Knighthood by assailing everything that is memorable in old institutions." But the "Mad-caps" put the Van Burenites, who were known popularly as Bucktails, in the awkward position of opposing the more democratic proposals. The Bucktails went along with the majority in abolishing the old two-class system of voting, but they rejected universal suffrage as "cheapening the privilege" and pushed through a taxpaying qualification for voting. The convention voted unanimously to abolish the Council of Appointment, and a committee recommended that all but a handful of military officers should be elected by "the privates and officers of the militia," and that justices of the peace should be elected by townspeople. But the 2500 justices of the peace, along with their extensive courthouse connections, were the key to any system of political patronage. Power was at stake! So the Bucktails fought vigorously against popular election of these local magistrates, and the positions remained appointive.

"Mad-caps" and Bucktails marched shoulder to shoulder, however, on the question of race. Against the protests of conservatives, they pushed through a provision that disfranchised most of New York's thirty thousand free blacks. Previously, black men voted on equal terms with white; they too had to possess $50 worth of property or pay $5 yearly rent to vote for assemblymen. Under the new constitution, they had to possess a freehold estate worth at least $250. Van Buren, who was capable of devising an argument to support almost anything, maintained that this requirement would not close the door on Negro suffrage. It would instead encourage black men to become more provident! Another Bucktail leader, Samuel Young, was at least forthright: "Public sentiment demands it! . . . No white man will stand shoulder to shoulder with a negro in the train band [militia] or jury-room. He will not invite him to a seat at his table, nor in his pew in the church. And yet some say he must be put on a footing of equality in the right of voting . . . Sir, he will not stand for it!"

Young's argument had wide support throughout the North. Connecticut, which served as a model for many New York delegates, stripped blacks of their right to vote in 1818; New Jersey followed suit in 1820; Pennsylvania in 1838. Black men could vote in nine northern states in 1815; only five by 1840. By the latter date, 93 percent of black Northerners lived in states where they were legally barred from voting. In five states where they could vote, aversion to Negro suffrage was often so great that "the voters absolutely drive them from the polls at an election, and scorn and spit upon them." And in race baiting, no one exceeded the supporters of Old Hickory. They were so vicious, noted an English visitor in 1833, that he never met a black man who was not "an anti-Jackson man."

Once New York settled on a white man's constitution in 1821, the Bucktails marketed themselves as the champions of democracy. They did this by exaggerating the influence of Chancellor James Kent and other "aristocrats" who spoke strongly in favor of the old two-class system of voting. It took strong, pragmatic, "responsible" democrats like themselves—not "Mad-caps" like Erastus Root—to overcome the "insidious influence of Federalist aristocracy." They triumphed easily over Clinton, who in 1822 decided to retire rather than face defeat. They took control of the state legislature. Then, suddenly, their image was shattered by the emergence of a new issue.

Choosing Presidential Electors.

The new issue was the method of choosing presidential electors. Since the founding of the Republic, there was anything but unanimity on how electors would be chosen. But the trend was toward popular election. In 1800, electors were chosen by state legislatures in ten states, and by popular election of one kind or another in five states. By 1823, popular election was the rule in all but six of twenty-four states. New York was one of the six. The Bucktails were not only the party in control of the legislature, but they had also decided to support William Crawford, who had little chance, if any, in a popular election. The Bucktails thus had a clear stake in the old system.

Led initially by Calhoun men, supporters of other presidential contenders raised a hue and cry for popular election of presidential electors. That was the only way "democracy" would be served! A People's party soon formed to lead the charge. The Bucktails resisted, and by the time the next state election rolled around their control of the legislature was in danger. Said one stalwart, Jacob Barker: "You may rely upon it this universal Yankee notion will take out of the Republican ranks so many . . . the Federalists, Clintonians, and dissatisfied will unite and together make a majority." Barker was wrong only because many of his fellow Republicans backed down, promised to revamp the "aristocratic" electoral law, and barely hung on to their seats.

The Bucktails faced a showdown when revamping the electoral law came up for a vote in 1824. Would they support an extremely popular electoral bill? Or would they follow party strategy by defeating the bill and then delivering New York's entire electoral vote to Crawford? Van Buren urged that "Republican members of both houses act in concert and magnanimously sacrifice individual preferences for the general good." Seventeen state senators followed the dictates of their party, and thereby killed the bill. They paid dearly. People were so angry that most of the seventeen never again held elective office. And to the dismay of the Bucktail leadership, DeWitt Clinton returned to power as the candidate of the People's party. Overnight, the hated aristocrat had suddenly become a democrat, while last year's democrats had become hated "aristocrats."

Anti-Masonry.

Of all the campaigns against "aristocracy," perhaps the most revealing was anti-Masonry. It highlights, as much as anything else, the temper of the times. It was, for one thing, one of the very few movements that was started by ordinary people. Most movements in behalf of the "people" or in behalf of "democracy" were clearly the work of politicians from the outset. And power, not democratic principle, was usually their primary concern. The Bucktails, as we just noticed, used democracy to get into power; the Clintonians in turn used it to drive them out. In the beginning at least, the anti-Masons were somewhat different. They were hardly tools of established politicians. Indeed, astute politicians were caught by surprise when anti-Masonry burst out, and many became its victims.

Then (as now) the Masons were a secret fraternal organization, which was not open to all members of the community. Some men were asked to join; others were blackballed; most were never even considered. Over the years, the Masons had developed the reputation of only accepting the "better sort": George Washington and Benjamin Franklin had been Masons, and so were Jackson and Clay. Masons had boasted for years that they held "almost every place of power where POWER IS OF ANY IMPORTANCE," and that their membership consisted of "men of RANK, wealth, office and talent, in power and out of power." They had bragged, too, of their ability to work in concert. After 1826, many Masons wished they had minced their words.

In the summer of 1826 bands of Masons tried to stop the printing of a manuscript revealing Freemasonry's secret, but innocuous rituals. After botching several attempts to steal the manuscript and to burn the publisher's office, they kidnapped its author, a disgruntled Mason named William Morgan, from his home in upstate New York. First, they threw Morgan in jail in a neighboring town, and then they hauled him over one hundred miles to Fort Niagara. No one knows for certain what happened to Morgan, but the kidnappers left a wide trail of evidence that indicates that they drowned him in the Niagara River. In fact, the trail was so wide that indignant citizens in four counties launched investigations to find out what happened to poor Morgan. Everywhere they were blocked by Masonic judges, Masonic sheriffs, and Masonic officeholders who sought to squelch the entire affair. Soon the investigators became convinced that they had uncovered a gigantic conspiracy to subvert the rule of law. The idea of a conspiracy, in turn, happened to coincide with a suspicion held by many churchgoers. For years they had wondered if Freemasonry, with its secret rituals and strange ceremonies, was really an organized plot to overthrow Christianity. In France, they noted, Masonic lodges had been centers of anticlerical propaganda at the time of the French Revolution, as well as bastions of the aristocracy.

Hence anti-Masonry was born. And, to the dismay of seasoned politicians, it spread like wildfire—first through New York, and then through Vermont, Connecticut, Massachusetts, Pennsylvania, Ohio, and the Michigan Territory. Suddenly, ordinary citizens began counting the number of Masons in town and state offices. There were hundreds. Indeed, in some states lists of lodge members resembled a roll call of the legislature and the bar. Were they conspiring against the people, too? All anti-Masons had to do was to take some well-known Masonic boasts, add a few embellishments of their own, and rail against "this vile conspiracy which benefited the *few* at the expense of the *many*," which preferred "corrupt 'brothers' to honest citizens in appointments to office," which "hated democracy and cherished aristocratic and regal forms of power." To this basic argument, evangelical anti-Masons added that Masonry was "an infidel society at war with true Christianity." Here and there, throughout the countryside, thousands soon flocked to the polls to do battle with "the Beast with seven heads and ten horns" and "to restore equal rights, equal laws, and equal privileges to all men."

The results were startling. In the fall election of 1827, just a year after Morgan's disappearance, anti-Masons carried fifteen assembly seats in central and western New York. "The result of the election," wrote one commentator, "astonished all—even the anti-Masons themselves—and opened the eyes of politicians to the growing power of the new political group." By 1830 anti-Masons could boast of 124 newspapers across the country; 45 percent of the gubernatorial vote in Pennsylvania; 48 percent in New York; 35 percent in Vermont; 150 assembly seats in Massachusetts. Skillful leaders like Thurlow Weed and William Seward of New York, and Thaddeus Stevens of Pennsylvania, emerged to lead the charge, and even old warhorses like John Quincy Adams joined the crusade. Half of the Masonic lodges in Pennsylvania "voluntarily" surrendered their charters; college fraternities went underground; and Phi Beta Kappa saved itself by becoming an honorary society.

Eventually, the crusade subsided in some states or became part of a major party in others. Historians usually mark its death soon after the presidential election of 1832, when its national candidate, William Wirt, captured only Vermont. Yet in many parts of the Northeast, candidates continued to run until the 1850s as "Anti-Mason and Whig" or "Anti-Mason and Democrat." For many voters, that was the badge of an honest man; for others, a sign of infamy. As late as 1868, when the Senate was about to try President Andrew Johnson for "high crimes and misdemeanors," Thaddeus Stevens asked the clerk of the House for the names of all senators who were Masons. Even after more than thirty years, he would never trust a Mason to vote right!

The crusade for democracy, then, was unpredictable. Spokesmen for the "common man" always denounced the "aristocracy" and sang the praises of "democracy." They always campaigned against "privilege" and "exclusivism." Yet they invariably ended up excluding someone from "democracy" or at least tried and failed, as in the case of the anti-Masons. The demand for popular government came from so many quarters, its appeal was so broad and diverse, that no party could embrace it fully. The Bucktails, the People's party, the anti-Masons—all claimed to be instruments of the common man. They all developed political apparatuses to bring thousands of ordinary citizens out of the hills, down the streams, and to the polls. But spokesmen for the common man never rallied around the same banner. Van Buren and the Bucktails went with Old Hickory, while the anti-Masons, led by Thurlow Weed and William Seward, joined the opposition. As for "Mad-cap" Erastus Root, he continued to perplex Van Buren by switching sides.

The Fall of Adams and Clay

Nationally, the Jackson party began in earnest when the House of Representatives, thanks to Henry Clay, elected John Quincy Adams to the Presidency in 1825, and Adams promptly nominated Clay to be his Secretary of State. Convinced that Clay had cheated him out of the White House, Andrew Jackson began immediately to campaign for the next election in 1828. He voted against Clay's confirmation, resigned from the Senate, and went home to Tennessee to organize his shock troops against the "corrupt bargainers". . . .

The campaign of 1828 marked the return of a two-man presidential race. Adams' position was clear, but Jackson was foxy on key issues. In the South, his partisans said he was against protection, but in Pennsylvania Samuel Ingham assured everyone that the Old Hero would "raise the tariff every time he touched it." In general, partisans favoring Jackson pictured him as the people's man while Adams' men depicted him as a seasoned statesman, and then both quickly descended into scurrility. The old story that Jackson had run off with another man's wife was revived. Although terribly unfair, it had some truth in it and could be expected. But the Cincinnati journalist who dug up this story concocted still another: "General Jackson's mother was a COMMON PROSTITUTE brought to this country by British soldiers! She afterwards married a MULATTO MAN, with whom she had several children, of which number General JACKSON IS ONE!!" The Jacksonians, of course, responded in kind: Isaac Hill of New Hampshire spread the fantastic story that John Quincy Adams had once pimped for the Tsar, and with straight faces Democrats in the West maintained that the President's fabulous success as a diplomat had finally been explained!

The two-man race returned in 1828, and so did dirty politics. But did a new two-party system emerge in 1828? Did the nasty fight between the Adams men and the Jackson men mark the emergence of a new system of national politics? Unfortunately, the election of 1828 has become so much a part of national mythology that it is difficult to strip away the myth—and then keep fact separate from fiction. The two always seem to get tangled once again.

First of all, the election resulted in a smashing victory for the Hero in the only place it counted: the electoral college. Jackson received 178 electoral votes to Adams' 83. And as the totals mounted, many Democrats came to believe their own propaganda: the people had revolted against the privileged few: the poor and unwashed had turned on the rich; the democratic masses had spoken. And, when herds of enthusiastic partisans romped through the Executive mansion on Inauguration Day, smashing the china and jumping enthusiastically to get a glimpse of the tall President dressed in a plain black suit and black cravat, the propagandist Amos Kendall reported: "It was a proud day for the *people*—General Jackson is *their own* president." Even the opposition was amazed. "I never saw such a crowd here before," said Daniel Webster. "Persons have come five hundred miles to see General Jackson, and *they really seem to think that the country is rescued from some dreadful danger!*" And thus the fiction gradually developed . . . . that democracy triumphed in 1828.

Was it really fiction? Yes it was, and historians should have known better. Even the old President spotted a basic fact in the election returns that historians long ignored. Sour and uncharitable, Adams read the returns as a defeat for democracy and a victory for the South: behind the public issues, as he always expected, lay the hidden issue of slavery. Adams was hardly an unbiased observer, of course, but neither were the Jacksonians. And like the Jacksonians, he failed to give the opposition their due. Jackson had been trounced in New England, . . . Adams' home ground, but Old Hickory had done well in other northern states, and . . . had won 50.3 percent of the northern vote.

There is no doubt, however, that the magnitude of Jackson's victory

The Election of 1828.

was due to the South. He carried most southern states by whopping majorities, and won 72.6 percent of the southern vote. And, thanks to the mechanics of the three-fifths clause and the electoral college, his 200,000 southern supporters provided him with far more help, man for man, than some 400,000 Northerners: 105 electoral votes as compared to 73. Hence, unless one is willing to say that the slaveholding states were much more democratic than the free states, or that Virginia was less aristocratic than states like Ohio and Vermont, then the old thesis about triumphant democracy must be laid aside.

The fact that looms largest in 1828 was the sectional appeal of the two candidates. As a result, real contests were held in no more than seven or eight of the twenty-four states; in the remainder one candidate or the other ran away with the election. The same pattern was repeated once again in 1832 when Jackson ran against Clay. The Old Hero won by a landslide in most of the South, capturing:

75 percent of the vote in Virginia
84 percent in North Carolina
95 percent in Tennessee
100 percent in Georgia and
Alabama

By contrast, he lost four of the six New England states by substantial margins, and even came in third in Massachusetts and Vermont where anti-Masons made strong showings. Jackson won just

43 percent of the vote in Rhode Island
35 percent in Connecticut
24 percent in Vermont
23 percent in Massachusetts

Two-party politics, then, was largely talk in much of the nation when Jackson triumphed in 1828 and 1832. It was real enough in a handful of states, such as New York and Maryland in the East, and Ohio and Kentucky in the West, but in most states one of the major contenders simply had no chance at all on election day. In the South especially, where nearly every politician was nominally a Jacksonian, one-party politics still prevailed. In short, Jackson's candidacy came far short of nationalizing political conflict; that would come later. . . .

Sources

The Election of 1828

The opposition fought Jackson with cartoons and broadsides as well as with speeches. In the 1828 election they made much of Jackson's violent nature, his street fights, and his many executions of army deserters and enemies. Do you think such propaganda had any effect on the voters? Undoubtedly it made little difference in states that Jackson either won or lost by big margins. But what about the close states? Who do you think would be influenced by such appeals? One thing is missing in the coffin handbill: the many duels Jackson had fought. Why do you think the opposition decided not to emphasize dueling?

The Bettmann Archive.   "Jackson is to be President, and you will be HANGED."

New-York Historical Society.

"King Andrew"

Later, when Jackson was president and vetoed more bills than all his predecessors combined and simply ignored the Supreme Court, the opposition tried to portray him as a tyrannical monarch. The first cartoon below, which is quite famous, has Jackson placing his will above that of the Constitution, the courts, and the good of the country. The second cartoon draws upon violent episodes from Jackson's military past and likens him to the English monarch Richard III, who was accused of murdering two young princes in the Tower of London. Which of the two cartoons do you think was more effective?

The
Bettmann
Archive.

RICHARD III.

American
Antiquarian
Society.

Davy Crockett

The Art of Democratic Politics

**Jackson was a rich Tennessee planter with over one hundred slaves,
but sometimes he was portrayed by his followers as a man of the
people, an unlettered hero of the West, who spoke common sense
and easily routed the learned Eastern establishment. To counter this
propaganda, anti-Jacksonians eventually found good copy in Davy
Crockett, who had served in Congress since 1826 and had roasted
Jackson for betraying the backwoodsmen of western Tennessee.
Crockett played the role of a comic backwoods hero who claimed to
be half-alligator, half-horse, with a touch of the snapping turtle.
Here Crockett explains to a Little Rock audience the tricks of democratic politics.**

From David Crockett, *The Life of Colonel David Crockett* (Philadelphia: Porter and Coates, 1865),
pp. 275–278.

Having gone through with the regular toasts, the president of the day drank, "Our distinguished guest, Col. Crockett," which called forth a prodigious clattering all around the table, and I soon saw that nothing would do, but I must get up and make them a speech. I had no sooner elongated my outward Adam, than they at it again, with renewed vigor, which made me sort of feel that I was still somebody, though no longer a member of Congress.

In my speech I went over the whole history of the present administration; took a long shot at the flying deposites, and gave an outline, a sort of charcoal sketch, of the political life of "the Government's" heir-presumptive. I also let them know how I had been rascaled out of my election, because I refused to bow down to the idol; and as I saw a number of young politicians around the table, I told them, that I would lay down a few rules for their guidance, which, if properly attended to, could not fail to lead them on the highway to distinction and public honor. I told them, that I was an old hand at the business, and as I was about to retire for a time I would give them a little instruction gratis, for I was up to all the tricks of the trade, though I had practised but few.

"Attend all public meetings," says I "and get some friends to move that you take the chair; if you fail in this attempt, make a push to be appointed secretary; the proceedings of course will be published, and your name is introduced to the public. But should you fail in both undertakings, get two or three acquaintances, over a bottle of whisky, to pass some resolutions, no matter on what subject; publish them even if you pay the printer—it will answer the purpose of breaking the ice, which is the main point in these matters. Intrigue until you are elected an officer of the militia; this is the second step towards promotion, and can be accomplished with ease, as I know an instance of an election being advertised, and no one attending, the innkeeper at whose house it was to be held, having a military turn, elected himself colonel of his regiment." Says I, "You may not accomplish your ends with as little difficulty, but do not be discouraged—Rome wasn't built in a day.

"If your ambition or circumstances compel you to serve your country, and earn three dollars a day, by becoming a member of the legislature, you must first publicly avow that the constitution of the state is a shackle upon free and liberal legislation; and is, therefore, of as little use in the present enlightened age, as an old almanac of the year in which the instrument was framed. There is policy in this measure, for by making the constitution a mere dead letter, your headlong proceedings will be attributed to a bold and unshackled mind; whereas, it might otherwise be thought they arose from sheer mulish ignorance. 'The Government' has set the example in his attack upon the constitution of the United States, and who should fear to follow where 'the Government' leads?

"When the day of election approaches, visit your constituents far and wide. Treat liberally, and drink freely, in order to rise in their estimation, though you fall in your own. True, you may be called a drunken dog by some of the clean shirt and silk stocking gentry, but the real rough necks will style you a jovial fellow, their votes are certain, and frequently count double. Do all you can to appear to advantage in the eyes of the women. That's easily done you have but to kiss and slabber their children, wipe their noses, and pat them on the head; this cannot fail to please their mothers, and you may rely on your business being done in that quarter.

"Promise all that is asked," said I, "and more if you can think of anything. Offer to build a bridge or a church, to divide a county, create a batch of new offices, make a turnpike, or anything they like. Promises cost nothing, therefore deny nobody who has a vote or sufficient influence to obtain one.

"Get up on all occasions, and sometimes on no occasion at all, and make long-winded speeches, though composed of nothing else than wind— talk of your devotion to your country, your modesty and disinterestedness, or on any such fanciful subject. Rail against taxes of all kinds, office-holders, and bad harvest weather; and wind up with a flourish about the heroes who fought and bled for our liberties in the times that tried men's souls. To be sure you run the risk of being considered a bladder of wind, or an empty barrel, but never mind that, you will find enough of the same fraternity to keep you in countenance.

"If any charity be going forward, be at the top of it, provided it is to be advertised publicly; if not, it isn't worth your while. None but a fool would place his candle under a bushel on such an occasion.

"These few directions," said I, "if properly attended to, will do your business; and when once elected, why a fig for the dirty children, the promises, the bridges, the churches, the taxes, the offices, and the subscriptions, for it is absolutely necessary to forget all these before you can become a thoroughgoing politician, and a patriot of the first water."

My speech was received with three times three, and all that; and we continued speechifying and drinking until nightfall, when it was put to vote, that we would have the puppet show over again, which was carried *nem. con.* The showman set his wires to work, just as "the Government" does the machinery in his big puppet show; and we spent a delightful and rational evening. We raised a subscription for the poor showman; and I went to bed, pleased and gratified with the hospitality and kindness of the citizens of Little Rock. There are some first-rate men there, of the real half horse, half alligator breed, with a sprinkling of the steamboat, and such as grow nowhere on the face of the universal earth, but just about the back bone of North America.

The Election of 1840

By 1840, political strategists of all stripes were willing to try what one newsman called the "Davy Crockett Line" and portray their candidates as simple backwoodsmen who had been raised on possum

fat and hominy. The Harrison campaign for president in 1840 probably carried political hoopla to an extreme. As you look at the picture
below, and read the newspaper account of a St. Louis political rally
that follows, you will begin to understand not only why Harrison
won but also why the election brought 78 percent of the electorate
out to vote. In many ways the Harrison campaign was the first modern political campaign.

F.D.R. Library.

Rally for William Henry Harrison in
St. Louis, Missouri

We cannot believe that any friend of Harrison could, in his most sanguine moments, have anticipated so glorious a day, such a turn-out of the people, as was witnessed on Tuesday last in this city. Everything was auspicious. The heavens, the air, the earth all seemed to have combined to assist in doing honor to the services, the patriotism and the virtues of William Henry Harrison. Never have we seen so much enthusiasm, so much honest, impassioned and eloquent feeling displayed in the countenances and bursting from the lips of freemen. It was a day of jubilee. The people felt that the time had come when they could breathe freely—when they were about to cast from them the incubus of a polluted and abandoned party, and when they could look forward to better and happier days in store for them and for the country.

Preparations had been made for the reception and entertainment of the company, by the proper committees, at Mrs. Ashley's residence. The extensive park was so arranged as to accommodate the throng of persons who were expected. Seats were erected for the officers of the day, for the speakers and for the ladies. At the hour appointed by the marshal of the day, the people commenced to assemble at the court house, and several associations and crafts were formed in the procession as they advanced on the ground. While this was going on, the steamboats bringing delegations from St. Charles, Hannibal, Adams county, Ill., and Alton, arrived at the wharf, with banners unfurled to the breeze, and presenting a most cheering sight. The order of procession, so far as we have been able to obtain it, was as follows:

Music: Brass band.

1. Banner, borne by farmers from the northern part of St. Louis township. This banner represented the "Raising of the Siege of Fort Meigs" and bore as its motto, "It Has Pleased Providence, We Are Victorious." (Harrison's dispatch.)

2. Officers and members of the Tippecanoe club, preceded by the president, Col. John O'Fallon, with a splendid banner, representing a hemisphere surmounted by an American eagle, strangling with his beak a serpent, its fold grasped within its talons, and its head having the face of a fox in the throes of death.

3. Log cabin committee, six abreast.

4. The president and vice-presidents of the day.

5. Soldiers who served under Harrison in the late war—in a car, adorned with banners on each side—one, a view of a steamboat named Tippecanoe, with a sign board, "For Washington City."

6. Invited guests in carriages.

7. Citizens on foot, six abreast, bearing banners inscribed, "Harrison, the Friend of Pre-emption Rights," "One Term for the Presidency," "Harri-

From "Rally for William Henry Harrison in St. Louis, Missouri," as reported by the St. Louis *New Era*, in A. B. Norton, ed., *The Election of 1840*, Vol. I (1888), pp. 141–146.

son, the People's Candidate;" "Harrison, the People's Sober Second Thought;" "Harrison, He Never Lost a Battle;" "Harrison, the Protector of the Pioneers of the West;" "Harrison, Tyler and Reform;" "Harrison, the Poor Man's Friend;" "Harrison, the Friend of Equal Laws and Equal Rights."

8. Citizens on horseback, six abreast.

9. Delegation from Columbia Bottom.

10. Canoe, "North Bend."

11. Boys with banners, upon one of which was inscribed, "Our Country's Hope," and on another, "Just as the Twig is Bent, the Tree's Inclined."

12. Laborers, with their horses and carts, shovels, picks, etc., with a banner bearing the inscription, "Harrison, the Poor Man's Friend—We Want Work."

13. A printing press on a platform with banners, and the pressman striking off Tippecanoe songs, and distributing them to the throng of people as they passed along, followed in order by the members of the craft.

14. Drays, with barrels of hard cider.

15. A log cabin mounted on wheels, and drawn by six beautiful horses, followed by the craft of carpenters in great numbers. Over the door of the cabin, the words, "The String of the Latch Never Pulled In."

16. The blacksmiths, with forge, bellows, etc., mounted on cars, the men at work. Banner, "We Strike for Our Country's Good."

17. The joiners and cabinet-makers; a miniature shop mounted on wheels; men at work; the craft following it.

18. A large canoe, drawn by six horses, and filled with men.

19. Two canoes, mounted, and filled by sailors.

20. Fort Meigs, in miniature, 40 by 15 feet, drawn by nine yoke of oxen.

Arrived at the southern extremity of the park, the procession halted and formed in open order, the rear passing to the front.

The people were then successively addressed by Mr. John Hogan, of Illinois.

Colonel John O'Fallon was then called for, and mounted on Fort Meigs, he thus addressed the people:

My Fellow Citizens:

I feel deeply sensible of the honor you confer upon me by calling me to address this vast concourse of intelligent freemen.

I had the honor of serving under General Harrison at the battle of Tippecanoe, during the siege of Fort Meigs, and at the battle of the Thames. I can say that, from the commencement to the termination of his military services in the last war, I was almost constantly by his side. I was familiar with his conduct as governor and superintendent of Indian affairs of the Territory of Indiana, and after the return of peace, as commissioner to treat with all the hostile Indians of the last war in the Northwest, for the establishment of a permanent reconciliation and peace. I saw also much of General Harrison whilst he was in the Congress of the United States.

Opportunities have thus been afforded me of knowing him in all the relations of life, as an officer and as a man, and of being enabled to form a pretty correct estimate of his military and civil services, as well as his qualifications and fitness for office.

As a military man, his daring, chivalrous courage inspired his men with confidence and spread dismay and terror to his enemies. In all his plans he was successful. In all his engagements he was victorious. He has filled all the various civil and military offices committed to him by his country, with sound judgment and spotless fidelity. In every situation he was cautious and prudent, firm and energetic, and his decisions always judicious. His acquirements as a scholar are varied and extensive, his principles as a statesman sound, pure and republican.

If chosen President he will be the President of the people rather than of a party. The Government will then be administered for the general good and welfare.

His election will be drawn of a new era! The reform of the abuses of a most corrupt, profligate and oppressive Government. Then will end the ten years' war upon the currency and institutions of the country. The hard-money cry and hard times will disappear altogether. Then will cease further attempts to increase the wages of the office-holders and reduce the wages of the people to the standard of European labor.

Then shall we see restored the general prosperity of the people, by giving them a sound local currency, mixed with a currency of a uniform value throughout the land. The revival of commerce, of trade, enterprise and general confidence. Then the return of happier, more peaceful and more prosperous days, when cheerfulness and plenty will, once more, smile around the poor man's table.

George Caleb Bingham

The Artist's View of Politics

What were ordinary elections like? Fortunately, the painter George Caleb Bingham of Missouri provided some answers to this question. He broke into Western politics in 1840 as an enthusiastic young orator for Harrison, and he eventually won a seat in the Missouri House of Representatives. He knew that every vote counted; he won one election by a mere three votes and another by twenty-five votes.

He painted these memorable political scenes out of his own experience. The first one, called "Canvassing for a Vote," shows a campaigner with a saddlebag full of literature trying to win a vote outside a highway tavern. The second, "County Election," shows the voters lined up to cast their ballots verbally, with candidates on top of the steps tipping their hats politely, and the inevitable barrel of cider (or whiskey) on the left. The third, "Verdict of the People," shows a clerk reading election results aloud from the steps of the courthouse. The fourth, "Stump Speaking," is Bingham's masterpiece. It shows an experienced politician who has grown gray in the pursuit of office trying to influence a crowd. The man taking notes is his opponent, and the fat man at the far left is the former governor of Missouri, Meredith Miles Marmaduke. He was so angry when he saw this painting that he challenged Bingham to a duel.

Compare these pictures with some earlier ones on pages 160–163 and 206. Do they help you understand why Jacksonian politics was regarded as being new and different? Was it really a complete break with the past? Or can you see some carry-over from earlier days?

Canvassing for a Vote. By George Bingham. *Nelson Gallery—Atkins Museum.*

County Election. By George Bingham. *St. Louis Mercantile Library Association/City Art Museum.*

Verdict of the People. By George Bingham. *Collection of the Boatman's National Bank of St. Louis.*

Stump Speaking. By George Bingham. *Collection of the Boatman's National Bank of St. Louis.*

12

Antislavery

There was one issue that leaders of both parties, Whigs and Democrats alike, wanted to keep out of politics. And that issue was slavery. Politicians of all stripes knew that slavery could easily shatter their national parties—and perhaps the Union itself. They preferred to fight over "safe" political issues like banking, tariffs, roads, and canals. And they fought over such issues year in and year out. In working to keep slavery out of the limelight, of course, politicians were effectively supporting slavery, which was an old and well-established institution by Jackson's time.

Keeping slavery out of politics, however, became increasingly difficult. For one thing, the old institution of slavery, which had been "normal" throughout the Atlantic world since the 1500s, began to give way rapidly after the American Revolution. By 1804 all Northern states had either freed their slaves or adopted programs of gradual emancipation. And by the time of Jackson's second administration (1833–1837) programs to abolish slavery had been adopted in Haiti, Argentina, Chile, Colombia, Central America, Mexico, Bolivia, and the British West Indies. The American South was beginning to stand out as a sore thumb.

For another thing, "reform" was in the air after the War of 1812, especially in the North, where all sorts of reformers suddenly emerged and tromped across the countryside. In contrast to the South, where one could go for weeks without hearing the cry of reform, there were parts of New England, upstate New York, and the Ohio Valley that seemed to be overrun with revivalists, reformers, and enthusiasts espousing one cause or another.

Why? The answers have been almost as numerous as the reformers and abolitionists. One point of view is that the reformers, especially the men and women who came out against slavery, were simply working out the logic of modern egalitarianism. Did not the Declaration of Independence assert simply the equality of all men? How could such a faith coexist with slavery? Other historians have argued that reform, especially in its connection with revivalism, was a product of the experience of the frontier. Others have claimed that the reform leaders were members of an old elite that was afraid of being displaced by a new class of people whose wealth came from business, and so turned to reform to relieve their anxiety at losing control of the nation's social and political life.

Another point of view is that the prime recruits for reform movements were to be found among people whose ethnic and regional identities led them to undergo conversion to a militant Protestant revivalism. Immigrants from England and Wales, and migrants from New England to the West, so this argument goes, were the people most likely to answer the evangelical preachers' calls that they dedicate their lives to Christ. Out of this wave of revival, on both sides of the Atlantic, came an army of hundreds of thousands of converts. And it was from among them that a tiny minority was chosen, a minority who turned now to try to perfect society in the image of Christ, and in so doing to try to perfect themselves.

Interpretive Essay

James Brewer Stewart

The Commitment to Immediate Emancipation

The following essay, by the historian James Brewer Stewart, examines the relationship between nineteenth-century Protestantism and the commitment to the immediate end of slavery. There were a variety of antislavery positions, some favoring gradual abolition, others immediate; some advocating sending ex-slaves to Africa; others involving paying their former owners something like their market value. The most radical position, which gained ground after 1830, was the uncompromising demand for the immediate, unconditional emancipation of the slaves without compensation to their owners— and without regard for the consequences. Only a minority of Americans with antislavery opinions adopted this position, and this selection is a guide to understanding who they were and why they embarked on such a course.

From James Brewer Stewart, *Holy Warriors: The Abolitionists and American Slavery* (New York: Hill and Wang, 1976), pp. 33–49. Copyright © 1976 by James Brewer Stewart. Reprinted with the permission of Hill and Wang, a division of Farrar, Straus & Giroux, Inc.

American society in the late 1820's presented the pious, well-informed Yankee with tremendous challenges. For the better part of a decade, Protestant spokesmen had warned him against the nation's all-absorbing interest in material wealth, geographic expansion, and party politics. Infidelity, he was told, flourished on the Western and Southern frontiers; vice reigned supreme in the burgeoning Eastern cities. In politics, he was exhorted to combat atheist demagogues called Jacksonians who insisted on popular rule and further demanded that the clerical establishment be divorced from government. Urban workingmen and frontier pioneers, morally numbed by alcoholism and illiteracy, were being duped in massive numbers by the blandishments of these greedy politicos. America, he was assured, faced moral bankruptcy and the total destruction of its Christian identity. Exaggerated as such claims may seem, they had some grounding in reality. Yankee Protestantism was indeed facing immense new challenges from a society in the throes of massive social change. As Protestants struggled to overcome these adversities, the abolitionists' crusade for immediate emancipation also took form.

By the end of the 1820's, America was in the midst of unparalleled economic growth. Powerful commercial networks were coming to link all sections of the country; canals, mass-circulation newspapers, and (soon) railroads reinforced this thrust toward regional interdependency. Northern business depended as never before on trade with the South. The "cotton revolution" which swept the Mississippi-Alabama-Georgia frontier in turn stimulated textile manufacturing and shipping in the Northeast. In the Northwest, yet another economic boom took shape as businessmen and farmers in Ohio, Indiana, and Illinois developed lucrative relationships with the Eastern seaboard, and the population of Northern cities grew apace. Politicians organized party machines which catered to these new interests and to the "common man's" mundane preferences.

The cosmopolitan forces of economic interdependence, urbanization, democratic politics, and mass communication posed major challenges to provincial New England culture. The Protestant response, in John L. Thomas's apt phrase, was "to fight democratic excess with democratic remedies." Throughout the 1820's New Englanders mounted an impressive counterattack against the forces of "immorality" by commandeering the tools of their secular opponents: the printing press, the rally, and the efficiently managed bureaucratic agency. With the hope of renovating American religious life, the American Tract Society spewed forth thousands of pamphlets which exhorted readers to repent. The Temperance Union carried a similar message to the nation's innumerable hard drinkers. Various missionary societies sent witnesses to backcountry settlements, the waterfront haunts of Boston's seamen, the bordellos of New York City. These societies envisioned a reassertion of traditional New England values on a national scale. At the same time, although unintentionally, these programs for Christian restoration were stimulating in pious young men and women stirrings of spiritual revolt.

All of these reform enterprises drew their vitality from revivalistic religion. Once again, social discontent and political alienation found widespread expression through the conversion experience; the Great Revivals announced the Protestant resurgence of the 1820's. Like their eighteenth-century predecessors, powerful evangelists such as Charles G. Finney and Lyman Beecher urged their audiences that man, though a sinner, should nonetheless strive for holiness and choose a new life of sanctification. Free will once again took precedence over original sin, which was again redefined as voluntary selfishness. As in the 1750's, God was pictured as insisting that the "saved" perform acts of benevolence, expand the boundaries of Christ's kingdom, and recognize a personal responsibility to improve society. Men and women again saw themselves playing dynamic roles in their own salvation and preparing society for the millennium. By the thousands they flocked to the Tract Society, the Sunday School Union, the temperance and peace organizations, and the Colonization Society. Seeking prevention, certainly not revolution, evangelicals thus dreamed of a glorious era of national reform: rid of liquor, prostitution, atheism, and popular politics, the redeemed masses of America would gladly submit to the leadership of Christian statesmen. So blessed, Americans would no longer fall prey to the blandishments of that hard-drinking gambler, duelist, and unchurched slaveowner, President Andrew Jackson.

From this defensive setting sprang New England's crusade against slavery. Indeed, radical reformers of all varieties, not just abolitionists, traced their activism to the revivals of the 1820's. . . .

While revivalism's ambiguities stimulated anxiety in the 1820's, its network of benevolent agencies opened opportunities for young Americans which their eighteenth-century counterparts could never have foreseen. The missionary agencies and even the revivals themselves were organized along complex bureaucratic lines. Volunteers were always needed to drum up donations or to organize meetings. New careers were also created. For the first time in American history, young people could regard social activism as a legitimate profession. Earnest ministerial candidates began accepting full-time positions as circuit riders, regional agents, newspaper editors, and schoolteachers, with salaries underwritten by the various benevolent agencies. One important abolitionist-to-be, Joshua Leavitt, spent his first years after seminary editing the *Seaman's Friend,* an evangelical periodical for sailors. Another, Elizur Wright, Jr., was employed by the American Tract Society.

Most important to abolitionism was the effect of revivalism on the ministry itself. Once open to only an elite, the ministry had by the 1820's become a common profession. Spurred by expanding geography, seminaries increased their enrollments as they attracted young New Englanders who burned to aid in America's regeneration. Included were some destined to number among abolitionism's dominant figures: Samuel J. May, Amos A. Phelps, Theodore D. Weld, Joshua Leavitt, and Stephen S. Foster, to name only a few. First as seminarians, then as volunteers, paid agents, clergymen, and teachers, many pious young Americans dedicated themselves to fighting sin and disbelief. Given the intensity of the evangelical temperament, the results of such experiences were to suggest, to some, far more radical courses of action, and there can be no question that these abolitionists-to-be took their responsibilities in deadly earnest.

There is some persuasive evidence that family background and upbringing predisposed young New Englanders toward a radical outlook. Over twenty years ago, David Donald gathered information which suggests the influence of parental guidance on abolitionism's most prominent spokesmen. Abolitionism, he reported, was a revolt of youth raised by old New England families of farmers, teachers, ministers, and businessmen. The parents of abolitionists were usually well-educated Presbyterians, Congregationalists, Quakers, and Unitarians who participated heavily in revivalism and its attendant benevolent projects. Many scholars have effectively criticized Donald's methods and have raised serious questions about the reliability of his evidence regarding the movement's rank-and-file. Donald also erred in concluding that commitments to abolitionism were reactions to a loss of social status to nouveau riche neighbors. Actually, abolitionism flourished among groups with rising social prospects during the 1830's. Nevertheless, Donald's findings remain extremely suggestive as to the influence of parental guidance of abolitionism's most prominent leaders.

In such families, as numerous biographers have since attested, a stern emphasis on moral uprightness and social responsibility generally prevailed. In the words of Bertram Wyatt-Brown, young men and women "learned that integrity came not from conformity to the ways of the world, but to the principles by which the family tried to live." Parents were usually eager to inculcate a high degree of religious and social conscience. In their reminiscences, abolitionists commonly paid homage to strong-minded mothers or fathers whose intense religious fervor dominated their households. In his early years, Wendell Phillips constantly turned to his mother for instruction, and after her death he confessed that "whatever good is in me, she is responsible for." Thomas Wentworth Higginson, Arthur and Lewis Tappan, and William Lloyd Garrison became, like Phillips, leading abolitionists and also internalized the religious dictates of dominating mothers. Sidney Howard Gay, James G. Birney, Elizur Wright, Jr., and Elijah P. Lovejoy are examples of abolitionists who modeled their early lives to fit the intentions of exacting fathers. Young women who were to enter the movement usually sought the advice of their fathers, as in the cases of Elizabeth Cady Stanton and Maria Weston Chapman. Yet whatever the child's focus, the expectations of parents seldom varied. Displays of conscience and upright behavior brought the rewards of parental love and approval.

Children also learned that sexual self-control was a vital part of righteous living. Parents stressed prayer and benevolent deeds as substitutes for "carnal thoughts" and intimacy; they associated sexual sublimation with family stability and personal redemption. During his years at boarding school and later at Harvard, Wendell Phillips strove to satisfy his mother on all these counts. Lewis Tappan, too, remembered how hard he had worked "to be one of the best scholars, often a favorite with the masters, and a leader among the boys in our plays." When he was twenty and living away from home, Tappan still received admonitions from his mother about the pitfalls of sex. Recalling a dream, she wrote, "Methought you had, by frequenting the theatre, been drawn into the society of lewd women, and had contracted a disease that was preying upon your constitution." For his part, Tappan had already sworn to "enjoy a sound mind and body, untainted by vice." A strong sense of their individuality, a deadly earnestness about moral issues, confidence in their ability to master themselves and to improve the world—these were the qualities which so often marked abolitionists in their early years. Above all, these future reformers believed in their own superiority and fully expected to become leaders.

Of course, not all children of morally assertive New England parents became radical abolitionists. William Lloyd Garrison's brother, for example, emerged from his mother's tutelage and lapsed into alcoholism. Still, the predisposition to rebellion remains hard to dismiss. Alienation and self-doubt certainly ran especially deep among these sensitive, socially conscious young people. Besides, America in the 1820's appeared to many a complex and bewildering place. Certain social realities were soon to seem disturbingly at variance with their high expectations and fixed moral codes.

These future abolitionists entered young adulthood at a time when rapid mobility, technological advance, and dizzying geographic expansion were transforming traditional institutions. Those who took up pastorates, seminary study, or positions in benevolent agencies were shocked to discover that the Protestant establishment was hardly free from the acquisitive taint and bureaucratic selfishness that they had been brought up to disdain. Expecting to lead communities of godfearing, Christian families, young ministers like Amos A. Phelps, Elizur Wright, Jr., and Charles T. Torrey confronted instead a fragmented society of entrepreneurs. Theodore Dwight Weld, for example, wrote critically to the great evangelist Charles G. Finney that "*revivals* are fast becoming with you a sort of trade, to be worked at so many hours a day." Promoters of colonization, such as James G. Birney and Joshua Leavitt, became increasingly disturbed that many of their co-workers were far less interested in Christian benevolence than in ridding the nation of inferior blacks. In politics, Lewis Tappan, William Jay, and William Lloyd Garrison searched desperately and without success for a truly Christian leader, an alternative to impious Andrew Jackson and the godless party he led.

Predictably, misgiving became ever more frequent among young evangelicals. They began to question their abilities, to rethink their choices of career, and to doubt the Christianity of the churches, seminaries, and benevolent societies. Just possibly, the nation was far more deeply mired in sin than anyone had imagined. Just possibly, parental formulas for godly reformation were fatally compromised. And, most disturbing of all, just possibly the idealist-reformer himself needed reforming—a new relationship with God, a new vision of his responsibility as a Christian American.

The powerful combination in the 1820's of Yankee conservatism, revivalist benevolence, New England upbringing, and social unrest was leading young evangelicals toward a genuinely radical vision. Given this setting, it hardly seems surprising that a militant abolitionist movement began to take shape. Opposition to slavery certainly constituted a dramatic affirmation of one's Christian identity and commitment to a life of Protestant purity. Economic exploitation, sexual license, gambling, drinking and dueling, disregard for family ties—all traits associated with slaveowning—could easily be set in bold contrast with the pure ideals of Yankee evangelicalism.

There were a few militant antislavery spokesmen in the upper South in the 1820's, but their influence on young New Englanders was negligible. The manumission societies organized largely by evangelical Quakers and Moravian Brethren in Tennessee, Kentucky, and other border areas were already collapsing at the start of New England's crusade for immediate emancipation. The Southern antislavery movement's chief spokesman, editor Benjamin Lundy, had retreated northward from Tennessee. By 1829 he was living in Baltimore and had hired a zealous young editorial assistant from Newburyport, Massachusetts: William Lloyd Garrison.

The sudden emergence of immediate abolitionism in New England thus cannot be explained as a predictable offshoot of Yankee revivalism or a legacy from the upper South. Instead, one must emphasize the interaction between the rebellious feelings of these religious men and women and the events of the early 1830's. As the 1830's opened in an atmosphere of crisis, their attentions became intensely fixed on slavery. As in the early 1820's, the nation was again beset by black rebellions and threats of southern secession. Concurrently, events in England and in its sugar islands empire seemed to confirm the necessity of demanding the immediate emancipation of all slaves, everywhere. An unprecedented array of circumstances and jarring events suddenly converged on these anxious young people and launched them upon the lifetime task of abolishing slavery.

By far the most alarming was the ominous note of black militancy on which the new decade opened. In Boston in 1829, an ex-slave from North Carolina, David Walker, published the first edition of his famous *Appeal*. A landmark in black protest literature, Walker's *Appeal* condemned colonization as a white supremacist hoax, excoriated members of his own race for their passivity, and called, as a last resort, for armed resistance. "I do declare," wrote Walker, "that one good black man can put to death six white men." Whites had never hesitated to kill blacks, he advised, so "if you commence . . . do not trifle, for they will not trifle with you." Other events, even more shocking, were to follow. In 1831, William Lloyd Garrison, now living in Boston, issued a call for immediate emancipation in the *Liberator*. Soon after, Southampton County, Virginia, erupted in the bloody Nat Turner insurrection, the largest slave revolt in antebellum America. Still another massive slave rebellion broke out in British Jamaica in 1831. Coinciding with these racial traumas was the Nullification Crisis of 1831–32, a confrontation ignited by South Carolina's opposition to national tariff policy and by the deeper fear that the federal government might someday abolish slavery. Intent on preserving state sovereignty and hence slavery, South Carolina politicians led by John C. Calhoun temporarily defied national authority, threatened secession, and risked occupation by federal troops.

As these frightening events unfolded, young evangelicals cast aside their self-doubt. Unfocused discontent gave way to soul-wrenching commitments to eradicating the sin of slavery. The combined actions of Nat Turner, the South Carolina "Nullifiers," and David Walker suggested with dramatic force that slavery was the fundamental cause of society's degraded state. As Theodore D. Weld observed, the abolitionist cause "not only *overshadows* all others, but . . . absorbs them into itself. Revivals, moral Reform etc. will remain stationary until the temple is cleansed." The step-by-step solutions advocated by their parents suddenly appeared to invite only God's retribution. Like Garrison, Arthur Tappan, and many others, James G. Birney sealed his commitment to immediate abolition by decrying colonization. The Colonization Society, Birney charged, acted as "an opiate to the consciences" of those who would otherwise "feel deeply and keenly the sin of slavery."

In one sense, these sudden espousals of immediate abolition can be understood as a strategic innovation developed because of the manifest failures of gradualism. Slaveholders had certainly shown no sympathy to moderate schemes. In England, too, where immediatism was also gaining followers, the general public had remained unmoved by gradualist proposals. Demands for "immediate, unconditional, uncompensated emancipation" thus appealed to young American idealists—at least the slogan was free of moral qualifications. Indeed, in 1831 the British government, responding to immediatist demands, enacted a massive program of gradual, compensated emancipation in the West Indies. But, even more important, by dedicating themselves to immediatism, the young reformers performed acts of self-liberation akin to the experience of conversion.

By freeing themselves from the shackles of gradualism, American abolitionists had finally triumphed over their feelings of selfishness, unworthiness, and alienation. Now they were morally fit to take God's side in the struggle against all the worldliness, license, cruelty, and selfishness that slaveowning had come to embody. Immediatists sensed themselves involved in a cosmic drama, a righteous war to redeem a fallen nation. They now felt ready to make supreme sacrifices and prove their fitness in their new religion of antislavery. "Never were men called on to die in a holier cause," wrote Amos A. Phelps in 1835 as he began his first tour as an abolitionist lecturer. It was far better, he thought, to die "as the negro's plighted friend" than to "sit in silken security, the consentor to & abettor of the manstealer's sin."

The campaign for Protestant reassertion had thus brought forth a vibrant romantic radicalism. Orthodox evangelicals quite rightly recoiled in fear. Abolitionists now put their faith entirely in the individual's ability to recognize and redeem himself from sin. No stifling traditions, no restrictive loyalties to institutions, no timorous concern for moderation or self-interest should be allowed to inhibit the free reign of Christian conscience. In its fullest

sense, the phrase "immediate emancipation" described a transformed state
of mind dominated by God and wholly at war with slavery. "The doctrine,"
wrote Elizur Wright, Jr., in 1833, "may be thus briefly stated":

> It is the duty of the holders of slaves to restore them to their liberty, and to
> extend to them the full protection of the law . . . to restore to them the profits
> of their labors, . . . to employ them as voluntary laborers on equitable wages.
> Also it is the *duty* of all men . . . to proclaim this doctrine, to urge upon slavehold-
> ers *immediate emancipation,* so long as there is a slave—to agitate the consciences
> of tyrants, so long as there is a tyrant on the globe.

Embedded in this statement was a vision of a new America, a daring
affirmation that people of both races could reestablish their relationships on
the basis of justice and Christian brotherhood. Like many other Americans
who took up the burdens of reform, abolitionists envisioned their cause as
leading to a society reborn in Christian brotherhood. Emancipation, like temperance, women's rights and communitarianism, became synonymous with
the redemption of mankind and the opening of a purer phase of human history.

Abolitionists constantly tried to explain that they were not expecting
some sudden Day of Jubilee when, with a shudder of collective remorse,
the entire planter class would abruptly strike the shackles from all two million
slaves and beg their forgiveness. Emancipation, they expected, would be
achieved gradually; still it must be immediately begun. Immediatists were
also forced to rebut the recurring charge that their demand promoted emancipation by rebellion on the plantations. "Our objects are to save life, not
destroy it," Garrison exclaimed in 1831. "Make the slave free and every
inducement to revolt is taken away." Few Americans believed these disclaim-
ers. Instead, most suspected that immediate emancipation would suddenly
create a large and mobile free population of inferior blacks. Most in the
North were quite content to discriminate harshly against their black neighbors
while the slaves remained at a safe distance on far-away plantations. According
to Alexis de Tocqueville, the unusually acute foreign observer of antebellum
society of the early 1830's: "Race prejudice seems stronger in those states
that have abolished slavery than in those states where it still exists, and nowhere is it more intolerant than in those states where it has never been known."
White supremacy and support for slavery were thus inextricably bound up
with all phases of American political, economic, and religious life. Immediatist
agitation was bound to provoke hostility from nearly every part of the social
order.

As we have seen, by the 1830's the Northeast and Midwest enjoyed a
thriving trade with the South, and the nation's economic well-being had
become firmly tied to slave labor. Powerful financial considerations could
thus dictate that abolitionism be harshly suppressed. Religious denominations
were also deeply enmeshed in slavery, for Southerners were influential among
the Methodists, Presbyterians, Anglicans, and Baptists. Little wonder that
most clergymen vigorously rejected demands that their churches declare slaveholders in shocking violation of God's Law.

But by far the most consistent opponents of the abolitionist crusade were found in politics. Young reformers had long ago come to abhor what they saw as the hollow demagoguery and secularism of Jacksonian mass politics. By 1830 they were fully justified in adding the politician's unstinting support of slavery to their bill of particulars. As Richard H. Brown has shown, Jackson's Democratic Party was deliberately designed to uphold the planters' interests. Jacksonian ideology soon became synonymous with racism and anti-abolition. In the North, men who aspired to careers in Democratic Party politics had to solicit the approval of slaveholding party chiefs like Amos Kendall, John C. Calhoun, and Jackson himself. When anti-Jacksonian dissidents finally coalesced into the Whig Party during the 1830's, they, too, relied upon this formula for getting votes and recruiting leaders. Obviously, neither party dared to alienate proslavery interests in the South or racist supporters in the North. Moreover, as the Missouri and Nullification controversies had shown, political debates about slavery caused party allegiances to break ominously along sectional lines. For these reasons, party loyalty meant the suppression of all discussions of slavery.

The challenges which the abolitionists faced as they began their crusade were thus enormous. So was their own capability for disruption, although they were hardly aware of it at first. The ending of slavery whether peacefully or violently would require great changes in American life. Yet, if immediate emancipation provoked fear and violent hostility, it was nevertheless a doctrine appropriate to the age. The evangelical outlook with its rejection of tradition and expedience both embodied and challenged the culture that had created it. In retrospect, moderate approaches to the problem of slavery hardly seemed possible in Jacksonian America.

As a result, immediatist goals were anything but limited. Abolitionists now proposed to transform hundreds of millions of dollars worth of slaves into millions of black citizens by eradicating two centuries of American racism. Nevertheless, they sincerely felt that they promoted a conservative enterprise, and in certain respects this was an understandable (if misleading) self-assessment. Their unqualified attacks on slavery were, as they understood them, simply emulations of well-established evangelical methods. The Temperance Society's assault on liquor and the revivalist's denunciation of unbelief had hardly been characterized by restraint. Besides, immediatists were simply proposing an ideal by which all Christians were to measure themselves. They were not planning bloody revolution. They relied solely on voluntary conversion and rejected violence. As agitators, they defined their task as restoring time-honored American freedoms to an unjustly deprived people. Except for their opposition to racism, they offered no criticism of ordinary Protestant values. Was it anarchy, they wondered, to urge that pure Christian morality replace what they believed was the sexual abandon of the slave quarters? "Are we then fanatics," Garrison asked, "because we cry, *Do not rob! Do not murder!?*"

In their own eyes, then, abolitionists were hardly behaving like incendiaries as they opened their crusade. In slaveholding they discovered the ultimate source of the moral collapse which so deeply disturbed them. The race violence of Nat Turner and the secession threats of the "Nullifiers" constituted evidence that the nation had jettisoned all her moral ballasts. But immediate abolition seemed to hold forth the promise of Christian reconciliation between races, sections, and individuals. All motive for race revolt, all reason for political strife, and all inducement for moral degeneracy would be swept away. Indeed, the alternative of silence only invited the further spread of anarchy in a nation which Garrison described in 1831 as already "full of the blood of innocent men, women and babies—full of adultery and concupiscence—full of blasphemy, darkness and woeful rebellion against God—full of wounds and bruises and putrefying sores." Abolitionists were thus filled "with burning earnestness" when they insisted, as Elizur Wright did, that "the instant abolition of the whole slave system is safe." Most other Americans remained firm in their suspicions to the contrary.

Nevertheless, the abolitionists launched their crusade on a note of glowing optimism. Armed with moral certitude, they were also completely naïve politically. "The whole system of slavery will fall to pieces with a rapidity which will astonish," wrote Samuel E. Sewall, one of the first adherents to immediatism. Weld predicted in 1834 that complete equality for all blacks in the upper South was but two years away, and that "scores of clergymen in the slaveholding states . . . *are really with us.*" Anxious for the millennium, abolitionists had wholly misjudged the depth of Northern racism, not to mention the extent of Southern tolerance.

All the same, there was wisdom in the naïveté. Without this romantic faith that God would put all things right, abolitionists would have lacked the incentive and creative stamina necessary for sustained assaults against slavery. Moreover, by stressing intuition as a sure guide to reality, abolitionists made an unprecedented attempt to establish empathy with the slave. One result, to be sure, was racist sentimentalism, a not surprising outcome considering the gulf which separated a Mississippi field hand from an independently wealthy Boston abolitionist. Yet the abolitionists were trying hard to imagine what it was like to be stripped of one's autonomy, prevented from protecting one's family, and deprived of legal safeguards and the rewards of one's own labor. This view of slavery made piecemeal reform completely unacceptable. To give slaves better food, fewer whippings, and some education was not enough. They deserved immediate justice, not charity. So convinced, and certain of ultimate victory, abolitionists set out to induce each American citizen to repent the sin of slavery.

Sources

Commission to
Theodore Dwight Weld, 1834

Abolitionists have often been pictured as rampant individualists who wanted to throw off the shackles of the existing social order. But, like other reformers of their day, most of them belonged to organizations that put a premium upon concerted action, the power of numbers, rather than individual initiative. The American Anti-Slavery Society, which was formed in 1833, wanted to build up massive followings, which through pressure-group tactics would force others in line. By 1838 the society had organized 1,350 auxiliaries in the North. Here are the society's instructions to its most famous organizer, Theodore Dwight Weld.

American Anti-Slavery Society.[*]

Commission To Theodore D. Weld

Dear Sir,

You are hereby appointed and commissioned, by the Executive Committee of the American Anti-Slavery Society, instituted at Philadelphia in 1833, as their Agent, for the space of one year commencing with the first day of January, 1834, in the State of Ohio and elsewhere as the Committee may direct.

The Society was formed for the purpose of awakening the attention of our whole community to the character of American Slavery, and presenting the claims and urging the rights of the colored people of the United States; so as to promote, in the most efficient manner, the immediate abolition of Slavery, and the restoration of our colored brethren to their equal rights as citizens.

For a more definite statement of the objects of your agency, and the methods of its prosecution, the Committee refer you to their printed "Particular Instructions," communicated to you herewith; a full acquaintance and compliance with which, according to your ability, you will, on accepting this commission, consider as indispensable.

The Committee welcome you as a fellow-laborer in this blessed and

[*] This commission is a printed form, with the name of Theodore Weld, the dates, etc., written in.

From Gilbert H. Barnes and Dwight L. Dumond, eds., *Letters of Theodore Dwight Weld, Angelina Grimké Weld, and Sarah Grimké, 1822–1844* (Washington, D.C.: American Historical Association, 1934), pp. 124–128. Reprinted by permission.

responsible work; the success of which will depend, in no small degree, under God, on the results of your efforts. Their ardent desires for your success will continually attend you; you will have their sympathy in trials; and nothing, they trust, will be wanting, on their part, for your encouragement and aid.

They commend you to the kindness and co-operation of all who love Zion; praying that the presence of God may be with you, cheering your heart, sustaining you in your arduous labors, and making them a means of a speedy liberation of all the oppressed.

Given at the Society's Office, No. 130 Nassau-street, New-York, the twentieth day of February in the year of our Lord eighteen hundred and thirty-four.

Arthur Tappan
Chairman of the Executive Committee

Attest,
   E. Wright Jr.
    Secretary of Domestic Correspondence.

Particular Instructions

To Mr. T. D. Weld

Dear Sir—You have been appointed an Agent of the American Anti-Slavery Society; and will receive the following instructions from the Executive Committee, as a brief expression of the principles they wish you to inculcate, and the course of conduct they wish you to pursue in this agency.

The general principles of the Society are set forth in the Declaration, signed by the members of the Convention which formed it at Philadelphia, Dec. 7, 1833. Our object is, the overthrow of American slavery, the most atrocious and oppressive system of bondage that has ever existed in any country. We expect to accomplish this, mainly by showing to the public its true character and legitimate fruits, its contrariety to the first principles of religion, morals, and humanity, and its special inconsistency with our pretensions, as a free, humane, and enlightened people. In this way, by the force of truth, we expect to correct the common errors that prevail respecting slavery, and to produce a just public sentiment, which shall appeal both to the conscience and love of character, of our slaveholding fellow-citizens, and convince them that both their duty and their welfare require the immediate abolition of slavery.

You will inculcate every where, the great fundamental principle of IMMEDIATE ABOLITION, as the duty of all masters, on the ground that slavery is both unjust and unprofitable. Insist principally on the SIN OF SLAVERY, because our main hope is in the consciences of men, and it requires little logic to prove that it is always safe to do right. To question this, is to impeach the superintending Providence of God.

We reprobate the idea of compensation to slave holders, because it implies the right of slavery. It is also unnecessary, because the abolition of slavery will be an advantage, as free labor is found to be more profitable than the labor of slaves. We also reprobate all plans of expatriation, by whatever specious pretences covered, as a remedy for slavery, for they all proceed from prejudice against color; and we hold that the duty of the whites in regard to this cruel prejudice is not to indulge it, but to repent and overcome it.

The people of color ought at once to be emancipated and recognized as citizens, and their rights secured as such, equal in all respects to others, according to the cardinal principle laid down in the American Declaration of Independence. Of course we have nothing to do with any *equal* laws which the states may make, to prevent or punish vagrancy, idleness, and crime, either in whites or blacks.

Do not allow yourself to be drawn away from the main object, to exhibit a detailed PLAN of abolition; for men's consciences will be greatly relieved from the feeling of present duty, by any objections or difficulties which they can find or fancy in your plan. Let the *principle* be decided on, of immediate abolition, and the plans will easily present themselves. What ought to be done can be done. If the *great* question were decided, and if half the ingenuity now employed to defend slavery were employed to abolish it, it would impeach the wisdom of American statesmen to say they could not, with the Divine blessing, steer the ship through.

You will make yourself familiar with FACTS, for they chiefly influence reflecting minds. Be careful to use only facts that are well authenticated, and always state them with the precision of a witness under oath. You cannot do our cause a greater injury than by overstating facts. Clarkson's "Thoughts," and Stuart's "West India Question," are Magazines of facts respecting the safety and benefit of immediate emancipation. Mrs. Child's Book, Stroud's Slave Laws, Paxton's and Rankin's Letters, D. L. Child's Address, are good authorities respecting the character of American slavery. The African Repository and Garrison's Thoughts will show the whole subject of expatriation.

The field marked out by the Committee for your agency is the State of Ohio.

The Committee expect you to confine your labors to that field, unless some special circumstances call you elsewhere. And in such case you will confer with the Committee before changing your field, if time will allow. And if not, we wish immediate notice of the fact.

In traversing your field, you will generally find it wise to visit first several prominent places in it, particularly those where it is known our cause has friends. In going to a place, you will naturally call upon those who are friendly to our objects, and take advice from them. Also call on ministers of the gospel and other leading characters, and labor specially to enlighten them and secure their favor and influence. Ministers are the hinges of community, and ought to be moved, if possible. If they can be gained, much is gained. But if not, you will not be discouraged; and if not plainly inexpedient, attempt to obtain a house of worship; or if none can be had, some other convenient place—and hold a public meeting, where you can present our cause, its facts, arguments and appeals, to as many people as you can collect, by notices in pulpits and newspapers, and other proper means.

From Auxiliary Societies, both male and female, in every place where it is practicable. Even if such societies are very small at the outset, they may do much good as centres of light, and means of future access to the people. Encourage them to raise funds and apply them in purchasing and circulating anti-slavery publications gratuitously; particularly the Anti-Slavery Reporter, of which you will keep specimens with you, and which can always be had of the Society at $2.00 per 100. You are at liberty, with due discretion, to recommend other publications, *so far* as they advocate our views of immediate abolition. We hold ourselves responsible only for our own.

You are not to take up collections in your public meetings, as the practice often prevents persons from attending, whom it might be desirable to reach. Let this be stated in the public notice of the meeting. If you find individuals friendly to our views, who are able to give us money, you will make special personal application, and urge upon them the duty of liberally supporting this cause. You can also give notice of some place where those disposed can give you their donations. Generally, it is best to invite them to do this *the next morning*.

We shall expect you to write frequently to the Secretary for Domestic Correspondence, and give minute accounts of your proceedings and success. If you receive money for the Society, you will transmit it *by mail,* WITHOUT DELAY, to the Treasurer.

Always keep us advised, if possible, of the place where letters may reach you.

Believing as we do, that the hearts of all men are in the hand of Almighty God, we wish particularly to engage the prayers of all good men in behalf of our enterprise. Let them pray that *we* and our agents may have Divine guidance and zeal; and slave-holders, penitence; and slaves, patience; and statesmen, wisdom; so that this grand experiment of moral influence may be crowned with glorious and speedy success. Especially stir up ministers and others to the duty of making continual mention of the oppressed slaves in all social and public prayers. And as far as you can, procure the stated observance of the LAST MONDAY EVENING in every month, as a season of special prayer in behalf of the people of color.

We will only remind you, that the Society is but the almoner of the public—that the silver and the gold are the Lord's—that the amount as yet set apart by his people for promoting this particular object is small—our work is great and our resources limited—and we therefore trust that you will not fail to use a faithful economy in regard to the expenses of traveling, and reduce them as low as you can without impairing your usefulness.

The Anti-Slavery Record, 1835–1836

In 1835, thanks to a sudden reduction in the costs of printing, the American Anti-Slavery Society was able to flood the country with propaganda. Able agitators, abolitionists were among the first to use lithographs for political ends. Images of women being whipped or separated from their children and of men being beaten were the bread-and-butter of the antislavery message. Here are some of the pictographs that appeared on the front page of the *Anti-Slavery Record*, the pamphlet with by far the greatest circulation.

Anti-Slavery Record/
New York Public Library.

See p. 27.

A punishment, practised in the United States, for the crime of loving liberty.

Anti-Slavery Record/
New York Public Library.

Anti-Slavery Record/*New York Public Library*.

Anti-Slavery Record/*New York Public Library*.

Anti-Slavery Record/*New York Public Library*.

Anti-Slavery Record/*New York Public Library*.

"Fathers and Rulers" Petition

The abolitionists, like other reformers of the age, relied heavily on churchwomen. While lacking the right to vote, women were generally regarded to be inherently more moral than men, and hence their opinions on moral questions were highly respected. Capitalizing on this sentiment, women gathered thousands of signatures for massive petitions to Congress calling for the end of slavery in Washington, D.C. To shut off the flood, Congress in 1836 passed a "gag law," which was designed to keep the petitions from being read, printed, or considered by Congress. The law remained in effect until 1844. Here is one of the more famous "female petitions."

[November (?) 1834]

To the Hon. the Senate and House of Representatives of the U. States, in Congress Assembled

Petition of Ladies resident in _____ County, State of Ohio.*

Fathers and Rulers of our Country,

Suffer us, we pray you, with the sympathies which we are constrained to feel as wives, as mothers, and as daughters, to plead with you in behalf of a long oppressed and deeply injured class of native Americans, residing in that portion of our country which is under your exclusive control. We should poorly estimate the virtues which ought ever to distinguish your honorable body could we anticipate any other than a favorable hearing when our appeal is to men, to philanthropists, to patriots, to the legislators and guardians of a Christian people. We should be less than women, if the nameless and unnumbered wrongs of which the slaves of our sex are made the defenceless victims, did not fill us with horror and constrain us, in earnestness and agony of spirit to pray for their deliverance. By day and night, their woes and wrongs rise up before us, throwing shades of mournful contrast over the joys of domestic life, and filling our hearts with sadness at the recollection of those whose hearths are desolate.

---

*This is a printed form. The signatures of the petitioners were to be secured separately and pasted upon the form, and the whole petition then mailed to a Congressman in Washington. This was by far the most popular form for "female petitions" until 1840. Tens of thousands are in the files of the House of Representatives (boxes 85–126) in the Library of Congress. Except for short "sentence forms" distributed by the American Anti-Slavery Society during the period 1837–1840, it was the commonest form in the campaign.

From Gilbert H. Barnes and Dwight L. Dumond, eds., *Letters of Theodore Dwight Weld, Angelina Grimké Weld, and Sarah Grimké, 1822–1844* (Washington, D.C.: American Historical Association, 1934), pp. 175–176. Reprinted by permission.

Nor do we forget, in the contemplation of their other sufferings, the intellectual and moral degradation to which they are doomed; how the soul formed for companionship with angels, is despoiled and brutified, and consigned to ignorance, pollution, and ruin.

Surely then, as the representatives of a people professedly christian, you will bear with us when we express our solemn apprehensions in the language of the patriotic Jefferson "we tremble for our country when we remember that God is just, and that his justice cannot sleep forever," and when in obedience to a divine command "we remember them who are in bonds as bound with them." Impelled by these sentiments, we solemnly purpose, the grace of God assisting, to importune high Heaven with prayer, and our national Legislature with appeals, until this christian people abjure forever a traffic in the souls of men, and the groans of the oppressed no longer ascend to God from the dust where they now welter.

We do not ask your honorable body to transcend your constitutional powers, by legislating on the subject of slavery within the boundaries of any slaveholding State; but we do conjure you to abolish slavery in the District of Columbia where you exercise exclusive jurisdiction. In the name of humanity, justice, equal rights and impartial law, our country's weal, her honor and her cherished hopes we earnestly implore for this our humble petition, your favorable regard. If both in christian and in heathen lands, Kings have revoked their edicts, at the intercession of woman, and tyrants have relented when she appeared a suppliant for mercy, surely we may hope that the Legislators of a free, enlightened and christian people will lend their ear to our appeals, when the only boon we crave is the restoration of rights unjustly wrested from the innocent and defenceless.—And as in duty bound your petitioners will ever pray.

NAMES	NAMES

Theodore Dwight Weld

Slavery as It Is, 1839

The most impressive antislavery indictment was compiled by Theodore Dwight Weld, his wife, Angelina, and her sister, Sarah Grimké. The two women spent six months going through thousands upon thousands of Southern newspapers, looking for items in which slaveholders effectively condemned themselves. Weld then assembled the clippings into a book, *Slavery as It Is: The Testimony of a Thousand Witnesses,* which was published in 1839 and quickly sold 22,000 copies. Here is an excerpt from that book.

From Theodore Dwight Weld, *American Slavery as It Is* (New York: American Anti-Slavery Society, 1839), pp. 79–81.

The slaves are often branded with hot irons, pursued with firearms and *shot,* hunted with dogs and torn by them, shockingly maimed with knives, dirks, &c.; have their ears cut off, their eyes knocked out, their bones dislocated and broken with bludgeons, their fingers disfigured with scars and gashes, *besides* those made with the lash.

We shall adopt, under this head, the same course as that pursued under previous ones,—first give the testimony of the slaveholders themselves, to the mutilations, &c. by copying their own graphic descriptions of them, in advertisements published under their own names, and in newspapers published in the slave states, and, generally, in their own immediate vicinity. We shall, as heretofore, insert only so much of each advertisement as will be necessary to make the point intelligible.

Testimony

"Ranaway, a Negro woman and two children; a few days before she went off, *I burnt her with a hot iron,* on the left side of her face, *I tried to make the letter M.*"

"Ranaway a Negro man named Henry, *his left eye out,* some scars from a *dirk* on and under his left arm, and *much scarred* with the whip."

"One hundred dollars reward for a Negro fellow Pompey, 40 years old, he is *branded* on the *left jaw.*"

"Ranaway a Negro named Arthur, has a considerable *scar* across his *breast* and *each arm,* made by a knife; loves to talk much of the goodness of God."

"Ranaway a Negro named Mary, has a small scar over her eye, *a good many teeth missing,* the letter A. *is branded on her cheek and forehead.*"

"Ranaway a Negro named Hambleton, *limps* on his left foot where he was *shot* a few weeks ago, while runaway.

"Ranaway a Negro boy name Mose, he has a *wound* in the right shoulder near the backbone, which was occasioned by *a rifle shot.*"

"Was committed to jail a Negro man, says his name is Josiah, his back very much scarred by the whip, and *branded on the thigh and hips, in three or four places,* thus (J.M.) the *rim of his right ear has been bit or cut off.*

"Ranaway from the plantation of James Surgette, the following Negroes, Randal, *has one ear cropped;* Bob, *has lost one eye,* Kentucky Tom, *has one jaw broken.*"

"Was committed, a Negro man, has a *scar* on his right side by a burn, one on his knee, and one on the calf of his leg *by the bite of a dog.*"

"Fifty dollars reward, for the Negro Jim Blake—has a *piece cut out of each ear,* and the middle finger of the left hand cut off to the second joint."

"Ranaway, the mulatto wench Mary—has a *cut on the left arm, a scar on the shoulder, and two upper teeth missing.*"

"Ranaway, my man Fountain—has *holes in his ears,* a *scar* on the right side of his forehead—has been *shot in the hind parts of his legs*—is marked on the back with the whip."

13

Western Expansion

Andrew Jackson and his colleagues were anxious to silence the abolitionists and to keep slavery out of politics. But at the same time they were zealous expansionists. Arguing that it was God's will for the United States to expand over North America, Jackson and his followers drove the Indians off their ancestral lands in Georgia, Alabama, Mississippi, and other states in the 1830s, annexed Texas in 1845, secured by treaty much of the vast Oregon country in 1846, and took California and the Southwest from Mexico in 1848. Jacksonian expansionism doubled the size of the country, but the process left ugly scars. Force, fraud, and murder were necessary to get choice Indian lands. And war was necessary to get lands from Mexico.

Expansion also brought slavery into the center of American politics. What was to become of the "new country"? Was it to become a covey of slave states—or free states? Texas was admitted to the Union in 1845 as a slave state, with the right to subdivide into as many as four additional states. Having lost Texas to slavery, antislavery forces in Congress were determined to keep slavery out of the territory seized from Mexico during the Mexican War. In 1846 an obscure Pennsylvania congressman named David Wilmot added to a money bill a proviso declaring that none of the territory acquired from Mexico should ever be open to slavery. Although solid opposition from the South, plus crucial votes from some Northern Democrats, killed the Wilmot Proviso, it was added to bill after bill. It was never adopted, but it infuriated Southern congressmen, who became angrier still when California in 1850 gained admission to the Union as a free state. The issue of slavery in the territories caused trouble time and again, snapping the bonds of union, shattering the national political parties, and by 1861 splitting the country itself into two warring nations.

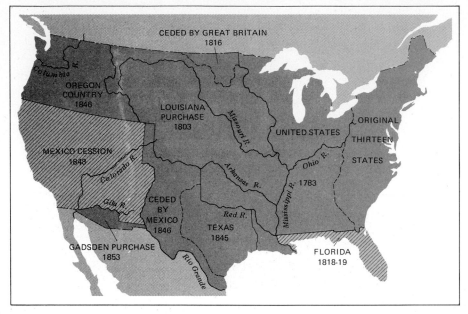

Westward Expansion.

Interpretive Essay

William L. Barney

The Quest for Room

**It was one thing for politicians in Washington to debate the future of
the West, and another for New England and New York reformers to
see the West as a fateful breeding ground for slavery. But what of the
Southerners themselves, the men who actually owned the slaves?
Many historians have argued that the West was really irrelevant, that
no white Southerner in his right mind would have thought seriously
of taking slaves into Nebraska, let alone California or Arizona. But
another argument, represented in the following essay by William L.
Barney, holds that the West *was* important to the slaveholders as a
place where they might transport their "peculiar institution."**

From William L. Barney, *The Road to Secession: A New Perspective on the Old South* (New York:
Praeger, 1972), pp. 6–17. Reprinted by permission of William L. Barney.

The history of slavery in the South was largely the story of its expansion. This expansion, from the tidewater of Virginia and the Carolinas in the late seventeenth century to the river valleys of eastern Texas by the mid-nineteenth century, enabled successive generations of Southerners to carry slavery into new territories. These surges of growth not only were converted into political power in Washington through increased representation but also satisfied two basic internal needs of the South. Additional slave territory sustained the economic viability of slavery by providing fresh land to replace the exhausted soil of the older plantation regions, creating markets for the sale of surplus and agriculturally unprofitable slaves from the Upper South, and enlarging opportunities for both the slaveholders and those striving to attain that status. Moreover, the diffusion of slaves through expansion permitted Southerners to avoid the fundamental problem of how to maintain control over a growing number of slaves confined to a closed area. The slaves had to be kept ignorant and tied to the land, because urbanization and industrialization entailed too grave a risk of slackened discipline and eventual race warfare. But a given amount of land subjected to an exploitive agriculture could support both whites and blacks for only a limited period before losing its fertility. Meanwhile, the concentration of slaves would grow ever denser until it reached unmanageable proportions. Soon—within a generation, some Southerners prophesied—the master would be fleeing his slaves. This was the Southern dilemma. The continual maturation of slavery within a fixed geographical area created class and racial stresses that could be relieved only through expansion. The extension of slavery, in turn, generated powerful opposition, capped in 1860 by the triumph of the Republican party, which was pledged to the strict containment of slavery within its existing limits. For the South, the dilemma had become a question of survival.

Land as the Economic Elixir

Of the many myths spawned by the plantation legend of the Old South, few are as alluring, or as deceptive, as the languorous, timeless image of the white-columned plantation, the homestead of the planter—that polished aristocrat with deep ties to the land, moving with grace and ease in a milieu of wealth, stability, and refinement. In fact, most planters were grasping parvenus, and their homes were simply overgrown log cabins. But what most distorts reality in this image is the absence of a sense of time and movement. It was precisely the restlessness and dynamism of most planters that attracted the attention of contemporaries. Thomas Cobb, a leading jurist of antebellum Georgia, described the planters as a class that was "never settled. Such a population is almost nomadic." Cobb explained this mobility by noting that the prime determinant of a planter's wealth and status was not his land but his slaves. As a result, his surplus income was invested in more slaves rather than in improvements to the land.

The homestead is valued only so long as the adjacent lands are profitable to cultivation. The planter himself having no local attachments, his children inherit none. On the contrary, he encourages in them a disposition to seek new lands. His valuable property (his slaves) are easily removed to fresh lands, much more easily than to bring the fertilizing materials to the old.

Mobility was characteristic of all Southerners and appears to have been a function of economic class. In Jefferson County, Mississippi, an alluvial planting area on the banks of the Mississippi, about 87 per cent of the nonslave-holders left the county during the 1850's. This percentage dropped among slaveholders in proportion to the number of slaves held, until it reached a low of 17 per cent for those owning 100 slaves or more. The main flow of migration was from the worn-out lands of the Southern Atlantic states to the virgin soils of the Southwest and across Louisiana into Texas. By 1860, South Carolina, an older state, had lost to emigration nearly half of all white natives born after 1800. (The annual and even seasonal movement was also quite heavy, but, because of gaps in the census returns, it cannot be measured.) Writing from the newly opened Alabama frontier in the mid-1830's, a planter's daughter noted that there were "a great many persons moving away from the place and going to the Choctaw [P]urchase and [a] great many coming in which keeps the number pretty much the same."

Whole counties were virtually depopulated by the Texas land fever, only to be refilled by a new wave of settlers. So prevalent was the wanderlust that many resorted to religious metaphor or cited positive secular values to explain their drive. In explaining his life-style, which had seen him constantly on the move, the yeoman farmer Gideon Linecum pointed to his "belief and faith in the pleasure of frequent change of country." Eli Lide, a planter's son who had moved to Alabama from South Carolina in the 1830's, rational-ized his move to Texas twenty years later in terms of "something within me [that] whispers onward onward and urges me on like a prisoner who has been 58 years and idles in his Lord['] s vineyard and lived on his bounty and made no returns for the favors received."

Southern institutions were transplanted across the Appalachians with but minimal disruptions. Planters frequently sent ahead a younger son or a trusted overseer with a few field hands to stake out the new territory and clear the land. When the planter arrived with his wagons, livestock, family, and slaves, he quickly re-established the community leadership to which he was accus-tomed. He assumed the responsibility of meeting the frontier's rudimentary cultural needs by hiring private tutors, perhaps setting up one of the few schools, and donating land or funds for the upkeep of an imported minister. In a few years, his slaves would have carved out of the wilderness the plantation on which his economic primacy rested. Finally, as long as he catered to the democratic sensibilities of the yeoman farmers, he could be virtually assured of political influence and, even, office. No concessions of substance were required, only of style. For example, it was always politically wise to express anti-aristocratic sentiments and to show an acceptably egalitarian spirit in one's personal dealings, no matter what one's natural inclinations. These were the rules of the game, and to violate them brought opprobrium—as one Virginia planter newly arrived in Mississippi discovered. A local farmer, observing that the good gentleman disdained soiling his hands, did not hesitate to tell him that, if he had "taken hold of a plough" and worked by the farmer's side, his help would have been welcomed, but "to see him sitting up on his horse with his gloves on, directing his Negroes how to work," was not to the farmer's taste. Most planters learned the rules soon enough. Generally speaking, then, there was a remarkably successful transfer of the prior structure of institutions and leadership from the Old South of Jefferson to the newer one of Jefferson Davis.

A potential source of conflict in the spread of the plantation was class competition for the better lands. This was usually not a problem, however, because the emigrants, naturally enough, sought out a region similar in soil and climate to what they had left behind. Traditionally, the yeomanry had avoided the heavy, sticky prairie soils and the wet, marshy bottomlands. These areas were thought to be unhealthy and required a much greater initial investment to cultivate than the lighter soils in the uplands or the sandy loam back on the ridges. As a result, when the Southwest was opened up, much of the prairie and alluvial soils, the most productive and fertile in the South, were left by default to the planters. Where competition did exist, it was usually short-lived. The average farmer was a speculator. For him, it was good business to enter a new region, put up a log cabin, clear the forest and make other improvements, and then sell out for a profit after a few years. If a wealthy planter should want the land, all the better. With plenty of land to the west, one could repeat the process several times in a lifetime.

The expansion of the South meant a continual renewal of slave society. Yet, Southerners always had the nagging doubt that the process itself had not solved any problems but only perpetuated them. The doubt, akin to a fear of overdependence, can be understood by looking at the economic forces that fueled the South's search for land.

The nature of plantation agriculture and the consistently low ratio of land to labor costs explain much of the South's outward thrust. Besides initially requiring large units of land, staple-crop production on the plantations exhausted the soil at an alarming rate. Throughout most of the antebellum period, good land was so cheap and available in such quantity, especially relative to slave labor, that it was more profitable to ruin a plantation, pick up stakes, and start anew on virgin soil than to practice soil-conserving agriculture through crop rotation, deep plowing, and the use of fertilizers. Soil erosion and sterility became serious problems not only in scattered localities but in entire districts. By the early 1850's, the plantation belt of middle Georgia was described as a region of "red old hills stripped of their native growth and virgin soil, and washed with deep gullies, with here and there patches of Bermuda grass, and stunted pine shrubs, struggling for a scanty subsistence on what was one of the richest soils in America." Before 1860, the supposedly inexhaustible new cotton lands of the Southwest had already exhibited the "painful signs of senility and decay" familiar to residents of the seaboard states. The complaint of a Georgia editor in 1858 that from the Chesapeake to the Mississippi there was "something fundamentally wrong in Southern agriculture" was little more than a stock refrain.

Within a generation, the planters monopolized the agricultural wealth of any given area with the land and transportation facilities suitable for plantation agriculture. Five per cent of the South's farmers owned 36 per cent of the region's agricultural wealth; the poorest 50 per cent of all farmers owned only 6 per cent of the land. Indeed, even in the uplands and pine barrens— regions where the plantation never took root and that were supposedly the haven of the small farmer—a slaveholding elite controlled more land and more valuable land than the majority of the yeomanry. With their large labor force, extensive credit arrangements, and the capital resources to buy and utilize the best lands, the planters enjoyed competitive advantages over their small farmer neighbors and gradually were able to displace them.

This encroachment of the planter was not a matter of economic necessity only. As much as the planter needed fresh land to replace what he had destroyed or as a hedge for the future, he was also concerned about the security problems of having his slaves come into contact with nonslaveholders. The poorer whites were accused of interfering with slave discipline by setting an example of shiftlessness and by encouraging the slaves to steal plantation property to exchange for liquor and cheap trinkets. A Louisiana sugar planter told Frederick Law Olmsted, perhaps the most perceptive of all Northern travelers in the South, that he wanted to buy out all the poor whites living around his plantation.

> It was better that negroes never saw anybody off their own plantation; that they had no intercourse with other white men than their owner or overseer; especially, it was best that they should not see white men who did not command their respect, and whom they did not always feel to be superior to themselves, and able to command them.

Wasteful agricultural practices, monopolistic patterns of land ownership, and displacement of the yeomanry combined to create the South's land hunger. Down to the 1850's, there had always been a new cotton frontier—whether in the Georgia-Carolina uplands before the War of 1812, the prairies of Alabama and Mississippi in the Jacksonian period, or the river valleys of Arkansas and Texas just before and after the Mexican War—to satisfy this hunger and prevent social tensions from building up. "The way we have been able to give land to the lacklanders, to extend this great country, and to supply the landless with land, has been by the extension of the empire by arms and by money," boasted Senator Robert Toombs of Georgia, as he argued in 1859 for the acquisition of Cuba. Even the moderate Jefferson Davis claimed an economic right of expansion: "We at the South are an agricultural people, and we require an extended territory. Slave labor is a wasteful labor, and it therefore requires a still more extended territory than would the same pursuits if they could be prosecuted by the more economical labor of white men."

The Failure of Expansionism

The 1850's witnessed a widening gap between the South's desire to gain more territory and her ability to do so within the Union. The decade opened with the loss of California to the free-soil North. California was the great prize in the lands recently wrested from Mexico. Already noted for its deep ocean ports and its rich valley agriculture, the area became, with the discovery of gold, a mecca for fortune-seeking Americans.

The antislavery forces, with some backing from Southern Whigs, argued that the United States was honor-bound to respect the Mexican decrees that had prohibited slavery in the provinces of California and New Mexico. Southern Democrats reacted scornfully to this position. They stressed that the South had contributed more than her fair share of men and arms to the conquest of these territories and thus had a military, as well as a constitutional, right to carry slaves there. Racial stereotypes were employed. "Do they mean to assert," wondered Senator Albert Gallatin Brown of Mississippi, "that the victorious and proud-hearted American is to go, cap in hand, to the miserable, cringing Mexican peon, and ask his permission to settle on the soil won by the valor of our troops at Buena Vista, or before the walls of Mexico?"

To arguments that the climate and soil of these territories were unsuitable for slavery, that the institution was debarred by a "decree of Nature," Southerners responded by citing the great profitability of slavery in mining. "Slave labor is never more profitably employed than in mining," said Brown in a letter to his constituents, "and you may judge whether slaves could be advantageously introduced into that country, when I inform you . . . that an able-bodied negro is worth in California from two to six thousand dollars per annum." The slaves were so valuable in the mines, contended a Virginia senator, that, unless the black race were excluded altogether from California, slaveholders could bring them in by the thousands under contracts calling for their manumission within a few years, work them until then, and still show a large profit. Senator Jefferson Davis of Mississippi was certain that, with irrigation, southern California could support a lucrative commercial agriculture in cotton, grapes, and olives. This agriculture, however, required slave labor. The individual pioneer could not settle upon this dry land and support his family with his own exertions as he had traditionally done in the more humid East. Associated labor was needed to establish and maintain the irrigation system. Because Mexican peonage was clearly inconsistent with American law, Davis concluded that black slavery was the only solution.

The admission of California as a free state was a bitter blow to the South. A small but strategically placed proslavery wing of the California Democracy continued to fight for the introduction of slavery and even succeeded by its control of the judiciary in allowing a limited use of slave labor in the mines until the mid-1850's. But the battle had been lost. Although they alleged improper executive interference by the administration of President Taylor with the statehood movement, Southerners generally blamed their defeat on the constant antislavery agitation of Northerners and the refusal of slaveholders to risk their property under such unsettling conditions. Had it not been for this agitation, insisted Representative Thomas Clingman of North Carolina, "our southern slaveholders would have carried their negroes into the mines of California in such numbers, that I have no doubt but that the majority there would have made it a slaveholding State."

Clingman, however, underestimated the extent of antislavery feelings. S. R. Thurston, the territorial representative from Oregon, explained that white Californians had excluded slavery not from any hostility to the South, nor even from opposition to slavery in the abstract, but solely out of economic self-interest: They feared that the slaveholders would monopolize the wealth of the mines. "One man might work a thousand [slaves], and consequently, on the ground that a slave will do as much work as a white man, the southerner might make a thousand dollars to the northerner['s] one." The miners would never permit such an aristocracy of wealth to arise. So, it was fortunate, Thurston continued, that slavery had never gained legal protection; for, if any man had taken large numbers of slaves into the mines, "they would have been cut down—yes, sir, cut down—cut down by white men. . . . To have maintained slave labor there, during this last year, would have required a standing army of fifty thousand men; and whenever it is desired to redden those mountain streams with human gore, take your slaves there."

Kansas, although economically less significant than California, represented an even more serious psychological defeat for the South. Badly misjudging the strength and sensitivity of the antislavery movement, many Southerners had deluded themselves into believing that the Kansas-Nebraska Act, by expressly revoking the Missouri Compromise line of 36° 30′, would take the issue of territorial slavery out of politics and allow the settlers to decide the question for themselves. Even Alexander Stephens of Georgia, a very cautious and moderate politician and a leading congressional spokesman for the Whigs, interpreted the Act as a moral victory for the South by its removal of the stigma of slavery exclusion. Far more perceptive was the comment of a Tennessee congressman who predicted that passage of the Act would result in a "most impolitic and mad moment for the South, no practical good can come of it because there is none in it."

Infuriated by the organized efforts of some abolitionist groups to send free-soil settlers into Kansas, the South committed herself to an ideological contest that she could not win. Most slaveholders simply were not interested in the flat, windy prairies of Kansas. Hemp and tobacco could be grown profitably in the eastern river valleys of the region, as they were in neighboring Missouri, but few planters wanted to hazard their slaves for such limited economic returns. Although led by slaveholders, the Southern bands that made the long trek to Kansas were composed mainly of land-hungry adventurers. These men were outnumbered by the free-soil settlers, more mobile than slave labor, who moved rapidly into the territory, and who were determined to keep slavery out.

Southern Democrats fought desperately to gain legal recognition of slavery in Kansas. Entrenched among the territorial office-holders, the proslavery forces pushed through the Kansas Lecompton Constitution in a boycotted election. This document, which could not be amended for several years, protected the slave property already within the territory. In attempting to bring Kansas into the Union under this constitution, the Southern Democrats downplayed economic motives. They insisted that the issue was whether slavery would ever again be permitted to expand. John Slidell of Louisiana told the Senate that the South was "struggling for the maintenance of a principle, barren, it is true, of present practical fruits, but indispensable for our future protection. . . ." If Kansas was refused admission because slavery "nominally and temporarily exists there, what may we expect," he asked, "when application shall be made by a State of which it will be a real and enduring institution?" Representative William Porcher Miles of South Carolina wanted Kansas as a "wall of defense" for Missouri—and for the two additional proslavery votes she would provide in the Senate. In a racist appeal, Brown of Mississippi accused the free-soilers of wanting to force a government upon the white settlers and thereby create a free Kansas that "makes the negro free by enslaving the white man; but my free Kansas makes the white man free, and leaves the negro where the Constitution left him—subject to the authority of his master." As to charges of corruption and irregularities surrounding the Lecompton Constitution, Southern Democrats replied that these were no worse than similar problems that had beset California. "Are we of the South to be made to see California hurried into the Union against all law and all precedent *because she is a free state* and Kansas subjected to the rigors of the inquisition because she *has a chance* of being a slave state?" demanded a Mississippi congressman.

In March of 1855, David Atchison, a Missouri senator and leader in the struggle to open up Kansas for slavery, offered an early version of the domino theory: "If we win we carry slavery to the Pacific Ocean; if we fail we lose Missouri, Arkansas, and Texas and all the territories; the game must be played boldly. I know that the Union as it exists is in the other scale, but I am willing to take the holyland." In the view of Python, a pseudonymous contributor to *DeBow's Review* in the late 1850's, all the dominoes would fall if the South lost Kansas; for the entire western flank of slavery would be endangered. The emboldened abolitionists, he warned, would first attack slavery in Missouri, then move south into the Oklahoma Indian territories and Texas, and finally turn west into New Mexico and Arizona. The Upper South would be the next target, and soon slavery would end up confined to the Gulf states.

Southern Whigs, on the other hand, while conceding that the admission of new slave states was vital to Southern interests, refused to believe that Kansas represented slavery's Armageddon. For one thing, the South, they

argued, was capable of standing on higher ground than the Lecompton Constitution, which one Whig denounced as the "most barefaced fraud and cheating
the world ever saw." For another, few of them expected slavery to take
permanent hold in Kansas. Senator John Bell of Tennessee, for example,
pointed out, in the spring of 1858, that the number of slaves in Kansas had
declined in the previous year from about three hundred to no more than
one hundred.

In the end, the South was hoist with her own petard. If the eventual
admission of Kansas as a free state was a humiliating defeat, it was largely
because too many Southerners had made the issue a test of sectional strength
and determination. "It will be useless to attempt explanations and excuses,
we are condemned, and I think justly," wrote a Georgia judge to Alexander
Stephens in June of 1857. "We have made the people believe it will be a
slave state and we ought to make it good or not assume to hold the reins of
power."

Cuba and Mexico offered unique advantages to Southern expansionists.
The former was already a slave society, and the latter seemed ripe for the
taking. Although the unyielding Republican opposition to the expansion of
slavery was sufficient to block most designs on these areas, internal resistance
within the South was itself a major deterrent.

The pro-Cuban forces were centered in the Democratic party, and they
had some support from the Northern wing of the party, as exemplified by
James Buchanan's acquiescence in the Ostend Manifesto of 1854. In this declaration, three American foreign ministers crudely served warning on Spain
that the United States meant to have Cuba. Many of their arguments would
sound familiar a century later. Cuba, lying just ninety miles off Florida, was
deemed the key to the commerce and defenses of the Caribbean. But, of
course, slavery was the overriding issue. "I want Cuba, and I know that
sooner or later we must have it. . . . I want Tamaulipas, Potosi, and one
or two other Mexican States; and I want them all for the same reason—for
the planting or spreading of slavery," announced Albert Gallatin Brown in
a speech at Hazlehurst, Mississippi. Cuba was to be the linchpin in a tropical
empire founded on outright annexation or on the creation of satellite states.
This empire, by giving the South a virtual monopoly over the production
of tropical goods, would ensure the perpetuation of slavery.

The annexationists charged that the British were scheming to effect emancipation in Cuba. Furthermore, they warned that the unstable Spaniards might
decree emancipation in order to punish the rebellious Creole planters or to
make the island unattractive to Americans. A free black government in Cuba
was depicted as a threat to slave security all along the Gulf Coast. "Indeed,"
in the vivid phrase of John Van Evrie, a proslavery propagandist, "Cuba
would be a volcano of 'free negroism', constantly vomiting fire and blood
on the neighboring coast. . . ." Annexation not only would eliminate this
threat but would also prove a boon to the Cuban slaves. Stephen Mallory
of Key West assured his Senate colleagues that, under the paternalism of a
Southern master, "the plantation negro in Cuba would be what he is in

Florida, the freest from disease and care, the happiest and the most enduring of his race on the face of the earth.''

The Southern opposition, once again led by the Whigs, contended that, if Cuban sugar were admitted duty-free, the sugar planters of Louisiana, Texas, and Florida would be ruined. These planters depended on tariff protection for their economic survival. If hurt by Cuban competition, they might shift their resources to cotton production, thus depressing the price of that staple. The Whigs stressed that Cuba, unlike Texas in the 1840's, was a settled, heavily populated country that had no room for Southern emigrants. The living conditions of the slaves would improve under American rule, but this would result in an even higher population density, which could not absorb the South's own rapidly increasing slave population. ''We want land without people on it, and not land and people together,'' said a Tennessee representative. The problems of assimilating the Cuban people were seen as insurmountable. Their language, religion, and extraction differed from ours, stressed Senator John Thompson of Kentucky, ''and our people have regarded them as aliens and outlaws from the pale of humanity and civilization. . . . Saying nothing about color, I think I have been at more respectable weddings than it would be to bring her into the household.'' The Republicans agreed. Cuban whites were ''ignorant, vicious, and priest-ridden,'' according to one Republican senator, and another wondered what the United States would do with the 200,000 free blacks on the island.

The Whigs could not see how Cuban annexation would strengthen slavery. The old fear of the future of slavery in the Upper South was revived. If, as most people expected, the African slave trade with Cuba were prohibited under the Americans, the planters would turn to the Upper South to replenish their labor supply and thereby hasten the abolitionizing of these states. One Whig congressman based his opposition on the ground that he did not want to see the area of slavery contracted. Because Spain hated and feared the United States, he reasoned, she would spitefully free the Cuban slaves if she ever became convinced that the island was about to fall into American hands. On the other hand, if Cuba, by some unexpected stroke of good fortune, were acquired with slavery intact, the Whigs foresaw an explosion of antislavery agitation. England and France, suspecting that the United States coveted, and would therefore try to seize, other West Indian islands, would be poised for war.

Despite considerable influence within the Pierce and Buchanan administrations, the Cuban annexationists got nowhere. Their most flamboyant leader, Governor John Quitman of Mississippi, was in constant difficulty with federal authorities over his open defiance of the neutrality laws through his filibustering activities. Quitman was convinced that the South would be able to expand within the Union only if she forced a drastic revision of these neutrality statutes, which barred Americans from private military enterprises against other sovereign powers. Then, Southern armies, privately financed and recruited, would be free, he hoped, to carry slavery into the Caribbean and Central America. Quitman was immensely popular in Mississippi, but most Southerners rejected his dramatic program. After all, even in the case of Cuba, the expansionists had not resolved certain paradoxes.. On the one hand, they predicted that, as a result of the closing of the African slave trade and of American paternalism, the Cuban slave population would be better treated and would increase rapidly by natural causes. With a longer life expectancy, their value would rise, and this, in turn, would inflate the production costs of Cuban sugar, making it more competitive with American sugar. Yet, if the slave population grew after annexation, the island could hardly serve as the outlet the South demanded for her own increasing numbers of slaves.

For some, Mexico could serve as that outlet. In a speech before Congress, Representative O. R. Singleton of Mississippi reasoned that, because there was no settled government in Mexico, the United States had every right to intervene to promote order and set up a stable government. And, "when we have wound it up, there being no better heirs than ourselves, we will be compelled to hold that territory." Such altruism had its rewards. Much of Mexico, Singleton declared, was suitable for cotton, rice, and sugar cultivation. The South would have her outlet. "In my opinion we must, and we are compelled to, expand in that direction, and thus perpetuate it [slavery]— a hundred or a thousand years it may be."

In 1858, William Burwell of Virginia, in urging Senator R. M. T. Hunter of Virginia to exert pressure for a more aggressive Mexican policy, suggested that the acquisition of all Mexico could serve both as a popular issue for the next Presidential election and as a means for the South to re-establish her political equality within the Union.

> . . . you have within your grasp a country accessible, abounding in all the metals and staples which civilised man most values, and a territory so extensive as that you can by only promoting the existing communities of Mexico to an equality with the present members of the Union preserve the balance in the Council of States, and so guarantee the peculiar rights of those States of which you are one of the guardians and representatives.

Burwell was confident that Southern whites could easily control the racially mixed population. Movement into Mexico would be relatively easy on the railroads, and, with the telegraph, communications would be no problem. In that sense, Mexico was no farther away from Washington than Alabama or Tennessee had been twenty years earlier. If Mexico were not won for slavery, Burwell contended, it would be abolitionized by the North. "And if the worst should befall us could we not cut loose from the Union, throw an emigrant army into Mexico and make it as safe as Texas?" There was no alternative. "The North has more states and more territory than the South. It has the immigration of Europe to aid it. Your subjugation is as certain as the unrelenting operation of these great causes can render it." Out of self-protection, the South must "seize upon all the territory which produces those great staples of social necessity which the world cannot go without. Do so and you are safe."

Southern Democrats did implement a pale replica of the Singleton–Burwell program. The Buchanan Administration tried to purchase the northern Mexican states or at least establish a protectorate over them, to extract commercial concessions, and to win diplomatic recognition of the right of the United States to intervene directly in Mexican affairs. These approaches, which met with some success, were held back by the same racial antipathies that had defeated the All-Mexico movement in the aftermath of the Mexican War. This racism was common to nearly all Americans. To Senator A. H. Sevier of Arkansas, the Mexicans were "a people bigoted, superstitious, cruel and ignorant; crossed, in the first place, in blood with the Moor and Spaniard, and recrossed with the negro and Indian." Representative C. Delano of Ohio believed that this intermixture produced a "slothful, indolent, ignorant race of beings." In his Barnwell, South Carolina, speech of 1858, Senator James Hammond used these racial slurs in denouncing any effort to take slavery into Mexico. Not only were Mexicans incapable of self-government, he asserted, but they could not even sustain slavery. Moreover, any attempt to incorporate them into the Union would result in a loss of racial purity.

> Sweep in Mexico at present, and it is the beginning of amalgamation. That is a people of mixed race and blood. So far from marking a line of discrimination between black and white, it is almost utterly obliterated, and would step over, and gradually spread itself over, and instead of aiding this country, debauch it.

There was no better indication of the difficulties, if not outright futility, plaguing the expansionists than the opposition within the South to the reopening of the African slave trade. There were many factors behind the opposition: the vested interest of the Upper South in high slave prices; fear of losing racial control by importing savage, heathen Africans; the wish to avoid agitating such a divisive issue; the threat of lower-class discontent if wages were severely depressed by cheap slave competition; and the conviction that the trade was morally wrong. These factors combined to hamstring the expansionists, for Southerners of both parties agreed that, without a surplus of cheap slave labor to throw into the territorial competition with free labor, the South had little chance of adding any more slave states. "This great truth seems to take the people by surprise," wrote the Georgia Whig, Alexander Stephens. "Some shrink from it as they would from death. Still it is as true as death." Albert Gallatin Brown realized this truth, but, ever sensitive to the land hunger of his piney-woods constituency and aware that land prices in Mississippi had more than doubled during the 1850's, he demanded more land before the trade was reopened. "If . . . labor is trenching, is close upon the lands— I mean lands worth cultivating—then we ought to get more land before we get more labor, since labor without land will be a burden rather than a profit."

The positions of Stephens and Brown were irreconcilable as long as the South remained in the Union. The South needed the slave trade in order to expand, but, even if the North consented to the reopening of the trade, the South feared that she had insufficient land on which to support the additional slaves. As an independent country, however, she would no longer face the political necessity of matching the Northern expansion of free labor with her slaves and, even without reviving the African slave trade, could stake out additional slave territory to be occupied whenever economic pressures dictated. . . .

Sources

The Kansas-Nebraska Act, 1854

Was there any way to quiet the slavery controversy? Senator Stephen A. Douglas, the North's leading Democrat, thought he had a way. In his eagerness to organize Kansas and Nebraska country, the Illinois senator gave in to Southern demands and in 1854 sponsored a bill that specifically repealed the Missouri Compromise of 1820, which barred slavery north of 36°30′. Douglas proposed that the fate of the territories be decided by "popular sovereignty." Under this system the actual settlers would have the opportunity to vote on slavery, either approving it or prohibiting it.

On page 305 is a map of the country after the Kansas-Nebraska Act was passed by Congress. Do you think the 36°30′ line was a real barrier to slavery or just of symbolic importance? Do you think its repeal was really a meaningless gesture to calm Southern nerves, as Douglas claimed? If you were a Northerner in 1854, would you have been concerned?

Two Portraits of the West

The Kansas-Nebraska Act raised a storm of protest throughout the North, and almost overnight Anti-Nebraska groups sprang up to fight the extension of slavery. Some called themselves "Republican," which had a nice Jeffersonian ring to it, and the name stuck. Douglas expected the storm to blow itself out once Northerners realized that his bill provided millions of acres for land-hungry farmers and a railroad route to the newly discovered gold fields of California. Moreover, argued Douglas, Kansas and Nebraska were obviously unsuited to slavery, and the "principle of dollars and cents" would keep slaveholders out.

But the storm did not blow itself out, and the brand-new Republican party did incredibly well at the polls, routing Northern Democrats in one congressional district after another, and carrying eleven of sixteen Northern states in the presidential election of 1856.

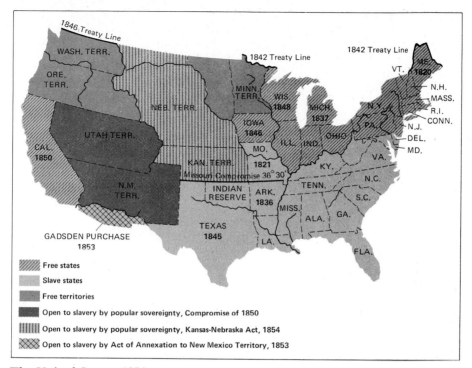

Free states
Slave states
Free territories
Open to slavery by popular sovereignty, Compromise of 1850
Open to slavery by popular sovereignty, Kansas-Nebraska Act, 1854
Open to slavery by Act of Annexation to New Mexico Territory, 1853

The United States, 1854.

Douglas had clearly misread Northern opinion. To many Northerners it did not matter that slavery was never likely to take root on the prairies. To them, merely allowing the possibility was an outrage, and even more outrageous was the fact that the federal government had reversed itself and legally opened free territory to slavery.

On page 306 are two documents to help you understand this outrage. The first is a painting by John Gast, "Manifest Destiny," which shows a typical Northern view of the American West. Moving westward from Eastern port cities is the goddess of Destiny bearing a schoolbook in one hand and a telegraph in the other. Below, white Americans push the Indians and the buffalo ever westward. What is the order of white settlement as envisioned by Gast? What kinds of people are the typical settlers? What do you make of the fact that there are no blacks in the picture? The second illustration is a Republican cartoon showing Douglas, with the help of other leading Northern Democrats, trying to force slavery down the throat of a Free-Soiler. What do you make of the Free-Soiler? Is he like the characters in Gast's painting? And why is he so concerned about his wife and children? Is the message of the cartoon racist as well as antislavery? Why do you think that keeping slavery out of the West had broad appeal, while abolishing slavery had very limited appeal?

"Manifest Destiny." By John Gast. *Library of Congress.*

The Lincoln-Douglas Debates, 1858

While Republicans were blasting the Kansas-Nebraska Act in national politics, Kansas itself became a battleground with Northerners and Southerners fighting for control. Proslavery forces in Kansas put forward the Lecompton Constitution, which the majority in Kansas clearly opposed. Nevertheless, President James Buchanan, a Pennsylvania Democrat, backed the Lecompton Constitution and tried to bring Kansas into the Union as a slave state. At the same time, the Supreme Court, in the Dred Scott case, declared that Congress had no right to bar slavery from the territories.

It was against this background that Senator Douglas, who broke with the White House over the Lecompton Constitution, ran for re-election in 1858. His opponent was a cunning Republican lawyer, Abraham Lincoln, who claimed that Douglas's policy of "squatter sovereignty" had become an invitation to chaos. Douglas attacked Lincoln as an abolitionist "Black Republican" whose principles would lead not only to disunion, but also to the "amalgamation" of the races and the downfall of white America. Across Illinois the two men battled in debate.

Here are some highlights from these famous debates. Douglas won re-election. Do you think he also won the debates? How did the two men differ on such basic issues as slavery, race, local self-government, the possibility of civil war? Today Lincoln is often referred to as a "racist." If Lincoln was a racist, how would you describe Douglas?

Lincoln, at Springfield

"A house divided against itself cannot stand." I believe this government cannot endure permanently half slave and half free. . . . I do not expect the house to fall; but I do expect it will cease to be divided. It will become all one thing, or all the other.

Douglas, at Chicago

Mr. Lincoln advocates boldly and clearly a war of sections, a war of the North against the South, of the Free States against the Slave States. . . . He objects to the Dred Scott decision because it does not put the negro in the possession of citizenship on an equality with the white man. I am opposed

From *Political Debates between Abraham Lincoln and Stephen A. Douglas in the Celebrated Campaign of 1858 in Illinois* (Cleveland, Ohio: The Arthur H. Clark Company, 1902), pp. 1, 14, 18, 33, 101–117 *passim*.

Illinois Senator Stephen A. Douglas. *The Bettman Archive.*

Abraham Lincoln in 1858. *The Lloyd Ostendorf Collection.*

to negro equality. . . . I am in favor of preserving, not only the purity of the blood, but the purity of the government from any mixture or amalgamation with inferior races.

Lincoln, at Chicago

I protest, now and forever, against that counterfeit logic which presumes that because I do not want a negro woman for a slave, I do necessarily want her for a wife. My understanding is that I need not have her for either, but, as God made us separate, we can leave one another alone, and do one another much good thereby. . . . The Judge regales us with the terrible enormities that take place by the mixture of races. . . . Why, Judge, if we do not let them get together in the Territories, they won't mix there.

Douglas, at Ottawa

Prior to 1854 this country was divided into two great political parties, known as the Whig and Democratic parties. Both were national and patriotic, advocating principles that were universal in their application. An Old Line Whig could proclaim his principles in Louisiana and Massachusetts alike. Whig principles had no boundary section line, they were not limited by the Ohio river, nor by the Potomac, nor by the line of the free and slave states, but applied and were proclaimed wherever the Constitution ruled or the American flag waved over the American soil. So it was, and so it is with the great Democratic party, which, from the days of Jefferson until this period, has proven itself to be the historic party of this nation. While the Whig and Democratic parties differed in regard to a bank, the tariff, distribution, the specie circular and the sub-treasury, they agreed on the great slavery question which now agitates the Union. I say that the Whig party and the Democratic party agreed on this slavery question while they differed on those matters of expediency to which I have referred. The Whig party and the Democratic party jointly adopted the compromise measures of 1850 as the basis of a proper and just solution of this slavery question in all its forms. Clay was the great leader, with Webster on his right and Cass on his left, and sustained by the patriots in the Whig and Democratic ranks, who had devised and enacted the compromise measures of 1850. . . .

Thus you see that up to 1853–'54, the Whig party and the Democratic party both stood on the same platform with regard to the slavery question. That platform was the right of the people of each state and each territory to decide their local and domestic institutions for themselves, subject only to the federal Constitution. . . .

In 1854, Mr. Abraham Lincoln and Mr. Trumbull entered into an arrangement, one with the other, and each with his respective friends, to dissolve the old Whig party on the one hand, and to dissolve the old Democratic party on the other, and to connect the members of both into an Abolition party under the name and disguise of a Republican party. . . . Lincoln went to work to abolitionize the Old Whig party all over the state, pretending that he was then as good a Whig as ever; and Trumbull went to work in his part of the state preaching abolitionism in its milder and lighter form, and trying to abolitionize the Democratic party, and bring old Democrats handcuffed and bound hand and foot into the abolition camp. . . .

Mr. Lincoln, following the example and lead of all the little Abolition orators, who go around and lecture in the basements of schools and churches, reads from the Declaration of Independence, that all men were created equal, and then asks how can you deprive a negro of that equality which God and the Declaration awards to him. . . . I do not question Mr. Lincoln's conscientious belief that the negro was made his equal, and hence is his brother, but for my own part, I do not regard the negro as my equal, and positively deny that he is my brother or any kin to me whatever. . . .

. . . He belongs to an inferior race, and must always occupy an inferior position. I do not hold that because the negro is our inferior that therefore he ought to be a slave. By no means can such a conclusion be drawn from what I have said. On the contrary, I hold that humanity and Christianity both require that the negro shall have and enjoy every right, every privilege, and every immunity consistent with the safety of the society in which he lives. On that point, I presume, there can be no diversity of opinion. You and I are bound to extend to our inferior and dependent being every right, every privilege, every facility and immunity consistent with the public good. The question then arises what rights and privileges are consistent with the public good. This is a question which each state and each territory must decide for itself. . . .

Lincoln, at Ottawa

Now gentlemen, I hate to waste my time on such things, but in regard to that general abolition tilt that Judge Douglas makes, when he says that I was engaged at that time in selling out and abolitionizing the old Whig party— I hope you will permit me to read a part of a printed speech that I made then at Peoria, which will show altogether a different view of the position I took in that contest of 1854.

VOICE: Put on your specs.
MR. LINCOLN: Yes, sir, I am obliged to do so; I am no longer a young man.

> . . . we have before us, the chief materials enabling us to correctly judge whether the repeal of the Missouri Compromise is right or wrong.
>
> I think, and shall try to show, that it is wrong; wrong in its direct effect, letting slavery into Kansas and Nebraska—and wrong in its prospective principle, allowing it to spread to every other part of the wide world, where men can be found inclined to take it.
>
> This *declared* indifference, but as I must think, covert *real* zeal for the spread of slavery, I can not but hate. I hate it because of the monstrous injustice of slavery itself. I hate it because it deprives our republican example of its just influence in the world—enables the enemies of free institutions, with plausibility, to taunt us as hypocrites—causes the real friends of freedom to doubt our sincerity, and especially because it forces so many really good men amongst ourselves into an open war with the very fundamental principles of civil liberty—criticising the Declaration of Independence, and insisting that there is no right principle of action but *self-interest*.
>
> Before proceeding, let me say I think I have no prejudice against the Southern

people. They are just what we would be in their situation. If slavery did not now exist amongst them, they would not introduce it. If it did now exist amongst us, we should not instantly give it up. This I believe of the masses North and South. Doubtless there are individuals, on both sides, who would not hold slaves under any circumstances; and others who would gladly introduce slavery anew, if it were out of existence. We know that some Southern men do free their slaves, go north, and become tip-top Abolitionists; while some Northern ones go south, and become most cruel slave-masters.

When Southern people tell us they are no more responsible for the origin of slavery, than we; I acknowledge the fact. When it is said that the institution exists, and that it is very difficult to get rid of it, in any satisfactory way, I can understand and appreciate the saying. I surely will not blame them for not doing what I should not know how to do myself. If all earthly power were given me, I should not know what to do, as to the existing institution. My first impulse would be to free all the slaves, and send them to Liberia,—to their own native land. But a moment's reflection would convince me, that whatever of high hope, (as I think there is) there may be in this, in the long run, its sudden execution is impossible. If they were all landed there in a day, they would all perish in the next ten days; and there are not surplus shipping and surplus money enough in the world to carry them there in many times ten days. What then? Free them all, and keep them among us as underlings? Is it quite certain that this betters their condition? I think I would not hold one in slavery, at any rate; yet the point is not clear enough to me to denounce people upon. What next? Free them, and make them politically and socially, our equals? My own feelings will not admit of this; and if mine would, we well know that those of the great mass of white people will not. Whether this feeling accords with justice and sound judgment, is not the sole question, if indeed, it is any part of it. A universal feeling, whether well or ill-founded, can not be safely disregarded. We can not, then, make them equals. It does seem to me that systems of gradual emancipation might be adopted; but for their tardiness in this, I will not undertake to judge our brethren of the South.

When they remind us of their constitutional rights, I acknowledge them not grudgingly, but fully, and fairly; and I would give them any legislation for the reclaiming of their fugitives, which should not in its stringency, be more likely to carry a free man into slavery, than our ordinary criminal laws are to hang an innocent one.

Now gentlemen, I don't want to read at any greater length, but this is the true complexion of all I have ever said in regard to the institution of slavery and the black race. This is the whole of it, and anything that argues me into his idea of perfect social and political equality with the negro, is but a specious and fantastic arrangement of words, by which a man can prove a horse chestnut to be a chestnut horse. I will say here, while upon this subject, that I have no purpose directly or indirectly to interfere with the institution of slavery in the states where it exists. I believe I have no lawful right to do so, and I have no inclination to do so. I have no purpose to introduce political and social equality between the white and the black races. There is a physical difference between the two, which in my judgment will probably forever forbid their living together upon the footing of perfect equality, and inasmuch as it becomes a necessity that there must be a difference, I, as well as Judge Douglas, am in favor of the race to which I belong, having the superior position. I have never said anything to the contrary, but I hold that notwithstanding all this, there is no reason in the world why the negro is not entitled to all the natural rights enumerated in the Declaration of Independence, the right to life, liberty and the pursuit of happiness. I hold that he is as much entitled to these as the white man. I agree with Judge Douglas he is not my equal in many respects—certainly not in color, perhaps not in moral or intellectual endowment. But in the right to eat the bread, without leave of anybody else, which his own hand earns, *he is my equal and the equal of Judge Douglas, and the equal of every living man.* . . .

When he [Douglas] undertakes to say that because I think this nation, so far as the question of slavery is concerned, will all become one thing or all the other, I am in favor of bringing about a dead uniformity in the various states, in all their institutions, he argues erroneously. The great variety of the local institutions in the states, springing from differences in the soil, differences in the face of the country, and in the climate, are bonds of union. They do not make "a house divided against itself," but they make a house united. If they produce in one section of the country what is called for by the wants of another section, and this other section can supply the wants of the first, they are not matters of discord but bonds of union, true bonds of union. But can this question of slavery be considered as among *these* varieties in the institutions of the country? I leave it to you to say whether, in the history of our government, this institution of slavery has not always failed to be a bond of union, and, on the contrary, been an apple of discord and an element of division in the house. . . . If so, then I have a right to say that in regard to this question, the Union is a house divided against itself, and when the Judge reminds me that I have often said to him that the institution of slavery has existed for eighty years in some states, and yet it does not exist in some others, I agree to the fact, and I account for it by looking at the position in which our fathers originally placed it—restricting it from the new territories where it had not gone, and legislating to cut off its source by the abrogation of the slave trade, thus putting the seal of legislation *against its spread.* The public mind *did* rest in the belief that it was in the course of ultimate extinction. But lately, I think—and in this I charge nothing on the Judge's motives—lately, I think, that he, and those acting with him, have placed that institution on a new basis, which looks to the *perpetuity and nationalization of slavery.* And while it is placed upon this new basis, I say, and I have said, that I believe we shall not have peace upon the question until the opponents of slavery arrest the further spread of it, and place it where the public mind shall rest in the belief that it is in the course of ultimate extinction; or, on the other hand, that its advocates will push it forward until it shall become alike lawful in all the states, old as well as new, North as well as South. Now, I believe if we would arrest the spread, and place it where Washington, and Jefferson, and Madison placed it, it *would be* in the course of ultimate extinction, and the public mind *would,* as for eighty years past, believe that it was in the course of ultimate extinction. The crisis would be past and the institution might be let alone for a hundred years, if it should live so long, in the states where it exists, yet it would be going out of existence in the way best for both the black and white races. . . .

When I made my speech at Springfield, of which the Judge complains, and from which he quotes, I really was not thinking of the things which he ascribes to me at all. I had no thought in the world that I was doing anything to bring about a war between the free and slave states. I had no thought in the world that I was doing anything to bring about a political and social equality of the black and white races. It never occurred to me that I was doing anything or favoring anything to reduce to a dead uniformity all the local institutions of the various states. But I must say, in all fairness to him, if he thinks I am doing something which leads to these bad results, it is none the better that I did not mean it. It is just as fatal to the country, if I have any influence in producing it, whether I intend it or not. But can it be true, that placing this institution upon the original basis—the basis upon which our fathers placed it—can have any tendency to set the Northern and the Southern states at war with one another, or that it can have any tendency to make the people of Vermont raise sugar cane, because they raise it in Louisiana, or that it can compel the people of Illinois to cut pine logs on the Grand Prairie, where they will not grow, because they cut pine logs in Maine, where they do grow? . . .

14

The Civil War

Americans have studied the Civil War with almost obsessive fascination. The main reason is that the Civil War was the nation's great trauma. It was the one instance where orderly democratic processes failed miserably. With Lincoln's election in 1860, the Lower South refused to abide by the dictates of the electorate, play democratic politics, and try to regain power in the next election. During the first seventy-two years of the American republic slaveholders had held the presidency for fifty years. Now the nation had a president who was committed to the "ultimate extinction" of slavery. Now the nation was governed by a Northern party that owed nothing to the South. Indeed, the Republicans were not even on the ballot in ten Southern states, and Lincoln captured only 26,000 votes in the slaveholding states as compared to 1,800,000 in the free states. With Lincoln's victory, the Lower South seceded from the Union, and when the first shots were fired four states in the Upper South followed suit.

The Civil War was also a brothers' war. If we wish, we can blame the American Revolution on the British, the Mexican War on the Mexicans, World War I on German submarines, World War II on the Japanese and Hitler, Korea and Vietnam on the Communists; but we can blame the Civil War on nobody but Americans. Thus, even though Americans have studied this war with fascination, they have never been able to agree which brother—if either—was to blame.

The Civil War was also a bloodbath. That, in fact, is what distinguished it from earlier American wars. The War of 1812 cost the country only 7,000 lives, with fewer than 2,000 men dying in action. The Mexican War cost the nation fewer than 2,000 lives on the battlefield and some 11,000 from diseases. Most Americans in 1861 expected the Civil War to be much the same. But it was not. By the time it was over, more than 600,000 men were dead, and many of the "lucky" survivors were missing arms and legs.

315

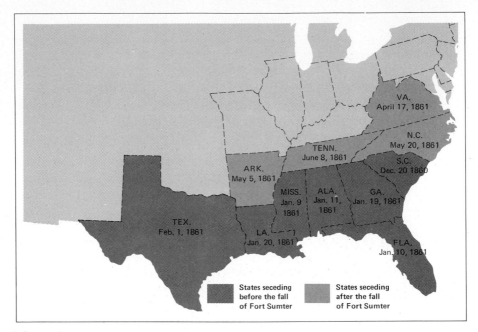

The Union Disintegrates.

The war has fascinated Americans, too, because of its totality. Indeed, some historians have argued that it was the first modern war not only because of its scale, but also because of the unprecedented extent to which both sides were mobilized. North and South, the war touched more aspects of more lives than any other had done. Factories and railroads became crucial objects of strategic concern. Women and children were involved as supporters—their traditional roles—but also as victims on a scale that Americans had not known before. Blacks were active participants in a war fought over the issue of slavery and its political consequences. In the end, too, the war

Deaths in the Civil War and Other Wars

	Total Deaths	*Deaths per 100,000 Population*
Civil War	618,000	1,967
World War II	318,000	241
Revolutionary War	4,000	144
World War I	115,000	109
Mexican War	13,270	57
War of 1812	2,200	31
Vietnam War	56,000	28
Korean War	33,000	22
Spanish-American War and Philippine Insurrection	9,700	13

sought not only a political settlement but a social and economic one
that went to the heart of the institutions by which half a nation had
ordered its life.

Interpretive Essay

Bruce Catton

Hayfoot, Strawfoot

**The way a society goes to war tells much about its economic and so-
cial life. In the following essay, one of the most popular historians of
the Civil War examines the military life of both sides. From such
portraits as this, we can learn much about the skills, the education,
and the attitudes of those plain men, Yankee and Confederate, who
bore the brunt of some of the most bloody fighting the world had
witnessed.**

The volunteer soldier in the American Civil War used a clumsy muzzle-
loading rifle, lived chiefly on salt pork and hardtack, and retained to the
very end a loose-jointed, informal attitude toward the army with which he
had cast his lot. But despite all of the surface differences, he was at bottom
blood brother to the G.I. Joe of modern days.

Which is to say that he was basically, and incurably, a civilian in arms.
A volunteer, he was still a soldier because he had to be one, and he lived
for the day when he could leave the army forever. His attitude toward discipline, toward his officers, and toward the whole spit-and-polish concept of
military existence was essentially one of careless tolerance. He refused to
hate his enemies—indeed, he often got along with them much better than
with some of his own comrades—and his indoctrination was often so imperfect
that what was sometimes despairingly said of the American soldier in World
War II would apply equally to him: he seemed to be fighting chiefly so that
he could some day get back to Mom's cooking.

What really set the Civil War soldier apart was the fact that he came
from a less sophisticated society. He was no starry-eyed innocent, to be sure—
or, if he was, the army quickly took care of that—but the America of the
1860's was less highly developed than modern America. It lacked the ineffable
advantages of radio, television, and moving pictures. It was still essentially
a rural nation; it had growing cities but they were smaller and somehow

From Bruce Catton, "Hayfoot, Strawfoot," *American Heritage,* Vol. 3, No. 3 (April 1957), pp.
31–37. © 1957 by American Heritage Publishing Co., Inc. Reprinted by permission from *American
Heritage.*

less urban than today's cities; a much greater percentage of the population lived on farms or in country towns and villages than is the case now, and there was more of a backwoods, hay-seed-in-the-hair flavor to the people who came from them.

For example: every war finds some ardent youngsters who want to enlist despite the fact that they are under the military age limit of eighteen. Such a lad today simply goes to the recruiting station, swears that he is eighteen, and signs up. The lad of the 1860's saw it a little differently. He could not swear that he was eighteen when he was only sixteen; in his innocent way, he felt that to lie to his own government was just plain wrong. But he worked out a little dodge that got him into the army anyway. He would take a bit of paper, scribble the number *18* on it, and put it in the sole of his shoe. Then, when the recruiting officer asked him how old he was, he could truthfully say: "I am over eighteen." That was a common happening, early in the Civil War; one cannot possibly imagine it being tried today.

Similarly, the drill sergeants repeatedly found that among the raw recruits there were men so abysmally untaught that they did not know left from right, and hence could not step off on the left foot as all soldiers should. To teach these lads how to march, the sergeants would tie a wisp of hay to the left foot and a wisp of straw to the right; then, setting the men to march, they would chant, "Hay-foot, straw-foot, hay-foot, straw-foot"—and so on, until everybody had caught on. A common name for a green recruit in those days was "strawfoot."

On the drill field, when a squad was getting basic training, the men were as likely as not to intone a little rhythmic chant as they tramped across the sod—thus:

> March! March! March old soldier march!
> Hayfoot, strawfoot,
> Belly-full of bean soup—
> March old soldier march!

Because of his unsophistication, the ordinary soldier in the Civil War, North and South alike, usually joined up with very romantic ideas about soldiering. Army life rubbed the romance off just as rapidly then as it does now, but at the start every volunteer went into the army thinking that he was heading off to high adventure. Under everything else, he enlisted because he thought army life was going to be fun, and usually it took quite a few weeks in camp to disabuse him of this strange notion. Right at the start, soldiering had an almost idyllic quality; if this quality faded rapidly, the memory of it remained through all the rest of life.

Early days in camp simply cemented the idea. An Illinois recruit, writing home from training camp, confessed: "It is fun to lie around, face unwashed, hair uncombed, shirt unbuttoned and everything uneverythinged. It sure beats clerking." Another Illinois boy confessed: "I don't see why people will stay at home when they can get to soldiering. A year of it is worth getting shot for to any man." And a Massachusetts boy, recalling the early days of army life, wrote that "Our drill, as I remember it, consisted largely of running around the Old Westbury town hall, yelling like Devils and firing at an imaginary foe." One of the commonest discoveries that comes from a reading of Civil War diaries is that the chief worry, in training camp, was a fear that the war would be over before the ardent young recruits could get into it. It is only fair to say that most of the diarists looked back on this innocent worry, a year or so afterward, with rueful amusement.

There was a regiment recruited in northern Pennsylvania in 1861—13th Pennsylvania Reserves officially, known to the rest of the Union Army as the Bucktails because the rookies decorated their caps with strips of fur from the carcass of a deer that was hanging in front of a butcher shop near their camp—and in mid-spring these youthful soldiers were ordered to rendezvous at Harrisburg. So they marched cross-country (along a road known today as the Bucktail Trail) to the north branch of the Susquehanna, where they built rafts. One raft, for the colonel, was made oversized with a stable; the colonel's horse had to ride, too. Then the Bucktails floated down the river, singing and firing their muskets and having a gay old time, camping out along the bank at night, and finally they got to Harrisburg; and they served through the worst of the war, getting badly shot up and losing most of their men to Confederate bullets, but they never forgot the picnic air of those first days of army life, when they drifted down a river through the forests, with a song in the air and the bright light of adventure shining just ahead. Men do not go to war that way nowadays.

Discipline in those early regiments was pretty sketchy. The big catch was that most regiments were recruited locally—in one town, or one county, or in one part of a city—and everybody more or less knew everybody else. Particularly, the privates knew their officers—most of whom were elected to their jobs by the enlisted men—and they never saw any sense in being formal with them. Within reasonable limits, the Civil War private was willing to do what his company commander told him to do, but he saw little point in carrying it to extremes.

So an Indiana soldier wrote: "We had enlisted to put down the Rebellion, and had no patience with the red-tape tomfoolery of the regular service. The boys recognized no superiors, except in the line of legitimate duty. Shoulder straps waived, a private was ready at the drop of a hat to thrash his commander—a thing that occurred more than once." A New York regiment, drilling on a hot parade ground, heard a private address his company commander thus: "Say, Tom, let's quit this darn foolin' around and go over to the sutler's and get a drink." There was very little of the "Captain, sir" business in those armies. If a company or regimental officer got anything especial in the way of obedience, he got it because the enlisted men recognized him as a natural leader and superior and not just because he had a commission signed by Abraham Lincoln.

Odd rivalries developed between regiments. (It should be noted that the Civil War soldier's first loyalty went usually to his regiment, just as a navy man's loyalty goes to his ship; he liked to believe that his regiment was better than all others, and he would fight for it, any time and anywhere.) The army legends of those days tell of a Manhattan regiment, camped near Washington, whose nearest neighbor was a regiment from Brooklyn, with which the Manhattanites nursed a deep rivalry. Neither regiment had a chaplain; and there came to the Manhattan colonel one day a minister, who volunteered to hold religious services for the men in the ranks.

The colonel doubted that this would be a good idea. His men, he said, were rather irreligious, not to say godless, and he feared they would not give the reverend gentleman a respectful hearing. But the minister said he would take his chances; after all, he had just held services with the Brooklyn regiment, and the men there had been very quiet and devout. That was enough for the colonel. What the Brooklyn regiment could do, his regiment could do. He ordered the men paraded for divine worship, announcing that any man who talked, laughed, or even coughed would be summarily court-martialed.

So the clergyman held services, and everyone was attentive. At the end of the sermon, the minister asked if any of his hearers would care to step forward and make public profession of faith; in the Brooklyn regiment, he said, fourteen men had done this. Instantly the New York colonel was on his feet.

"Adjutant!" he bellowed. "We're not going to let that damn Brooklyn regiment beat us at anything. Detail twenty men and have them baptized at once!"

Each regiment seemed to have its own mythology, tales which may have been false but which, by their mere existence, reflected faithfully certain aspects of army life. The 48th New York, for instance, was said to have an unusually large number of ministers in its ranks, serving not as chaplains but as combat soldiers. The 48th, fairly early in the war, found itself posted in a swamp along the South Carolina coast, toiling mightily in semitropical heat, amid clouds of mosquitoes, to build fortifications, and it was noted that all hands became excessively profane, including the one-time clergymen. A visiting general, watching the regiment at work one day, recalled the legend and asked the regiment's lieutenant colonel if he himself was a minister in private life.

"Well, no, General," said the officer apologetically. "I can't say that I was a regularly ordained minister. I was just one of these —— local preachers."

Another story was hung on this same 48th New York. A Confederate ironclad gunboat was supposed to be ready to steam through channels in the swamp and attack the 48th's outposts, and elaborate plans were made to trap it with obstructions in the channel, a tangle of ropes to snarl the propellers, and so on. But it occurred to the colonel that even if the gunboat was trapped the soldiers could not get into it; it was sheathed in iron, all its ports would be closed, and men with axes could never chop their way into it. Then the colonel had an inspiration. Remembering that many of his men had been recruited from the less savory districts of New York City, he paraded the regiment and (according to legend) announced:

"Now men, you've been in this cursed swamp for two weeks—up to your ears in mud, no fun, no glory and blessed poor pay. Here's a chance. Let every man who has had experience as a cracksman or a safe-blower step to the front." To the last man, the regiment marched forward four paces and came expectantly to attention.

Not unlike this was the reputation of the 6th New York, which contained so many Bowery toughs that the rest of the army said a man had to be able to show that he had done time in prison in order to get into the regiment. It was about to leave for the South, and the colonel gave his men an inspirational talk. They were going, he said, to a land of wealthy plantation owners, where each Southerner had riches of which he could be despoiled; and he took out his own gold watch and held it up for all to see, remarking that any deserving soldier could easily get one like it, once they got down to plantation-land. Half an hour later, wishing to see what time it was, he felt for his watch . . . and it was gone.

If the Civil War army spun queer tales about itself, it had to face a reality which, in all of its aspects, was singularly unpleasant. One of the worst aspects had to do with food.

From first to last, the Civil War armies enlisted no men as cooks, and there were no cooks' and bakers' schools to help matters. Often enough, when in camp, a company would simply be issued a quantity of provisions—flour, pork, beans, potatoes, and so on—and invited to prepare the stuff as best it could. Half a dozen men would form a mess, members would take turns with the cooking, and everybody had to eat what these amateurs prepared or go hungry. Later in the war, each company commander would usually detail two men to act as cooks for the company, and if either of the two happened to know anything about cooking the company was in luck. One army legend held that company officers usually detailed the least valuable soldiers to this job, on the theory that they would do less harm in the cook shack than anywhere else. One soldier, writing after the war, asserted flatly: "A company cook is a most peculiar being; he generally knows less about cooking than any other man in the company. Not being able to learn the drill, and too dirty to appear on inspection, he is sent to the cook house to get him out of the ranks."

When an army was on the march, the ration issue usually consisted of salt pork, hardtack, and coffee. (In the Confederate Army the coffee was often missing, and the hardtack was frequently replaced by corn bread; often enough the meal was not sifted, and stray bits of cob would appear in it.) The hardtack was good enough, if fresh, which was not always the case; with age it usually got infested with weevils, and veterans remarked that it was better to eat it in the dark.

In the Union Army, most of the time, the soldier could supplement his rations (if he had money) by buying extras from the sutler—the latter being a civilian merchant licensed to accompany the army, functioning somewhat as the regular post exchange functions nowadays. The sutler charged high prices and specialized in indigestibles like pies, canned lobster salad, and so on; and it was noted that men who patronized him regularly came down with stomach upsets. The Confederate Army had few sutlers, which helps to explain why the hungry Confederates were so delighted when they could capture a Yankee camp: to seize a sutler's tent meant high living for the captors, and the men in Lee's army were furious when, in the 1864 campaign, they learned that General Grant had ordered the Union Army to move without sutlers. Johnny Reb felt that Grant was really taking an unfair advantage by cutting off this possible source of supply.

If Civil War cooking arrangements were impromptu and imperfect, the same applied to its hospital system. The surgeons, usually, were good men by the standards of that day—which were low since no one on earth knew anything about germs or about how wounds became infected, and antisepsis in the operating room was a concept that had not yet come into existence; it is common to read of a surgeon whetting his scalpel on the sole of his shoe just before operating. But the hospital attendants, stretcher-bearers, and the like were chosen just as the company cooks were chosen; that is, they were detailed from the ranks, and the average officer selected the most worthless men he had simply because he wanted to get rid of men who could not be counted on in combat. As a result, sick or wounded men often got atrocious care.

A result of all this—coupled with the fact that many men enlisted without being given any medical examinations—was that every Civil War regiment suffered a constant wastage from sickness. On paper, a regiment was supposed to have a strength ranging between 960 and 1,040 men; actually, no regiment ever got to the battlefield with anything like that strength, and since there was no established system for sending in replacements a veteran regiment that could muster 350 enlisted men present for duty was considered pretty solid. From first to last, approximately twice as many Civil War soldiers died of disease—typhoid, dysentery, and pneumonia were the great killers—as died in action; and in addition to those who died a great many more got medical discharges.

In its wisdom, the Northern government set up a number of base hospitals in Northern states, far from the battle fronts, on the theory that a man recovering from wounds or sickness would recuperate better back home. Unfortunately, the hospitals thus established were under local control, and the men in them were no longer under the orders of their own regiments or armies. As a result, thousands of men who were sent north for convalescence never returned to the army. Many were detailed for light work at the hospitals, and in these details they stayed because nobody had the authority to extract them and send them back to duty. Others, recovering their health, simply went home and stayed there. They were answerable to the hospital authorities, not to the army command, and the hospital authorities rarely cared very much whether they returned to duty or not. The whole system was ideally designed to make desertion easy.

On top of all of this, many men had very little understanding of the requirements of military discipline. A homesick boy often saw nothing wrong in leaving the army and going home to see the folks for a time. A man from a farm might slip off to go home and put in a crop. In neither case would the man look on himself as a deserter; he meant to return, he figured he would get back in time for any fighting that would take place, and in his own mind he was innocent of any wrongdoing. But in many cases the date of return would be postponed from week to week; the man might end as a deserter, even though he had not intended to be one when he left.

This merely reflected the loose discipline that prevailed in Civil War armies, which in turn reflected the underlying civilian-mindedness that pervaded the rank and file. The behavior of Northern armies on the march in Southern territory reflected the same thing—and, in the end, had a profound effect on the institution of chattel slavery.

Armies of occupation always tend to bear down hard on civilian property in enemy territory. Union armies in the Civil War, being imperfectly disciplined to begin with—and suffering, furthermore, from a highly defective rationing system—bore down with especial fervor. Chickens, hams, cornfields, anything edible that might be found on a Southern plantation, looked like fair game, and the loose fringe of stragglers that always trailed around the edges of a moving Union army looted with a fine disregard for civilian property rights.

This was made all the more pointed by the fact that the average Northern soldier, poorly indoctrinated though he was, had strong feelings about the evils of secession. To his mind, the Southerners who sought to set up a nation of their own were in rebellion against the best government mankind had ever known. Being rebels, they had forfeited their rights; if evil things happened to them that (as the average Northern soldier saw it) was no more than just retribution. This meant that even when the army command tried earnestly to prevent looting and individual foraging the officers at company and regimental levels seldom tried very hard to carry out the high command's orders.

William Tecumseh Sherman has come down in history as the very archetype of the Northern soldier who believed in pillage and looting; yet during the first years of the war Sherman resorted to all manner of ferocious punishments to keep his men from despoiling Southern property. He had looters tied up by the thumbs, ordered courts-martial, issued any number of stern orders—and all to very little effect. Long before he adopted the practice of commandeering or destroying Southern property as a war measure, his soldiers were practicing it against his will, partly because discipline was poor and partly because they saw nothing wrong with it.

It was common for a Union colonel, as his regiment made camp in a Southern state, to address his men, pointing to a nearby farm, and say: "Now, boys, that barn is full of nice fat pigs and chickens. I don't want to see any of you take any of them"—whereupon he would fold his arms and look sternly in the opposite direction. It was also common for a regimental commander to read, on parade, some ukase from higher authority forbidding foraging, and then to wink solemnly—a clear hint that he did not expect anyone to take the order seriously. One colonel, punishing some men who had robbed a chicken house, said angrily: "Boys, I want you to understand that I am not punishing you for stealing but for getting caught at it."

It is more than a century since that war was fought, and things look a little different now than they looked at the time. At this distance, it may be possible to look indulgently on the wholesale foraging in which Union armies indulged; to the Southern farmers who bore the brunt of it, the business looked very ugly indeed. Many a Southern family saw the foodstuffs needed for the winter swept away in an hour by grinning hoodlums who did not need and could not use a quarter of what they took. Among the foragers there were many lawless characters who took watches, jewels, and any other valuables they could find; it is recorded that a squad would now and then carry a piano out to the lawn, take it apart, and use the wires to hang pots and pans over the campfire. . . . The Civil War was really romantic only at a considerable distance.

Underneath his feeling that it was good to add chickens and hams to the army ration, and his belief that civilians in a state of secession could expect no better fate, the Union soldier also came to believe that to destroy Southern property was to help win the war. Under orders, he tore up railroads and burned warehouses; it was not long before he realized that anything that damaged the Confederate economy weakened the Confederate war effort, so he rationalized his looting and foraging by arguing that it was a step in breaking the Southern will to resist. It is at this point that the institution of human slavery enters the picture.

Most Northern soldiers had very little feeling against slavery as such, and very little sympathy for the Negro himself. They thought they were fighting to save the Union, not to end slavery, and except for New England troops most Union regiments contained very little abolition sentiment. Nevertheless, the soldiers moved energetically and effectively to destroy slavery, not because they especially intended to but simply because they were out to do all the damage they could do. They were operating against Southern property—and the most obvious, important, and easily removable property of all was the slave. To help the slaves get away from the plantation was, clearly, to weaken Southern productive capacity, which in turn weakened Confederate armies. Hence the Union soldier, wherever he went, took the peculiar institution apart, chattel by chattel.

As a result, slavery had been fatally weakened long before the war itself came to an end. The mere act of fighting the war killed it. Of all institutions on earth, the institution of human slavery was the one least adapted to survive a war. It could not survive the presence of loose-jointed, heavy-handed armies of occupation. It may hardly be too much to say that the mere act of taking up arms in slavery's defense doomed slavery.

Above and beyond everything else, of course, the business of the Civil War soldier was to fight. He fought with weapons that look very crude to modern eyes, and he moved by an outmoded system of tactics, but the price he paid when he got into action was just as high as the price modern soldiers pay despite the almost infinite development of firepower since the 1860's.

Standard infantry weapon in the Civil War was the rifled Springfield—a muzzle-loader firing a conical lead bullet, usually of .54 caliber.

To load was rather laborious, and it took a good man to get off more than two shots a minute. The weapon had a range of nearly a mile, and its "effective range"—that is, the range at which it would hit often enough to make infantry fire truly effective—was figured at about 250 yards. Compared with a modern Garand, the old muzzle-loader is no better than a museum piece; but compared with all previous weapons—the weapons on which infantry tactics in the 1860's were still based—it was a fearfully destructive and efficient piece.

For the infantry of that day still moved and fought in formations dictated in the old days of smoothbore muskets, whose effective range was no more than 100 yards and which were wildly inaccurate at any distance. Armies using those weapons attacked in solid mass formations, the men standing, literally, elbow to elbow. They could get from effective range to hand-to-hand fighting in a very short time, and if they had a proper numerical advantage over the defensive line they could come to grips without losing too many men along the way. But in the Civil War the conditions had changed radically; men would be hit while the rival lines were still half a mile apart, and to advance in mass was simply to invite wholesale destruction. Tactics had not yet been adjusted to the new rifles; as a result, Civil War attacks could be fearfully costly, and when the defenders dug entrenchments and got some protection—as the men learned to do, very quickly—a direct frontal assault could be little better than a form of mass suicide.

It took the high command a long time to revise tactics to meet this changed situation, and Civil War battles ran up dreadful casualty lists. For an army to lose 25 per cent of its numbers in a major battle was by no means uncommon, and in some fights—the Confederate army at Gettysburg is an outstanding example—the percentage of loss ran close to one third of the total number engaged. Individual units were sometimes nearly wiped out. Some of the Union and Confederate regiments that fought at Gettysburg lost up to 80 per cent of their numbers; a regiment with such losses was usually wrecked, as an effective fighting force, for the rest of the war.

The point of all of which is that the discipline which took the Civil War soldier into action, while it may have been very sketchy by modern standards, was nevertheless highly effective on the field of battle. Any armies that could go through such battles as Antietam, Stone's River, Franklin or Chickamauga and come back for more had very little to learn about the business of fighting.

Perhaps the Confederate General D. H. Hill said it, once and for all. The battle of Malvern Hill, fought on the Virginia peninsula early in the summer of 1862, finished the famous Seven Days campaign, in which George B. McClellan's Army of the Potomac was driven back from in front of Richmond by Robert E. Lee's Army of Northern Virginia. At Malvern Hill, McClellan's men fought a rear-guard action—a bitter, confused fight which came at the end of a solid week of wearing, costly battles and forced marches. Federal artillery wrecked the Confederate assault columns, and at the end of the day Hill looked out over the battlefield, strewn with dead and wounded boys. Shaking his head, and reflecting on the valor in attack and in defense which the two armies had displayed, Hill never forgot about this. Looking back on it, long after the war was over, he declared, in substance:

"Give me Confederate infantry and Yankee artillery and I'll whip the world!"

Sources

The Photographers' War

The Civil War was the first war in history to be photographed on a large scale. Matthew Brady, Alexander Gardner, T. H. O'Sullivan, and others used large box cameras on tripods and collodion-coated glass plates that had to be sensitized in one chemical bath before exposure and developed immediately after in another chemical bath. The process was incredibly awkward and it was impossible to take action shots. But the photographers produced a magnificent record of the war.

Here are two memorable photographs that show the strain of war. Below, Abraham Lincoln in Springfield, Illinois, on June 3,

Chicago Historical Society.

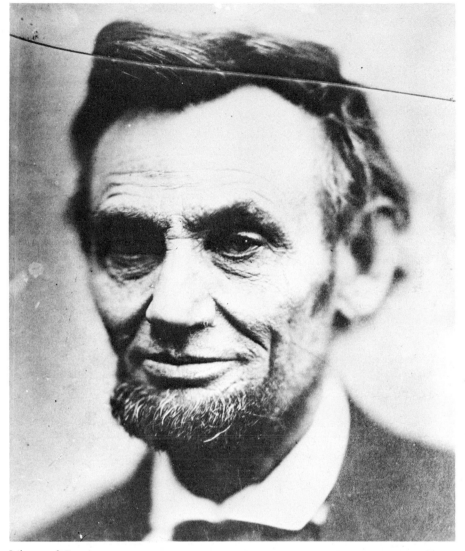

Library of Congress.

1860. Above, after four years of war, Lincoln in Washington, April 10, 1865.

And in the photograph at the top of page 328 one gets some idea why Lincoln aged so quickly. It shows the dead of both sides lying together after the battle of Gettysburg, where 150,000 men fired their muskets for several days, hour after hour, and left the ground littered with over 7,000 corpses.

Following is a series of pictures that more or less speak for themselves. Most are the work of Matthew Brady, who followed the Union army, and especially the wagons that collected the dead after battle.

Library of Congress.

**Private Edwin Francis Jennison,
Georgia Infantry.** Killed at Malvern Hill.
Library of Congress.

The 107th U.S. Colored Infantry.
Library of Congress.

**Powder Monkey,
USS New Hampshire.**
Off Charleston, South
Carolina, 1865.
*The Brady Collection/
Library of Congress.*

**Ruins of Charleston,
South Carolina, 1865.**
Library of Congress.

Union Dead. Trapped in the Sunken Road, Battle of Chancellorsville, May 3–5, 1863. *The Brady Collection/Library of Congress.*

Union Wounded. Battle of Chancellorsville, May 3–5, 1863. *Library of Congress.*

The Richmond and Petersburg Railroad Depot, 1865. *Library of Congress.*

Richmond, Virginia, at War's End. *Library of Congress.*

Freedmen in Richmond, Virginia. *Library of Congress.*

John Wilkes Booth's accomplices (Mary Surratt, David Herold, Lewis Paine, George Atserodt) in a Washington jailyard, July 7, 1865, three months after Lincoln's assassination. Booth himself had been shot and killed earlier, two weeks after he killed Lincoln. *Library of Congress.*

David P. Conyngham

Sherman's March Through Georgia, 1865

The South had lost the war by 1865, and Southerners knew it. One reason was General William Tecumseh Sherman's army, which in 1864 marched through Georgia and destroyed a civilization. Along with Sherman's army went a young newspaperman, David P. Conyngham, who was hired by the New York *Herald* to write on-the-spot reports. Here are some of his observations. What effect do you think they had on the people back home?

The Red Badge of Courage

Night had set in. The ground was strewn with the dead and wounded. Our men slept beside their arms, for the rebel lines were quite close to them. The living, the dying, and the dead slept beside one another. Rebel and Union officers and men lay piled together; some transfixed with bayonet wounds, their faces wearing that fierce, contorted look that marks those who have suffered agony. Others, who were shot dead, lay with their calm faces and glassy eyes turned to heaven. One might think they were but sleeping.

Others had their skulls crushed in by the end of a musket, while the owner of the musket lay stiff beside them, with the death grip tightened on the piece.

Clinging to one of the guns, with his hand on the spoke, and his body bent as if drawing it, lay a youth with the top of his head shot off. Another near him, with his body cut in two, still clung to the ropes.

Men writhing in pain, men stark and cold; broken caissons, rifles, and bayonets; bloody clothes and torn haversacks with all the other debris of war's havoc, were the price we paid for two old cannon.

A battle-field, when the carnage of the day is over; when the angry passions of men have subsided; when the death silence follows the din and roar of battle; when the victors have returned triumphant to their camps to celebrate their victory, regardless of the many comrades they have left behind; when the conquered sullenly fall back to a new position, awaiting to renew the struggle,—is a sad sight. It is hard to listen to the hushed groans and cries of the dying, and to witness the lacerated bodies of your fellow-soldiers strewn around, some with broken limbs, torn and mangled bodies, writhing in agony. How often has some poor fellow besought me to shoot him, and put him out of pain! It would be a mercy to do so, yet I dared not.

From David P. Conyngham, *Sherman's March Through Georgia* (New York: Sheldon and Company, 1865), *passim*.

Piled up together in a ditch, near a battery which they supported with their lines, I found several rebel dead and wounded. I dragged some of the wounded out under the shelter of the trees.

The ghouls of the army were there before me; they had rifled the pockets of the dead and wounded indiscriminately.

I gave many a poor fellow a reviving drink, amidst silent prayers.

In one place I found a mere boy of about fifteen. His leg was shattered with a piece of shell. I placed his knapsack under his head. Poor child! what stories he told me of his mother, away down in Carolina; and his little sisters, how glad they would be, now that he was wounded, to see him home.

They never saw him home, for he went to the home where the weary are at rest.

I came up to the corpse of a rebel soldier, over whom a huge Kentuckian federal soldier was weeping.

"My man," I exclaimed, "why do you weep over him? Look at your comrades around you."

"True, sir," he replied, wiping his eyes; and pointing to a federal soldier near, he said, "There is my brother; this man shot him: I killed him in return. He was my bosom friend. I loved him as a father loves his child."

Next morning, as we were removing our wounded to hospital, I saw a group collected. I rode up, and found that they were some raw troops jeering and insulting rebel wounded. Veteran troops will never do this, but share their last drink and bite with them. I rated them pretty roundly, and ordered the cowardly sneaks to their regiments. After another battle or two, these very boys would feel indignant at such conduct.

It is an affecting sight to witness the removal of the dead and wounded from a battle-field, and the manner in which the former are interred. In some cases, deep pits are sunk, and, perhaps, a hundred or more bodies are flung promiscuously into it, as if no one owned them, or cared for them.

In other cases, where the bodies had been recognized, they were buried with some semblance of decency. I was once riding with a column over a battle-field, in which the skeletons of the hastily buried were partly exposed. . . .

Women and children were dreadfully frightened at the approach of our army. It was almost painful to witness the horror and fear depicted on their features. They were schooled up to this by lying statements of what atrocious murders we were committing.

The country people trembled at our approach, and hid themselves away in woods and caves. I rode out one evening alone to pay a visit to another camp which lay some six miles beyond us. In trying to make a short way through the woods, I lost the road, and rambled on through the forest, trying to recover it. This is no easy matter, as I soon discovered; for I only got deeper and deeper into the forest. I then turned my horse's head down a valley that I knew would lead me out on a camp somewhere.

In riding along this, I thought I saw a woman among the trees. I rode in the direction, and saw her darting like a frightened deer towards a thick copse of tangled briers, wild vines, and underbrush.

Fearing some snare, I followed, with pistol in hand; and heavens, what a sight met my view! In the midst of the thicket, sheltered by a bold bluff, were about a dozen women, as many children, and three old men, almost crazy with fear and excitement.

Some of them screamed when they saw me, and all huddled closer, as if resolved to die together. I tied my horse, and assured them that they had no cause for fear; that I was not going to harm them, but would protect them, if needed. Thus assured, they became somewhat communicative.

They told me that they thought the soldiers would kill them, and that they hid here on our approach. Thinking that we were only passing through, they had brought nothing to eat or to cover them. They were here now near three days, and had nothing but the berries they picked up in the woods. They looked wretched, their features wan and thin, their eyes wild and haggard; and their lips stained from the unripe wild fruit. Some of them were lying down, huddled together to keep themselves warm; their clothes were all saturated from the dew and a heavy shower of rain which fell during the day.

I do not think one could realize so much wretchedness and suffering as that group presented. Some of the women were evidently planters' wives and daughters; their appearance and worn dresses betokened it; others were their servants, or the wives of the farm-laborers.

There were two black women, and some three picaninnies. Under the shelter of a tree, I saw a woman sitting down, rocking her body to and fro, as she wept bitterly.

I went over to her. Beside her was a girl of some fourteen years, lying at full length. As I approached, she looked so pale and statuelike, I exclaimed,—

"What's the matter. Is she in a faint?"

"Yes; in one that she won't waken from," said an old crone near.

"Dead!" I exclaimed.

"Well, stranger, I reckon so; better for her to go, poor darling, than have the Yankees cotch her."

It was so. She was dead. I understood she was delicate; and the hunger and cold had killed her. So much were they afraid of being discovered that they had not even a fire lighted.

I inquired my way to the camp, and soon returned with some provisions. The dead body was removed, and the sorrowing group returned to their homes; but some of them had no homes, for the soldiers, on the principle that all abandoned houses belong to rebels, had laid them in ashes. . . .

On one occasion General Johnston sent a flag of truce to Sherman, in order to give time to carry off the wounded and bury the dead, who were festering in front of their lines.

A truce followed, and Rebels and Federals freely participated in the work of charity. It was a strange sight to see friends, to see old acquaintances, and in some instances brothers, who had been separated for years, and now pitted in deadly hostility, meet and have a good talk over old times, and home scenes, and connections. They drank together, smoked together, appeared on the best possible terms, though the next day they were sure to meet in deadly conflict again.

Even some of the generals freely mixed with the men, and seemed to view the painful sight with melancholy interest.

An officer, speaking of this sad burial, said, "I witnessed a strange scene yesterday in front of Davis's division. During the burial of the dead, grouped together in seemingly fraternal unity, were officers and men of both contending armies, who, but five minutes before, were engaged in the work of slaughter and death."

Under the shelter of a pine, I noticed a huge gray Kentuckian rebel, with his arm affectionately placed around the neck of a Federal soldier, a mere boy. The bronzed warrior cried and laughed by turns, and then kissed the young Federal.

Attracted by such a strange proceeding, I went over to them, and said to the veteran, "Why, you seem very much taken by that boy; I suppose he is some old friend of yours."

"Old friend, sir! Why, he is my son!"

I have often seen a rebel and a Federal soldier making right for the same rifle-pit, their friends on both sides loudly cheering them on. As they would not have time to fight, they reserved their fire until they got into the pit, then woe betide the laggard, for the other was sure to pop him as soon as he got into cover. Sometimes they got in together, and then came the tug of war; for they fought for possession with their bayonets and closed fists. In some cases however, they made a truce, and took joint possession of it.

It was no unusual thing to see our pickets and skirmishers enjoying themselves very comfortably with the rebels, drinking bad whiskey, smoking and chewing worse tobacco, and trading coffee and other little articles. The rebels had no coffee, and our men plenty, while the rebels had plenty of whiskey; so they very soon came to an understanding. It was strange to see these men, who had been just pitted in deadly conflict, trading, and bantering, and chatting, as if they were the best friends in the world. They discussed a battle with the same gusto they would a cock-fight, or horse-race, and made inquiries about their friends, as to who was killed, and who not, in the respective armies. Friends that have been separated for years have met in this way. Brothers who parted to try their fortune have often met on the picket line, or on the battlefield. I once met a German soldier with the head of a dying rebel on his lap. The stern veteran was weeping, whilst the boy on his knee looked pityingly into his face. They were speaking in German, and from my poor knowledge of the language, all I could make out was, they were brothers; that the elder had come out here several years before; the younger followed him, and being informed that he was in Macon, he went in search of him, and got conscripted; while the elder brother, who was in the north all the time, joined our army. The young boy was scarcely twenty, with light hair, and a soft, fair complexion. The pallor of death on his brow, and the blood was flowing from his breast, and gurgled in his throat and mouth, which the other wiped away with his handkerchief. When he could speak, the dying youth's conversation was of the old home in Germany, of his brothers and sisters, and dear father and mother, who were never to see him again.

In those improvised truces, the best possible faith was observed by the men. These truces were brought about chiefly in the following manner. A rebel, who was heartily tired of his crippled position in his pit, would call out, "I say, Yank!"

"Well, Johnny Reb," would echo from another hole or tree.

"I'm going to put out my head; don't shoot."

"Well, I won't."

The reb would pop up his head; the Yank would do the same.

"Hain't you got any coffee, Johnny?"

"Na'r a bit, but plenty of rot-gut."

"All right; we'll have a trade."

They would meet, while several others would follow the example, until there would be a regular bartering mart established. In some cases the men would come to know each other so well, that they would often call out,— "Look out, reb; we're going to shoot," or, "Look out, Yank, we're going to shoot," as the case may be. . . .

The Siege of Atlanta

From several points along the lines we could plainly see the doomed city, with the smoke of burning houses and bursting shells enveloping it in one black canopy, hanging over it like a funeral pall.

The scene at night was sublimely grand and terrific! The din of artillery rang on the night air. In front of General Geary's headquarters was a prominent hill, from which we had a splendid view of the tragedy enacting before us. One night I sat there with the general and staff, and several other officers, while a group of men sat near us enjoying the scene, and speculating on the effects of the shells. It was a lovely, still night, with the stars twinkling in the sky. The lights from the campfires along the hills and valleys, and from amidst the trees, glimmered like the gas-lights of a city in the distance. We could see the dark forms reclining around them, and mark the solemn tread of the sentinel on his beat. A rattle of musketry rang from some point along the line. It was a false alarm. The men for a moment listened, and then renewed their song and revelry, which was for a while interrupted. The song, and music, and laughter floated to our ears from the city of camps, that dotted the country all round.

Sherman had lately ordered from Chattanooga a battery of four and a half inch rifles, and these were trying their metal on the city.

Several batteries, forts, and bastions joined in the fierce chorus. Shells flew from the batteries, up through the air, whizzing and shrieking, until they reached a point over the devoted city, when down they went, hurling the fragments, and leaving in their train a balloon-shaped cloud of smoke. From right, and left, and centre flew these dread missiles, all converging towards the city. From our commanding position we could see the flash from the guns, then the shells, with their burning fuses, hurtling through the air like flying meteors.

"War is a cruelty," said the general beside me; "we know not how many innocents are now suffering in this miserable city."

"I'm dog gone if I like it," said a soldier, slapping his brawny hand upon his thigh; "I can fight my weight of rattlesnakes; but this thing of smoking out women and children, darn me if it's fair."

On the night of September 1, Hood blew up all the magazines and ammunition, destroyed all the supplies he could not move, comprising eight locomotives, and near one hundred cars laden with ammunition, small arms, and stores, and then retreated. Our troops, advancing near the city, met with no resistance. Observing that it was evacuated, they entered it about 11 o'clock on the morning of September 2, 1864.

Atlanta was now in our hands, the crowning point of Sherman's great campaign. Hood had been outgeneraled, outmanoeuvred, and outflanked, and was now trying to concentrate his scattered army. On the night of the 1st, when the rebel army was vacating, the stampede was frightful to those engaged, but grandly ludicrous to casual spectators. . . .

The city had suffered much from our projectiles. Several houses had been burned, and several fallen down. In some places the streets were blocked up with the rubbish. The suburbs were in ruins, and few houses escaped without being perforated. Many of the citizens were killed, and many more had hairbreadth escapes. Some shells had passed through the Trout House Hotel, kicking up a regular muss among beds and tables.

One woman pointed out to me where a shell dashed through her house as she was sitting down to dinner. It upset the table and things, passed through the house, and killed her neighbor in the next house.

Several had been killed; some in their houses, others in the streets.

When the rebels were evacuating, in the confusion several of our sick and wounded escaped from the hospitals, and were sheltered by the citizens.

Almost every garden and yard around the city had its cave. These were sunk down with a winding entrance to them, so that pieces of shells could not go in. When dug deep enough, boards were placed on the top, and the earth piled upon them in a conical shape, and deep enough to withstand even a shell. Some of these caves, or bomb-proofs, were fifteen feet deep, and well covered. All along the railroad, around the intrenchments and the bluff near the city, were gopher holes, where soldiers and citizens concealed themselves.

In some cases it happened that our shells burst so as to close up the mouths of the caves, thus burying the inmates in a living tomb.

. . . The first fire burst out on the night of Friday, the 11th of November, in a block of wooden tenements on Decatur Street, where eight buildings were destroyed.

Soon after, fires burst out in other parts of the city. These certainly were the works of some of the soldiers, who expected to get some booty under cover of the fires. . . .

It was hard to restrain the soldiers from burning it down. With that licentiousness that characterizes an army they wanted a bonfire.

On Sunday night a kind of long streak of light, like an aurora, marked the line of march, and the burning stores, depots, and bridges, in the train of the army.

The Michigan engineers had been detailed to destroy the depots and public buildings in Atlanta. Everything in the way of destruction was now considered legalized. The workmen tore up the rails and piled them on the smoking fires. Winship's iron foundery and machine shops were early set on fire. This valuable property was calculated to be worth about half a million dollars.

An oil refinery near by next got on fire, and was soon in a fierce blaze. Next followed a freight warehouse, in which were stored several bales of cotton. The depot, turning-tables, freight sheds, and stores around, were soon a fiery mass. The heart was burning out of beautiful Atlanta. . . .

Atlanta to the Sea

It was pretty well known that Sherman was going to cut loose from all communications, and to destroy all the factories, founderies, railroads, mills, and all government property, thus preventing the rebels from using them in his rear. After the troops destroyed Rome, Kingston, and Marietta, tore up the track, and set fire to sleepers, railroad depots, and stores, Sherman issued a special field order:

"The army will forage liberally on the country during the march. To this end each brigade commander will organize a good and efficient foraging party, under command of one or more discreet officers. To regular foraging parties must be intrusted the gathering of provisions and forage at any distance from the roads travelled.

"As for horses, mules, wagons, &c., the cavalry and artillery may appropriate freely and without limit. Foraging parties may also take mules or horses to replace the jaded animals of their trains, or to serve as pack-mules for the regiments or brigades."

These orders were all right, if literally carried out; but they were soon converted into licenses for indiscriminate plunder. The followers of an army, in the shape of servants, hangers-on, and bummers, are generally as numerous as the effective force. Every brigade and regiment had its organized, foraging party, which were joined by every officer's servant and idler about the camps. . . .

"Living off the country" was fast becoming the order. The men knew that Sherman had started with some sixteen days' supplies, and they wished to preserve them if possible; besides, they thought that a change of diet would be good for their health. There was nothing to be got the first two days' march, as the country all around Atlanta had been foraged by Slocum's corps while hemmed in there. Now we were opening on a country where pits of sweet potatoes, yards of poultry and hogs, and cellars of bacon and flour. were making their appearance. A new spirit began to animate the men; they were as busy as so many bees about a honey-pot, and commenced important voyages of discovery, and returned well laden with spoils. Foragers, bummers, and camp followers scattered over the country for miles, and black clouds of smoke showed where they had been. Small lots of cotton were found near most of the plantation houses. These, with the gins and presses, were burned, oftentimes firing the houses and offices. Near Madison we passed some wealthy plantations; one, the property of a Mr. Lane, who was courteous enough to wait to receive us, was full of decrepit, dilapidated negroes, presided over by a few brimstone-looking white ladies. They were viciously rabid, and only wished they could eat us with the same facility that the troops consumed all the edibles on the place, and eloped with plump grunters and indignant roosters, and their families. . . .

15

Reconstruction

When it was first coined in the crisis months between the election of Lincoln and the beginnings of the Civil War, the term "Reconstruction" meant simply the reunification of the nation. By the time the war ended in 1865, the idea of Reconstruction was more complicated: it now meant more than simple political re-establishment of the Union; it meant reconstructing the South, refashioning its social and economic life to some degree or other. For the freedmen—many only days removed from slavery—Reconstruction would soon come to represent freedom itself. Even in 1865, most Southern blacks realized that without thoroughgoing Reconstruction, in which freedmen obtained land as well as the right to vote, freedom would mean only a new kind of economic oppression.

Twelve years later, in 1877, many people, North and South, realized that Reconstruction had ended. But by then the term had taken on intense moral meanings. To most white Southerners, it was a term of resentment, the name of a bleak period during which vindictive Yankee politicians had tried to force "black rule" on a "prostrate South." Tried and finally failed, for the South had in the end been "redeemed" by its own leaders. Slavery had ended, but white supremacy had been firmly re-established. To perhaps a majority of whites in the North, Reconstruction had over the years become a nuisance, and they were glad to let go of it, to reaffirm the value of the Union, and to let the bitter past die. There were other Northerners, however, who looked back from 1877 to twelve years of moral failure, of lost opportunities to force freedom and equality on an unrepentant South.

There were hundreds of thousands of freedmen who experienced this "moral failure" in very real ways. Instead of farming their own land, they farmed the lands of whites as tenants and sharecroppers. Far from benefiting from meaningful voting rights, most blacks were denied the franchise, and those who continued to exercise it did so in a climate of hostility hardly conducive to political freedom. Nonetheless, it was possible for blacks to look back positively at the Reconstruction experience. The 1866 Civil Rights Act granted blacks both citizenship and all the civil rights possessed by whites. When the constitutionality of that statute seemed in doubt, Congress made ratification of the Fourteenth Amendment (accomplished in 1868) a precondition for Southern restoration to the Union. In theory, that amendment made the federal government the protector of rights that might be invaded by the states. Under "Radical" reconstruction, carried out by Congress after 1867, hundreds of thousands of Southern blacks voted, and many held high elective office. And in 1875, when whites had re-established their authority throughout most of the region, a new civil rights act "guaranteed" blacks equal rights in theaters, inns, and other public places. If in the end it proved impossible to maintain these gains, Reconstruction still remained the bright spot in the lives of many former slaves.

Interpretive Essay

Elizabeth Rauh Bethel

Promised Land

Most accounts of the Reconstruction period have been written largely from the perspective of powerful white men such as presidents, Northern congressmen, or Southern "redeemers." As a result, students often get the impression that all decisions were made by whites, and blacks were idly sitting on their hands, just the beneficiaries or victims of white actions. That was not the case. Throughout the South black men and women, even though they were just months away from slavery, actively shaped their own futures and challenged the power and prejudices of their white neighbors. Most wanted to own land and become family farmers. The odds against them were immense, and many struggled valiantly only to see their hopes dashed by their lack of money, or by political decisions made in distant Washington, or by white terrorists such as the Ku Klux Klan. But some, as Elizabeth Rauh Bethel documents in the following selection, overcame great obstacles and established tightly-knit communities. What do you think accounts for the courage and determination of the families Bethel describes? Do you think the course of

American history would have been changed if most black families during Reconstruction had obtained a forty-acre farm? In what respect?

The opportunity to acquire land was a potent attraction for a people just emerging from bondage, and one commonly pursued by freedmen throughout the South. Cooperative agrarian communities, instigated in some cases by the invading Union Army and in other cases by the freedmen themselves, were scattered across the plantation lands of the South as early as 1863. Collective land purchases and cooperative farming ventures developed in the Tidewater area of Virginia, the Sea Islands of South Carolina and Georgia, and along the Mississippi River as refugees at the earliest contraband camps struggled to establish economic and social stability.

These initial land tenure arrangements, always temporary, stimulated high levels of industrious labor among both those fortunate enough to obtain land and those whose expectations were raised by their neighbors' good fortunes. Although for most freedmen the initial promise of landownership was never realized, heightened expectations resulted in "entire families laboring together, improving their material conditions, laying aside money that might hopefully be used to purchase a farm or a few acres for a homestead of their own" during the final years of the war.

The desire for a plot of land dominated public expressions among the freedmen as well as their day-to-day activities and behaviors. In 1864 Secretary of War Stanton met with Negro leaders in Savannah to discuss the problems of resettlement. During that meeting sixty-seven-year-old freedman Garrison Frazier responded to an inquiry regarding living arrangements by telling Stanton that "we would prefer to 'live by ourselves' rather than 'scattered among the whites.'" These arrangements, he added, should include self-sufficiency established on Negro-owned lands. The sentiments Frazier expressed were not unusual. They were repeated by other freedmen across the South. Tunis Campbell, also recently emancipated, testified before the congressional committee investigating the Ku Klux Klan that "the great cry of our people is to have land." A delegate to the Tennessee Colored Citizens' Convention of 1866 stated that "what is needed for the colored people is land which they own." A recently emancipated Negro representative to the 1868 South Carolina Constitutional Convention, speaking in support of that state's land redistribution program, which eventually gave birth to the Promised Land community, said of the relationship between landownership and the state's Negro population: "Night and day they dream" of owning their own land. "It is their all in all."

At Davis Bend, Mississippi and Port Royal, South Carolina, as well as similar settlements in Louisiana, North Carolina, and Virginia, this dream

From Ethel Rauh Bethel, *Promiseland: A Century of Life in a Negro Community* (Philadelphia: Temple University Press, 1981), pp. 5–8, 17–21, 23, 25–33, 39–40. © 1981 by Temple University. Reprinted by permission of Temple University Press.

was in fact realized for a time. Freedmen worked "with commendable zeal
. . . out in the morning before it is light and at work 'til darkness drives
them to their homes" whenever they farmed land which was their own.
John Eaton, who supervised the Davis Bend project, observed that the most
successful land experiments among the freedmen were those in which plantations were subdivided into individually owned and farmed tracts. These small
farms, rather than the larger cooperative ventures, "appeared to hold the
greatest chance for success." The contraband camps and federally directed
farm projects afforded newly emancipated freedmen an opportunity to "redis-
cover and redefine themselves, and to establish communities." Within the
various settlements a stability and social order developed that combined economic self-sufficiency with locally directed and controlled schools, churches,
and mutual aid societies. In the years before the Freedmen's Bureau or the
northern missionary societies penetrated the interior of the South, the freedmen, through their own resourcefulness, erected and supported such community institutions at every opportunity. In obscure settlements with names
like Slabtown and Acreville, Hampton, Alexandria, Saxtonville, and Mitchel-
ville, "status, experience, history, and ideology were potent forces operating
toward cohesiveness and community." . . .

    . . . In South Carolina, perhaps more intensely than any of the other
southern states, the thirst for land was acute. It was a possibility sparked
first by General William T. Sherman's military actions along the Sea Islands,
then dashed as quickly as it was born in the distant arena of Washington
politics. Still, the desire for land remained a goal not readily abandoned by
the state's freedpeople, and they implemented a plan to achieve that goal at
the first opportunity. Their chance came at the 1868 South Carolina Constitutional Convention.
    South Carolina was among the southern states which refused to ratify
the Fourteenth Amendment to the Constitution, the amendment which established the citizenship of the freedmen. Like her recalcitrant neighbors, the
state was then placed under military government, as outlined by the Military
Reconstruction Act of 1867. Among the mandates of that federal legislation
was a requirement that each of the states in question draft a new state constitution which incorporated the principles of the Fourteenth Amendment. Only
after such new constitutions were completed and implemented were the separate states of the defeated Confederacy eligible for readmission to the Union.
    The representatives to these constitutional conventions were selected by
a revolutionary electorate, one which included all adult male Negroes. Registration for the elections was handled by the Army with some informal assistance by "that God-forsaken institution, the Freedman's Bureau." Only South
Carolina among the ten states of the former Confederacy elected a Negro
majority to its convention. The instrument those representatives drafted called
for four major social and political reforms in state government: a state-wide
system of free common schools; universal manhood suffrage; a jury law which
included the Negro electorate in county pools of qualified jurors; and a land

redistribution system designed to benefit the state's landless population, primarily the freedmen.

White response to the new constitution and the social reforms which it outlined was predictably vitriolic. It was condemned by one white newspaper as "the work of sixty-odd Negroes, many of them ignorant and depraved." The authors were publicly ridiculed as representing "the maddest, most unscrupulous, and infamous revolution in history." Despite this and similar vilification, the constitution was ratified in the 1868 referendum, an election boycotted by many white voters and dominated by South Carolina's 81,000 newly enfranchised Negroes, who cast their votes overwhelmingly with the Republicans and for the new constitution.

That same election selected representatives to the state legislature charged with implementing the constitutional reforms. That body, like the constitutional convention, was constituted with a Negro majority; and it moved immediately to establish a common school system and land redistribution program. The freedmen were already registered, and the new jury pools remained the prerogative of the individual counties. The 1868 election also was notable for the numerous attacks and "outrages" which occurred against the more politically active freedmen. Among those Negroes assaulted, beaten, shot, and lynched during the pre-election campaign months were four men who subsequently bought small farms from the Land Commission and settled at Promised Land. Like other freedmen in South Carolina, their open involvement in the state's Republican political machinery led to personal violence.

Wilson Nash was the first of the future Promised Land residents to encounter white brutality and retaliation for his political activities. Nash was nominated by the Republicans as their candidate for Abbeville County's seat in the state legislature at the August 1868 county convention. In October of that year, less than two weeks before the general election, Nash was attacked and shot in the leg by two unidentified white assailants. The "outrage" took place in the barn on his rented farm, not far from Dr. Marshall's farm on Curltail Creek. Wilson Nash was thirty-three years old in 1868, married, and the father of three small children. He had moved from "up around Cokesbury" within Abbeville County, shortly after emancipation to the rented land further west. Within months after the Nash family was settled on their farm, Wilson Nash joined the many Negroes who affiliated with the Republicans, an alliance probably instigated and encouraged by Republican promises of land to the freedmen. The extent of Nash's involvement with local politics was apparent in his nomination for public office; and this same nomination brought him to the forefront of county Negro leadership and to the attention of local whites.

After the attack Nash sent his wife and young children to a neighbor's home, where he probably believed they would be safe. He then mounted his mule and fled his farm, leaving behind thirty bushels of recently harvested corn. Whether Nash also left behind a cotton crop is unknown. It was the unprotected corn crop that worried him as much as his concern for his own safety. He rode his mule into Abbeville and there sought refuge at the local

Freedman's Bureau office where he reported the attack to the local bureau agent and requested military protection for his family and his corn crop. Captain W. F. DeKnight was sympathetic to Nash's plight but was powerless to assist or protect him. DeKnight had no authority in civil matters such as this, and the men who held that power generally ignored such assaults on Negroes. The Nash incident was typical and followed a familiar pattern. The assailants remained unidentified, unapprehended, and unpunished. The attack achieved the desired end, however, for Nash withdrew his name from the slate of legislative candidates. For him there were other considerations which took priority over politics.

Violence against the freedmen of Abbeville County, as elsewhere in the state, continued that fall and escalated as the 1868 election day neared. The victims had in common an involvement with the Republicans, and there was little distinction made between direct and indirect partisan activity. Politically visible Negroes were open targets. Shortly after the Nash shooting young Willis Smith was assaulted, yet another victim of Reconstruction violence. Smith was still a teenager and too young to vote in the elections, but his age afforded him no immunity. He was a known member of the Union League, the most radical and secret of the political organizations which attracted freedmen. While attending a dance one evening, Smith and four other League members were dragged outside the dance hall and brutally beaten by four white men whose identities were hidden by hoods. This attack, too, was an act of political vengeance. It was, as well, one of the earliest Ku Klux Klan appearances in Abbeville. Like other crimes committed against politically active Negroes, this one remained unsolved.

On election day freedmen Washington Green and Allen Goode were precinct managers at the White Hall polling place, near the southern edge of the Marshall land. Their position was a political appointment of some prestige, their reward for affiliation with and loyalty to the Republican cause. The appointment brought them, like Wilson Nash and Willis Smith, to the attention of local whites. On election day the voting proceeded without incident until midday, when two white men attempted to block Negroes from entering the polling site. A scuffle ensued as Green and Goode, acting in their capacity as voting officials, tried to bring the matter to a halt and were shot by the white men. One freedman was killed, two others injured, in the incident which also went unsolved. In none of the attacks were the assailants ever apprehended. Within twenty-four months all four men—Wilson Nash, Willis Smith, Washington Green, and Allen Goode—bought farms at Promised Land.

Despite the violence which surrounded the 1868 elections, the Republicans carried the whole of the state. White Democrats refused to support an election they deemed illegal, and they intimidated the newly enfranchised Negro electorate at every opportunity. The freedmen, nevertheless, flocked to the polls in an unprecedented exercise of their new franchise and sent a body of legislative representatives to the state capitol of Columbia who were wholly committed to the mandates and reforms of the new constitution. Among the first legislative acts was one which formalized the land redistribution program through the creation of the South Carolina Land Commission.

The Land Commission program, as designed by the legislature, was financed through the public sale of state bonds. The capital generated from the bond sales was used to purchase privately owned plantation tracts which were then subdivided and resold to freedmen through long-term (ten years), low-interest (7 percent per annum) loans. The bulk of the commission's transactions occurred along the coastal areas of the state where land was readily available. The labor and financial problems of the rice planters of the low-country were generally more acute than those of the up-country cotton planters. As a result, they were more eager to dispose of a portion of the landholdings at a reasonable price, and their motives for their dealings with the Land Commission were primarily pecuniary.

Piedmont planters were not so motivated. Many were able to salvage their production by negotiating sharecropping and tenant arrangements. Most operated on a smaller scale than the low-country planters and were less dependent on gang labor arrangements. As a consequence, few were as financially pressed as their low-country counterparts, and land was less available for purchase by the Land Commission in the Piedmont region. With only 9 percent of the commission purchases lying in the up-country, the Marshall lands were the exception rather than the rule.

The Marshall sons first advertised the land for sale in 1865. These lands, like others at the eastern edge of the Cotton Belt, were exhausted from generations of cultivation and attendant soil erosion; and for such worn out land the price was greatly inflated. Additionally, two successive years of crop failures, low cotton prices, and a general lack of capital discouraged serious planters from purchasing the lands. The sons then advertised the tract for rent, but the land stood idle. The family wanted to dispose of the land in a single transaction rather than subdivide it, and Dr. Marshall's farm was no competition for the less expensive and more fertile land to the west that was opened for settlement after the war. In 1869 the two sons once again advertised the land for sale, but conditions in Abbeville County were not improved for farmers, and no private buyer came forth.

Having exhausted the possibilities for negotiating a private sale, the family considered alternative prospects for the disposition of a farm that was of little use to them. James L. Orr, a moderate Democrat, former governor (1865 to 1868), and family son-in-law, served as negotiator when the tract was offered to the Land Commission at the grossly inflated price of ten dollars an acre. Equivalent land in Abbeville County was selling for as little as two dollars an acre, and the commission rejected the offer. Political promises took precedence over financial considerations when the commission's regional agent wrote the Land Commission's Advisory Board that "if the land is not bought the (Republican) party is lost in this district." Upon receipt of his advice the commission immediately met the Marshall family's ten dollar an acre price. By January 1870 the land was subdivided into fifty small farms, averaging slightly less than fifty acres each, which were publicly offered for sale to Negro as well as white buyers.

The Marshall Tract was located in the central sector of old Abbeville County and was easily accessible to most of the freedmen who were to make the lands their home. . . .

The farms on the Marshall Tract were no bargain for the Negroes who bought them. The land was only partially cleared and ready for cultivation, and that which was free of pine trees and underbrush was badly eroded. There was little to recommend the land to cotton farming. Crop failures in 1868 and 1869 severely limited the local economy, which further reduced the possibilities for small farmers working on badly depleted soil. There was little credit available to Abbeville farmers, white or black; and farming lacked not only an unqualified promise of financial gain but even the possibility of breaking even at harvest. Still, it was not the fertility of the soil or the possibility of economic profit that attracted the freedmen to those farms. The single opportunity for landownership, a status which for most Negroes in 1870 symbolized the essence of their freedom, was the prime attraction for the freedmen who bought farms from the subdivided Marshall Tract.

Most of the Negroes who settled the farms knew the area and local conditions well. Many were native to Abbeville County. In addition to Wilson Nash, the Moragne family and their in-laws, the Turners, the Pinckneys, the Letmans, and the Williamses were also natives of Abbeville, from "down over by Bordeaux" in the southwestern rim of the county which borders Georgia. Others came to their new farms from "Dark Corner, over by McCormick," and another nearby Negro settlement, Pettigrew Station—both in Abbeville County. The Redd family lived in Newberry, South Carolina before they bought their farm; and James and Hannah Fields came to Promised Land from the state capitol, Columbia, eighty miles to the east.

Many of the settlers from Abbeville County shared their names with prominent white families—Moragne, Burt, Marshall, Pressley, Frazier, and Pinckney. Their claims to heritage were diverse. One recalled "my grandaddy was a white man from England," and others remembered slavery times to their children in terms of white fathers who "didn't allow nobody to mess with the colored boys of his." Others dismissed the past and told their grandchildren that "some things is best forgot." A few were so fair skinned that "they could have passed for white it they wanted to," while others who bought farms from the Land Commission "was so black there wasn't no doubt about who their daddy was."

After emancipation many of these former bondsmen stayed in their old neighborhoods, farming in much the same way as they had during slavery times. Some "worked for the marsters at daytime and for theyselves at night" in an early Piedmont version of sharecropping. Old Samuel Marshall was one former slave owner who retained many of his bondsmen as laborers by assuring them that they would receive some land of their own—promising them that "if you clean two acres you get two acres; if you clean ten acres you get ten acres" of farmland. It was this promise which kept some freedmen on the Marshall land until it was sold to the Land Commission. They cut and cleared part of the tract of the native pines and readied it for planting in anticipation of ownership. But the promise proved empty, and Marshall's death and the subsequent sale of his lands to the state deprived many of those who labored day and night on the land of the free farms they hoped would be theirs. "After they had cleaned it up they still had to pay for it." Other freedmen in the county "moved off after slavery ended but couldn't get no place" of their own to farm. Unable to negotiate labor or lease arrangements, they faced a time of homelessness with few resources and limited options until the farms became available to them. A few entered into labor contracts supervised by the Freedman's Bureau or settled on rented farms in the county for a time.

The details of the various postemancipation economic arrangements made by the freedmen who settled on the small tracts at Dr. Marshall's farm, whatever the form they assumed, were dominated by three conscious choices all had in common. The first was their decision to stay in Abbeville County following emancipation. For most of the people who eventually settled in Promised Land, Abbeville was their home as well as the site of their enslavement. There they were surrounded by friends, family and a familiar environment. The second choice this group of freedmen shared was occupational. They had been Piedmont farmers throughout their enslavement, and they chose to remain farmers in their freedom.

Local Negroes made a third conscious decision that for many had long-range importance in their lives and those of their descendents. Through the influence of the Union League, the Freedman's Bureau, the African Methodist Church, and each other, many of the Negroes in Abbeville aligned politically with the Republicans between 1865 and 1870. In Abbeville as elsewhere in the state, this alliance was established enthusiastically. The Republicans promised land as well as suffrage to those who supported them. If their political activities became public knowledge, the freedmen "were safe nowhere"; and men like Wilson Nash, Willis Smith, Washington Green, and Allen Goode who were highly visible Negro politicians took great risks in this exercise of freedom. Those risks were not without justification. It was probably not a coincidence that loyalty to the Republican cause was followed by a chance to own land.

. . . The Land Commission first advertised the farms on the Marshall Tract in January and February 1870. Eleven freedmen and their families established conditional ownership of their farms before spring planting that year. They were among a vanguard of some 14,000 Negro families who acquired small farms in South Carolina through the Land Commission program between 1868 and 1879. With a ten-dollar down payment they acquired the right to settle on and till the thin soil. They were also obliged to place at least half of their land under cultivation within three years and to pay all taxes due annually in order to retain their ownership rights.

Among the earliest settlers to the newly created farms was Allen Goode, the precinct manager at White Hall, who bought land in January 1870, almost immediately after it was put on the market. Two brothers-in-law, J. H. Turner and Primus Letman, also bought farms in the early spring that year. Turner was married to LeAnna Moragne and Letman to LeAnna's sister Francis. Elias Harris, a widower with six young children to raise, also came to his lands that spring, as did George Hearst, his son Robert, and their families. Another father-son partnership, Carson and Will Donnelly, settled on adjacent tracts. Willis Smith's father Daniel also bought a farm in 1870.

Allen Goode was the wealthiest of these early settlers. He owned a horse, two oxen, four milk cows, and six hogs. For the other families, both material resources and farm production were modest. Few of the homesteaders produced more than a single bale of cotton on their new farms that first year; but all, like Wilson Nash two years earlier, had respectable corn harvests, a crop essential to "both us and the animals." Most households also had sizable pea, bean, and sweet potato crops and produced their own butter. All but the cotton crops were destined for household consumption, as these earliest settlers established a pattern of subsistence farming that would prevail as a community economic strategy in the coming decades.

This decision by the Promised Land farmers to intensify food production and minimize cotton cultivation, whether intentional or the result of other conditions, was an important initial step toward their attainment of economic self-sufficiency. Small scale cotton farmers in the Black Belt were rarely free agents. Most were quickly trapped in a web of chronic indebtedness and marketing restrictions. Diversification of cash crops was inhibited during the 1870's and 1880's not only by custom and these economic entanglements but also by an absence of local markets, adequate roads, and methods of transportation to move crops other than cotton to larger markets. The Promised Land farmers, generally unwilling to incur debts with the local lien men if they could avoid it, turned to a modified form of subsistence farming as their only realistic land-use option. Through this strategy many of them avoided the "economic nightmare" which fixed the status of other small-scale cotton growers at a level of permanent peonage well into the twentieth century.

The following year, 1871, twenty-five more families scratched up their ten-dollar down payment; and upon presenting it to Hollinshead obtained conditional titles to farms on the Marshall Tract. The Williams family, Amanda and her four adult sons—William, Henry, James, and Moses—purchased farms together that year, probably withdrawing their money from their accounts at the Freedman's Savings and Trust Company Augusta Branch for their separate down payments. Three of the Moragne brothers—Eli, Calvin, and Moses—joined the Turners and the Letmans, their sisters and brothers-in-law, making five households in that corner of the tract soon designated "Moragne Town." John Valentine, whose family was involved in A.M.E. organizational work in Abbeville County, also obtained a conditional title to a farm, although he did not settle there permanently. Henry Redd, like the Williamses, withdrew his savings from the Freedman's Bank and moved to his farm from Newberry, a small town about thirty miles to the east. Moses Wideman, Wells Gray, Frank Hutchison, Samuel Bulow, and Samuel Burt also settled on their farms before spring planting.

As the cluster of Negro-owned farms grew more densely populated, it gradually assumed a unique identity; and this identity, in turn, gave rise to a name, Promised Land. Some remember their grandparents telling them that "the Governor in Columbia [South Carolina] named this place when he sold it to the Negroes." Others contend that the governor had no part in the naming. They argue that these earliest settlers derived the name Promised Land from the conditions of their purchase. "They only promised to pay for it, but they never did!" Indeed, there is some truth in that statement. For although the initial buyers agreed to pay between nine and ten dollars per acre for their land in the original promissory notes, few fulfilled the conditions of those contracts. Final purchase prices were greatly reduced, from ten dollars to $3.25 per acre, a price more in line with prevailing land prices in the Piedmont.

By the end of 1873 forty-four of the fifty farms on the Marshall Tract had been sold. The remaining land, less than seven hundred acres, was the poorest in the tract, badly eroded and at the perimeter of the community. Some of those farms remained unsold until the early 1880's, but even so the land did not go unused. Families too poor to consider buying the farms lived on the state-owned property throughout the 1870's. They were squatters, living there illegally and rent-free, perhaps working a small cotton patch, always a garden. Their condition contrasted sharply with that of the landowners who, like other Negroes who purchased farmland during the 1870's, were considered the most prosperous of the rural freedmen. The freeholders in the community were among the pioneers in a movement to acquire land, a movement that stretched across geographical and temporal limits. Even in the absence of state or federal assistance in other regions, and despite the difficulties Negroes faced in negotiating land purchases directly from white landowners during Reconstruction, by 1875 Negroes across the South owned five million acres of farmland. The promises of emancipation were fulfilled for a few, among them the families at Promised Land.

Settlement of the community coincided with the establishment of a public school, another of the revolutionary social reforms mandated by the 1868 constitution. It was the first of several public facilities to serve community residents and was built on land still described officially as "Dr. Marshall's farm." J. H. Turner, Larkin Reynolds, Iverson Reynolds and Hutson Lomax, all Negroes, were the first school trustees. The families established on their new farms sent more than ninety children to the one-room school. Everyone who could be spared from the fields was in the classroom for the short 1870 school term. Although few of the children in the landless families attended school regularly, the landowning families early established a tradition of school attendance for their children consonant with their new status. With limited resources the school began the task of educating local children.

The violence and terror experienced by some of the men of Promised Land during 1868 recurred three years later when Eli and Wade Moragne were attacked and viciously beaten with a wagon whip by a band of Klansmen. Wade was twenty-three that year, Eli two years older. Both were married and had small children. It was rumored that the Moragne brothers were among the most prominent and influential of the Negro Republicans in Abbeville County. Their political activity, compounded by an unusual degree of self-assurance, pride, and dignity, infuriated local whites. Like Wilson Nash, Willis Smith, Washington Green, and Allen Goode, the Moragne brothers were victims of insidious political reprisals. Involvement in Reconstruction politics for Negroes was a dangerous enterprise and one which addressed the past as well as the future. It was an activity suited to young men and those who faced the future bravely. It was not for the timid.

The Republican influence on the freedmen at Promised Land was unmistakable, and there was no evidence that the "outrages" and terrorizations against them slowed their participation in local partisan activities. In addition to the risks, there were benefits to be accrued from their alliance with the Republicans. They enjoyed appointments as precinct managers and school trustees. As candidates for various public offices, they experienced a degree of prestige and public recognition which offset the element of danger they faced. These men, born slaves, rose to positions of prominence as landowners, as political figures, and as makers of a community. Few probably had dared to dream of such possibilities a decade earlier.

During the violent years of Reconstruction there was at least one official attempt to end the anarchy in Abbeville County. The representative to the state legislature, J. Hollinshead—the former regional agent for the Land Commission—stated publicly what many local Negroes already knew privately, that "numerous outrages occur in the county and the laws cannot be enforced by civil authorities." From the floor of the General Assembly of South Carolina Hollinshead called for martial law in Abbeville, a request which did not pass unnoticed locally. The Editor of the *Press* commented on Hollinshead's request for martial law by declaring that such outrages against the freedmen "exist only in the imagination of the legislator." His response was probably typical of the cavalier attitude of southern whites toward the problems of their former bondsmen. Indeed, there were no further reports of violence and attacks against freedmen carried by the *Press,* which failed to note the murder of County Commissioner Henry Nash in February 1871. Like other victims of white terrorists, Nash was a Negro.

While settlement of Dr. Marshall's Farm by the freedmen proceeded, three community residents were arrested for the theft of "some oxen from Dr. H. Drennan who lives near the 'Promiseland.'" Authorities found the heads, tails, and feet of the slaughtered animals near the homes of Ezekiel and Moses Williams and Colbert Jordan. The circumstantial evidence against them seemed convincing; and the three were arrested and then released without bond, pending trial. Colonel Cothran, a former Confederate officer and respected barrister in Abbeville, represented the trio at their trial. Although freedmen in Abbeville courts were generally convicted of whatever crime they were charged with, the Williamses and Jordan were acquitted. Justice for Negroes was always a tenuous affair; but it was especially so before black, as well as white, qualified electors were included in the jury pool. The trial of the Williams brothers and Jordan signaled a temporary truce in the racial war, a truce which at least applied to those Negroes settling the farms at Promised Land.

In 1872, the third year of settlement, Promised Land gained nine more households as families moved to land that they "bought for a dollar an acre." There they "plow old oxen, build log cabin houses" as they settled the land they bought "from the Governor in Columbia." Colbert Jordan and Ezekiel Williams, cleared of the oxen stealing charges, both purchased farms that year. Family and kinship ties drew some of the new migrants to the community. Joshuway Wilson, married to Moses Wideman's sister Delphia, bought a farm near his brother-in-law. Two more Moragne brothers, William and Wade, settled near the other family members in "Moragne Town." Whitfield Hutchison, a jack-leg preacher, bought the farm adjacent to his brother Frank. "Old Whit Hutchison could sing about let's go down to the water and be baptized. He didn't have no education, and he didn't know exactly how to put his words, but when he got to singing he could make your hair rise up. He was a number one preacher." Hutchison was not the only preacher among those first settlers. Isaac Y. Moragne, who moved to Promised Land the following year, and several men in the Turner family all combined preaching and farming.

Not all of the settlers came to their new farms as members of such extensive kinship networks as the Moragnes, who counted nine brothers, four sisters, and an assortment of spouses and children among the first Promised Land residents. Even those who joined the community in relative isolation, however, were seldom long in establishing kinship alliances with their neighbors. One such couple was James and Hannah Fields who lived in Columbia before emancipation. While still a slave, James Fields owned property in the state capitol, which was held in trust for him by his master. After emancipation Fields worked for a time as a porter on the Columbia and Greenville Railroad and heard about the up-country land for sale to Negroes as he carried carpet bags and listened to political gossip on the train. Fields went to Abbeville County to inspect the land before he purchased a farm there. While he was visiting, he "run up on Mr. Nathan Redd," old Henry Redd's son. The Fieldses' granddaughter Emily and Nathan were about the same age, and Fields proposed a match to young Redd. "You marry my granddaughter, and I'll will all this land to you and her." The marriage was arranged before the farm was purchased, and eventually the land was transferred to the young couple.

By the conclusion of 1872 forty-eight families were settled on farms in Promised Land. Most of the land was under cultivation, as required by law; but the farmers were also busy with other activities. In addition to the houses and barns which had to be raised as each new family arrived with their few possessions, the men continued their political activities. Iverson Reynolds, J. H. Turner, John and Elias Tolbert, Judson Reynolds, Oscar Pressley, and Washington Green, all community residents, were delegates to the county Republican convention in August 1872. Three of the group were landowners. Their political activities were still not received with much enthusiasm by local whites, but reaction to Negro involvement in politics was lessening in hostility. The *Press* mildly observed that the fall cotton crop was being gathered with good speed and "the farmers have generally been making good use of their time." Cotton picking and politics were both seasonal, and the newspaper chided local Negroes for their priorities. "The blacks have been indulging a little too much in politics but are getting right again." Iverson Reynolds and Washington Green, always among the community's Republican leadership during the 1870's, served as local election managers again for the 1872 fall elections. The men from Promised Land voted without incident that year.

Civic participation among the Promised Land residents extended beyond partisan politics when the county implemented the new jury law in 1872. There had been no Negro jurors for the trial of the Williams brothers and Colbert Jordan the previous year. Although the inclusion of Negroes in the jury pools was a reform mandated in 1868, four years passed before Abbeville authorities drew up new jury lists from the revised voter registration rolls. The jury law was as repugnant to the whites as Negro suffrage, termed "a wretched attempt at legislation, which surpasses anything which has yet been achieved by the Salons in Columbia." When the new lists were finally completed in 1872 the *Press,* ever the reflection of local white public opinion, predicted that "many of [the freedmen] probably have moved away; and the chances are that not many of them will be forthcoming" in the call to jury duty. Neither the initial condemnation of the law nor the optimistic undertones of the *Press* prediction stopped Pope Moragne and Iverson Reynolds from responding to their notices from the Abbeville Courthouse. Both landowners rode their mules up Five Notch Road from Promised Land to Abbeville and served on the county's first integrated jury in the fall of 1872. Moragne and Reynolds were soon followed by others from the community— Allen Goode, Robert Wideman, William Moragne, James Richie, and Luther (Shack) Moragne. By 1874, less than five years after settlement of Dr. Marshall's farm by the new Negro landowners began, the residents of Promised Land remained actively involved in Abbeville County politics. They were undaunted by the *Press* warning that "just so soon as the colored people lose the confidence and support of the North their doom is fixed. The fate of the red man will be theirs." They were voters, jurors, taxpayers, and trustees of the school their children attended. Their collective identity as an exclusively Negro community was well established. . . .

The representatives to the 1868 South Carolina Constitutional Convention who formulated the state's land redistribution hoped to establish an economically independent Negro yeomanry in South Carolina. The Land Commission intended the purchase and resale of Dr. Marshall's farm to solidify the interests of radical Republicanism in Abbeville County, at least for a time. Both of these designs were realized. A third and unintended consequence also resulted. The land fostered a socially autonomous, identifiable community. Drawing on resources and social structures well established within an extant Negro culture, the men and women who settled Promised Land established churches and schools and a viable economic system based on landownership. They maintained that economic autonomy by subsistence farming and supported many of their routine needs by patronizing the locally owned and operated grist mills and general store. The men were actively involved in Reconstruction politics as well as other aspects of civil life, serving regularly on county juries and paying their taxes. Attracted by the security and prestige Promised Land afforded and the possible hope of eventual landownership, fifty additional landless households moved into the community during the 1870's, expanding the 1880 population to almost twice its original size. Together the eighty-nine households laid claim to slightly more than four square miles of land, and within that small territory they "carved out their own little piece of the world."

Sources

The Meaning of Freedom

What did it mean to be free? As Bethel's account of the settlers of Promised Land indicates, there were many obstacles in the path of every freedman and only a few succeeded in becoming independent small farmers. Some twentieth-century writers have argued that the gains for most blacks were minuscule, that being a poor tenant farmer or share-cropper was often even worse than being a slave. But these writers, of course, never experienced the change from slavery to freedom. Here is a man who did.

Dayton, Ohio, August 7, 1865

To My Old Master, Colonel P. H. Anderson,
Big Spring, Tennessee

Sir: I got your letter and was glad to find you had not forgotten Jourdon, and that you wanted me to come back and live with you again, promising to do better for me than anybody else can. I have often felt uneasy about you. I thought the Yankees would have hung you long before this for harboring Rebs they found at your house. I suppose they never heard about your going to Col. Martin's to kill the Union soldier that was left by his company

From Lydia Maria Child, ed., *The Freedmen's Book* (Boston, 1865), pp. 265–267.

in their stable. Although you shot at me twice before I left you, I did not want to hear of your being hurt, and am glad you are still living. It would do me good to go back to the dear old home again and see Miss Mary and Miss Martha and Allen, Esther, Green, and Lee. Give my love to them all, and tell them I hope we will meet in the better world, if not in this. I would have gone back to see you all when I was working in the Nashville hospital, but one of the neighbors told me Henry intended to shoot me if he ever got a chance.

I want to know particularly what the good chance is you propose to give me. I am doing tolerably well here; I get $25 a month, with victuals and clothing; have a comfortable home for Mandy (the folks here call her Mrs. Anderson), and the children, Milly, Jane and Grundy, go to school and are learning well; the teacher says Grundy has a head for a preacher. They go to Sunday-School, and Mandy and me attend church regularly. We are kindly treated; sometimes we overhear others saying, "Them colored people were slaves" down in Tennessee. The children feel hurt when they hear such remarks, but I tell them it was no disgrace in Tennessee to belong to Col. Anderson. Many darkies would have been proud, as I used to was, to call you master. Now, if you will write and say what wages you will give me, I will be better able to decide whether it would be to my advantage to move back again.

As to my freedom, which you say I can have, there is nothing to be gained on that score, as I got my free-papers in 1864 from the Provost-Marshal-General of the Department at Nashville. Mandy says she would be afraid to go back without some proof that you are sincerely disposed to treat us justly and kindly—and we have concluded to test your sincerity by asking you to send us our wages for the time we served you. This will make us forget and forgive old scores, and rely on your justice and friendship in the future. I served you faithfully for thirty-two years and Mandy twenty years. At $25 a month for me, and $2 a week for Mandy, our earnings would amount to $11,680. Add to this the interest for the time our wages has been kept back and deduct what you paid for our clothing and three doctor's visits to me, and pulling a tooth for Mandy, and the balance will show what we are in justice entitled to. Please send the money by Adams Express, in care of V. Winters, esq, Dayton, Ohio. If you fail to pay us for faithful labors in the past we can have little faith in your promises in the future. We trust the good Maker has opened your eyes to the wrongs which you and your fathers have done to me and my fathers, in making us toil for you for generations without recompense. Here I draw my wages every Saturday night, but in Tennessee there was never any pay day for the negroes any more than for the horses and cows. Surely there will be a day of reckoning for those who defraud the laborer of his hire.

In answering this letter please state if there would be any safety for my Milly and Jane, who are now grown up and both good-looking girls. You know how it was with poor Matilda and Catherine. I would rather stay here and starve and die if it comes to that than have my girls brought to shame by the violence and wickedness of their young masters. You will also please state if there has been any schools opened for the colored children in your neighborhood, the great desire of my life now is to give my children an education, and have them form virtuous habits.

P.S.—Say howdy to George Carter, and thank him for taking the pistol from you when you were shooting at me.

From your old servant,
Jourdon Anderson

The Cartoonist's View of Reconstruction

Thomas Nast was America's foremost political cartoonist. He also was a Radical Republican who had no love for the white South or the Democratic party. The touchstone cause of Radical Republicans was black civil rights—particularly the right to vote—and conflict with the Democrats and the white South often focused on this issue. Nast's drawings in *Harper's Weekly*, as you will notice, illustrated vividly this ongoing battle. The high point for Nast came when Hiram Revels, a black, occupied the Senate seat from Mississippi once held by Jefferson Davis. The low point came shortly afterwards. What effect do you think each cartoon had on the electorate? Were any more compelling than the others?

PARDON.

Columbia—"Shall I Trust These Men,

FRANCHISE.

And Not This Man?"
Thomas Nast, Harper's Weekly, *August 5, 1865. Courtesy of The Research Libraries, The New York Public Library, Astor, Lenox and Tilden Foundations.*

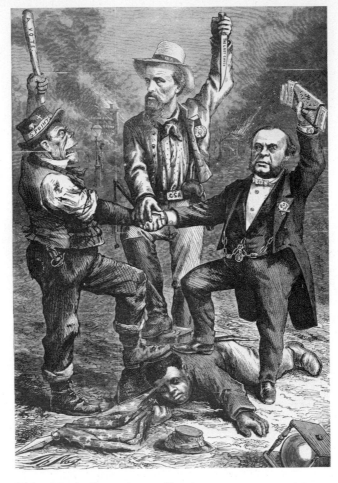

"This Is a White Man's Government."
"We regard the Reconstruction Acts (so called) of Congress as usurpations, and
unconstitutional, revolutionary, and void."–*Democratic Platform. Thomas Nast,*
Harper's Weekly, *September 5, 1868, Courtesy of The Research Libraries, The New
York Public Library, Astor, Lenox and Tilden Foundations.*

"TIME WORKS WONDERS."

IAGO.(JEFF DAVIS.) "FOR THAT I DO SUSPECT THE LUSTY MOOR
HATH LEAP'D INTO MY SEAT: THE THOUGHT WHEREOF
DOTH LIKE A POISONOUS MINERAL GNAW MY INWARDS." — OTHELLO.

Thomas Nast, Harper's Weekly, *April 9, 1870. Courtesy of The Research Libraries, The New York Public Library, Astor, Lenox and Tilden Foundations.*

The Commandments in South Carolina.
"We've pretty well smashed that; but I suppose, Massa Moses, you can get another one." *Thomas Nast,* Harper's Weekly, *September 26, 1874. Courtesy of The Research Libraries, The New York Public Library, Astor, Lenox and Tilden Foundations.*

Thomas Nast, Harper's Weekly, *October 24, 1874. Courtesy of The Research Libraries, The New York Public Library, Astor, Lenox and Tilden Foundations.*

The Target
"* * * They (Messrs. Phelps & Potter) seem to regard the White League as *innocent as a Target Company.*"–*Special Dispatch to the "N.Y. Times," from Washington,* Jan. 17, 1875. *Thomas Nast,* Harper's Weekly, *February 6, 1875. Courtesy of The Research Libraries, The New York Public Library, Astor, Lenox and Tilden Foundatons.*

"To Thine Own Self Be True."
Thomas Nast, Harper's Weekly, *April 24, 1875. Courtesy of The Research Libraries, The New York Public Library, Astor, Lenox and Tilden Foundations.*

"These Few Precepts in Thy Memory."

Beware of entrance to a quarrel: but, being in,
Bear it that the opposer may beware of thee.
Give every man thine ear, but few thy voice:
Take each man's censure, but reserve thy judgment.
Costly thy habit as thy purse can buy,
But not express'd in fancy; rich, not gaudy:
For the apparel oft proclaims the man.

This above all,—To thine own self be true;
And it must follow, as the night the day,
Thou canst not then be false to any man.
SHAKSPEARE.

The "Civil Rights" Scare Is Nearly Over.
The game of (Colored) fox and (White) goose. Thomas Nast, Harper's Weekly, *May 22, 1875. Courtesy of The Research Libraries, The New York Public Library, Astor, Lenox and Tilden Foundations.*

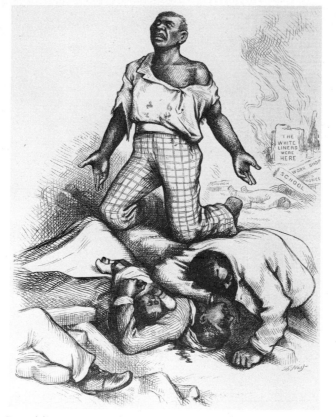

"Is *This* a Republican Form of Government? Is *This* Protecting Life, Liberty, or Property? Is *This* the Equal Protection of the Laws?"
Mr. Lamar (*Democrat, Mississippi*). "In the words of the inspired poet, 'Thy gentleness has made thee great.' " [Did Mr. Lamar mean the colored race?] *Thomas Nast,* Harper's Weekly, *September 2, 1876. Courtesy of The Research Libraries, The New York Public Library, Astor, Lenox and Tilden Foundations.*

The South Redeemed

As Nast's cartoons indicate, the crusade for black voting rights and
other civil rights ran into stiff opposition and eventually failed. By
1877, white supremacy was firmly re-established throughout the
South, and black political voices were almost completely stilled. The
South, according to many white Southerners, had been "redeemed"
by its white leaders. But the white South did not get back everything it wanted. Black men had refused to work as gang laborers,
and black families had refused to let women and children work long
hours in the field. Grudgingly, white land owners had let blacks
work the land in family plots, usually as either tenant farmers or
share-croppers. Thus, despite "redemption," the Southern landscape
would look startlingly different after Reconstruction. Here are maps
of the same Georgia plantation in 1860 and in 1880. What, in your
judgment, were the important features in the new and the old landscape? Do the changes match up with the kinds of attitudes discussed
in Bethel's essay? How many of the 1880 families, would you guess,
once lived in the old slave quarters?

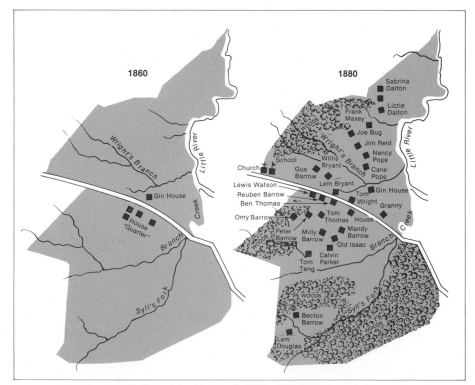

Adapted from Scribner's Monthly *21 (April 1881): 832–833.*

About the Editors

William Graebner is Professor of History at the State University of New York at Fredonia. He received the Frederick Jackson Turner Award from the Organization of American Historians for *Coal-Mining Safety in the Progressive Period: The Political Economy of Reform*. Another book, *A History of Retirement: The Meaning and Function of an American Institution, 1885–1978*, was published in 1980. He is also the author of *The Engineering of Consent: Democracy and Authority in Twentieth-Century America* (1987).

Leonard Richards is Professor of History at the University of Massachusetts at Amherst. He was awarded the 1970 Beveridge Prize by the American Historical Association for his book *"Gentlemen of Property and Standing": Anti-Abolition Mobs in Jacksonian America*. Professor Richards is also the author of *The Advent of American Democracy* and *The Life and Times of Congressman John Quincy Adams*. He is planning another book on the social history of industrial New England.